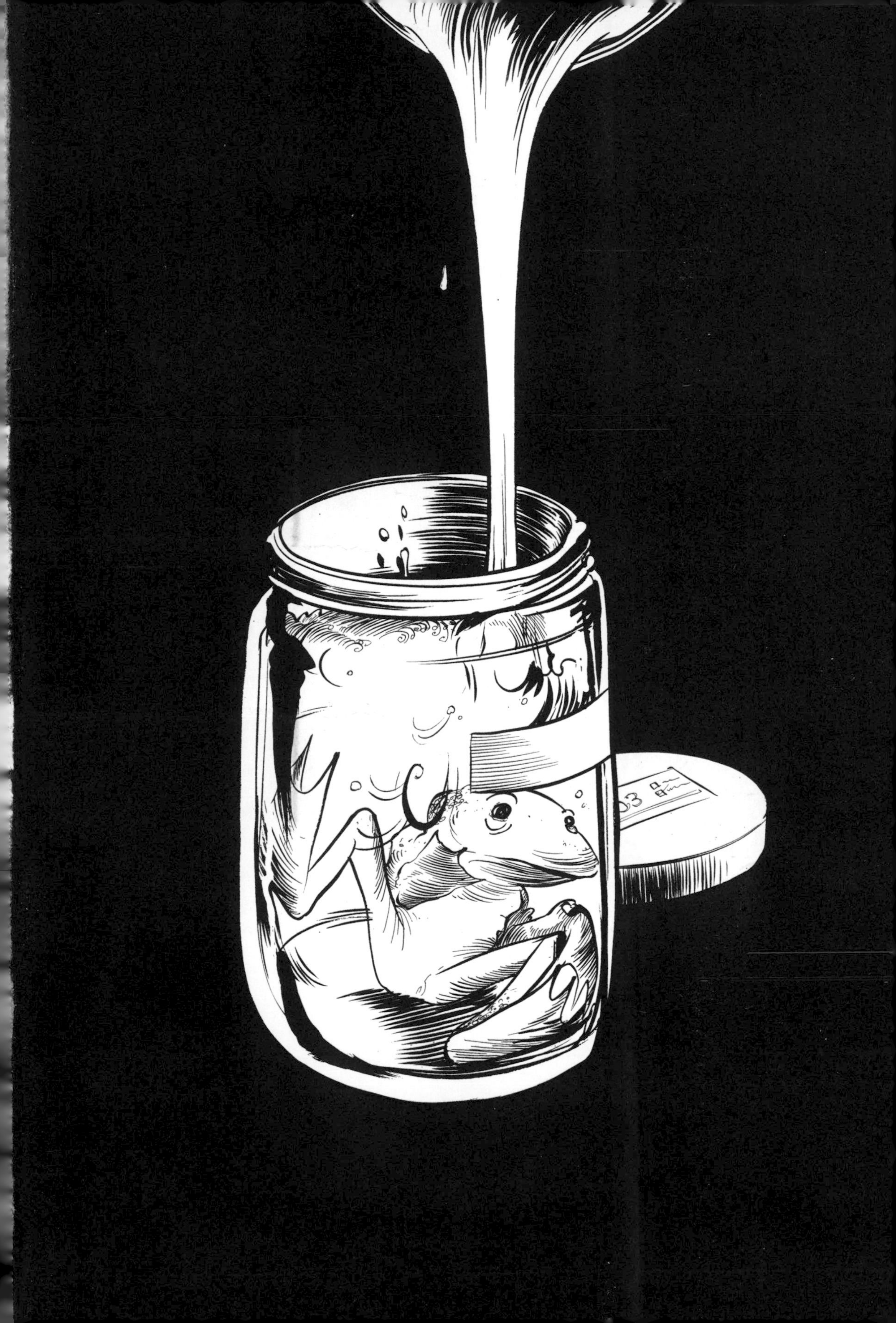

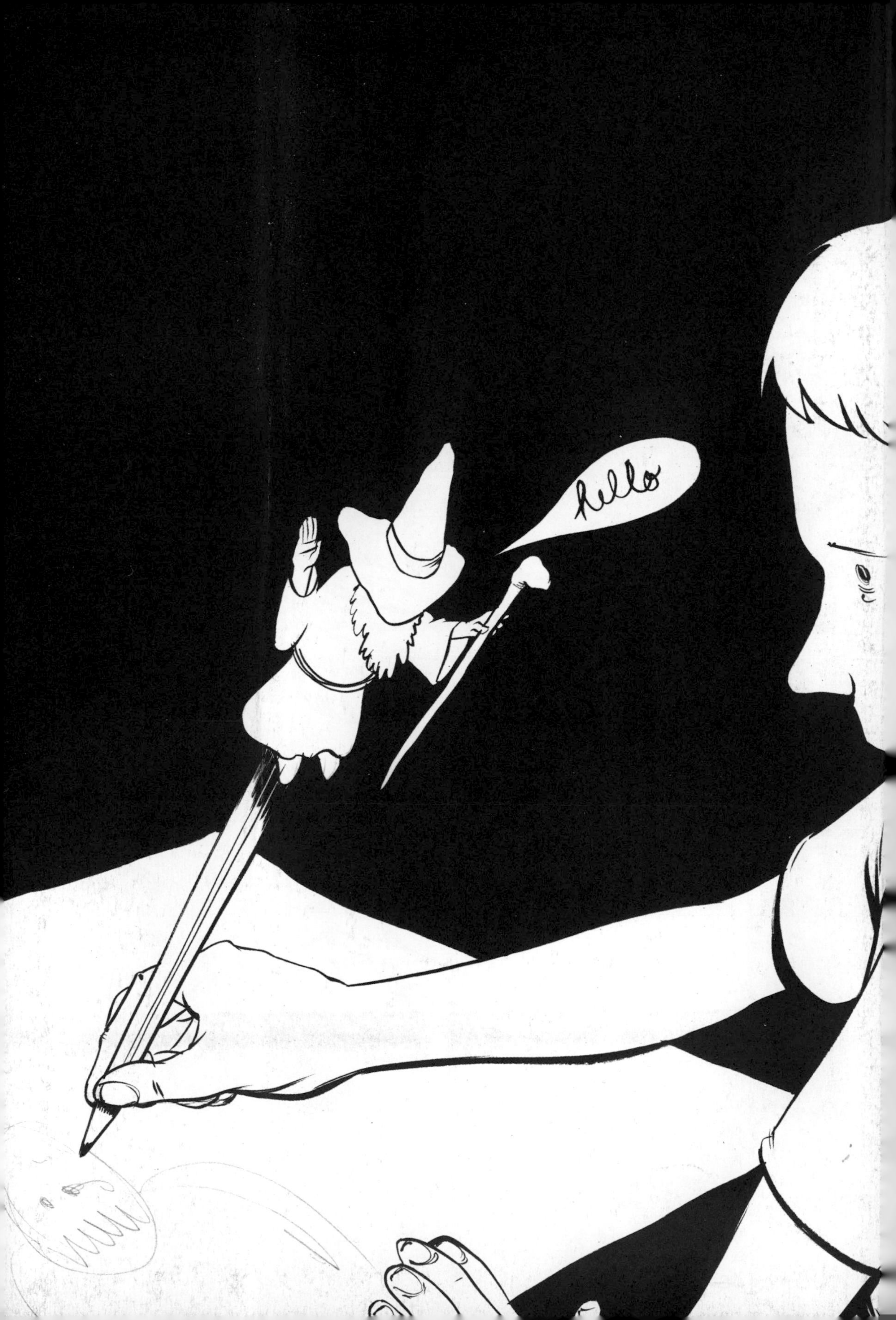
hello

NATE POWELL

and

Top Shelf Productions

present

ISBN 978-1-60309-033-9

1. Family Drama
2. Schizophrenia/Hallucination
3. Graphic Novels

 Edited by Chris Staros. Published by Top Shelf Productions, P.O. Box 1282, Marietta GA 30061-1282, USA. Publishers: Brett Warnock and Chris Staros. Visit our online catalog at www.topshelfcomix.com.

First Printing, September 2008. Printed in China.

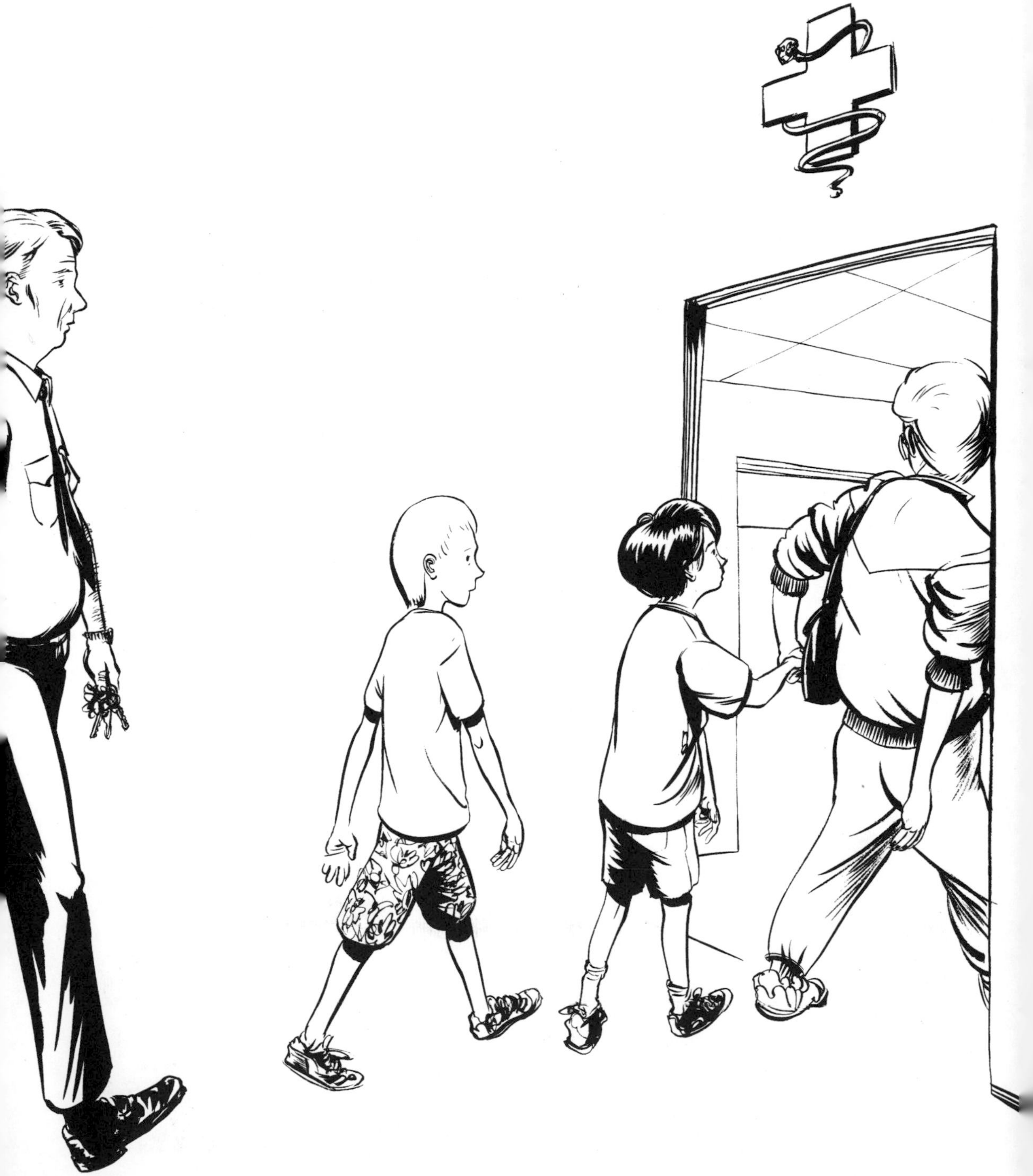

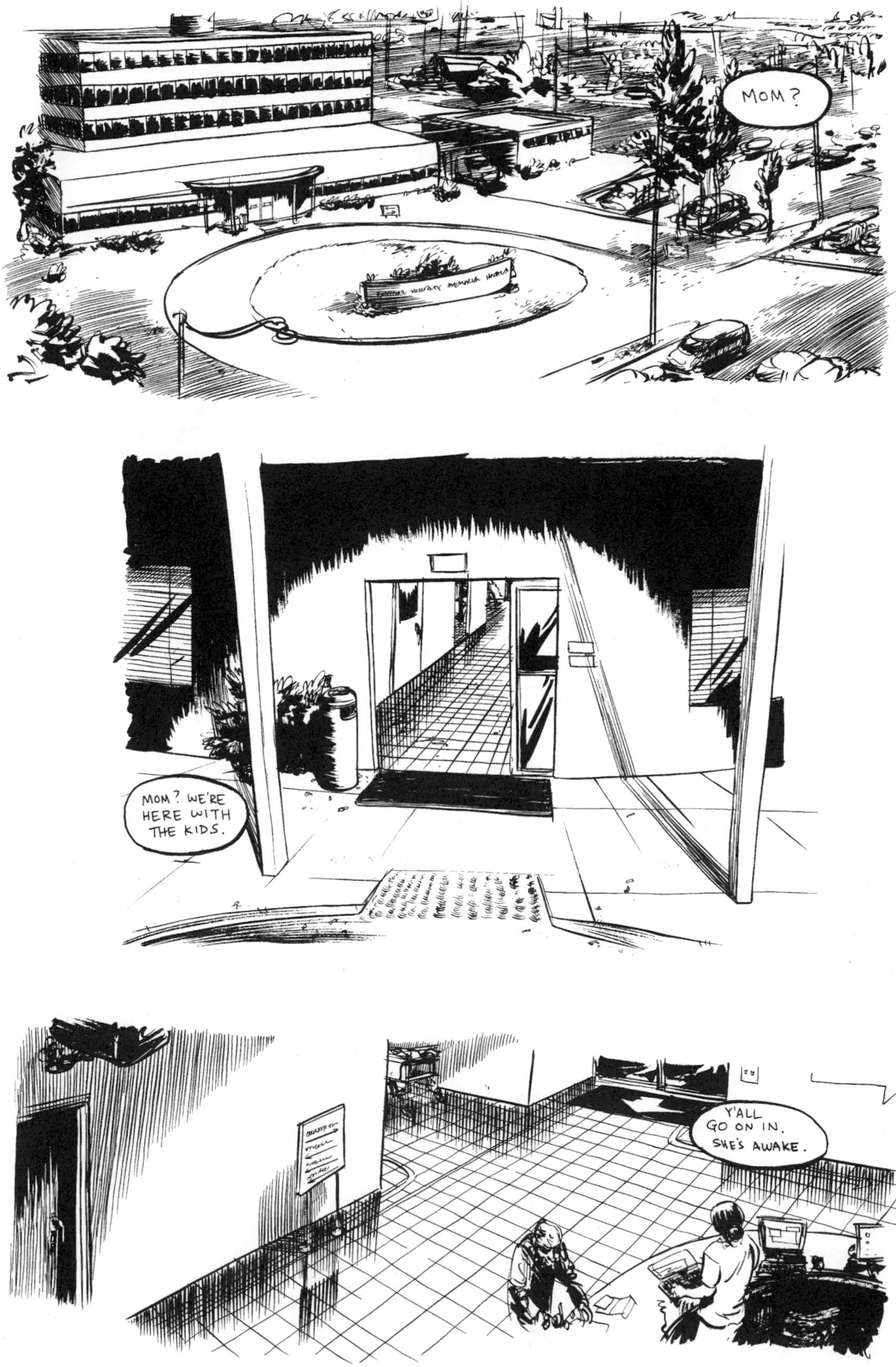
MOM?
MOM? WE'RE HERE WITH THE KIDS.
Y'ALL GO ON IN. SHE'S AWAKE.

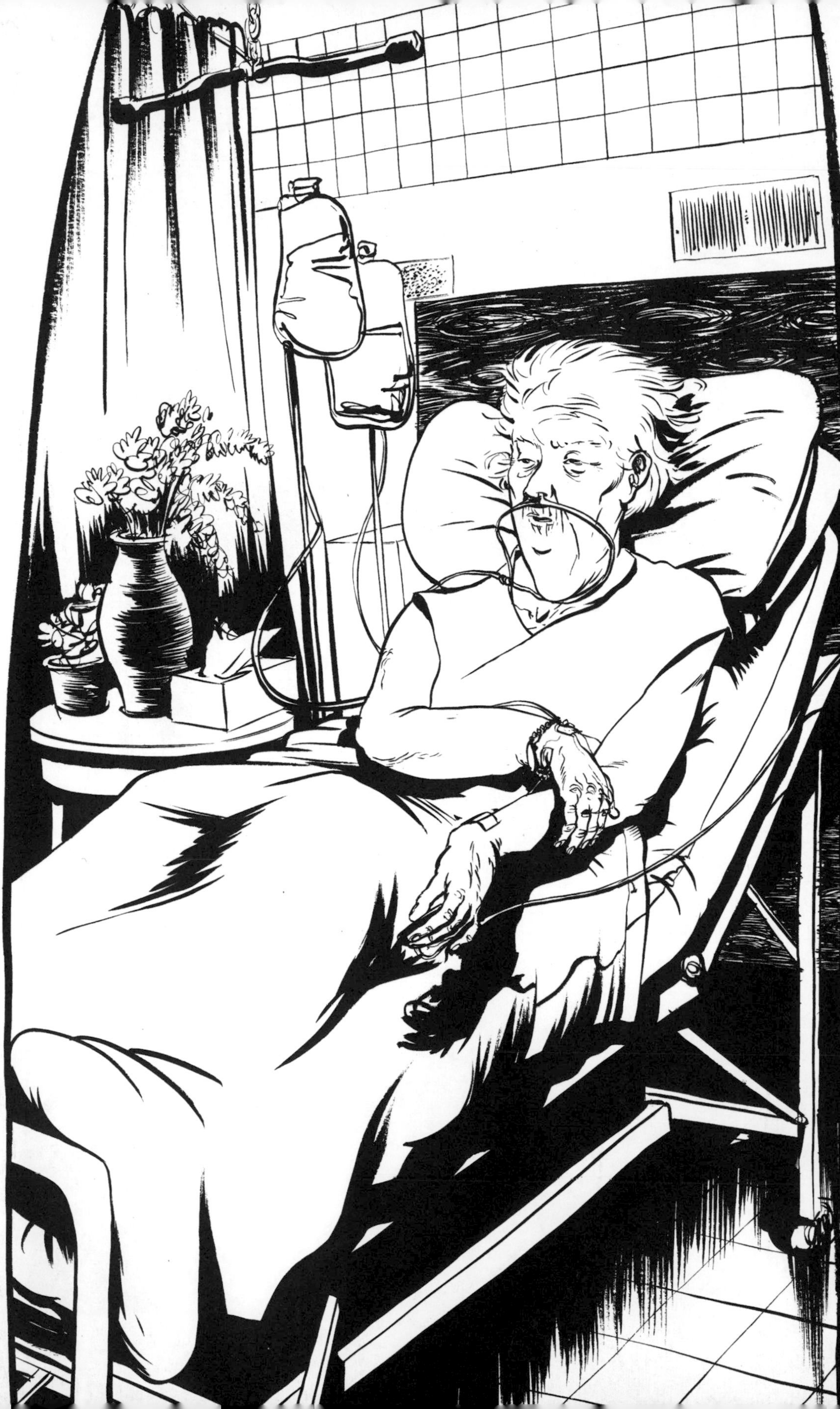

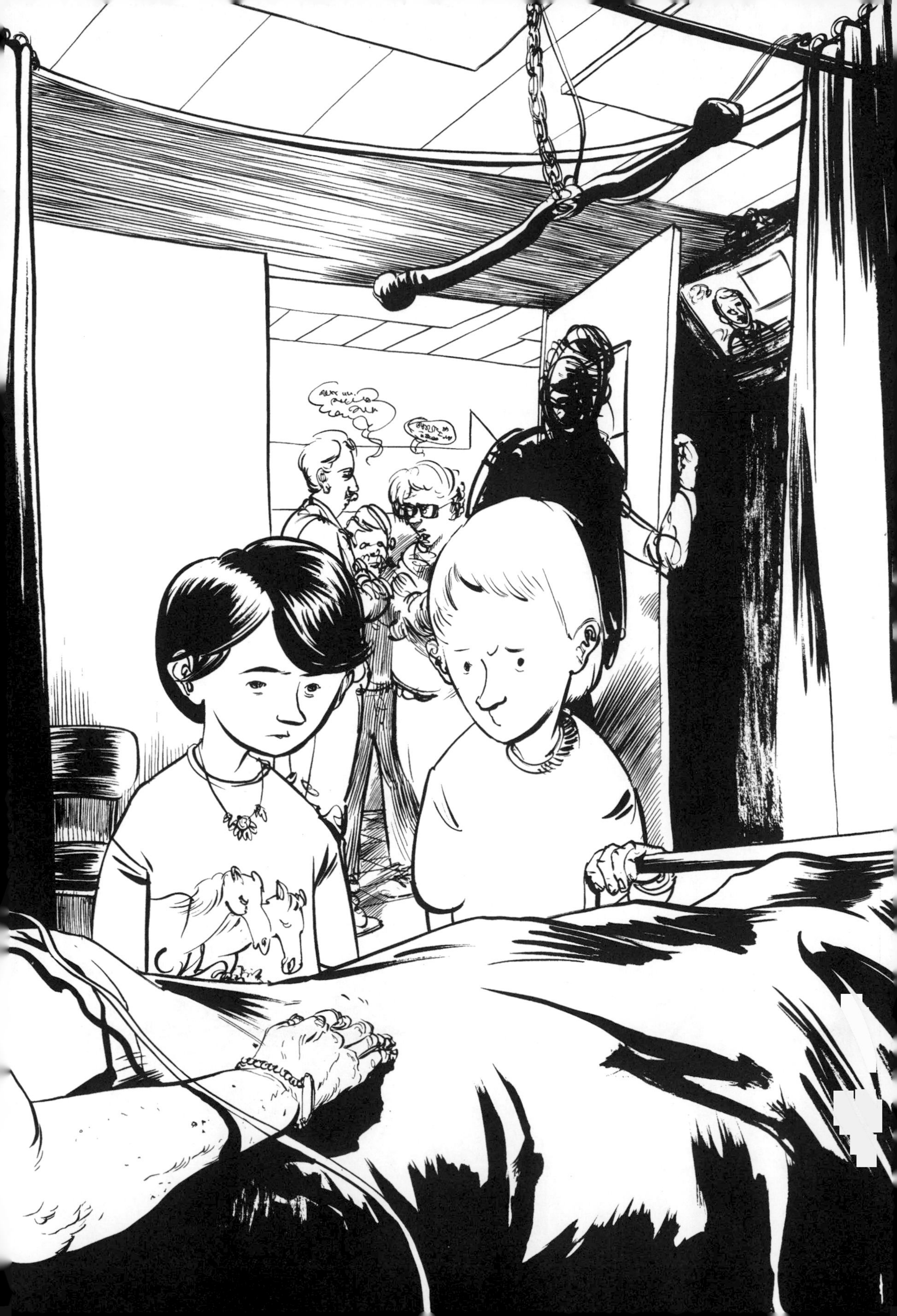

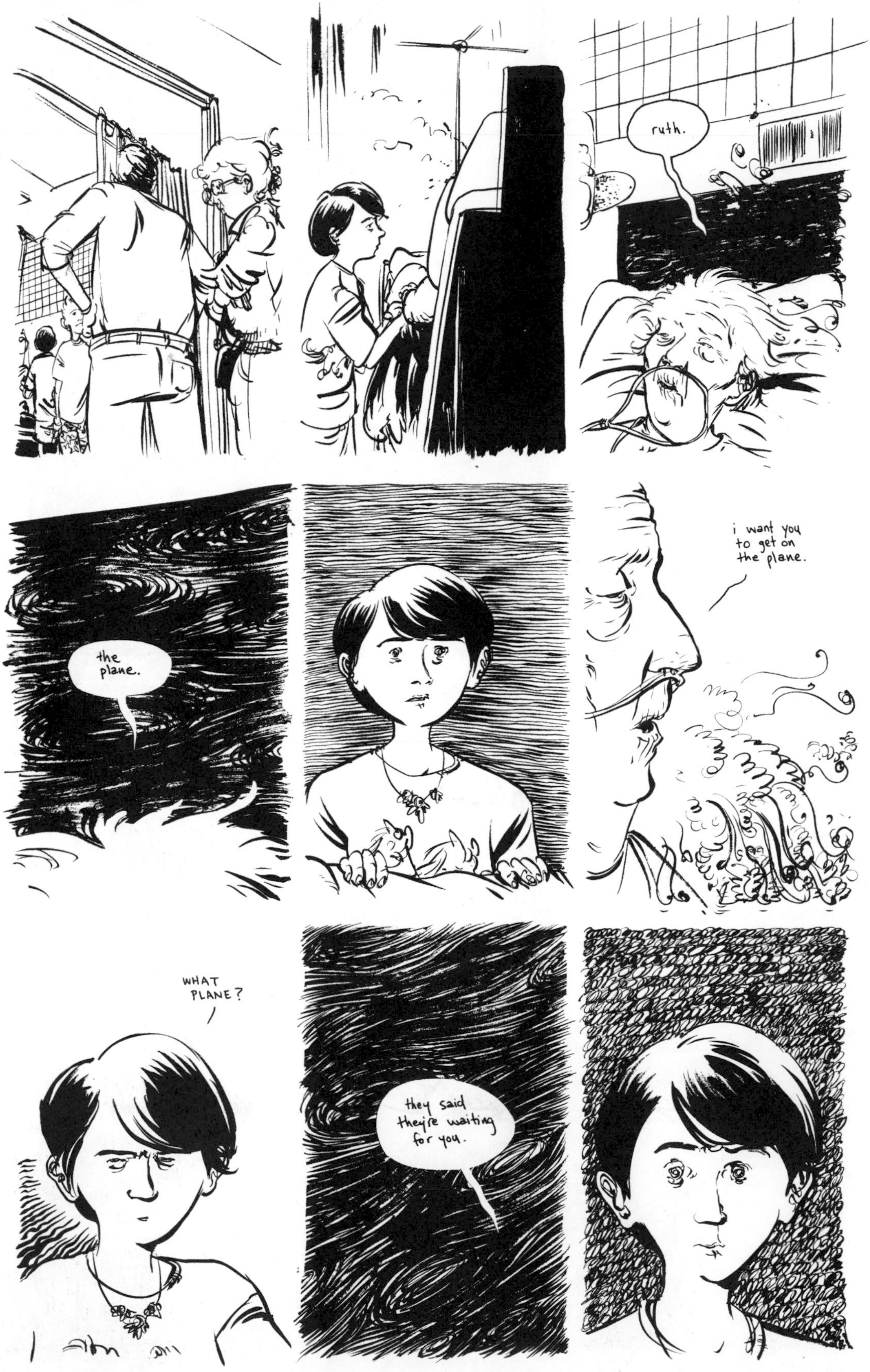
ruth.
the plane.
i want you to get on the plane.
WHAT PLANE?
they said they're waiting for you.

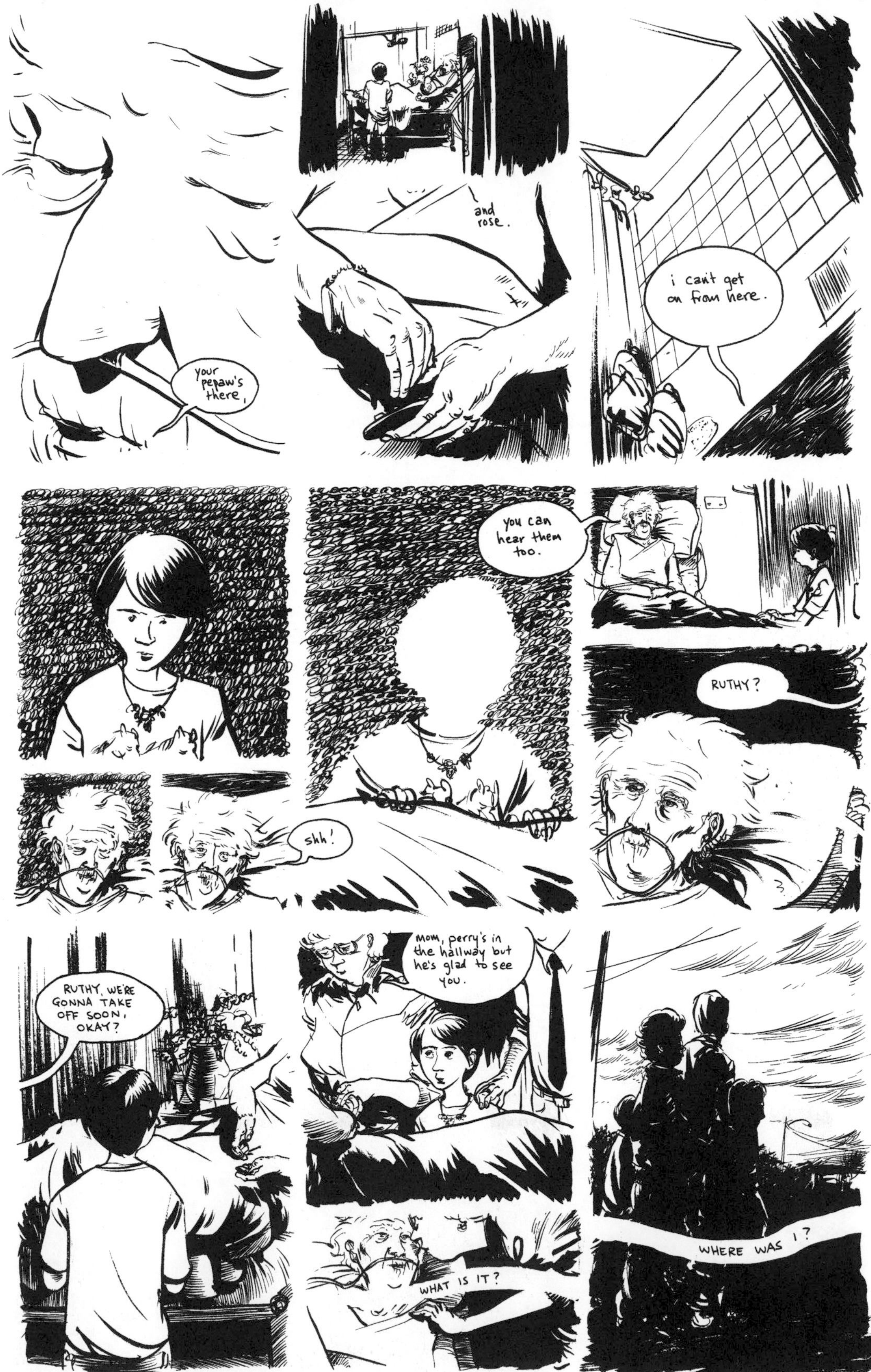
your pepaw's there,
and rose.
i can't get on from here.
you can hear them too.
shh!
RUTHY?
RUTHY, WE'RE GONNA TAKE OFF SOON, OKAY?
mom, perry's in the hallway but he's glad to see you.
WHAT IS IT?
WHERE WAS I?

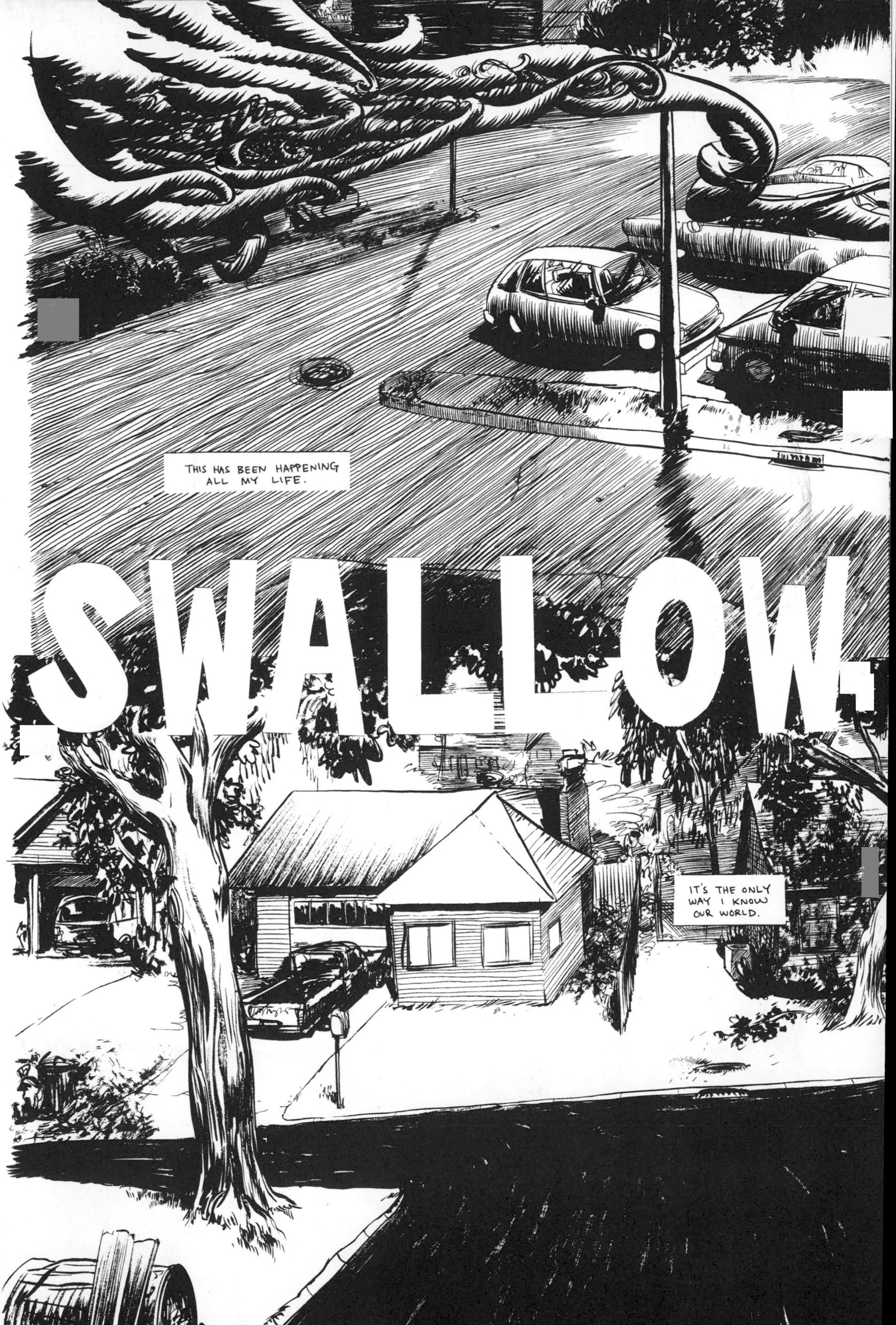
THIS HAS BEEN HAPPENING ALL MY LIFE.
SWALLOW
IT'S THE ONLY WAY I KNOW OUR WORLD.

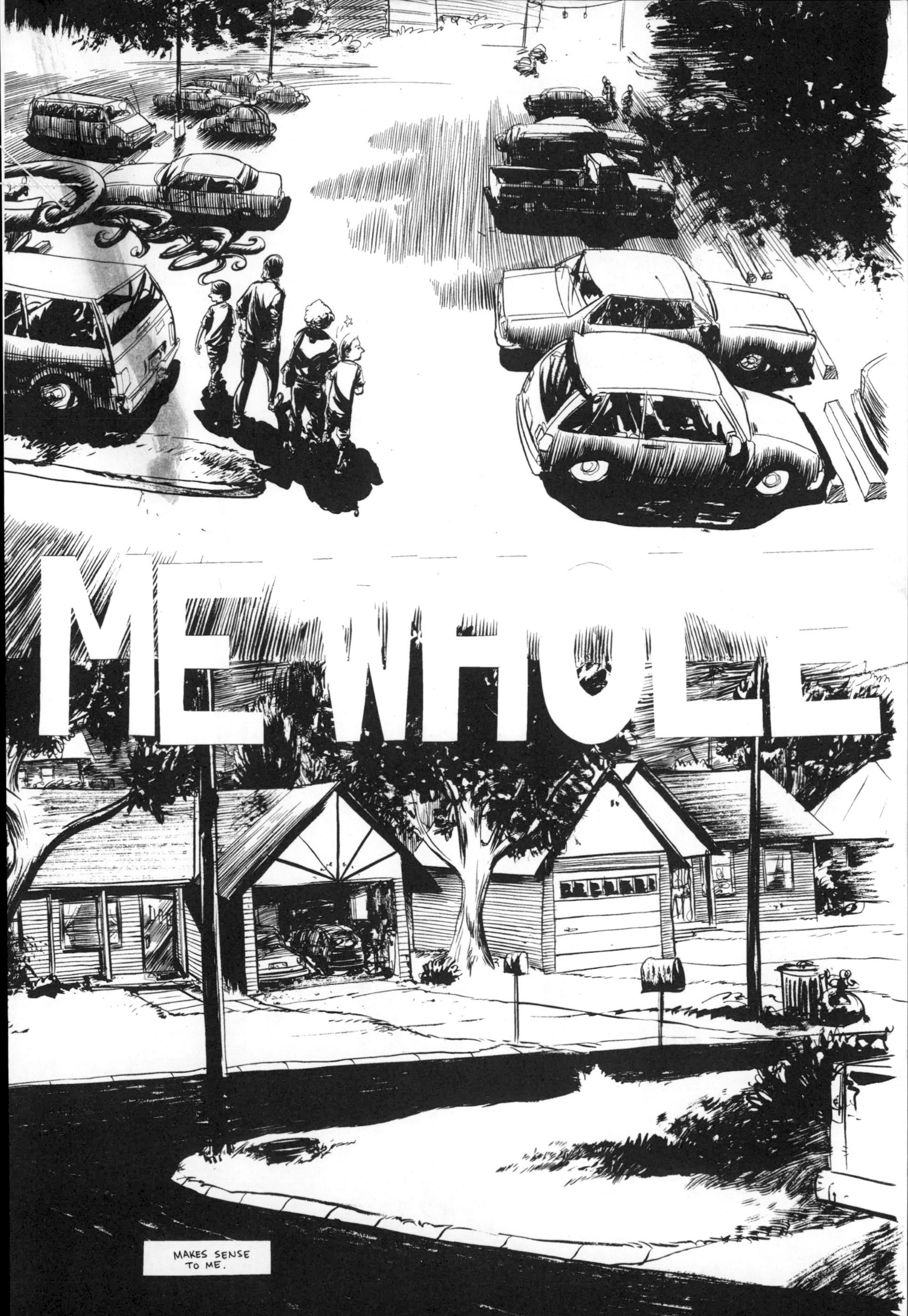
ME WHOLE
MAKES SENSE TO ME.

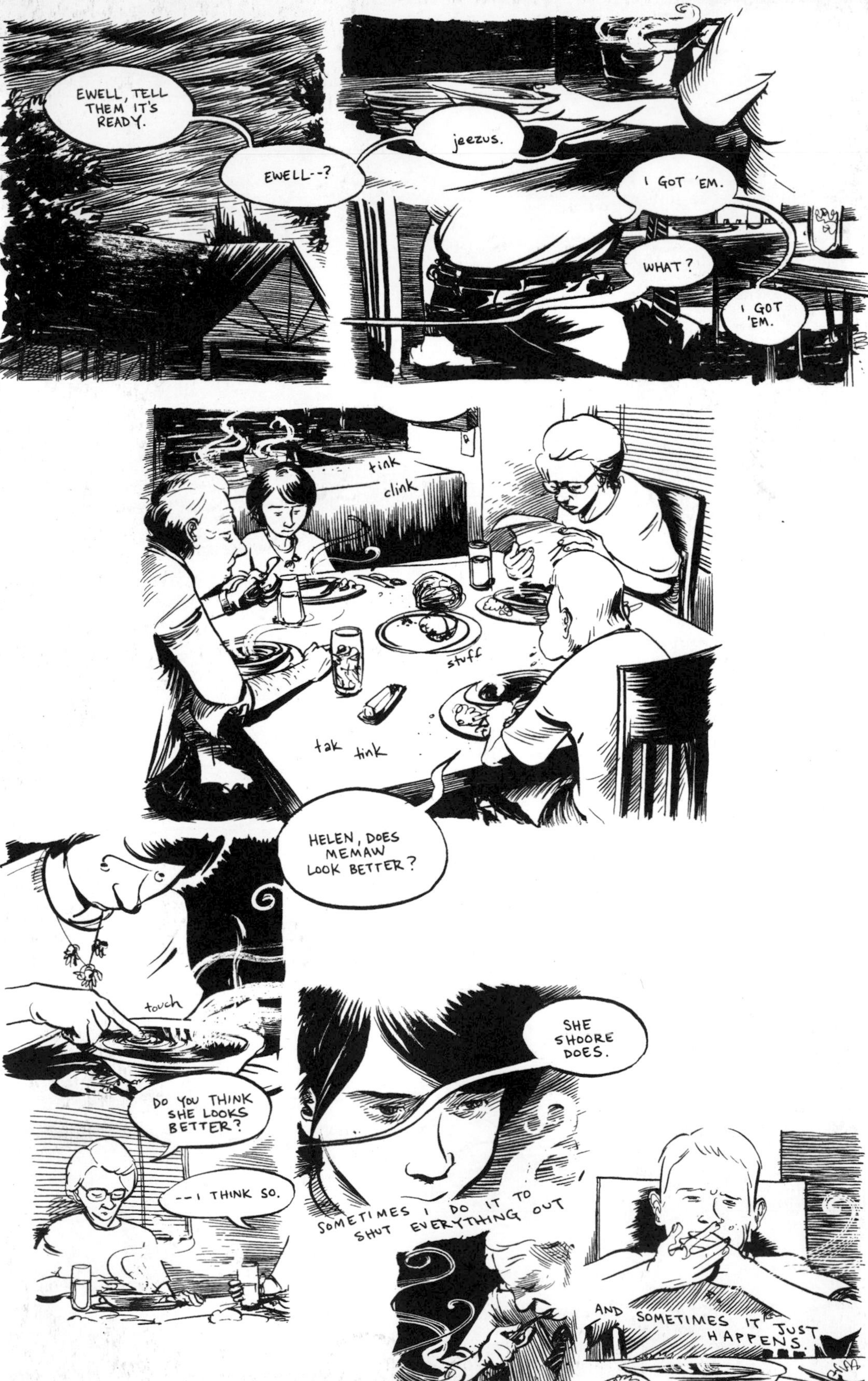
EWELL, TELL THEM IT'S READY.
EWELL--?
jeezus.
I GOT 'EM.
WHAT?
I GOT 'EM.
tink
clink
stuff
tak
tink
HELEN, DOES MEMAW LOOK BETTER?
touch
DO YOU THINK SHE LOOKS BETTER?
--I THINK SO.
SHE SHOORE DOES.
SOMETIMES I DO IT TO SHUT EVERYTHING OUT
AND SOMETIMES IT JUST HAPPENS.

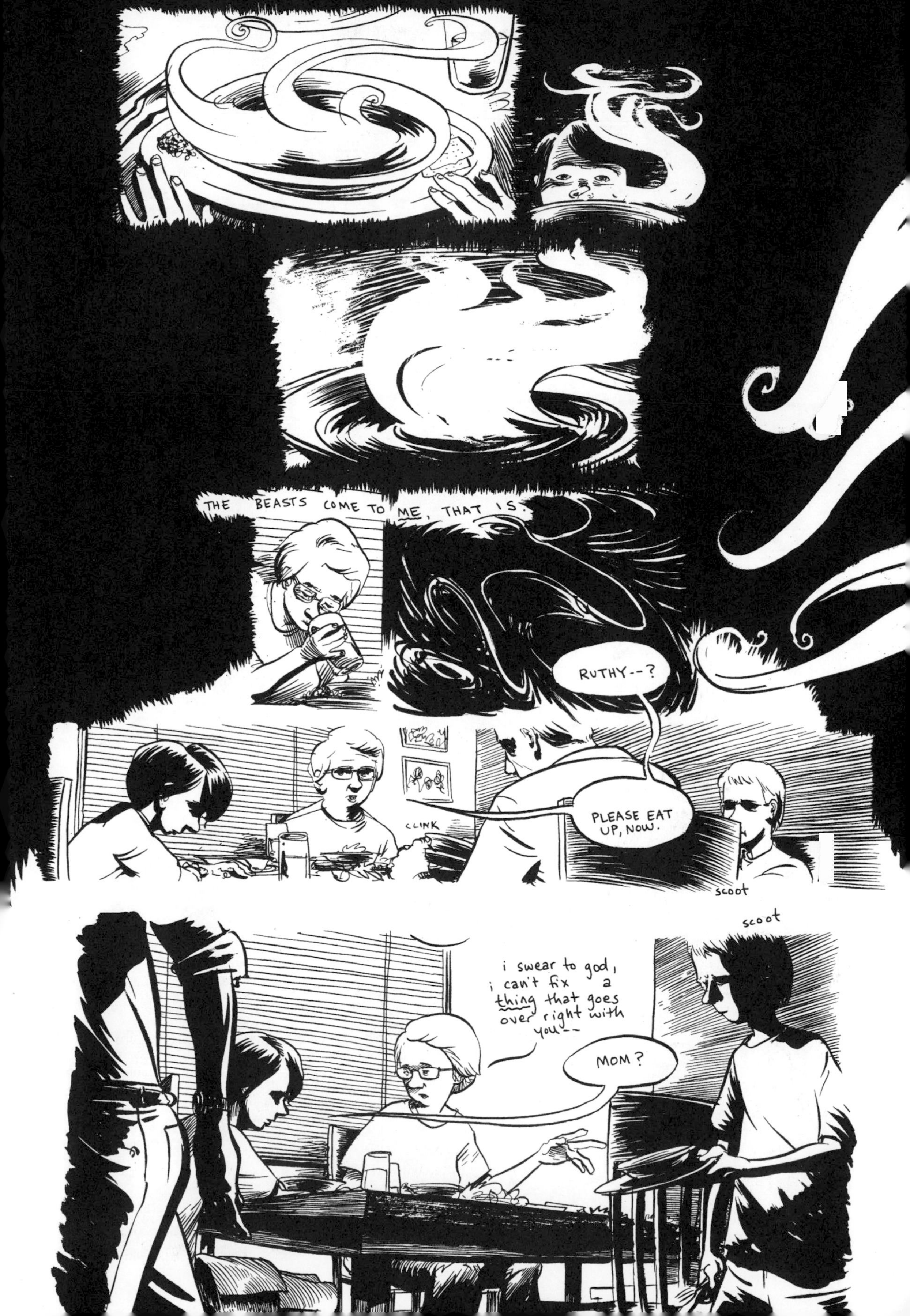
THE BEASTS COME TO ME, THAT IS.
RUTHY--?
CLINK
PLEASE EAT UP, NOW.
scoot
scoot
i swear to god, i can't fix a thing that goes over right with you--
MOM?

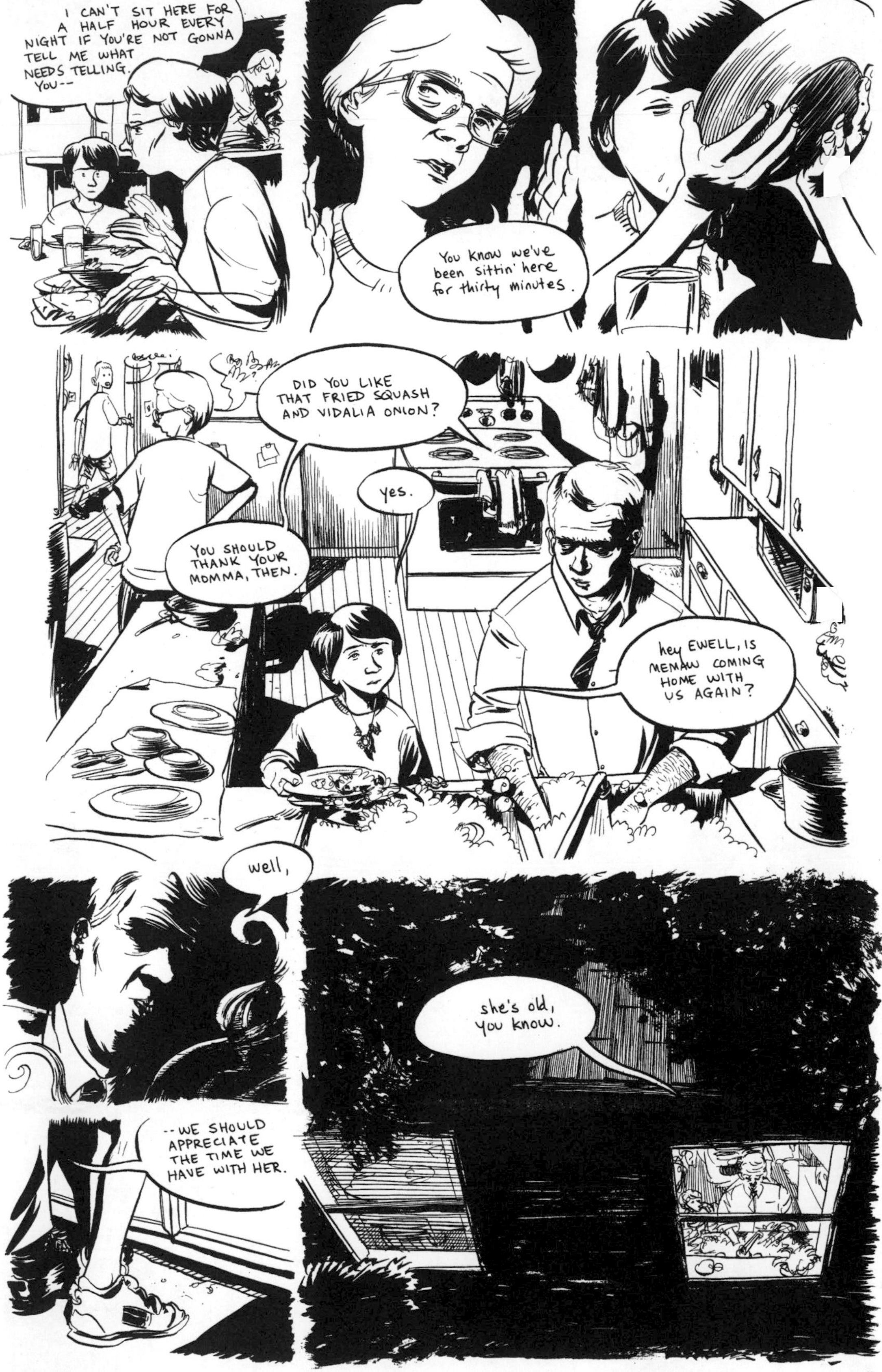
I CAN'T SIT HERE FOR A HALF HOUR EVERY NIGHT IF YOU'RE NOT GONNA TELL ME WHAT NEEDS TELLING. YOU--
You know we've been sittin' here for thirty minutes.
DID YOU LIKE THAT FRIED SQUASH AND VIDALIA ONION?
yes.
YOU SHOULD THANK YOUR MOMMA, THEN.
hey EWELL, IS MEMAW COMING HOME WITH US AGAIN?
well,
she's old, you know.
--WE SHOULD APPRECIATE THE TIME WE HAVE WITH HER.

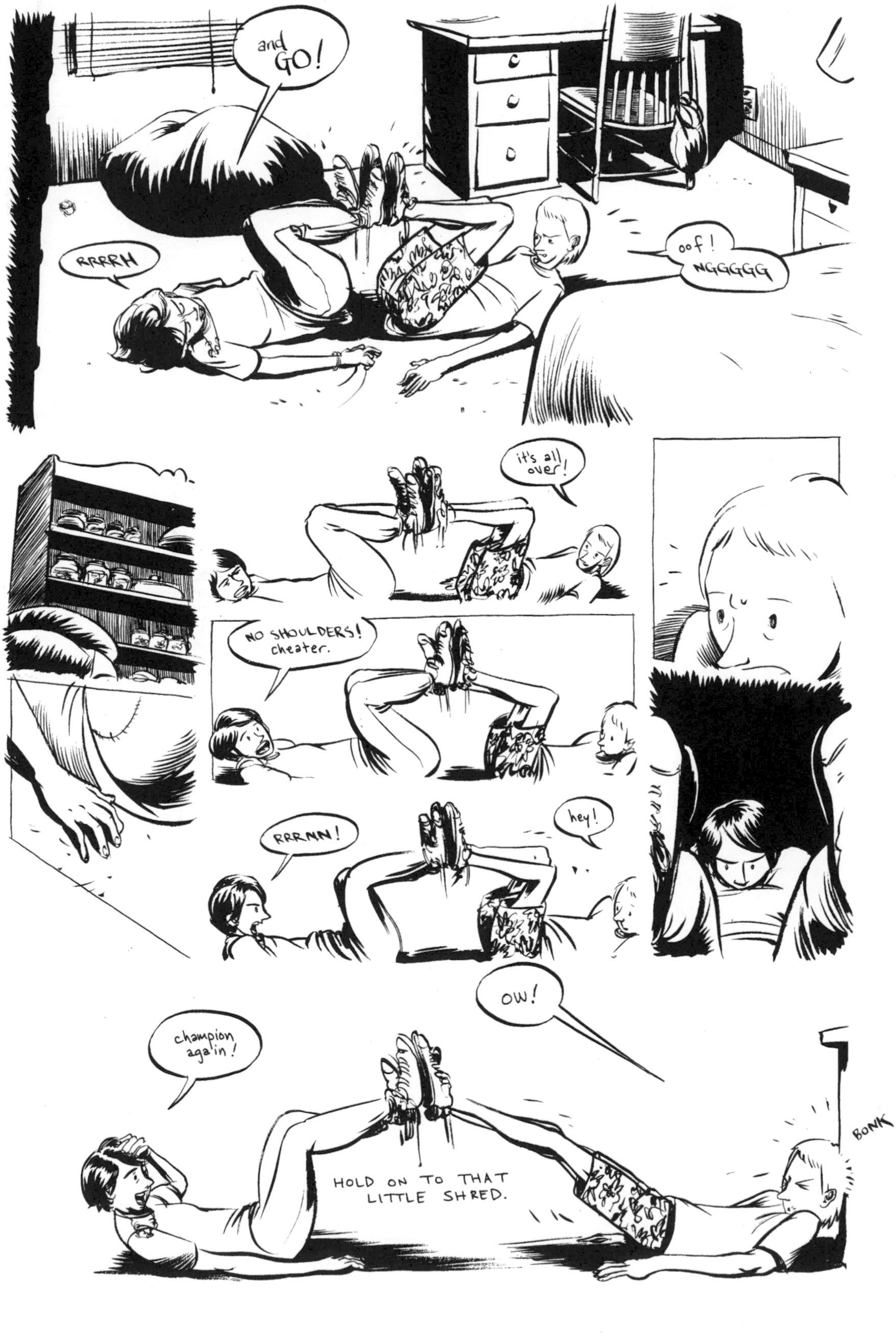

and GO!
RRRRH
oof! NGGGGG
it's all over!
NO SHOULDERS! cheater.
RRRNN!
hey!
champion again!
OW!
BONK
HOLD ON TO THAT LITTLE SHRED.

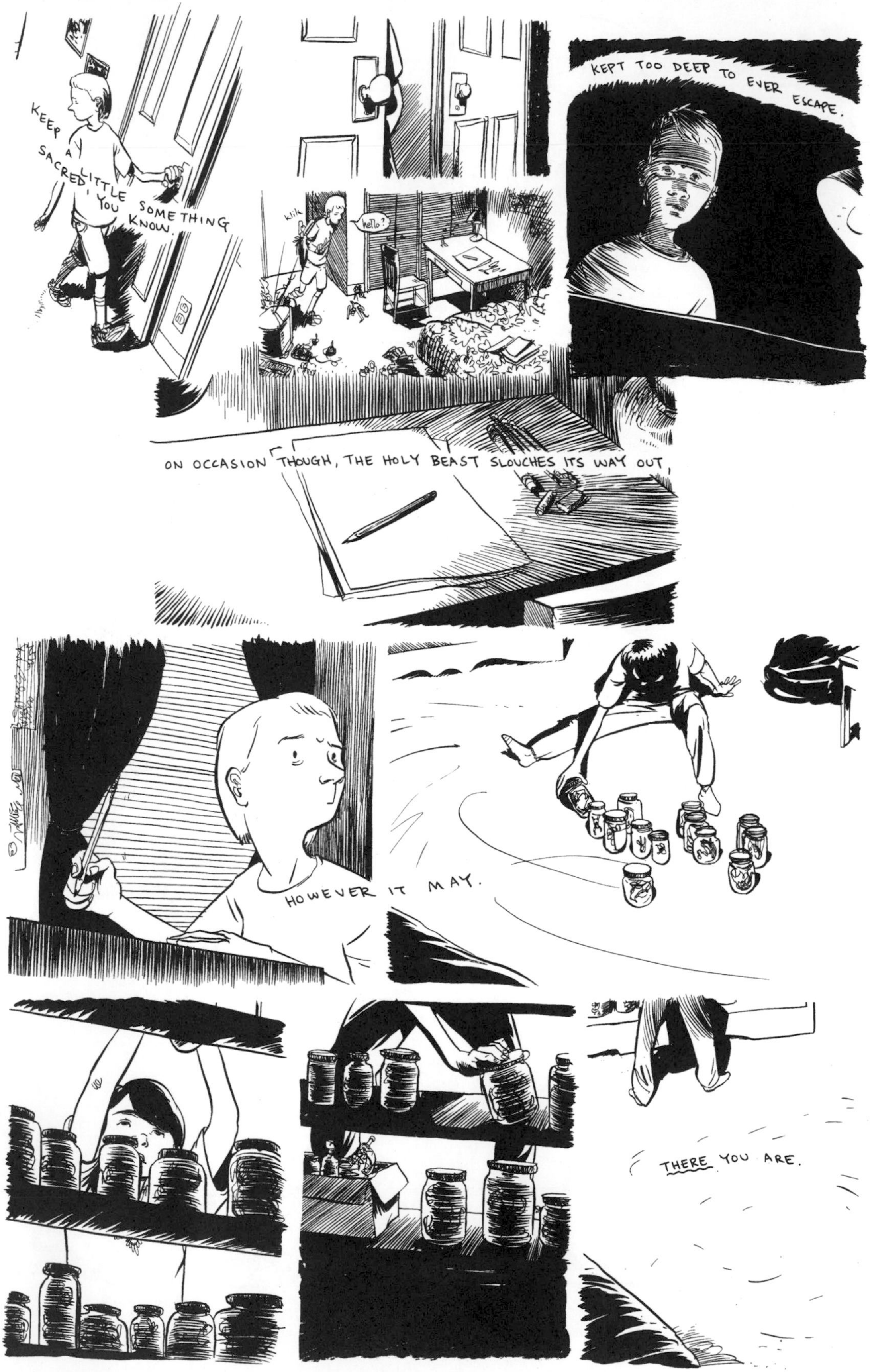
KEEP A LITTLE SOMETHING SACRED, YOU KNOW.
klik
hello?
KEPT TOO DEEP TO EVER ESCAPE.
ON OCCASION THOUGH, THE HOLY BEAST SLOUCHES ITS WAY OUT,
HOWEVER IT MAY.
THERE YOU ARE.

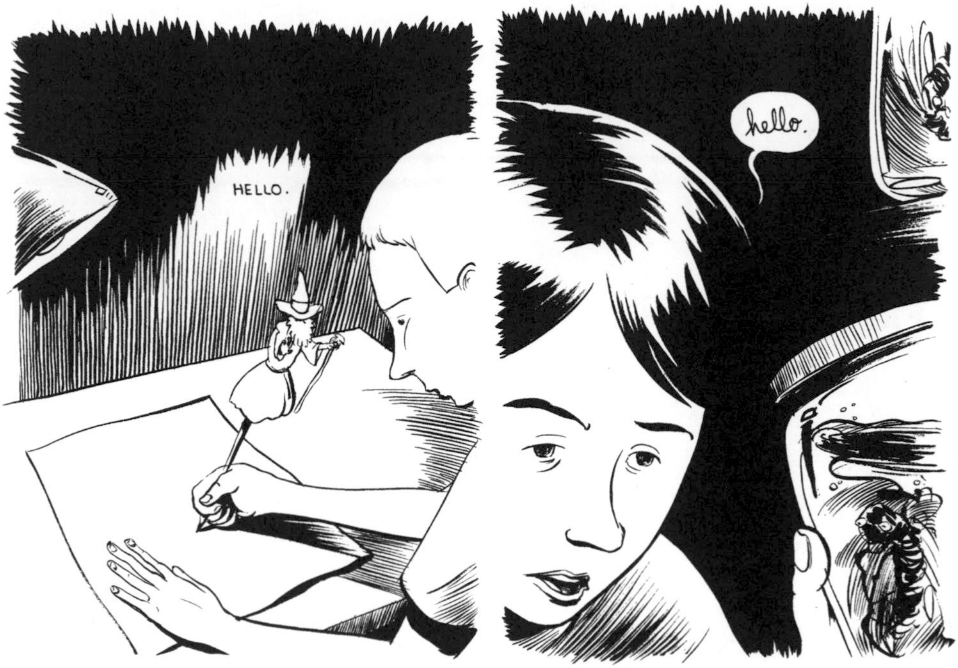
HELLO.
hello.

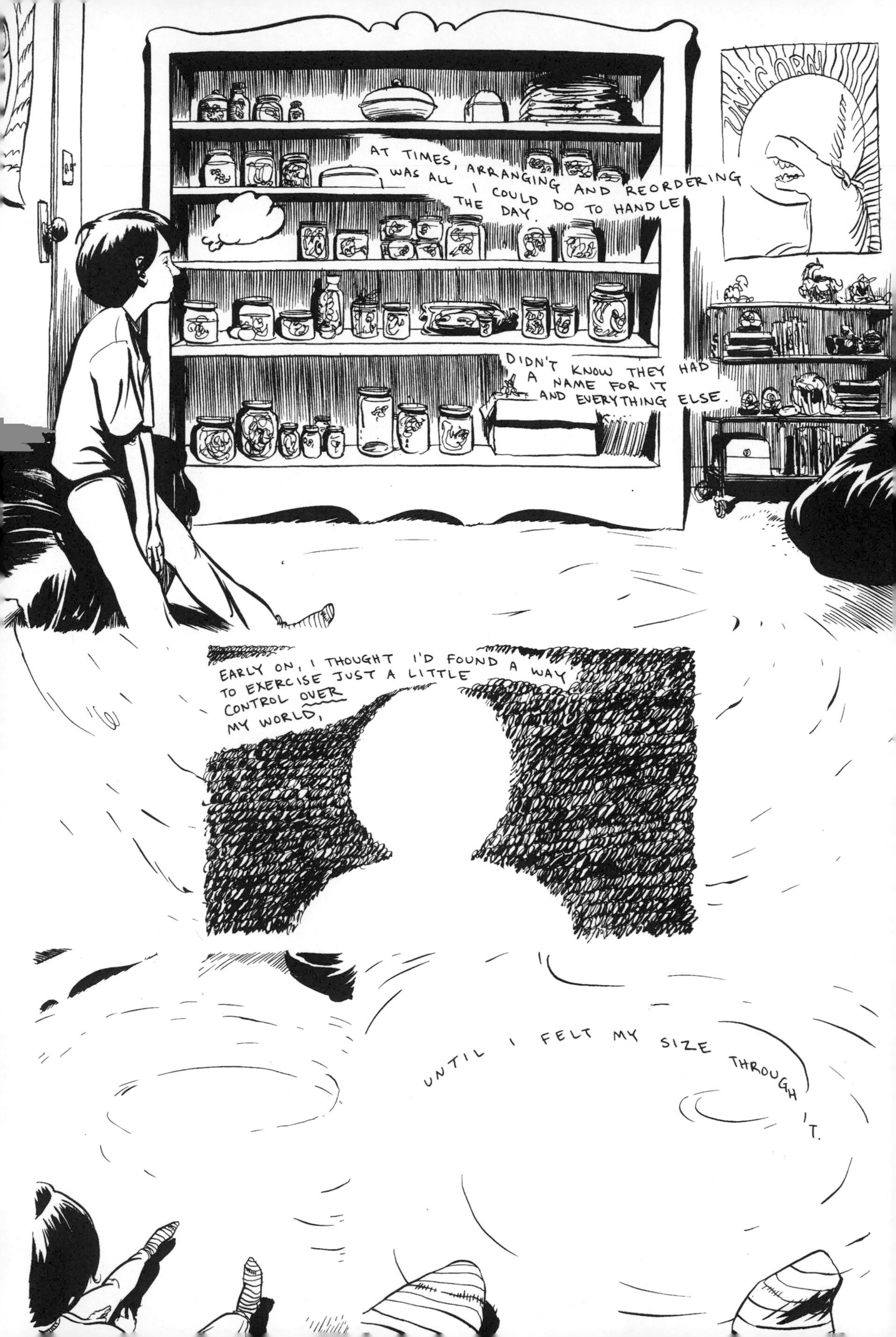
AT TIMES, ARRANGING AND REORDERING WAS ALL I COULD DO TO HANDLE THE DAY.
DIDN'T KNOW THEY HAD A NAME FOR IT AND EVERYTHING ELSE.
UNICORN
EARLY ON, I THOUGHT I'D FOUND A WAY TO EXERCISE JUST A LITTLE CONTROL OVER MY WORLD,
UNTIL I FELT MY SIZE THROUGH IT.

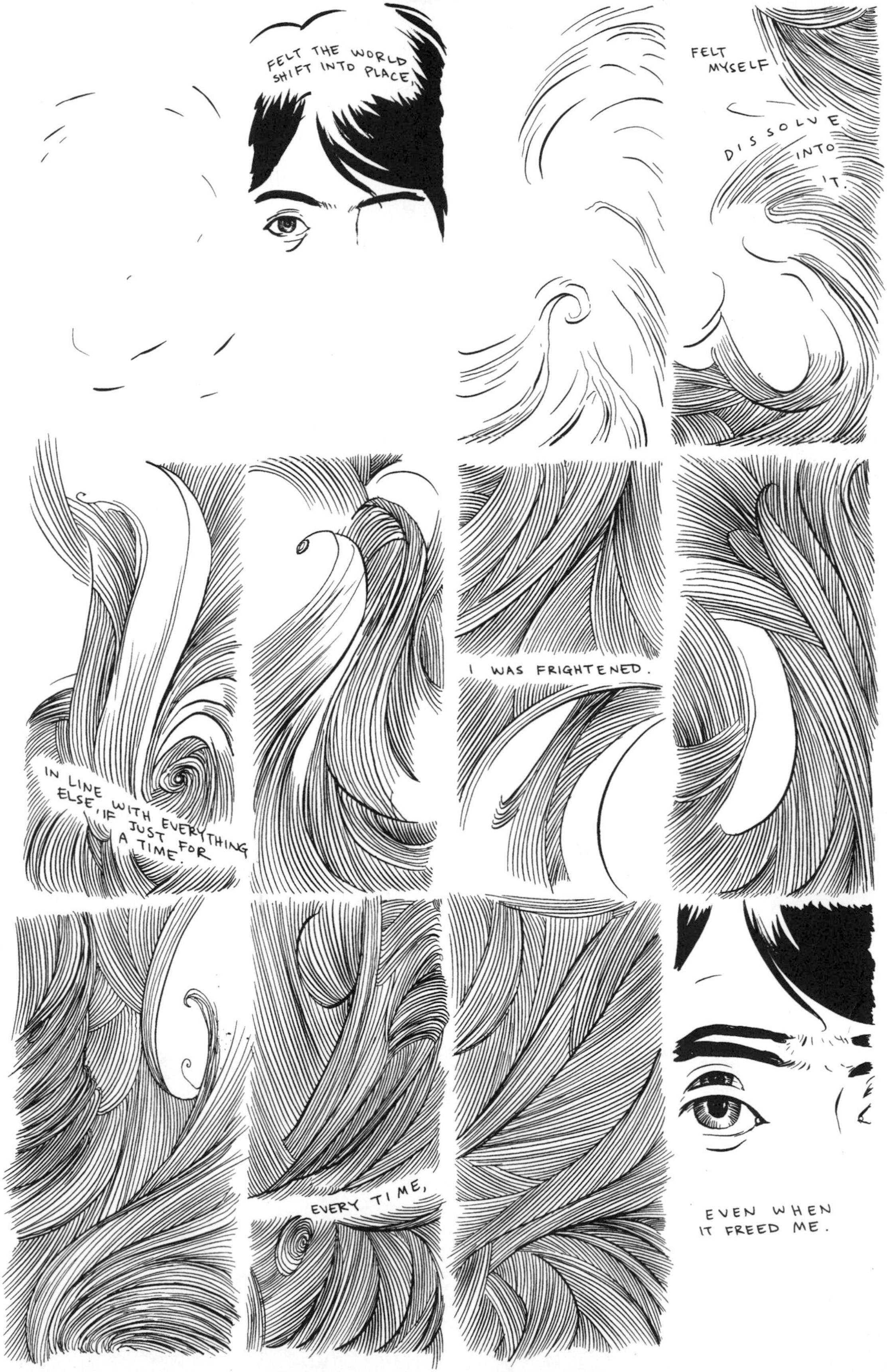
FELT THE WORLD SHIFT INTO PLACE,
FELT MYSELF
DISSOLVE INTO IT.
IN LINE WITH EVERYTHING ELSE, IF JUST FOR A TIME.
I WAS FRIGHTENED.
EVERY TIME,
EVEN WHEN IT FREED ME.

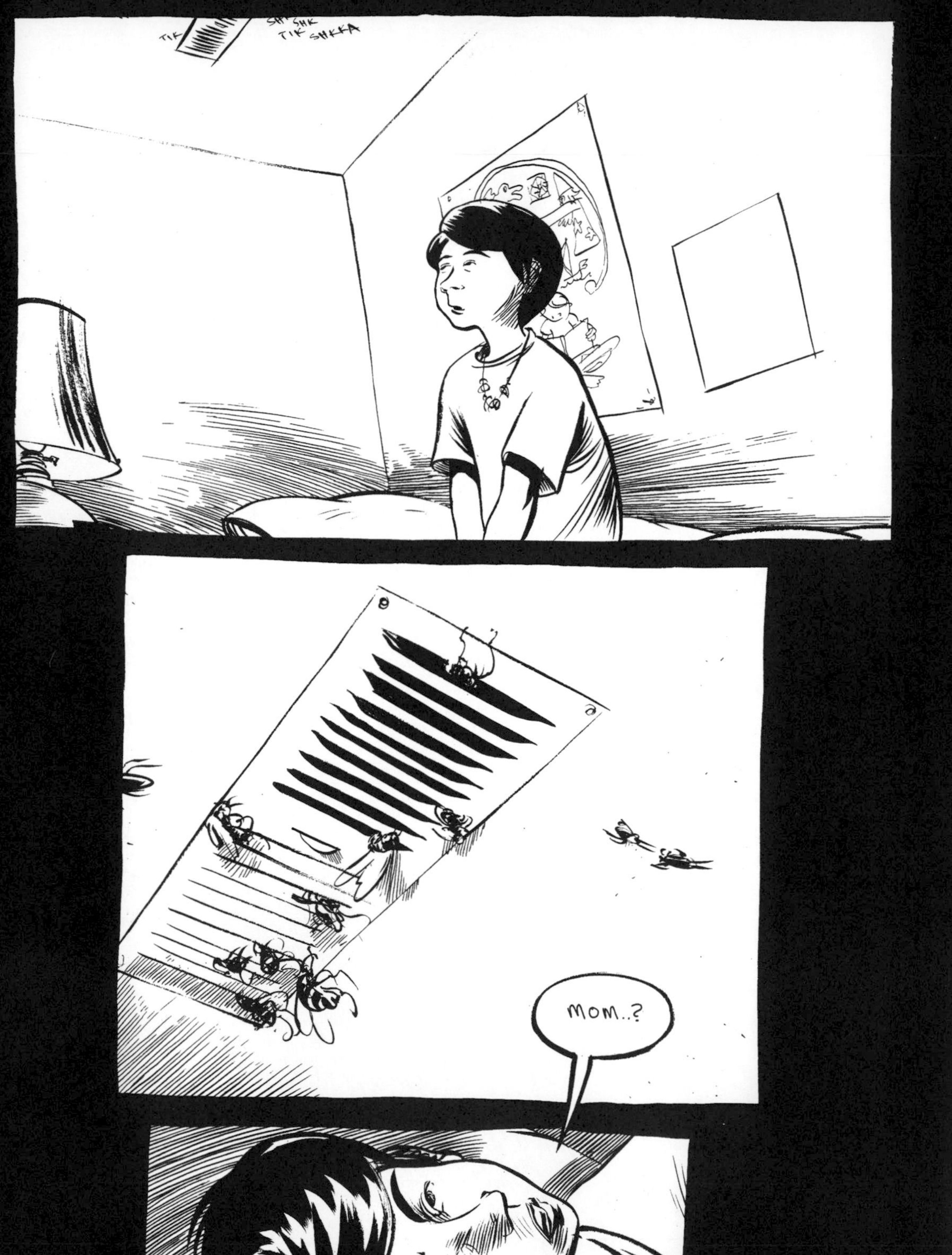
TIK
SHK
TIK
SHKKA
MOM..?

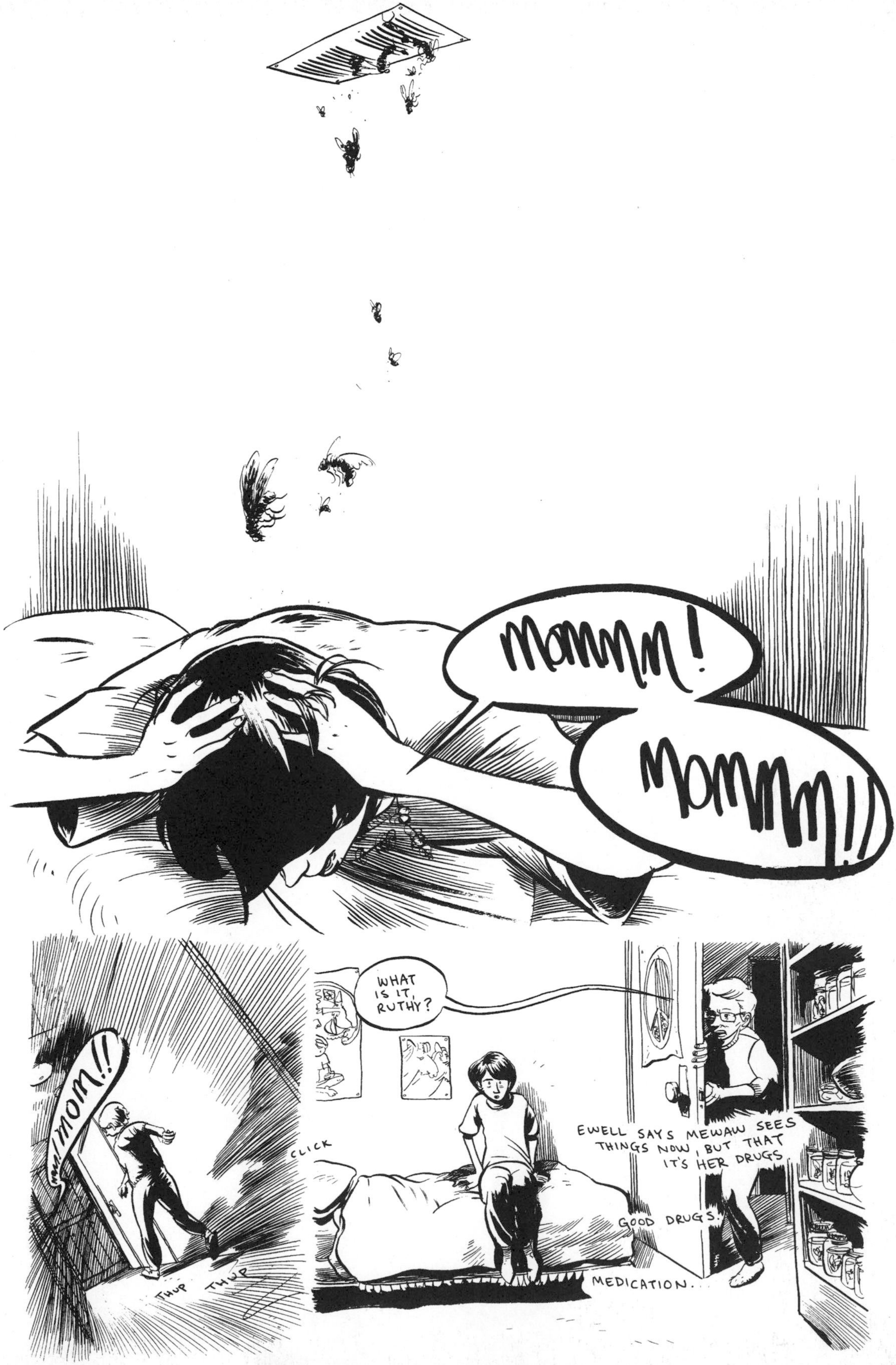

MOMMM!
MOMMM!!
MOM!!
CLICK
THUP THUP
WHAT IS IT, RUTHY?
EWELL SAYS MEWAW SEES THINGS NOW, BUT THAT IT'S HER DRUGS.
GOOD DRUGS.
MEDICATION..

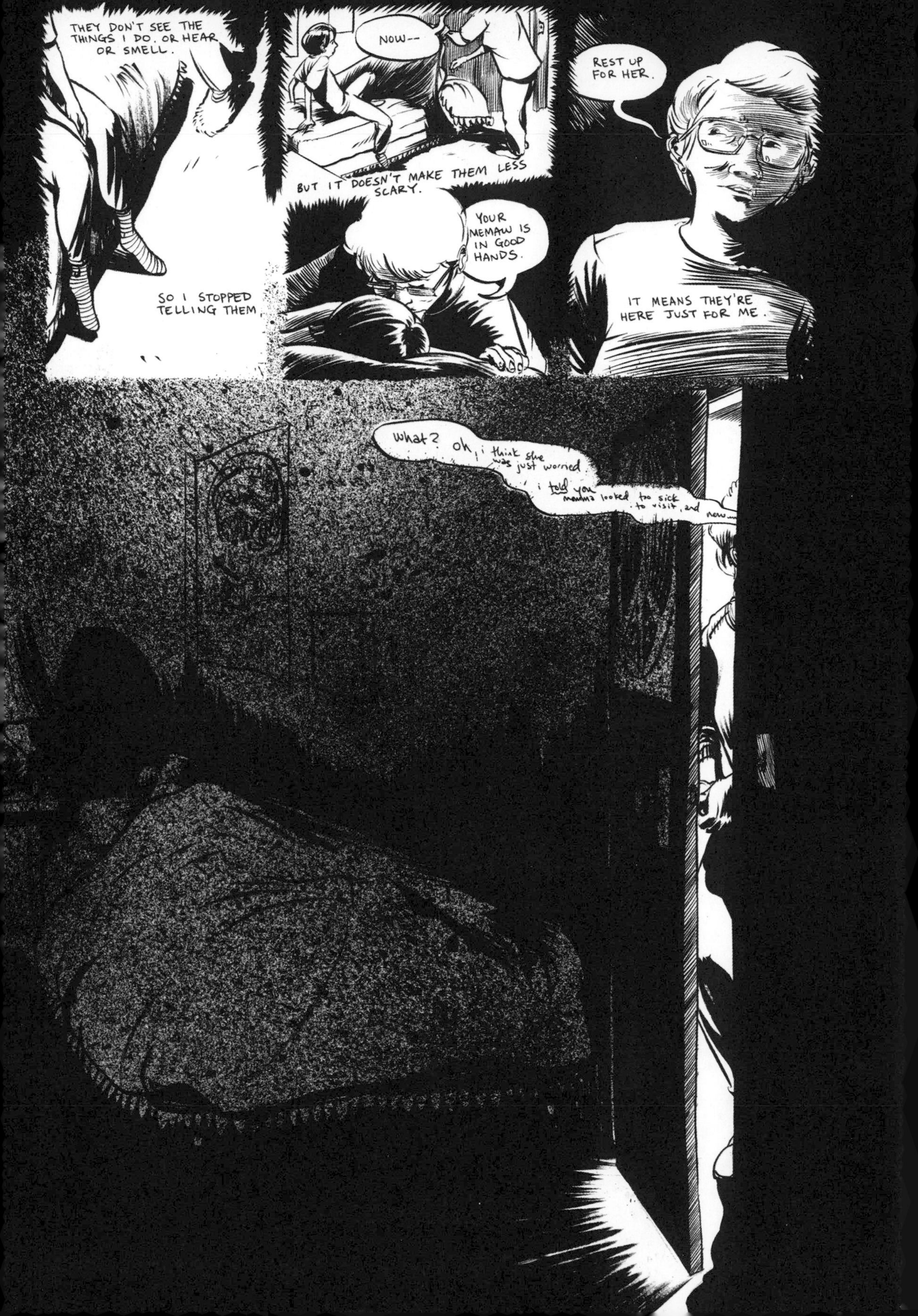
THEY DON'T SEE THE THINGS I DO, OR HEAR OR SMELL.
SO I STOPPED TELLING THEM.
NOW--
BUT IT DOESN'T MAKE THEM LESS SCARY.
YOUR MEMAW IS IN GOOD HANDS.
REST UP FOR HER.
IT MEANS THEY'RE HERE JUST FOR ME.
what? oh, i think she was just worried. i told you mamma looked too sick to visit, and now...

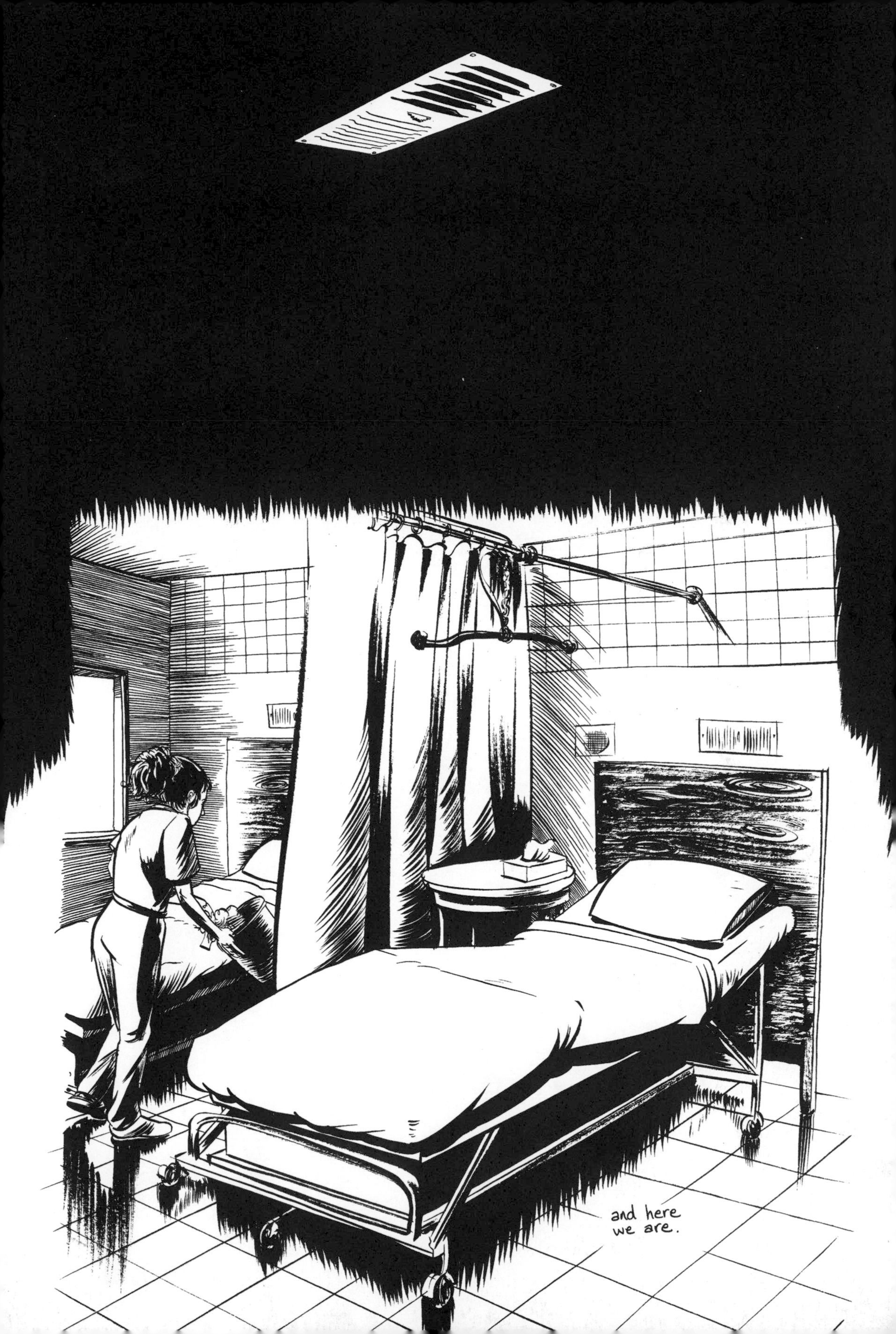
and here we are.

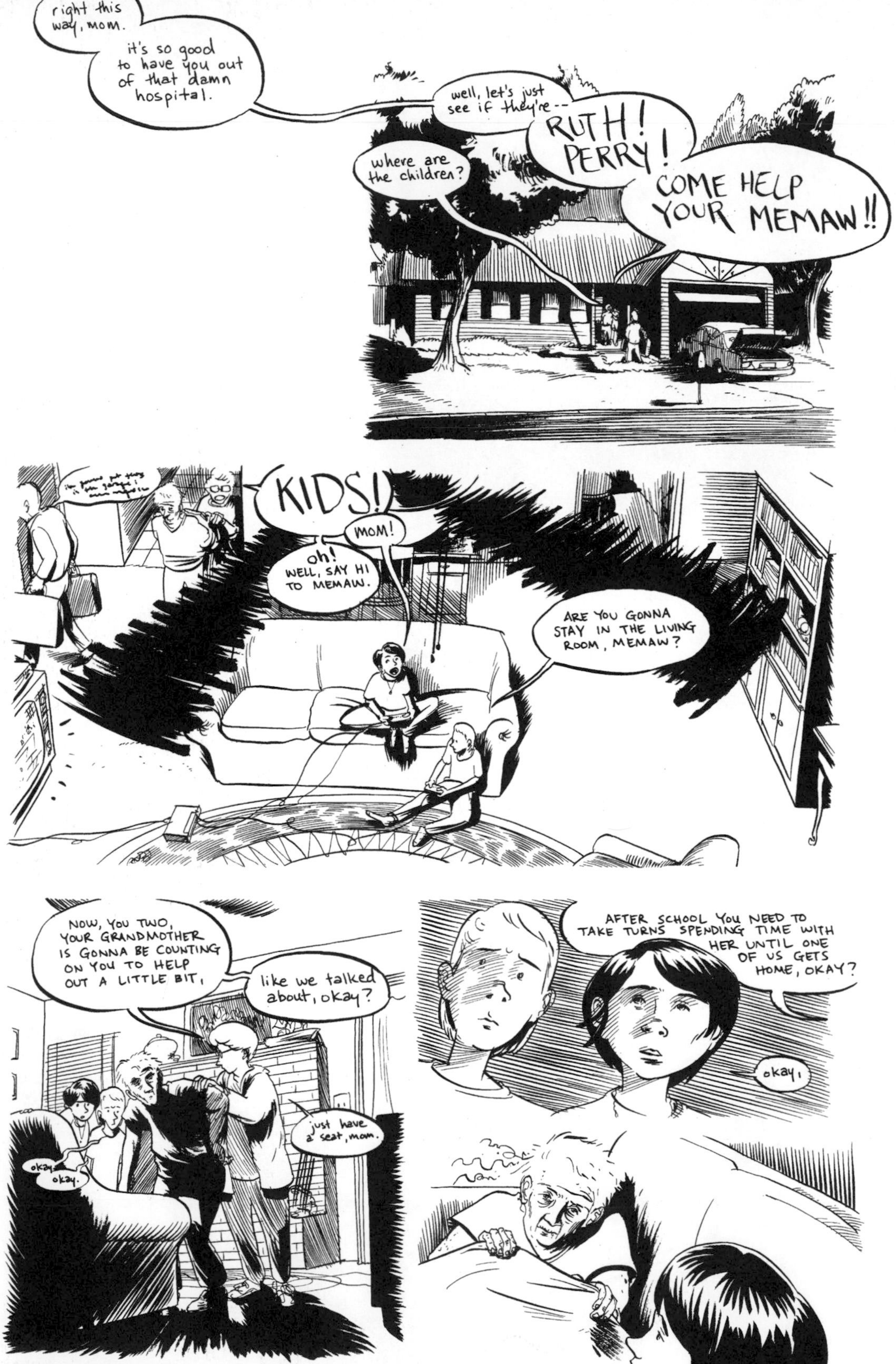
right this way, mom.
it's so good to have you out of that damn hospital.
well, let's just see if they're--
RUTH! PERRY!
COME HELP YOUR MEMAW!!
where are the children?
KIDS!
MOM!
oh! WELL, SAY HI TO MEMAW.
ARE YOU GONNA STAY IN THE LIVING ROOM, MEMAW?
NOW, YOU TWO, YOUR GRANDMOTHER IS GONNA BE COUNTING ON YOU TO HELP OUT A LITTLE BIT,
like we talked about, okay?
just have a seat, mom.
okay.
okay.
AFTER SCHOOL YOU NEED TO TAKE TURNS SPENDING TIME WITH HER UNTIL ONE OF US GETS HOME, OKAY?
okay.

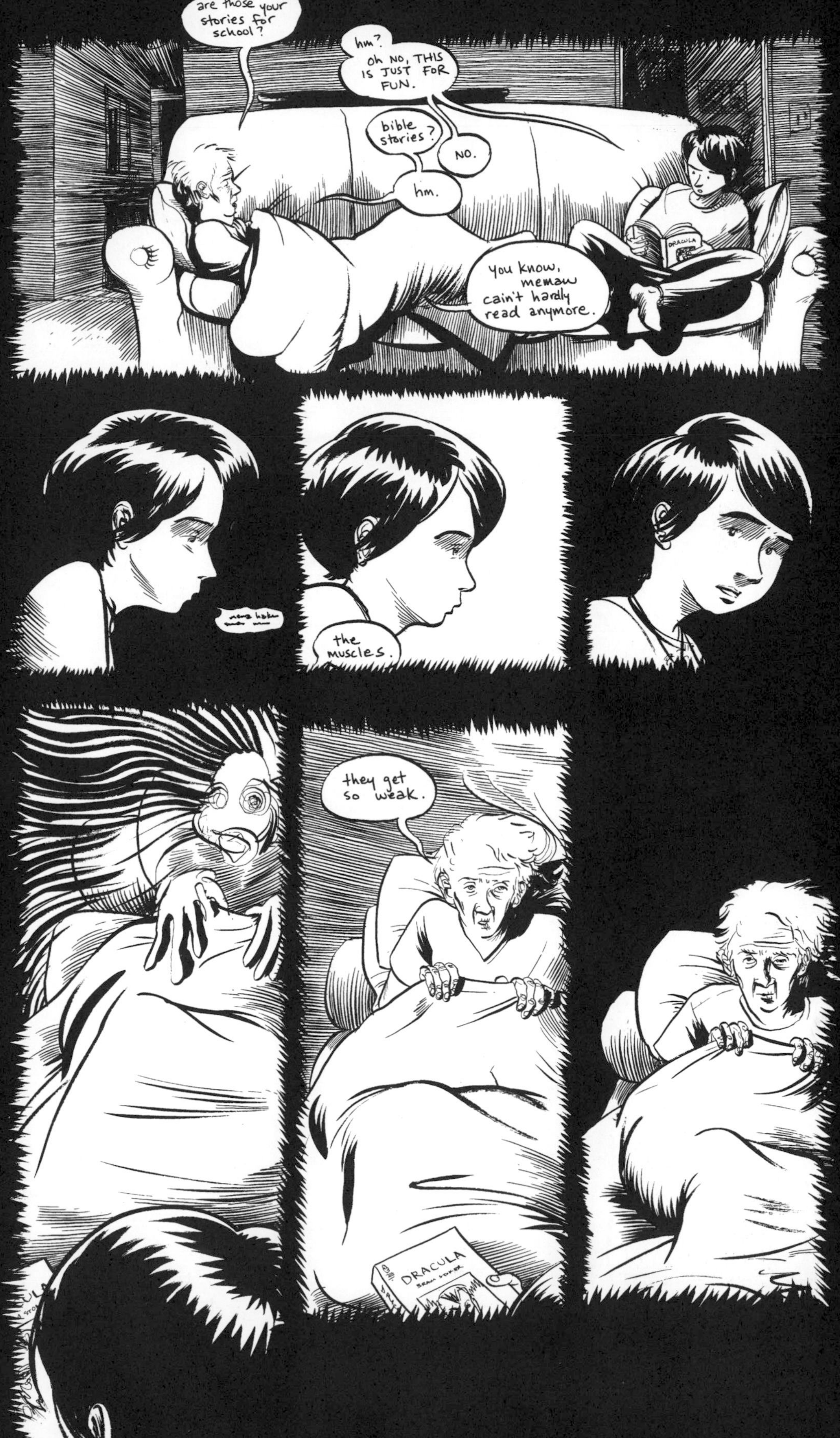

are those your stories for school?
hm? oh NO, THIS IS JUST FOR FUN.
bible stories?
NO.
hm.
DRACULA
you know, memaw cain't hardly read anymore.
the muscles.
they get so weak.
DRACULA

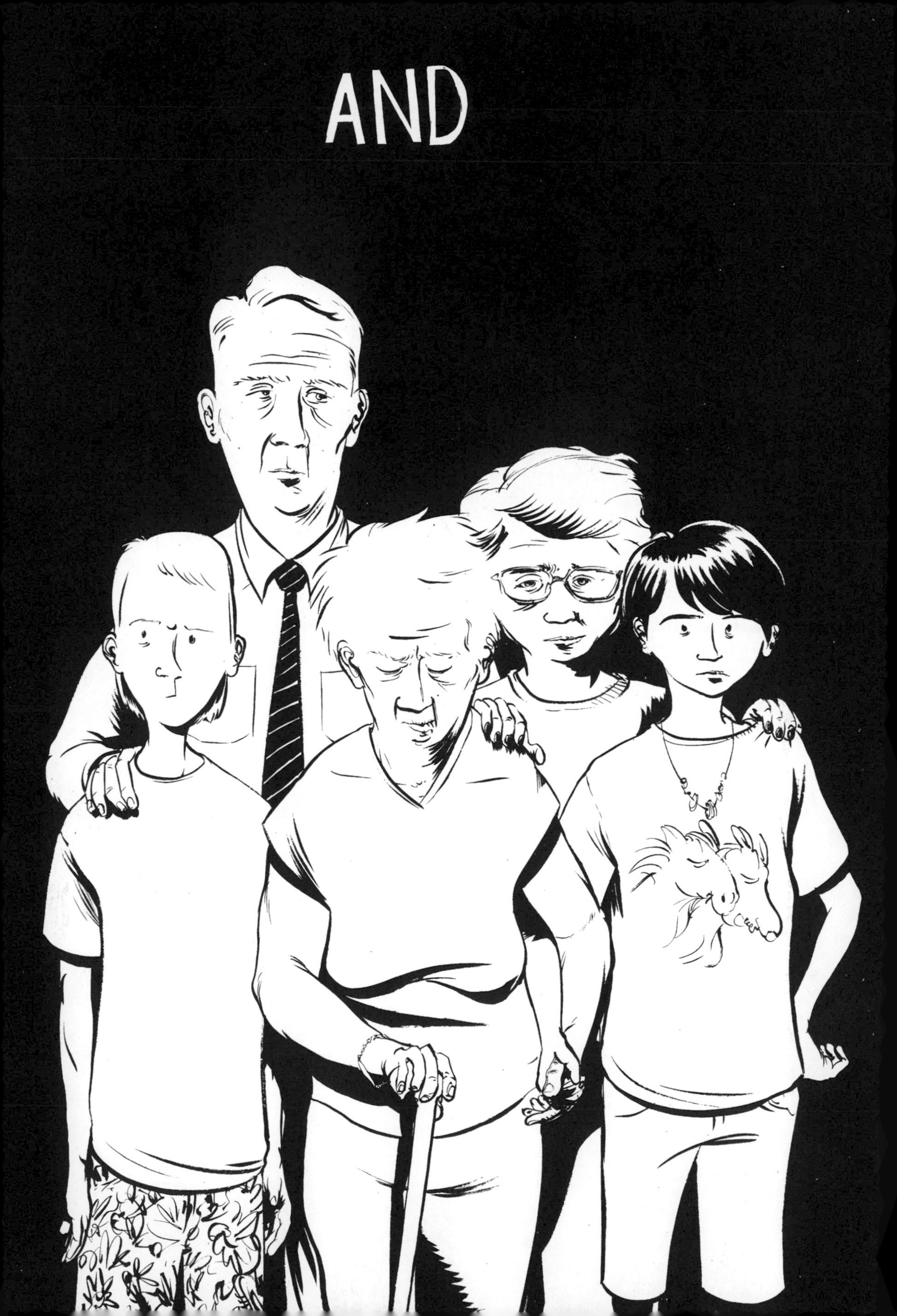
AND

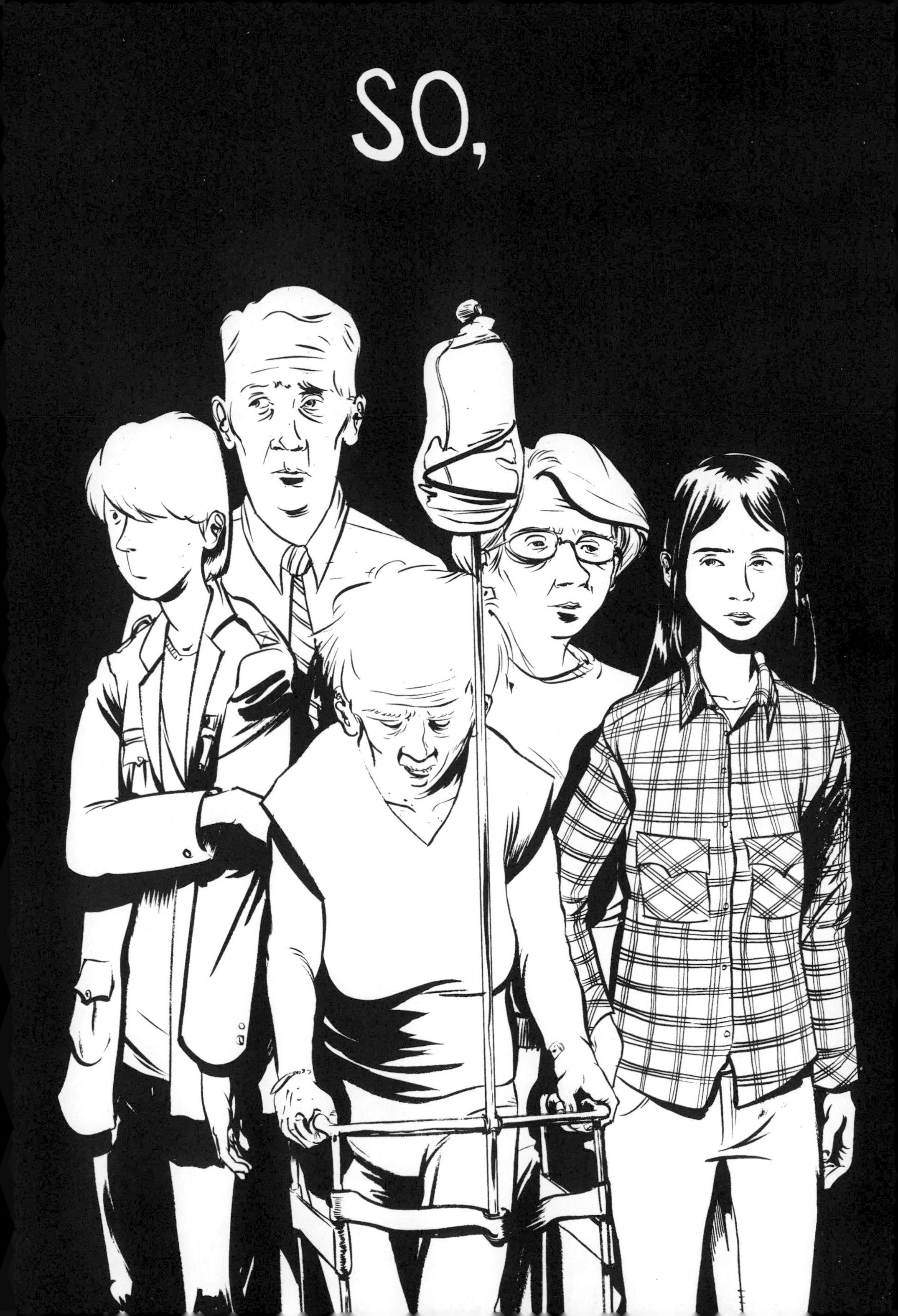
SO,

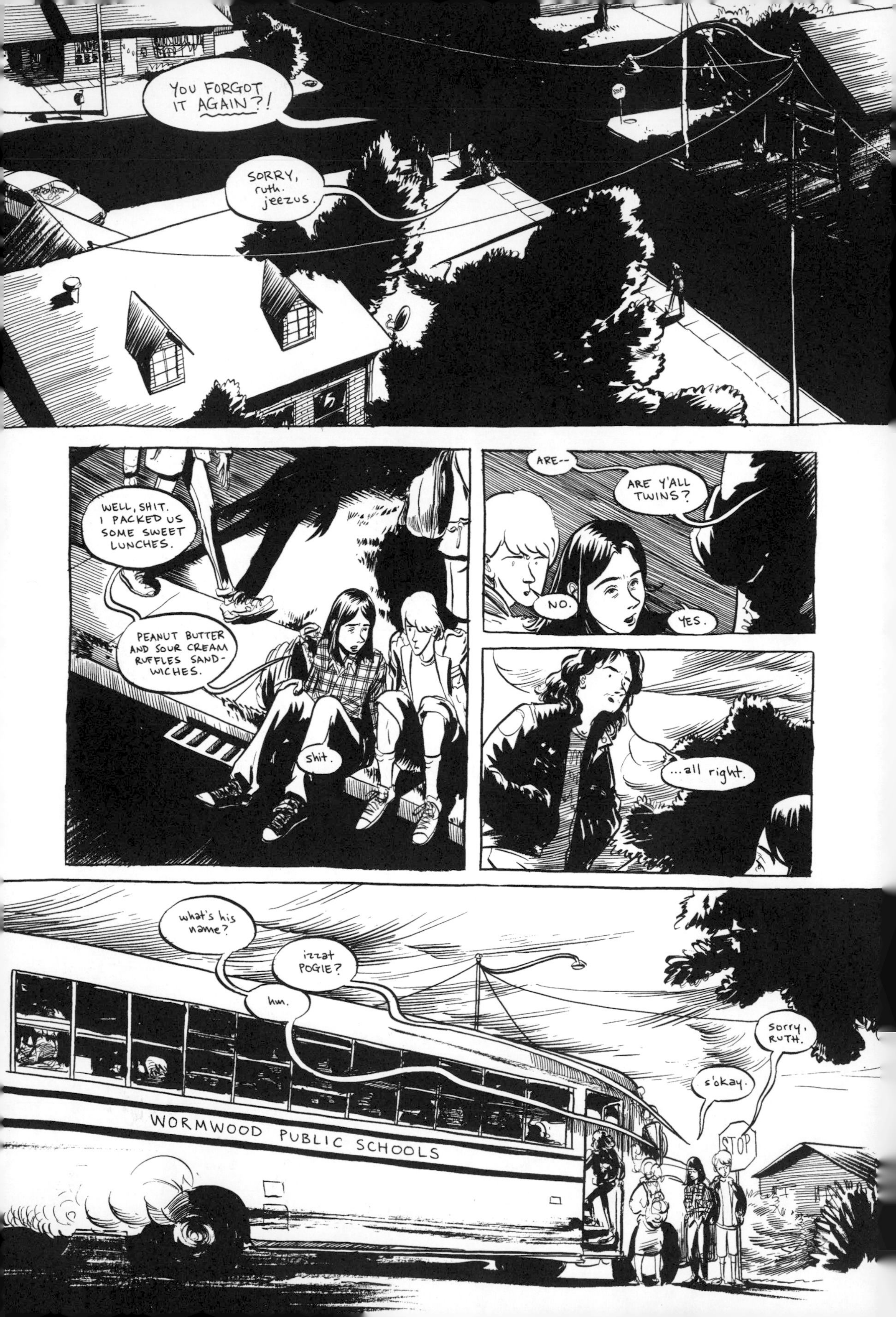
YOU FORGOT IT AGAIN?!
SORRY, ruth. jeezus.
WELL, SHIT. I PACKED US SOME SWEET LUNCHES.
PEANUT BUTTER AND SOUR CREAM RUFFLES SAND-WICHES.
shit.
ARE--
ARE Y'ALL TWINS?
NO.
YES.
...all right.
what's his name?
izzat POGIE?
hm.
sorry, RUTH.
s'okay.
WORMWOOD PUBLIC SCHOOLS
STOP

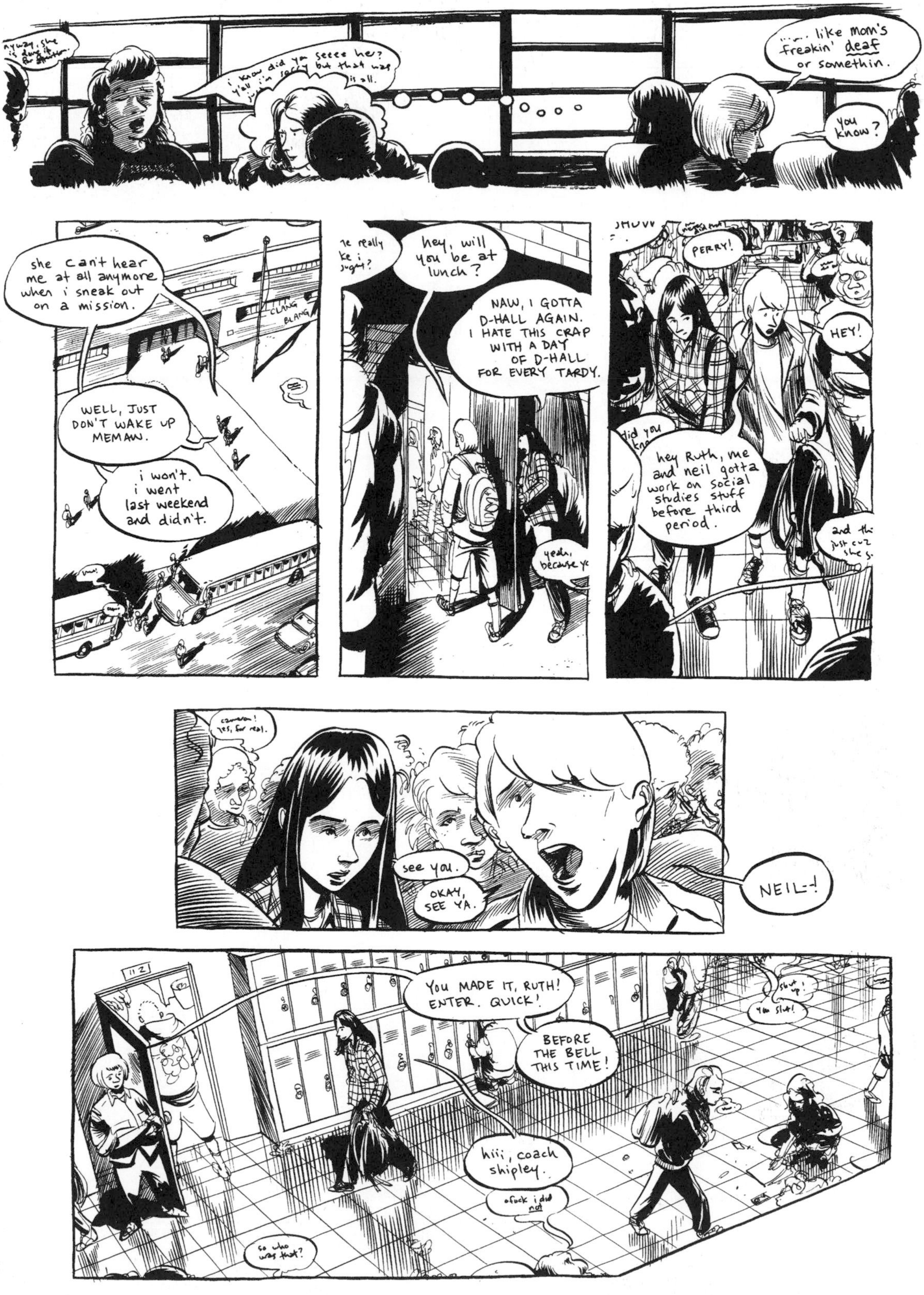
i know did you seeee her?
... like mom's freakin' deaf or somethin.
you know?
she can't hear me at all anymore when i sneak out on a mission.
CLANG BLANG
WELL, JUST DON'T WAKE UP MEMAW.
i won't. i went last weekend and didn't.
hey, will you be at lunch?
NAW, I GOTTA D-HALL AGAIN. I HATE THIS CRAP WITH A DAY OF D-HALL FOR EVERY TARDY.
PERRY!
HEY!
hey Ruth, me and neil gotta work on social studies stuff before third period.
see you.
OKAY, SEE YA.
NEIL--!
YOU MADE IT, RUTH! ENTER. QUICK!
BEFORE THE BELL THIS TIME!
hiii, coach shipley.
shut up!
You slut!
so who was that?

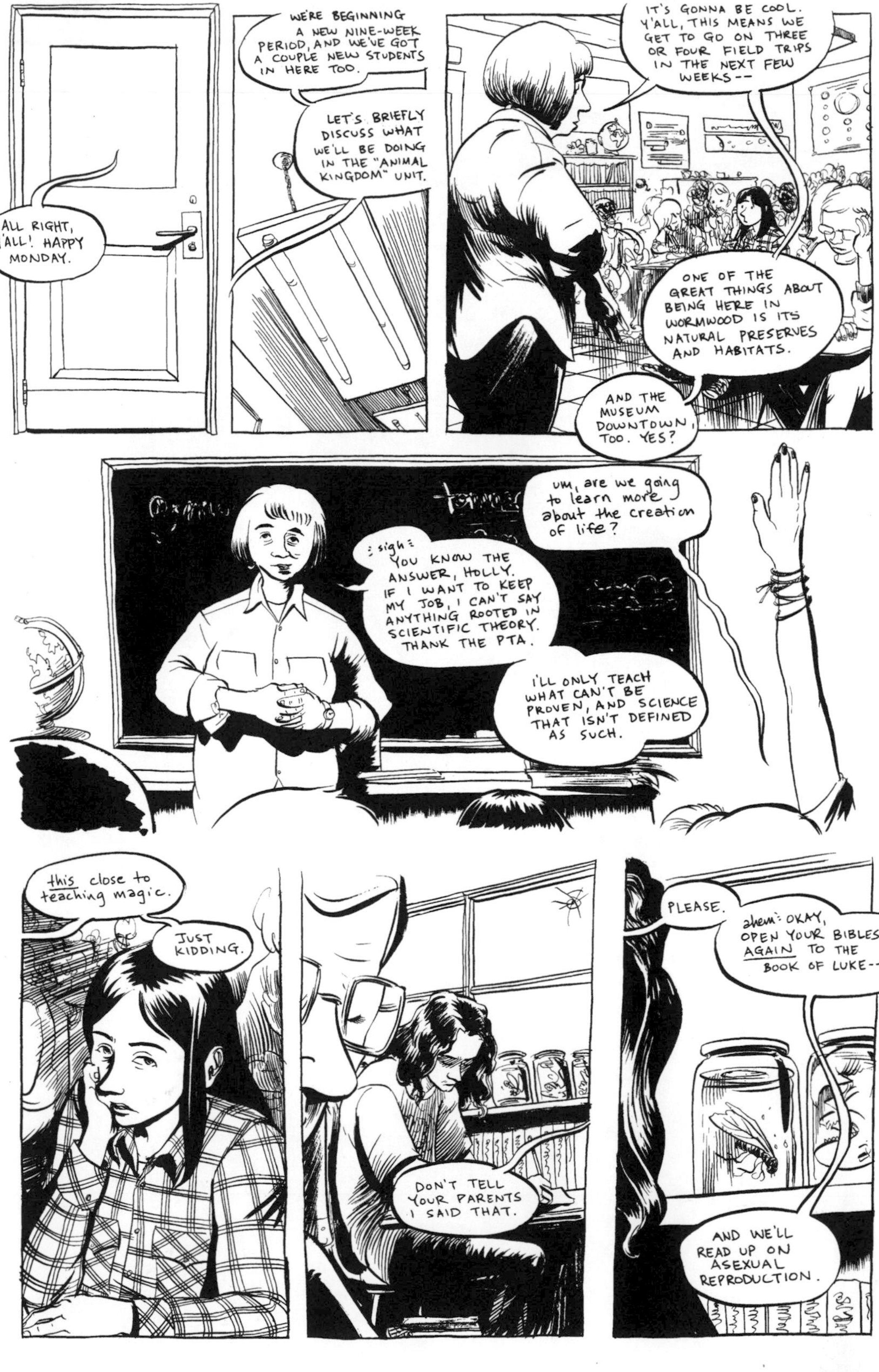
ALL RIGHT, Y'ALL! HAPPY MONDAY.
WE'RE BEGINNING A NEW NINE-WEEK PERIOD, AND WE'VE GOT A COUPLE NEW STUDENTS IN HERE TOO.
LET'S BRIEFLY DISCUSS WHAT WE'LL BE DOING IN THE "ANIMAL KINGDOM" UNIT.
NO, REALLY! IT'S GONNA BE COOL. Y'ALL, THIS MEANS WE GET TO GO ON THREE OR FOUR FIELD TRIPS IN THE NEXT FEW WEEKS--
ONE OF THE GREAT THINGS ABOUT BEING HERE IN WORMWOOD IS ITS NATURAL PRESERVES AND HABITATS.
AND THE MUSEUM DOWNTOWN, TOO. YES?
um, are we going to learn more about the creation of life?
:sigh: YOU KNOW THE ANSWER, HOLLY. IF I WANT TO KEEP MY JOB, I CAN'T SAY ANYTHING ROOTED IN SCIENTIFIC THEORY. THANK THE PTA.
I'LL ONLY TEACH WHAT CAN'T BE PROVEN, AND SCIENCE THAT ISN'T DEFINED AS SUCH.
this close to teaching magic.
JUST KIDDING.
DON'T TELL YOUR PARENTS I SAID THAT.
PLEASE.
ahem: OKAY, OPEN YOUR BIBLES AGAIN TO THE BOOK OF LUKE--
AND WE'LL READ UP ON ASEXUAL REPRODUCTION.

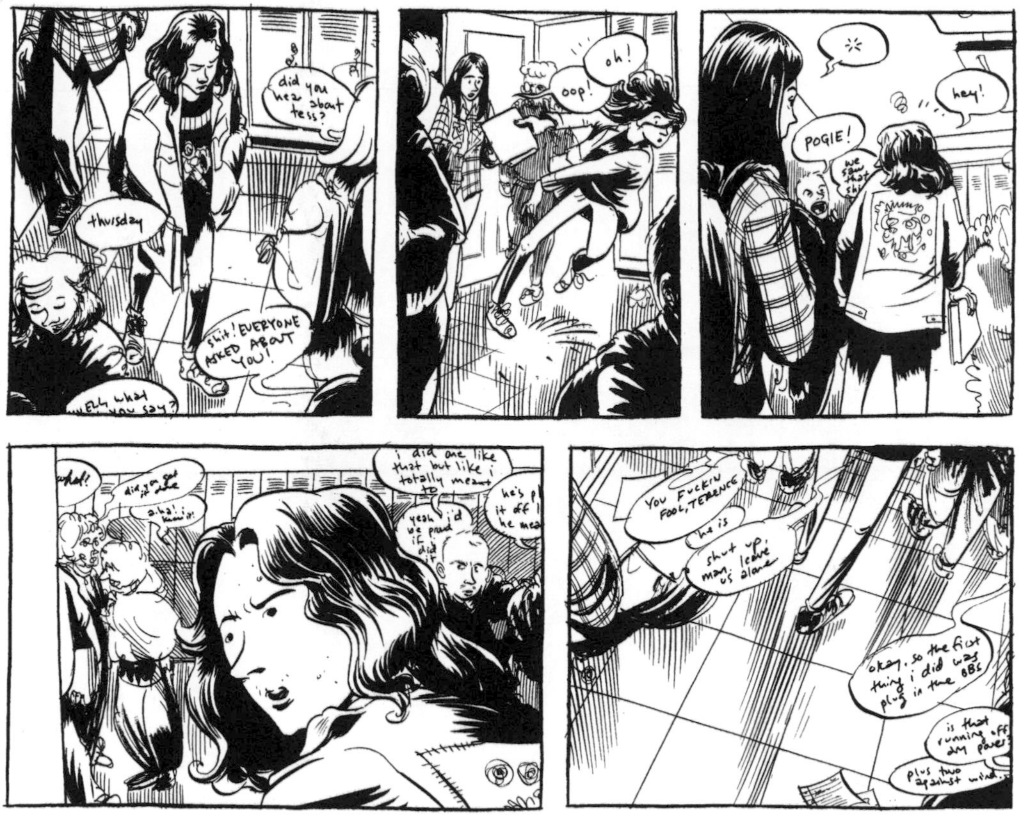
did you hear about tess?
thursday
shit! EVERYONE ASKED ABOUT YOU!
oop!
oh!
hey!
POGIE!
did you get it done
a-ha! knew it!
i did one like that but like i totally meant to
yeah i'd be proud if i did it
YOU FUCKIN FOOL, TERENCE
he is
shut up, man. leave us alone
okay, so the first thing i did was plug in the BBS
is that running off dry power?
plus two against wind

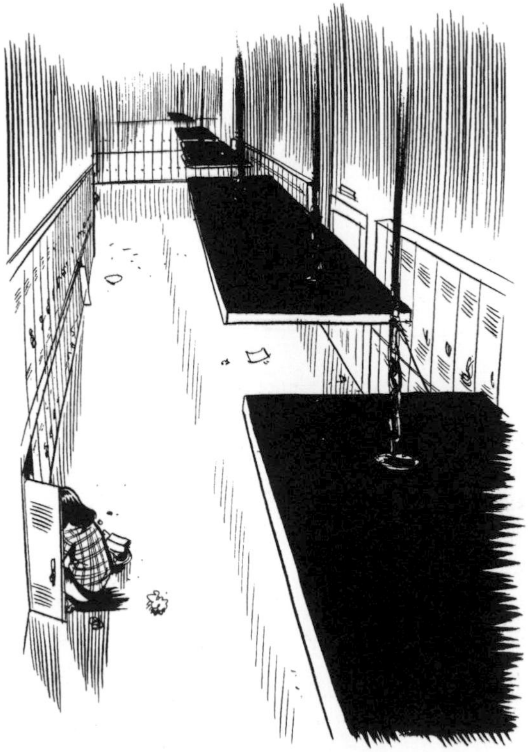

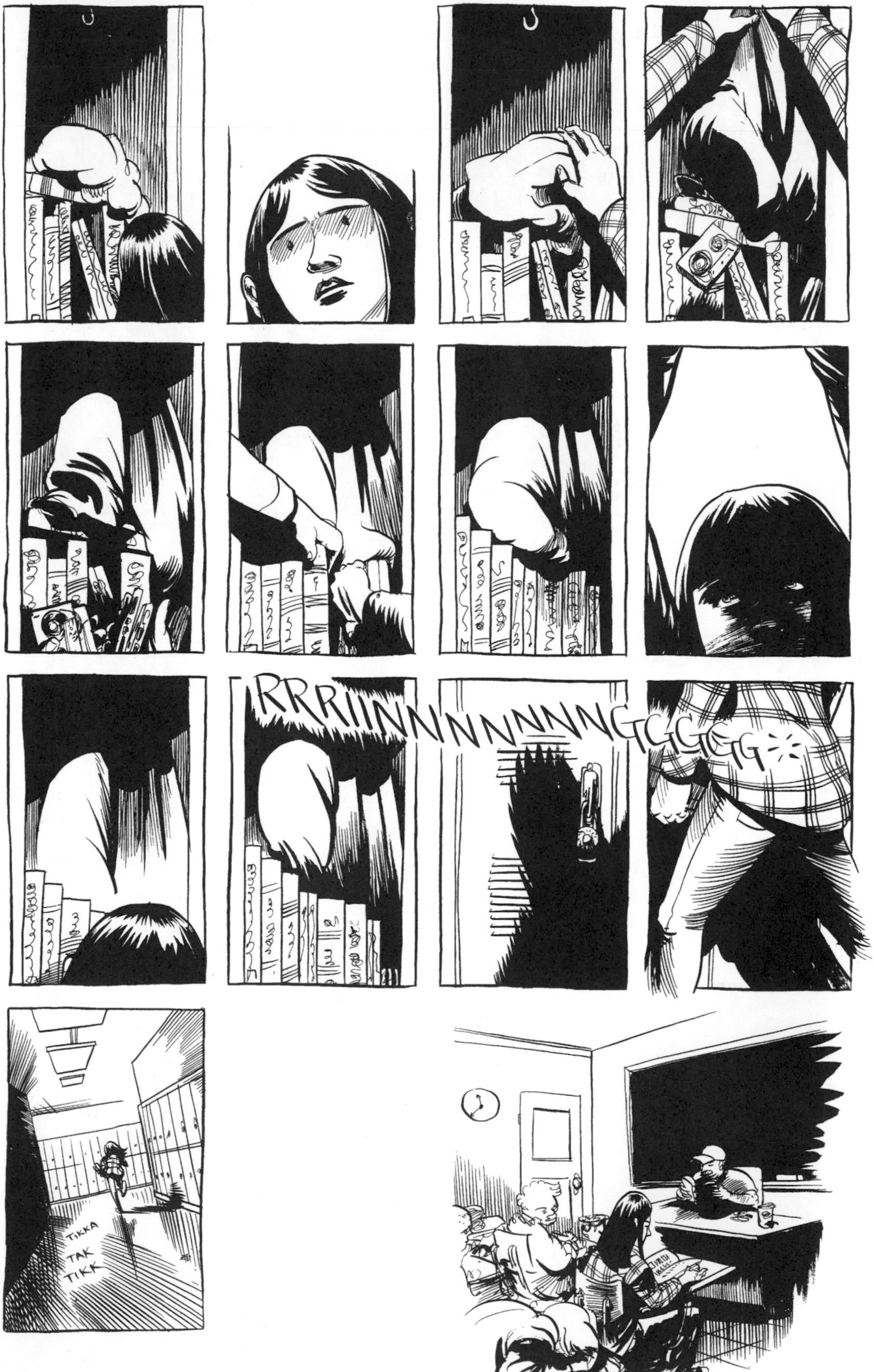
RRRIINNNNNNNNGGGGG
TIKKA
TAK
TIKK

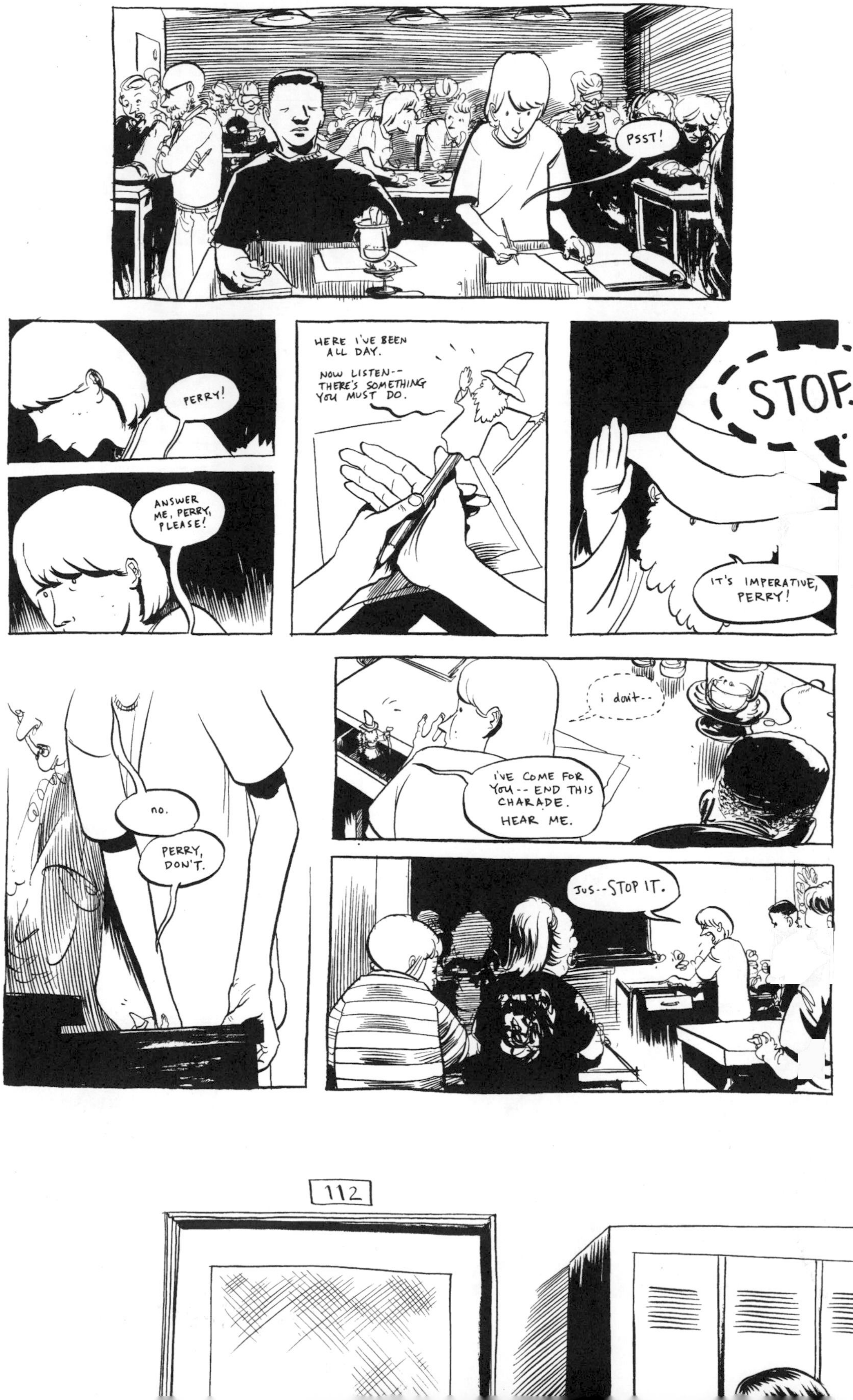
PSST!
PERRY!
ANSWER ME, PERRY, PLEASE!
HERE I'VE BEEN ALL DAY.
NOW LISTEN-- THERE'S SOMETHING YOU MUST DO.
STOP.
IT'S IMPERATIVE, PERRY!
no.
PERRY, DON'T.
i don't--
I'VE COME FOR YOU-- END THIS CHARADE.
HEAR ME.
JUS--STOP IT.
112

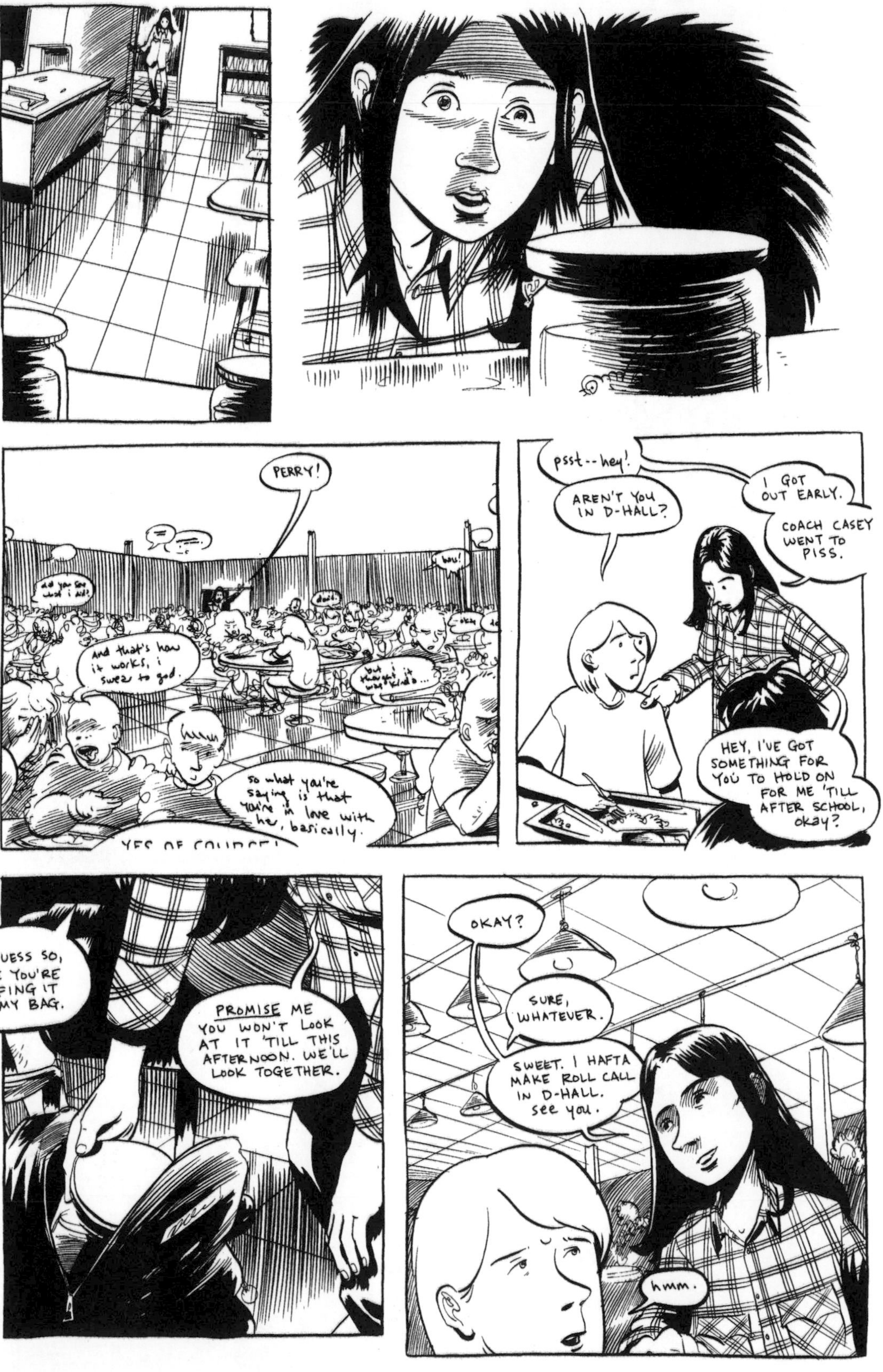
PERRY!
did you see what i did?
And that's how it works, i swear to god.
but i thought it was kinda...
so what you're saying is that you're in love with her, basically.
YES OF COURSE!
psst--hey!
AREN'T YOU IN D-HALL?
I GOT OUT EARLY.
COACH CASEY WENT TO PISS.
HEY, I'VE GOT SOMETHING FOR YOU TO HOLD ON FOR ME 'TILL AFTER SCHOOL, okay?
I GUESS SO, SINCE YOU'RE STUFFING IT IN MY BAG.
PROMISE ME YOU WON'T LOOK AT IT 'TILL THIS AFTERNOON. WE'LL LOOK TOGETHER.
OKAY?
SURE, WHATEVER.
SWEET. I HAFTA MAKE ROLL CALL IN D-HALL. see you.
hmm.

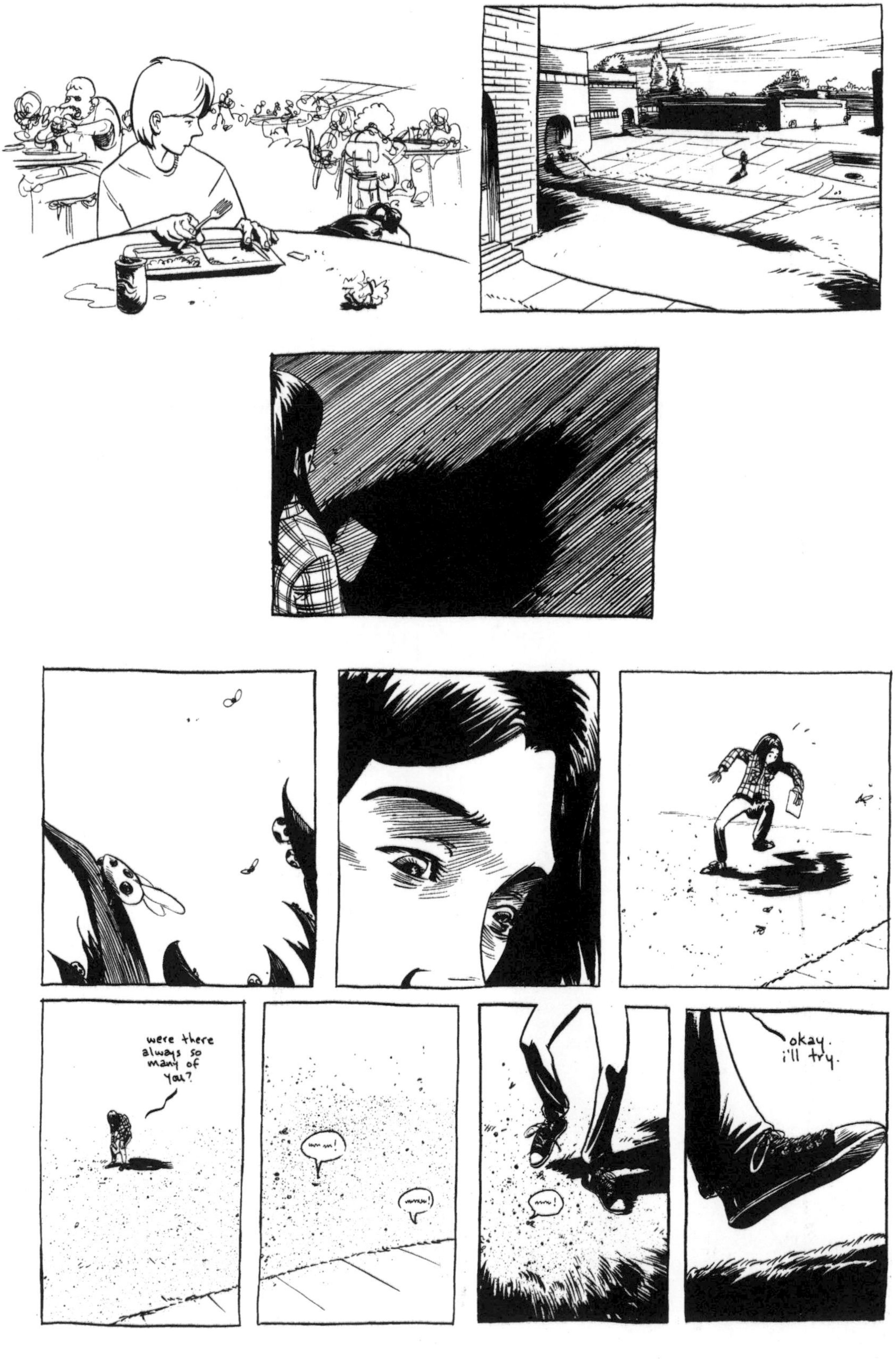
were there always so many of you?
mm!
mmm!
mm!
okay. i'll try.

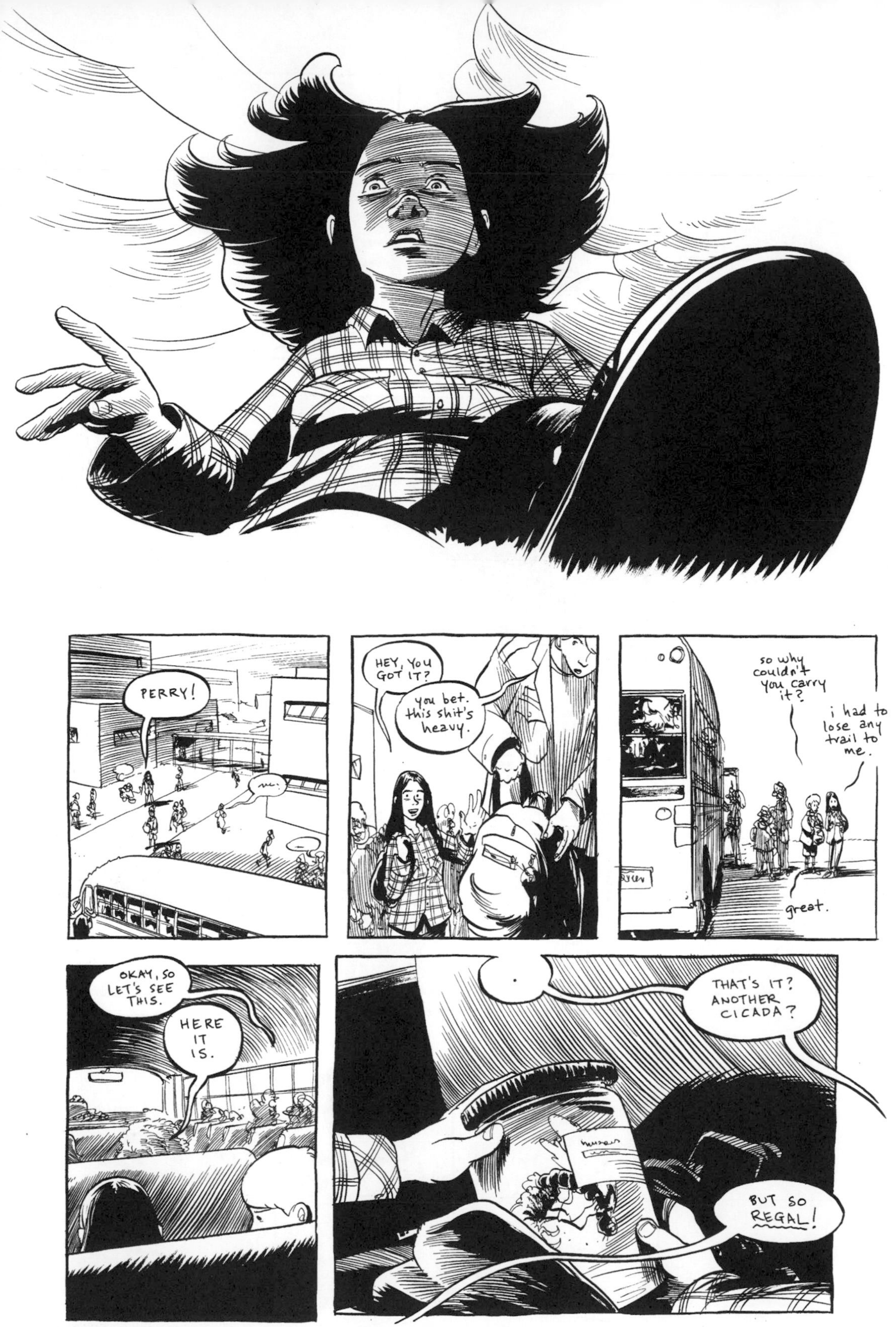
PERRY!
HEY, YOU GOT IT?
you bet. this shit's heavy.
so why couldn't you carry it?
i had to lose any trail to me.
great.
OKAY, SO LET'S SEE THIS.
HERE IT IS.
.
THAT'S IT? ANOTHER CICADA?
BUT SO REGAL!

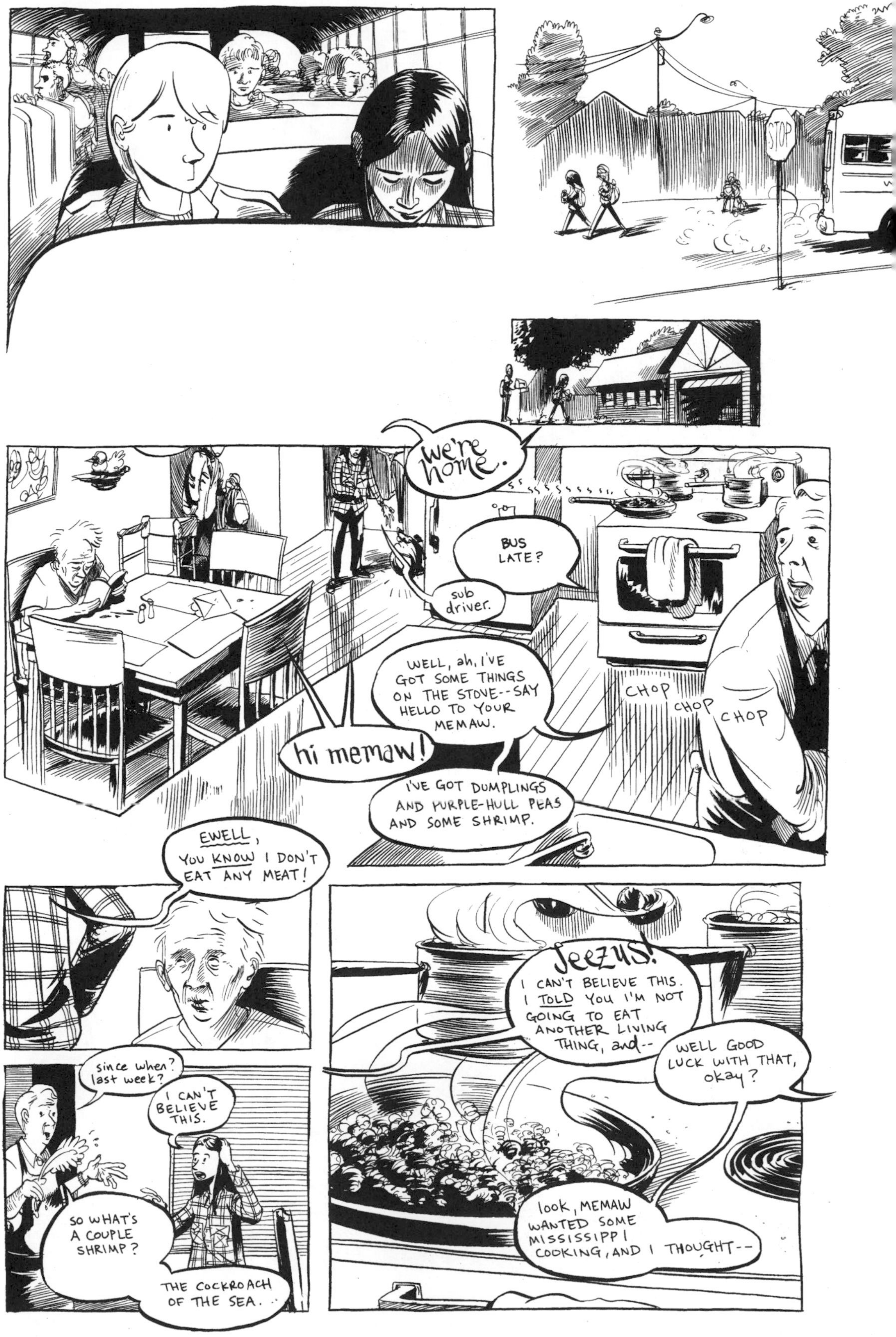
we're home.
BUS LATE?
sub driver.
WELL, ah, I'VE GOT SOME THINGS ON THE STOVE--SAY HELLO TO YOUR MEMAW.
CHOP CHOP CHOP
hi memaw!
I'VE GOT DUMPLINGS AND PURPLE-HULL PEAS AND SOME SHRIMP.
EWELL, YOU KNOW I DON'T EAT ANY MEAT!
Jeezus! I CAN'T BELIEVE THIS. I TOLD YOU I'M NOT GOING TO EAT ANOTHER LIVING THING, and--
WELL GOOD LUCK WITH THAT, okay?
since when? last week?
I CAN'T BELIEVE THIS.
SO WHAT'S A COUPLE SHRIMP?
THE COCKROACH OF THE SEA...
look, MEMAW WANTED SOME MISSISSIPPI COOKING, AND I THOUGHT--

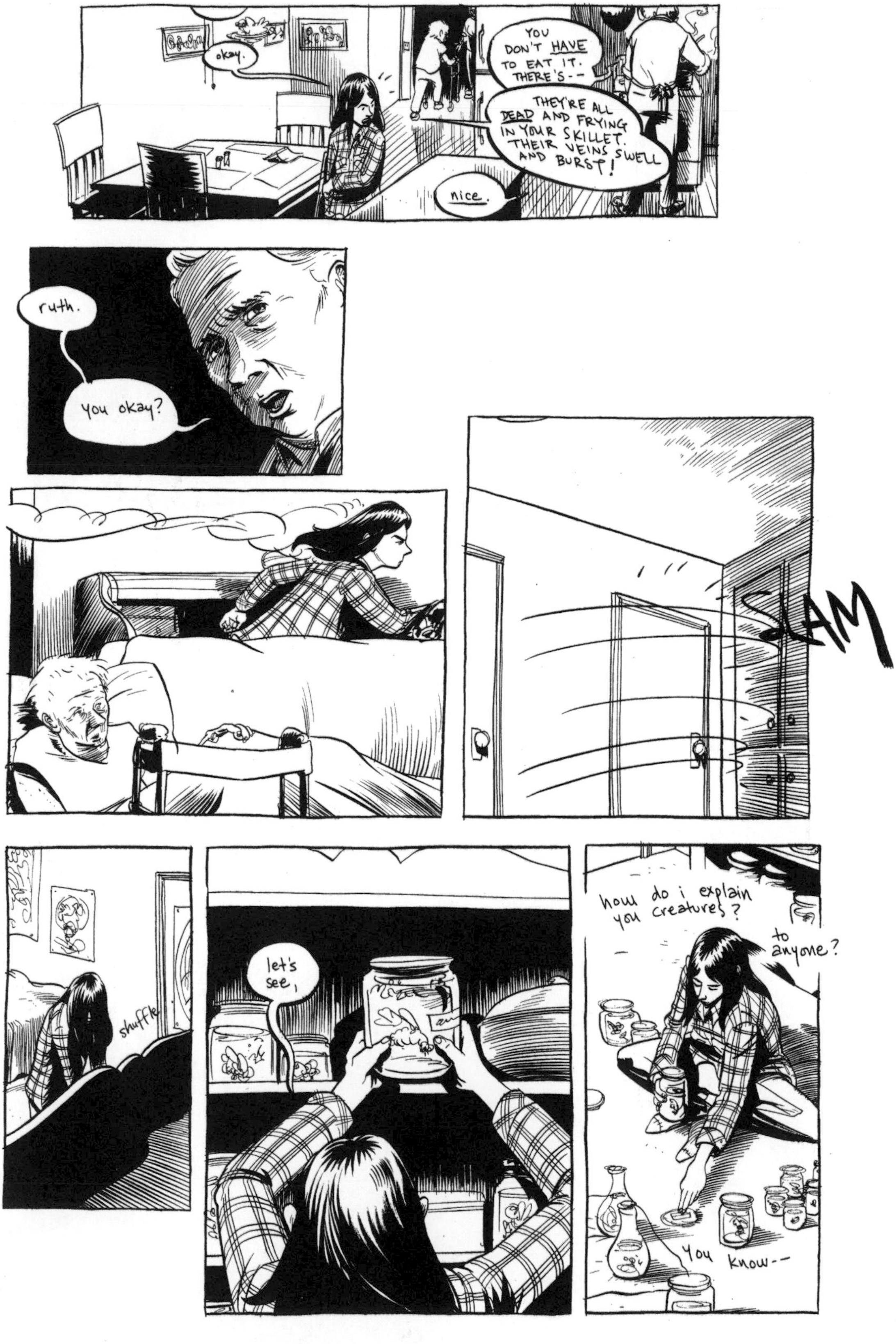
okay.
YOU DON'T HAVE TO EAT IT. THERE'S--
THEY'RE ALL DEAD AND FRYING IN YOUR SKILLET. THEIR VEINS SWELL AND BURST!
nice.
ruth.
you okay?
SLAM
shuffle
let's see,
how do i explain you creatures?
to anyone?
You know--

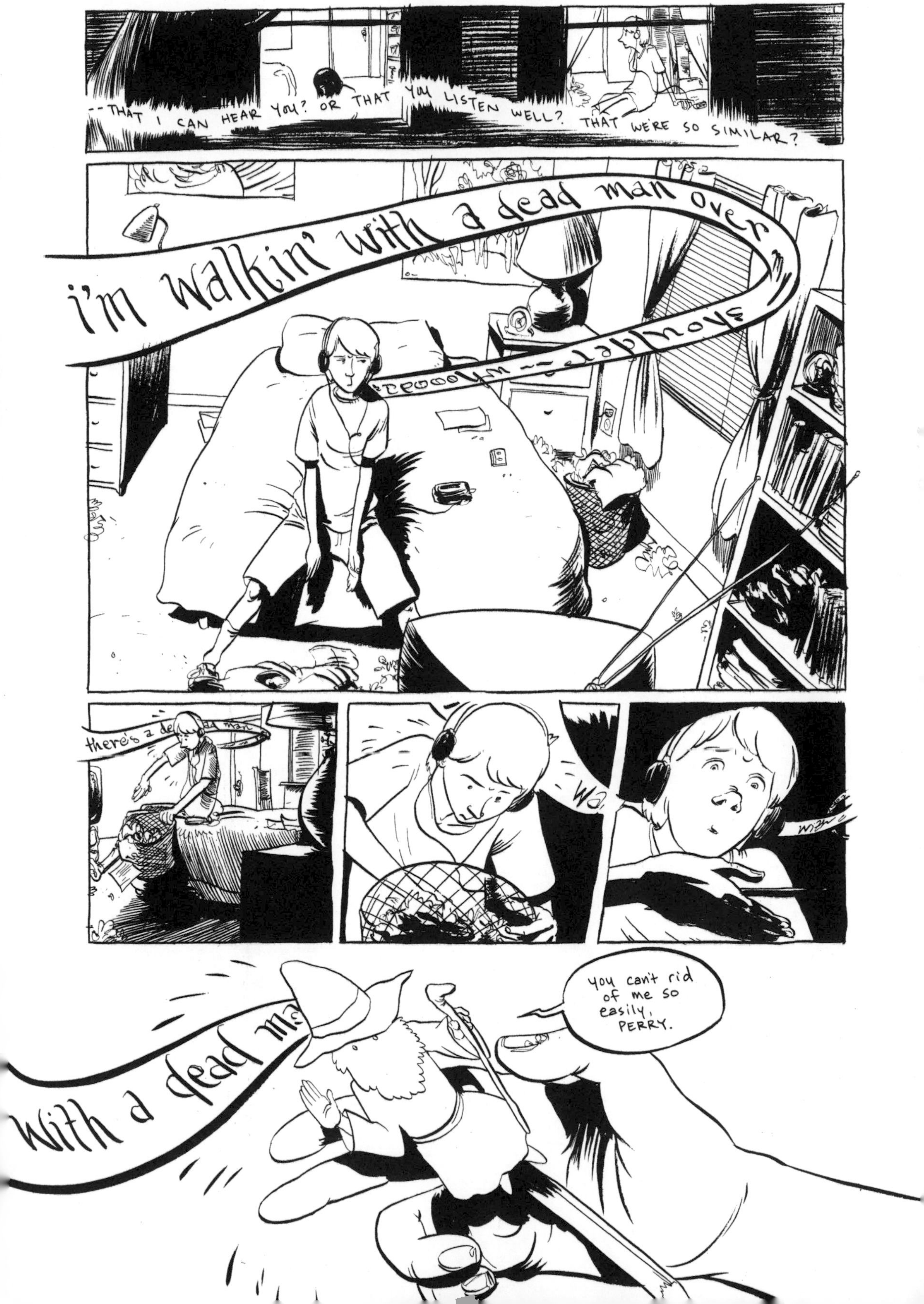
--THAT I CAN HEAR YOU? OR THAT YOU LISTEN WELL? THAT WE'RE SO SIMILAR?
i'm walkin' with a dead man over
shoulder--whoooa
there's a de
wa
with a dead m
you can't rid of me so easily, PERRY.

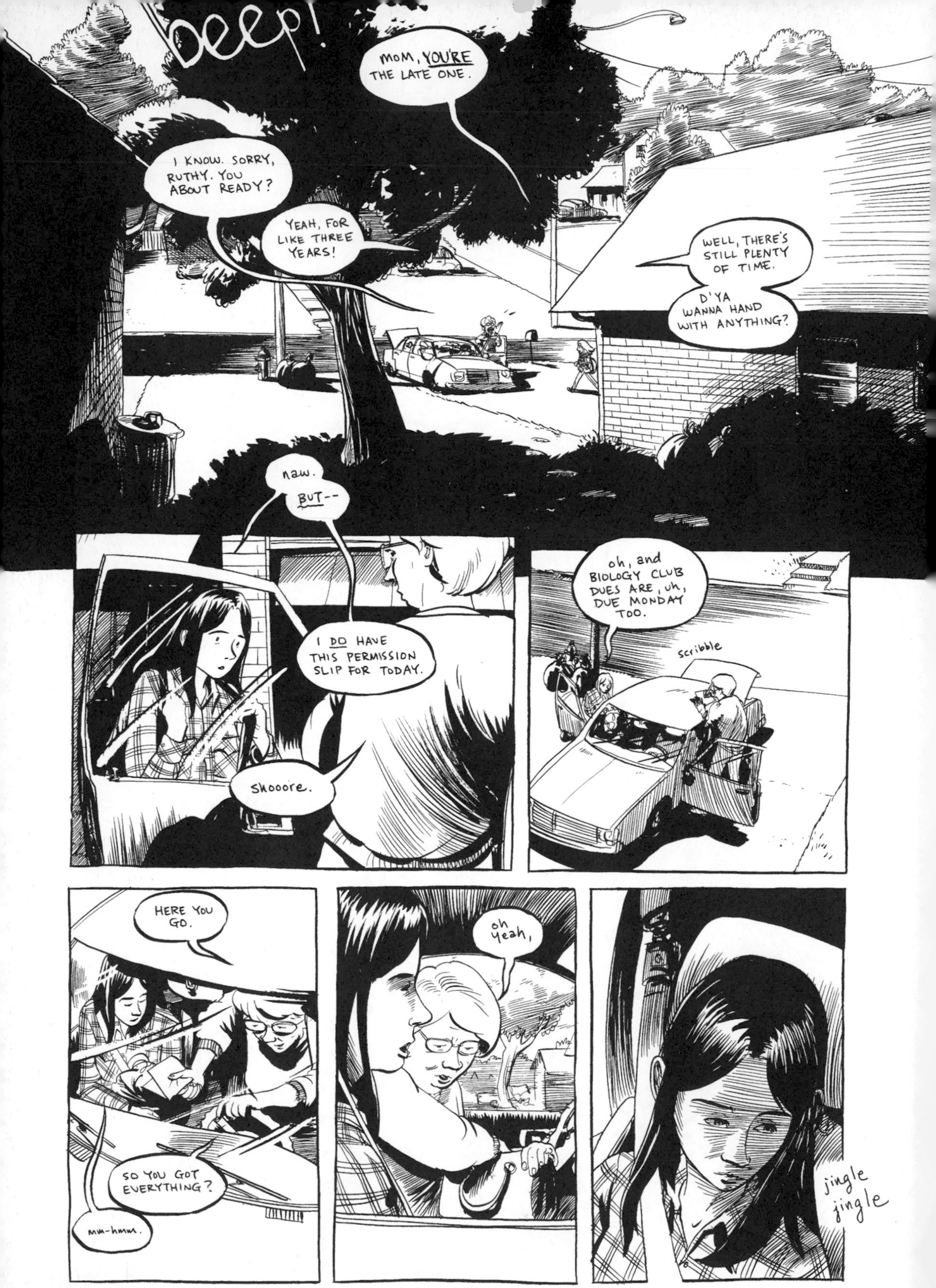
beep!
MOM, YOU'RE THE LATE ONE.
I KNOW. SORRY, RUTHY. YOU ABOUT READY?
YEAH, FOR LIKE THREE YEARS!
WELL, THERE'S STILL PLENTY OF TIME.
D'YA WANNA HAND WITH ANYTHING?
naw.
BUT--
I DO HAVE THIS PERMISSION SLIP FOR TODAY.
shooore.
oh, and BIOLOGY CLUB DUES ARE, uh, DUE MONDAY TOO.
scribble
HERE YOU GO.
SO YOU GOT EVERYTHING?
mm-hmm.
oh yeah,
jingle jingle

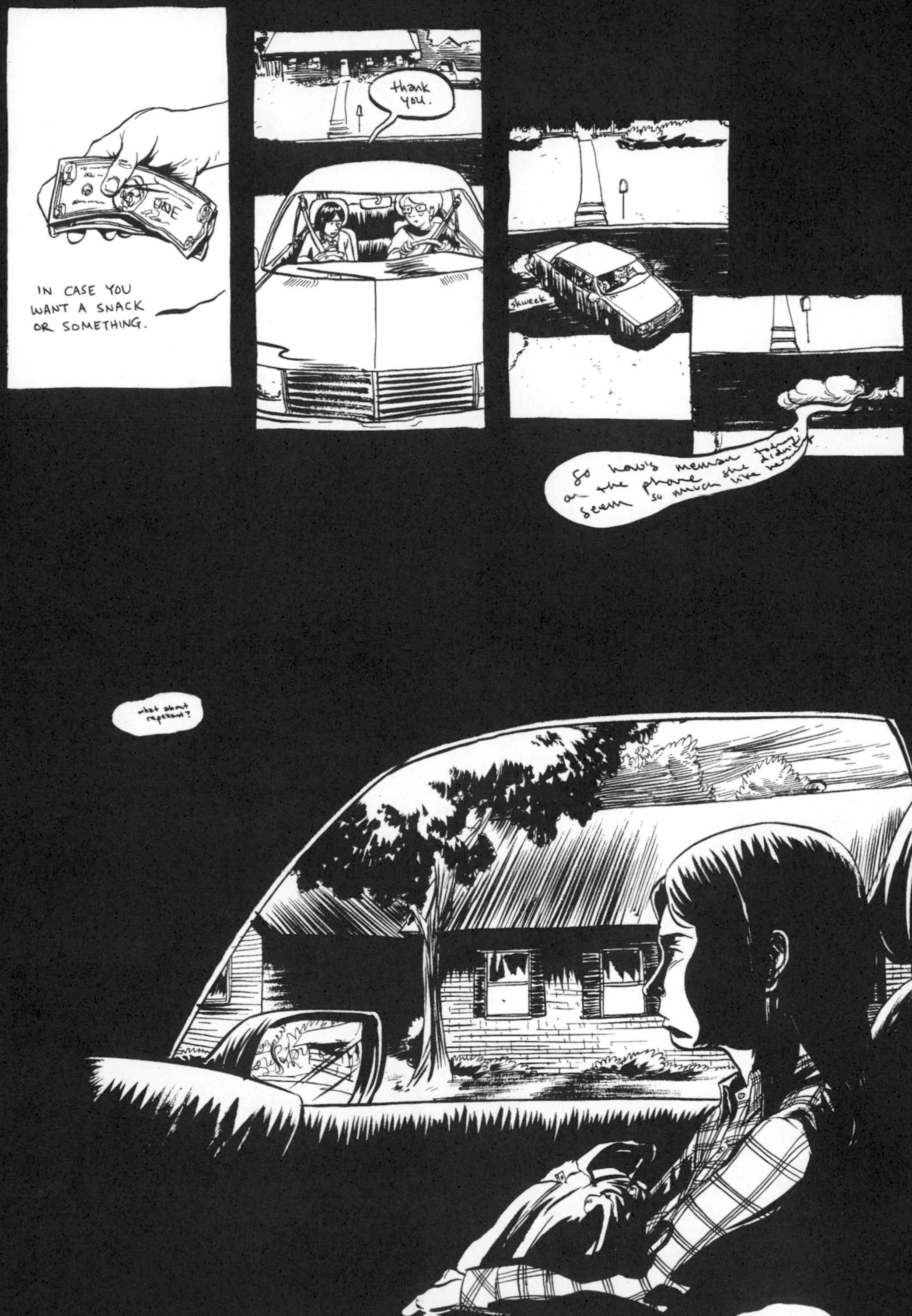
IN CASE YOU WANT A SNACK OR SOMETHING.
thank you.
skweek
So how's memaw today? on the phone she didn't seem so much like herself
what about repellant?
what about repellant?
are you listening?

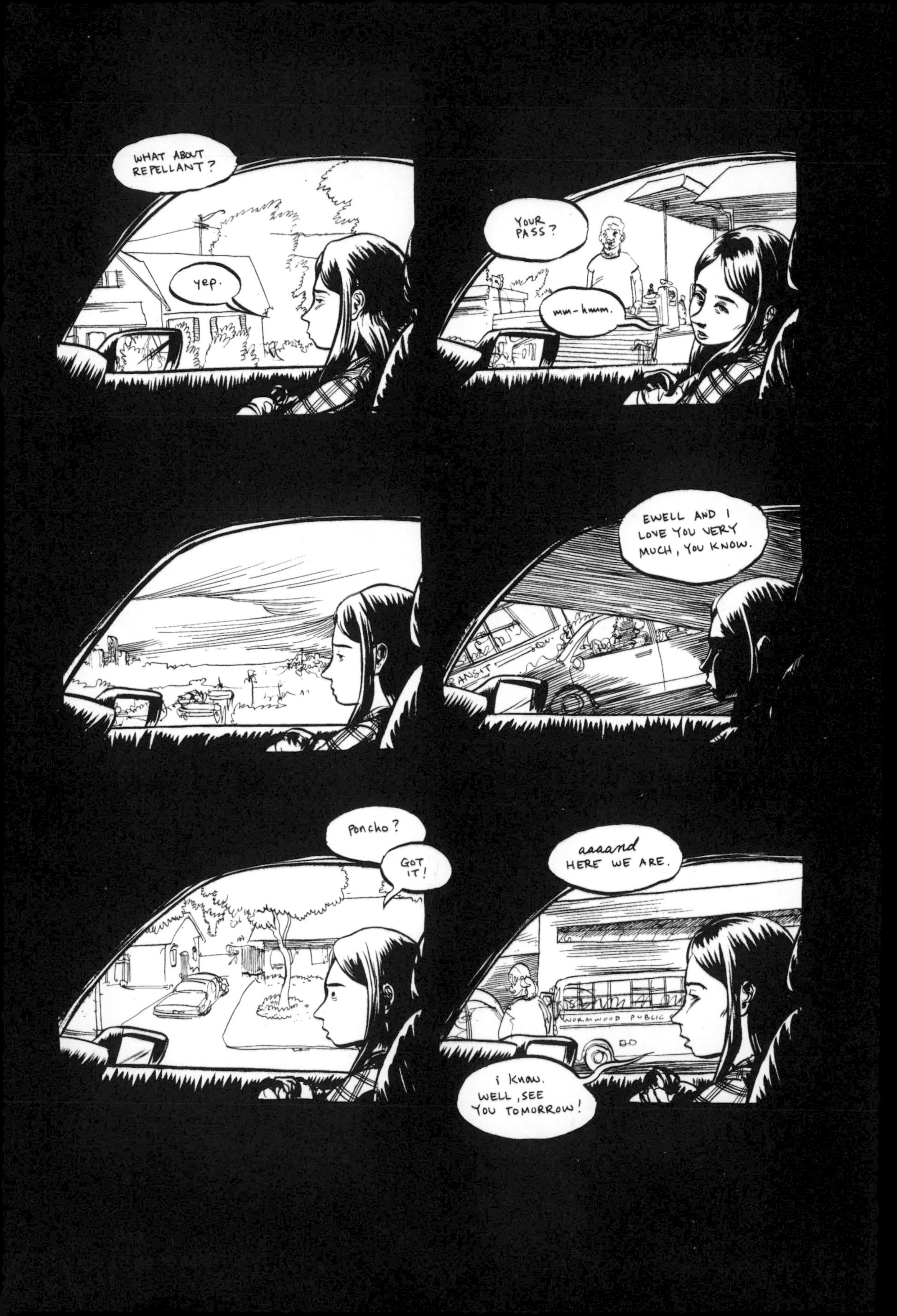

WHAT ABOUT REPELLANT?
yep.
YOUR PASS?
mm-hmm.
EWELL AND I LOVE YOU VERY MUCH, YOU KNOW.
Poncho?
GOT IT!
aaaand HERE WE ARE.
WORMWOOD PUBLIC
i KNOW. WELL, SEE YOU TOMORROW!

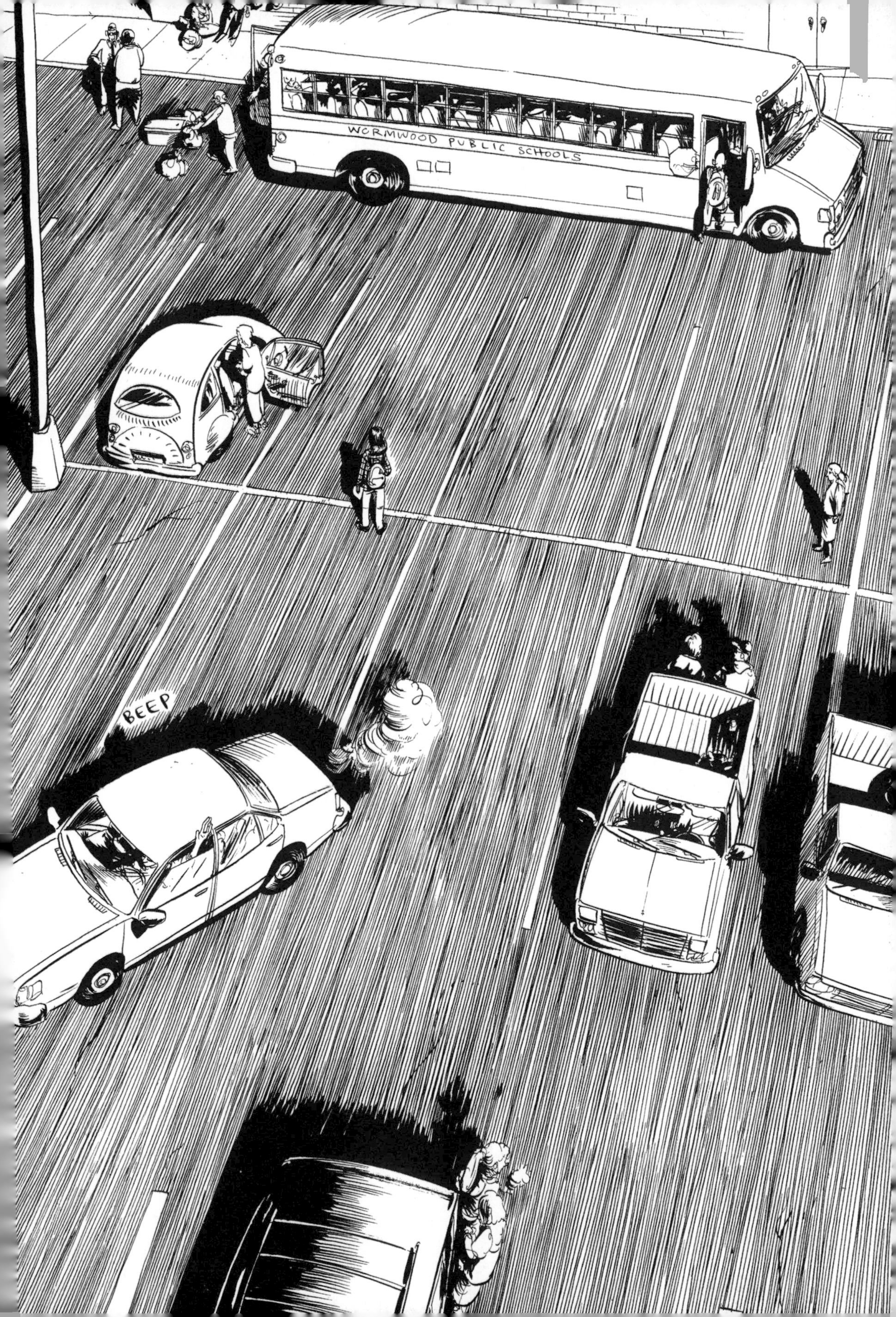
WORMWOOD PUBLIC SCHOOLS
BEEP

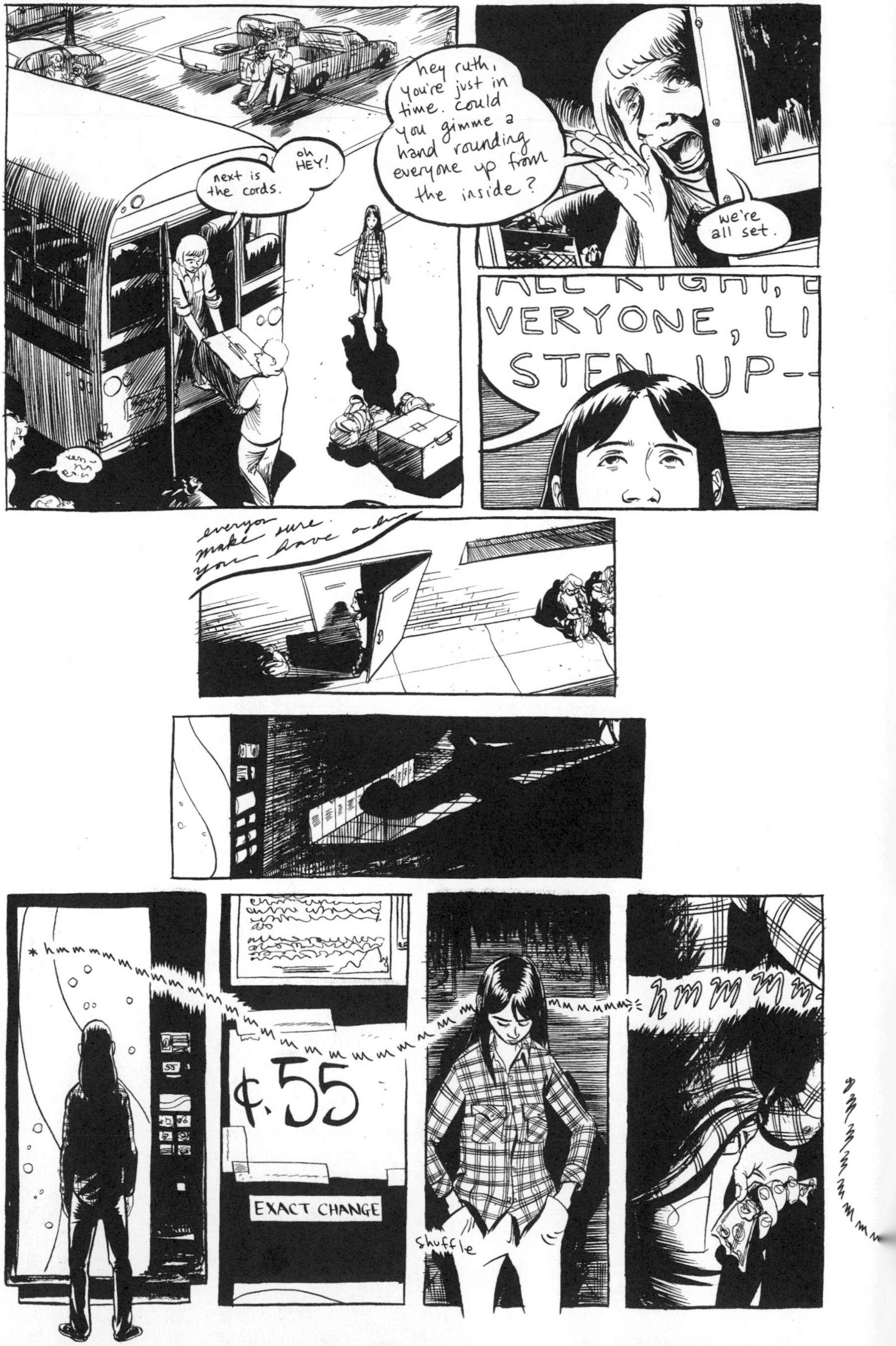
next is the cords.
oh HEY!
hey ruth, you're just in time. could you gimme a hand rounding everyone up from the inside?
we're all set.
ALL RIGHT, E
VERYONE, LI
STEN UP--
*hmmmmmmmmmmmmmmmmmmmmmmmmmm
¢.55
EXACT CHANGE
shuffle
hmmmmm

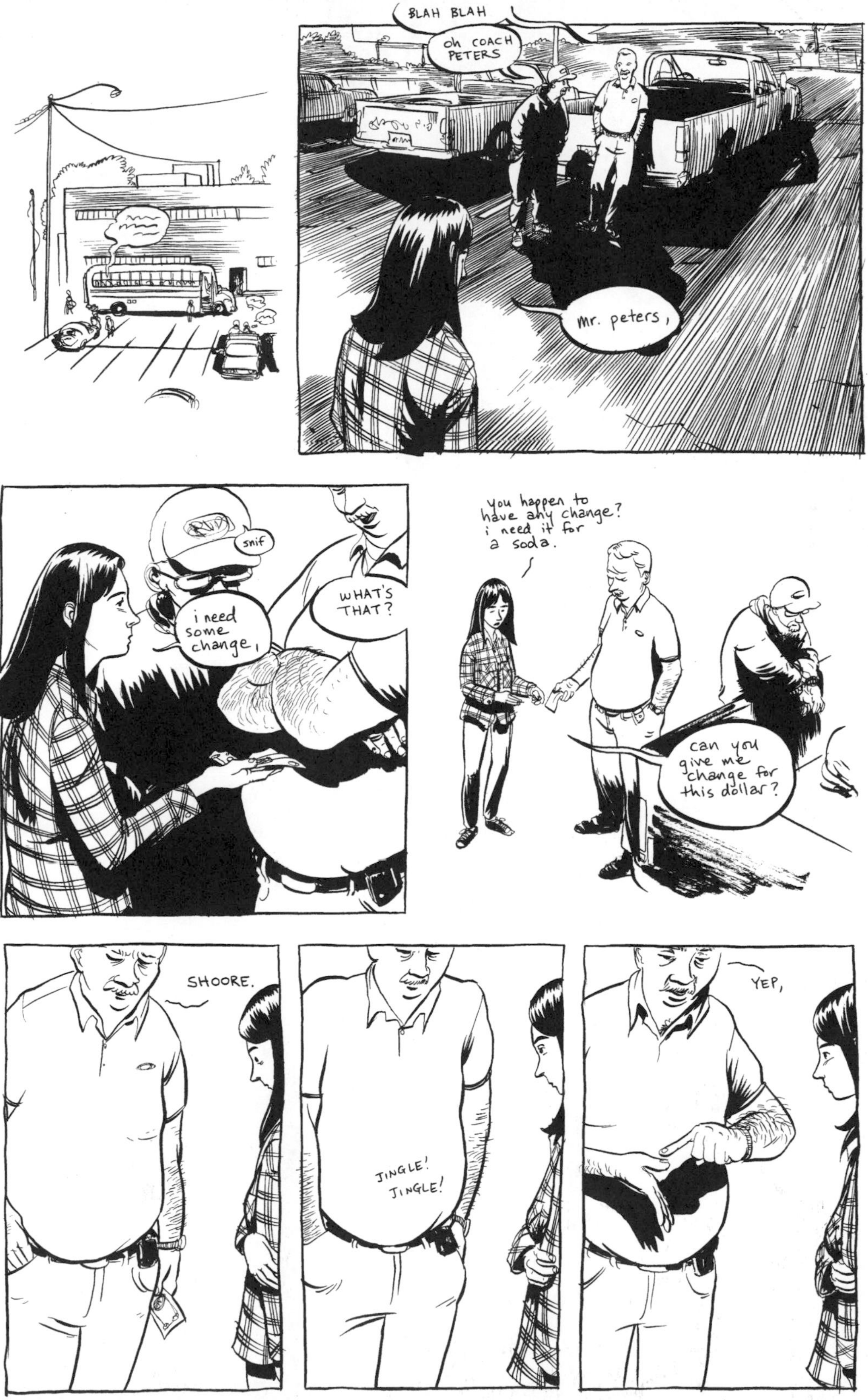
BLAH BLAH
oh COACH PETERS
mr. peters,
snif
i need some change,
WHAT'S THAT?
you happen to have any change? i need it for a soda.
can you give me change for this dollar?
SHOORE.
JINGLE! JINGLE!
YEP,

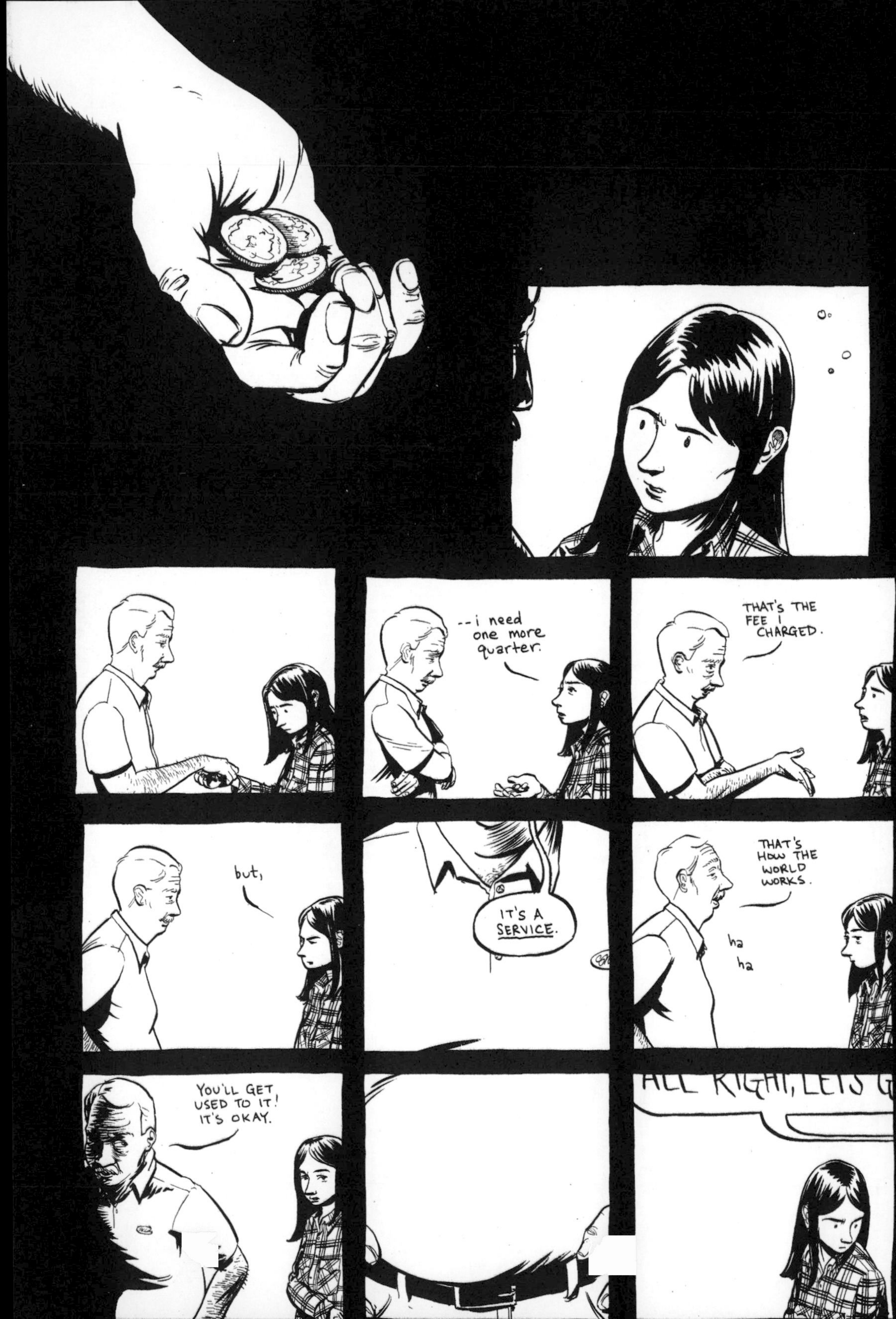
--i need one more quarter.
THAT'S THE FEE I CHARGED.
but,
IT'S A SERVICE.
THAT'S HOW THE WORLD WORKS.
ha ha
YOU'LL GET USED TO IT! IT'S OKAY.

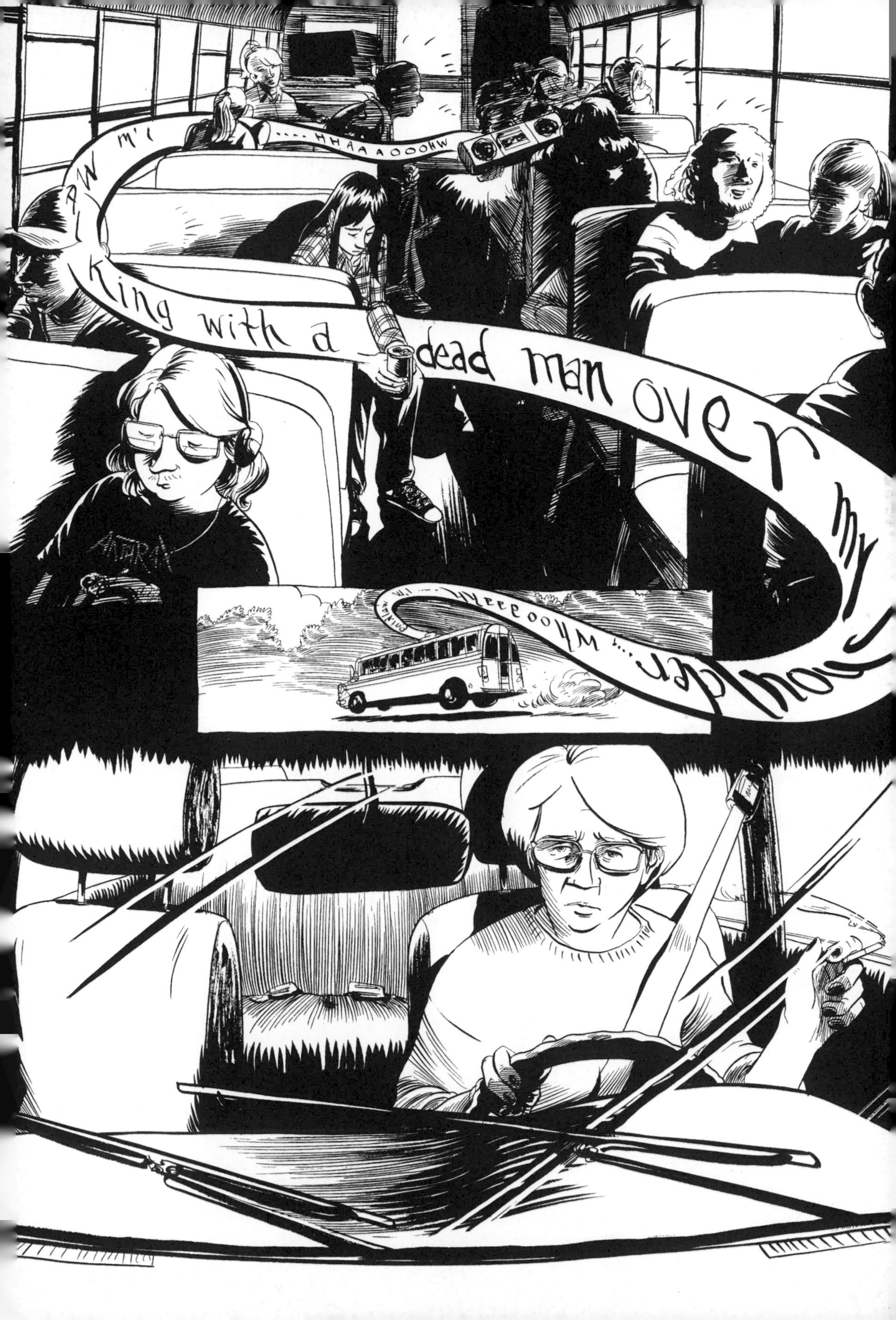
WHOOOAAAHH.... I'm WALking with a dead man over my shoulder.... Whooaaaeee.... I'm walkin

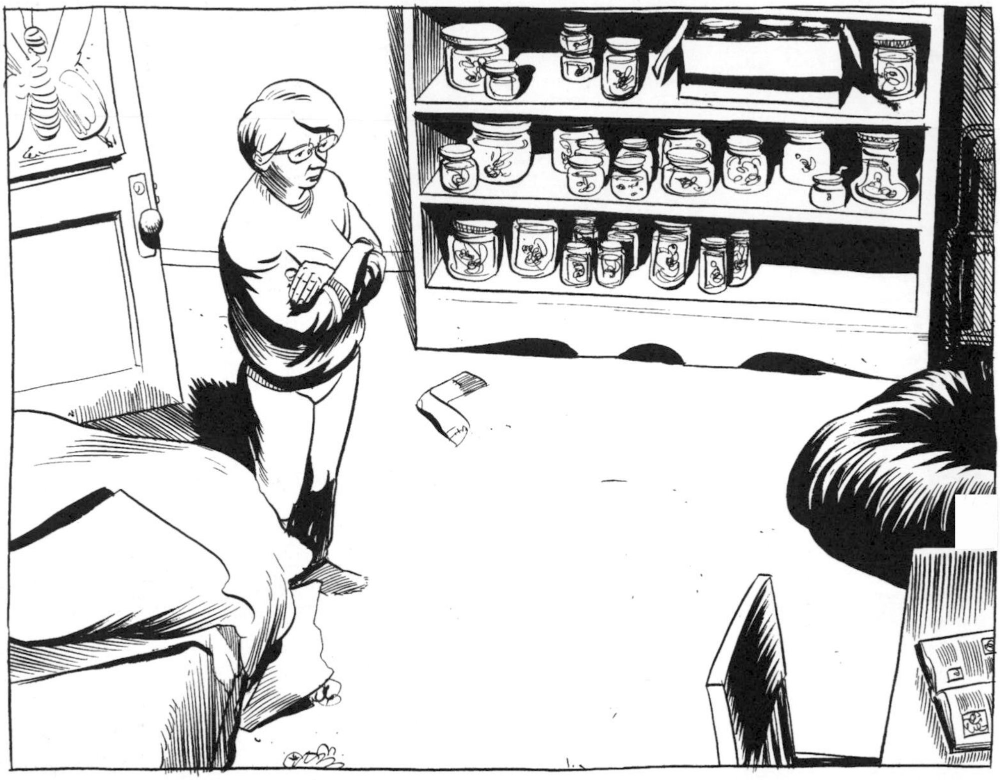

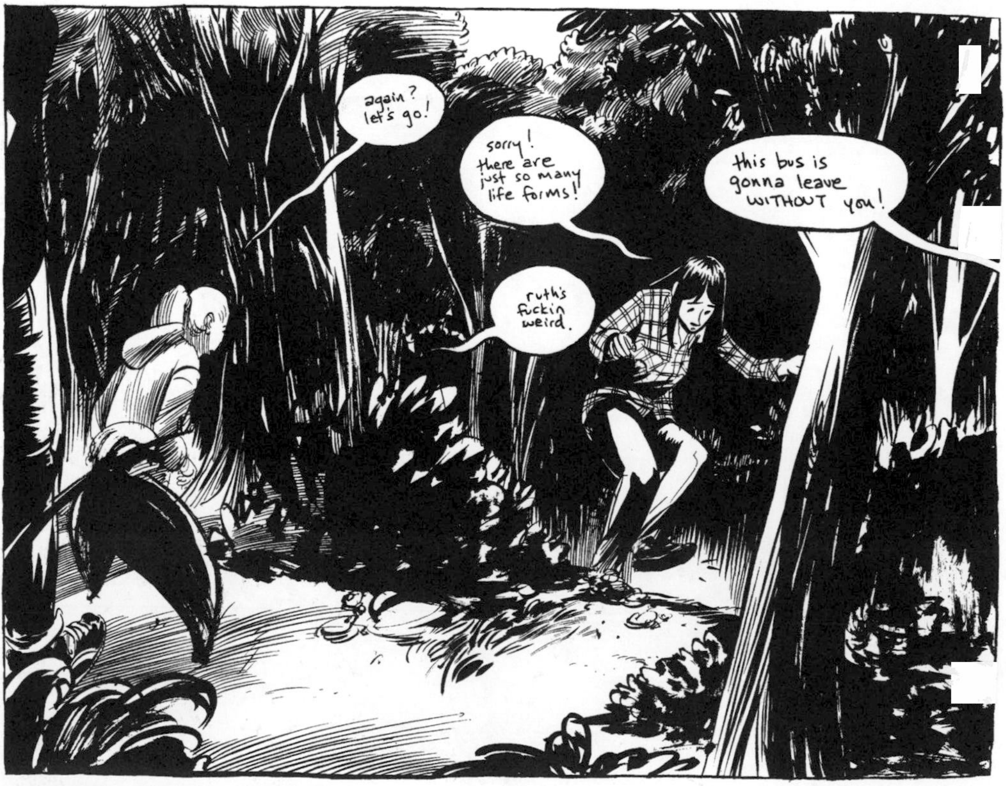
again? let's go!
sorry! there are just so many life forms!
this bus is gonna leave WITHOUT you!
ruth's fuckin weird.

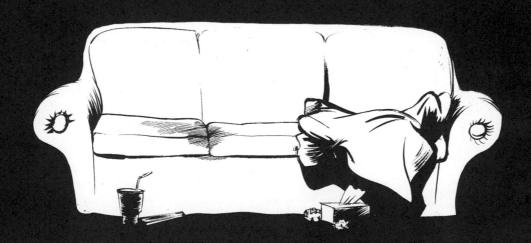

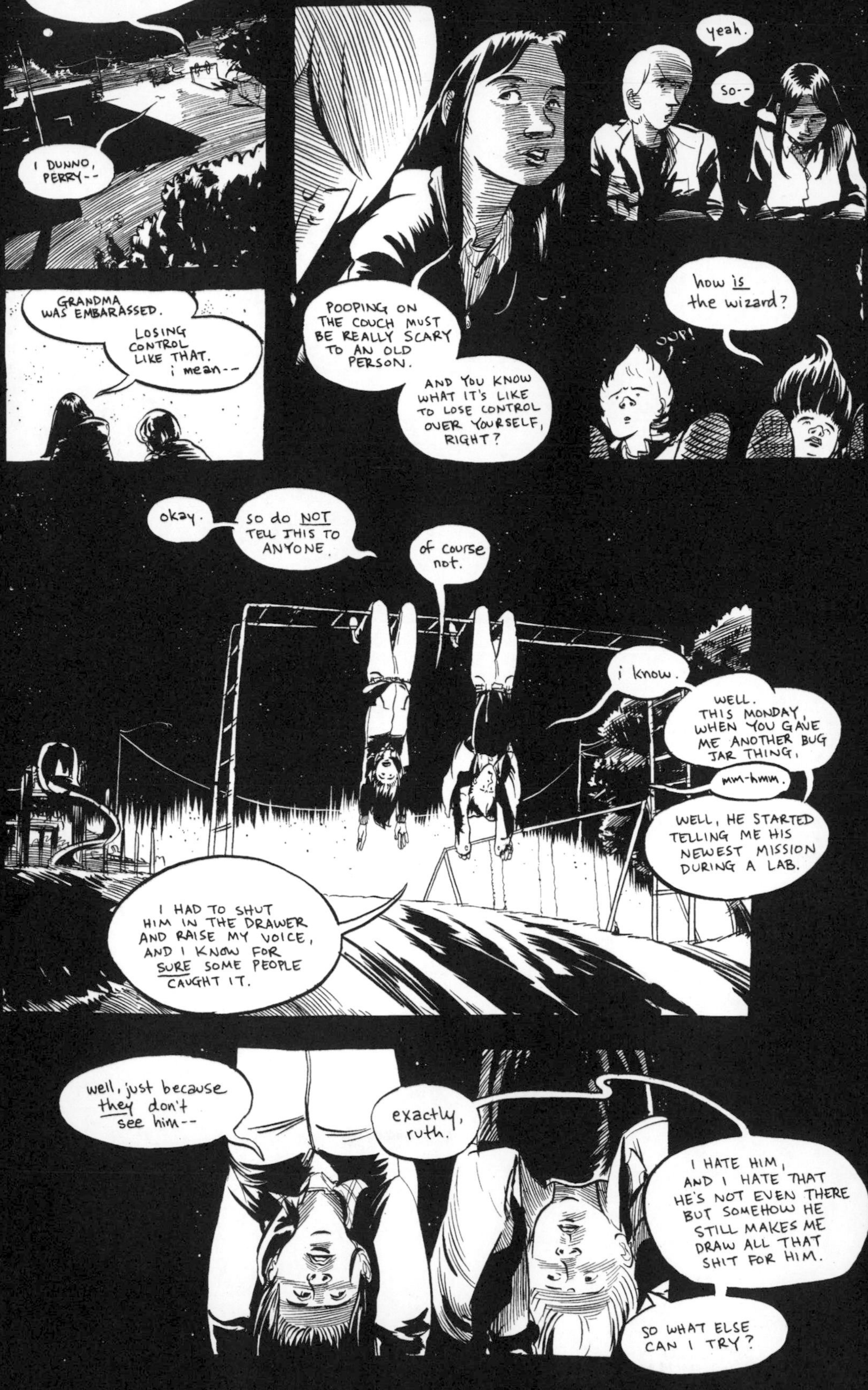

--AND BESIDES, THAT'S BULLSHIT, KICKING US OUT OF THE HOUSE LIKE THAT!
I DUNNO, PERRY--
POOPING ON THE COUCH MUST BE REALLY SCARY TO AN OLD PERSON.
AND YOU KNOW WHAT IT'S LIKE TO LOSE CONTROL OVER YOURSELF, RIGHT?
yeah.
so--
GRANDMA WAS EMBARASSED.
LOSING CONTROL LIKE THAT. i mean--
how is the wizard?
OOP!
okay.
so do NOT TELL THIS TO ANYONE.
of course not.
i know.
WELL. THIS MONDAY, WHEN YOU GAVE ME ANOTHER BUG JAR THING,
mm-hmm.
WELL, HE STARTED TELLING ME HIS NEWEST MISSION DURING A LAB.
I HAD TO SHUT HIM IN THE DRAWER AND RAISE MY VOICE, AND I KNOW FOR SURE SOME PEOPLE CAUGHT IT.
well, just because they don't see him--
exactly, ruth.
I HATE HIM, AND I HATE THAT HE'S NOT EVEN THERE BUT SOMEHOW HE STILL MAKES ME DRAW ALL THAT SHIT FOR HIM.
SO WHAT ELSE CAN I TRY?

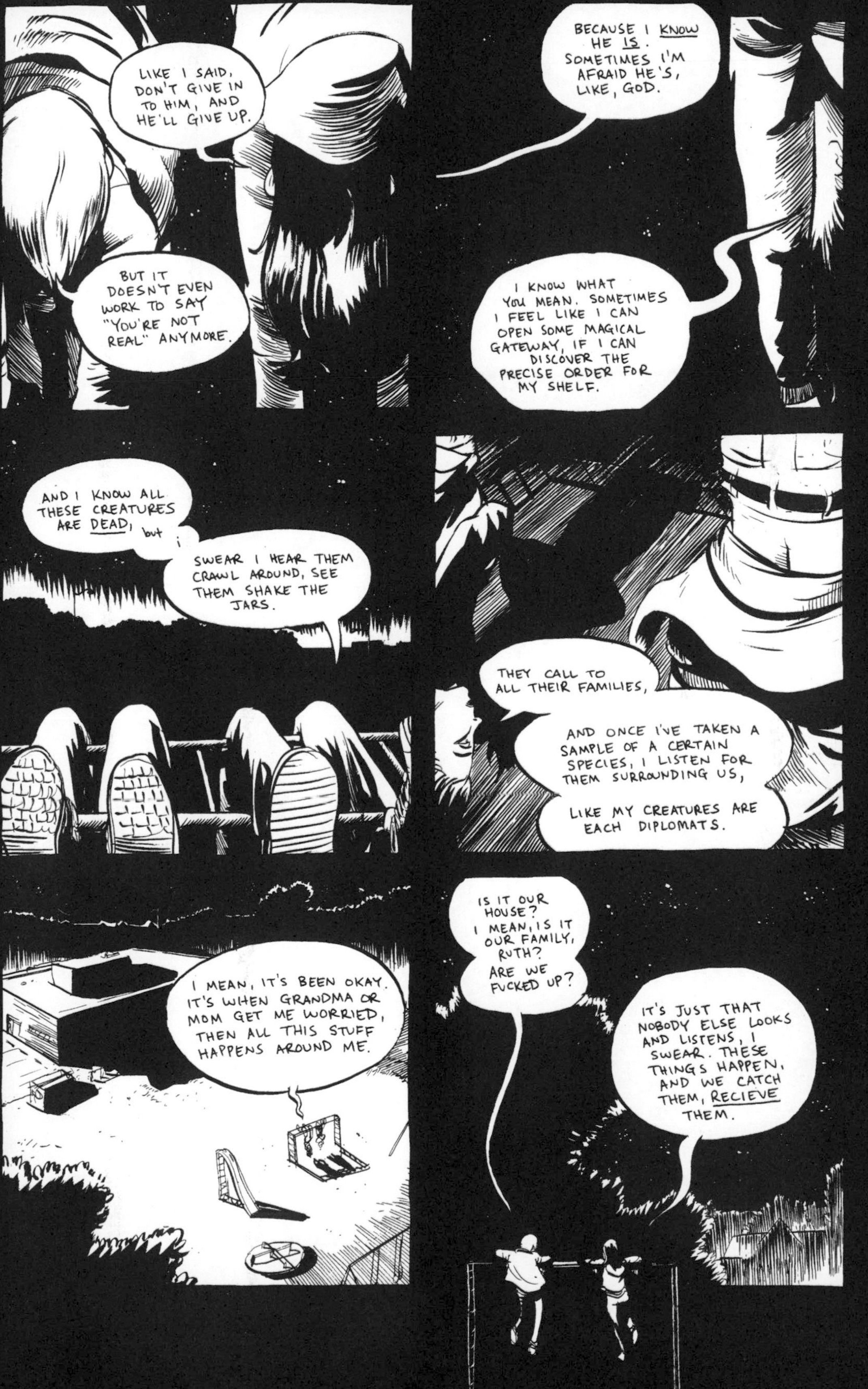
LIKE I SAID, DON'T GIVE IN TO HIM, AND HE'LL GIVE UP.
BUT IT DOESN'T EVEN WORK TO SAY "YOU'RE NOT REAL" ANYMORE.
BECAUSE I KNOW HE IS. SOMETIMES I'M AFRAID HE'S, LIKE, GOD.
I KNOW WHAT YOU MEAN. SOMETIMES I FEEL LIKE I CAN OPEN SOME MAGICAL GATEWAY, IF I CAN DISCOVER THE PRECISE ORDER FOR MY SHELF.
AND I KNOW ALL THESE CREATURES ARE DEAD, but i
SWEAR I HEAR THEM CRAWL AROUND, SEE THEM SHAKE THE JARS.
THEY CALL TO ALL THEIR FAMILIES,
AND ONCE I'VE TAKEN A SAMPLE OF A CERTAIN SPECIES, I LISTEN FOR THEM SURROUNDING US,
LIKE MY CREATURES ARE EACH DIPLOMATS.
I MEAN, IT'S BEEN OKAY. IT'S WHEN GRANDMA OR MOM GET ME WORRIED, THEN ALL THIS STUFF HAPPENS AROUND ME.
IS IT OUR HOUSE? I MEAN, IS IT OUR FAMILY, RUTH? ARE WE FUCKED UP?
IT'S JUST THAT NOBODY ELSE LOOKS AND LISTENS, I SWEAR. THESE THINGS HAPPEN, AND WE CATCH THEM, RECIEVE THEM.

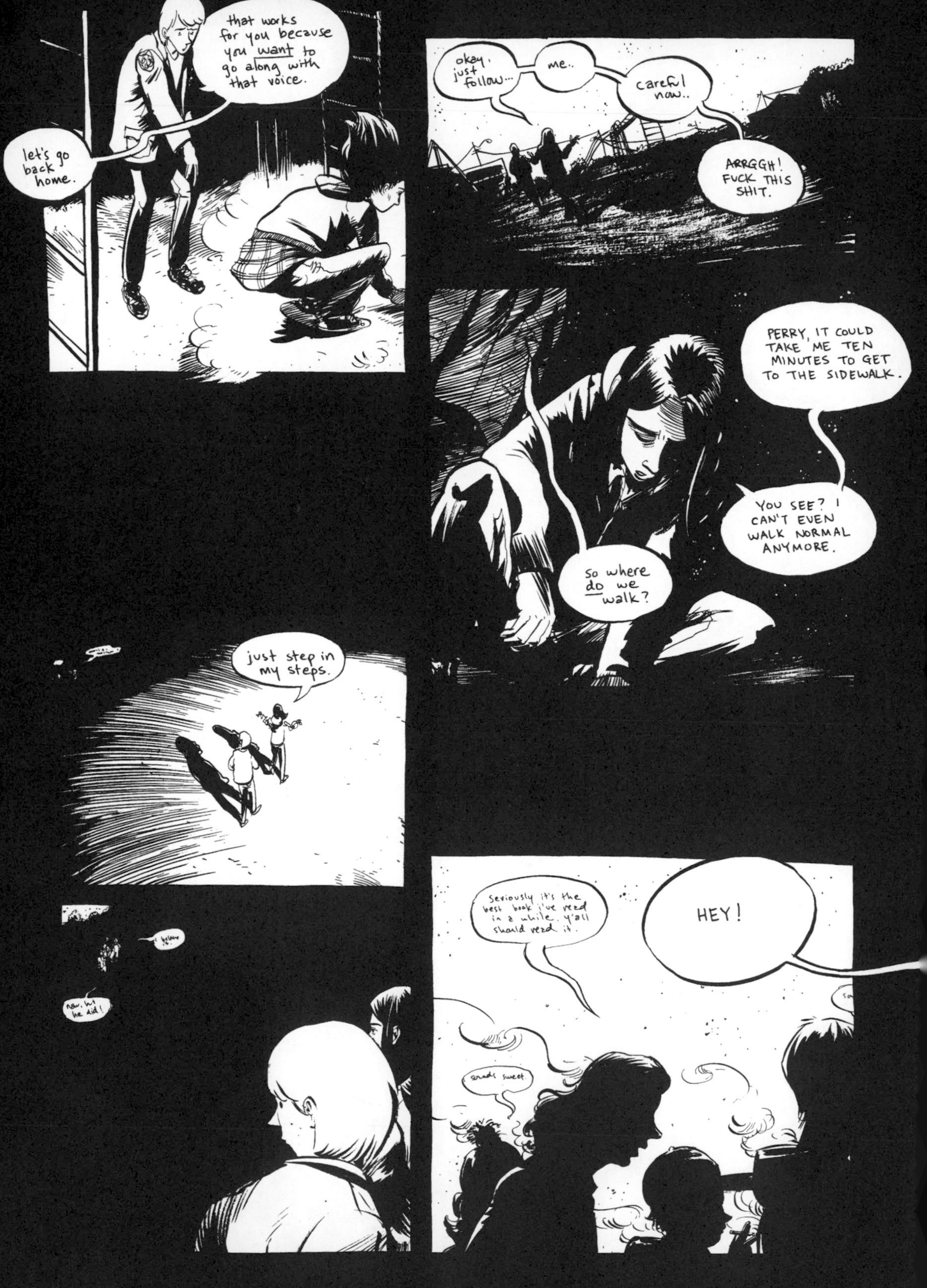
that works for you because you want to go along with that voice.
let's go back home.
okay. just follow...
me..
careful now..
ARRGGH! FUCK THIS SHIT.
PERRY, IT COULD TAKE ME TEN MINUTES TO GET TO THE SIDEWALK.
YOU SEE? I CAN'T EVEN WALK NORMAL ANYMORE.
so where do we walk?
just step in my steps.
i believe it.
naw, but he did!
seriously it's the best book i've read in a while. y'all should read it.
sounds sweet.
HEY!

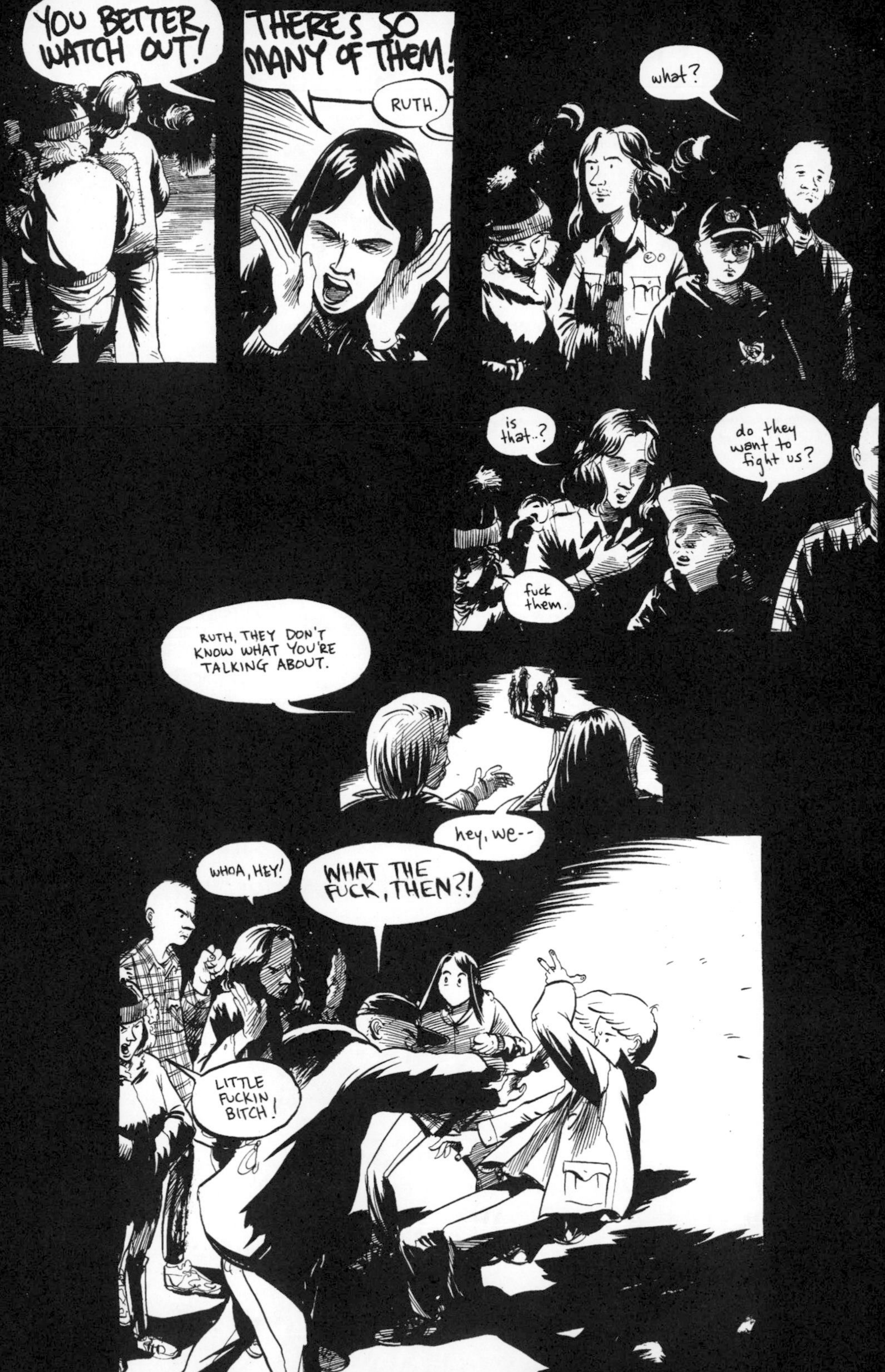
YOU BETTER WATCH OUT!
THERE'S SO MANY OF THEM!
RUTH.
what?
is that..?
do they want to fight us?
fuck them.
RUTH, THEY DON'T KNOW WHAT YOU'RE TALKING ABOUT.
hey, we--
WHOA, HEY!
WHAT THE FUCK, THEN?!
LITTLE FUCKIN BITCH!

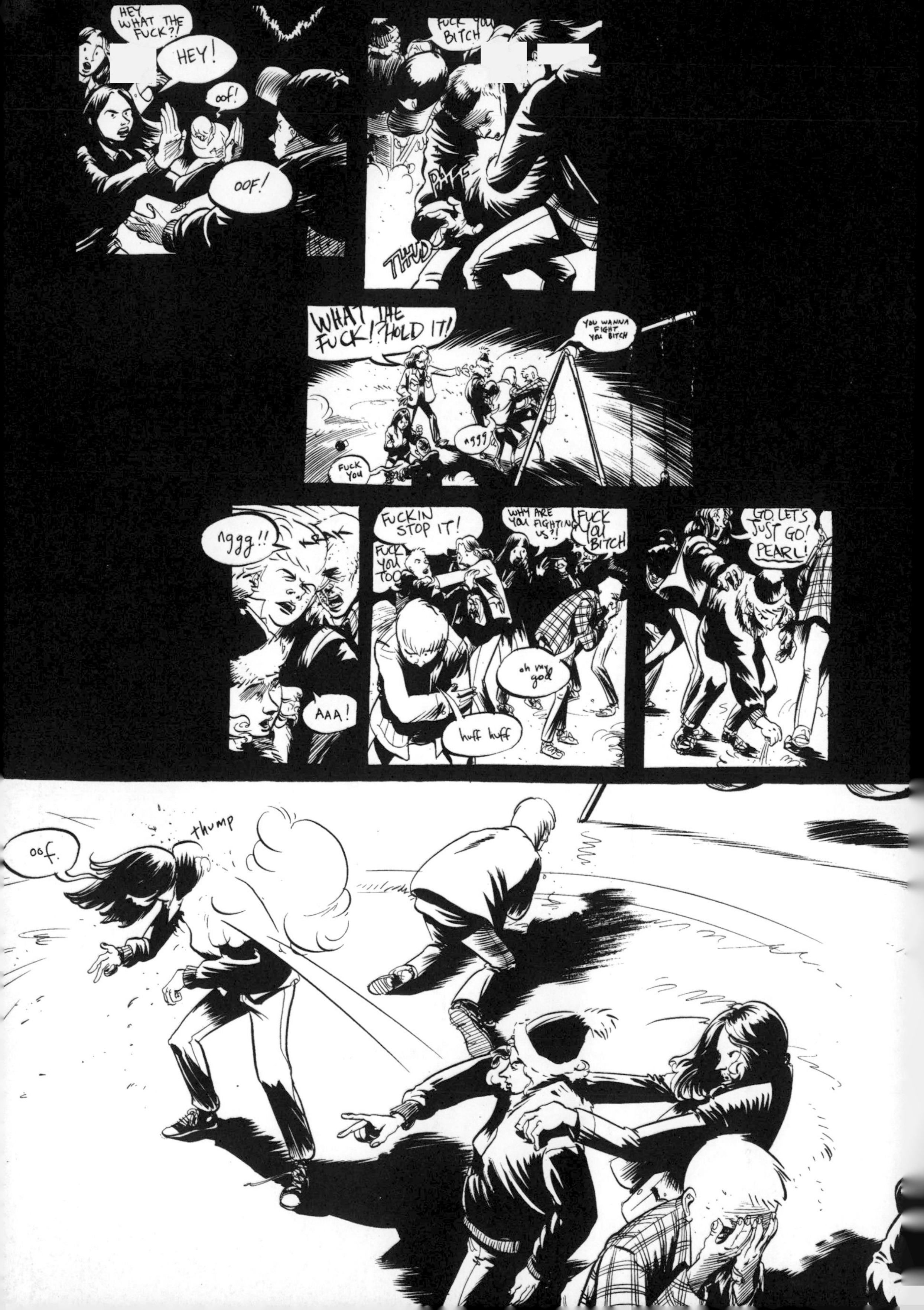
HEY WHAT THE FUCK?!
HEY!
oof!
OOF!
FUCK YOU BITCH
PAFF
THUD
WHAT THE FUCK!? HOLD IT!
YOU WANNA FIGHT YOU BITCH
nggg
FUCK YOU
nggg!!
AAA!
FUCKIN STOP IT!
FUCK YOU TOO
WHY ARE YOU FIGHTING US?!
FUCK YOU BITCH
oh my god
huff huff
GO, LET'S JUST GO! PEARL!
oof.
thump

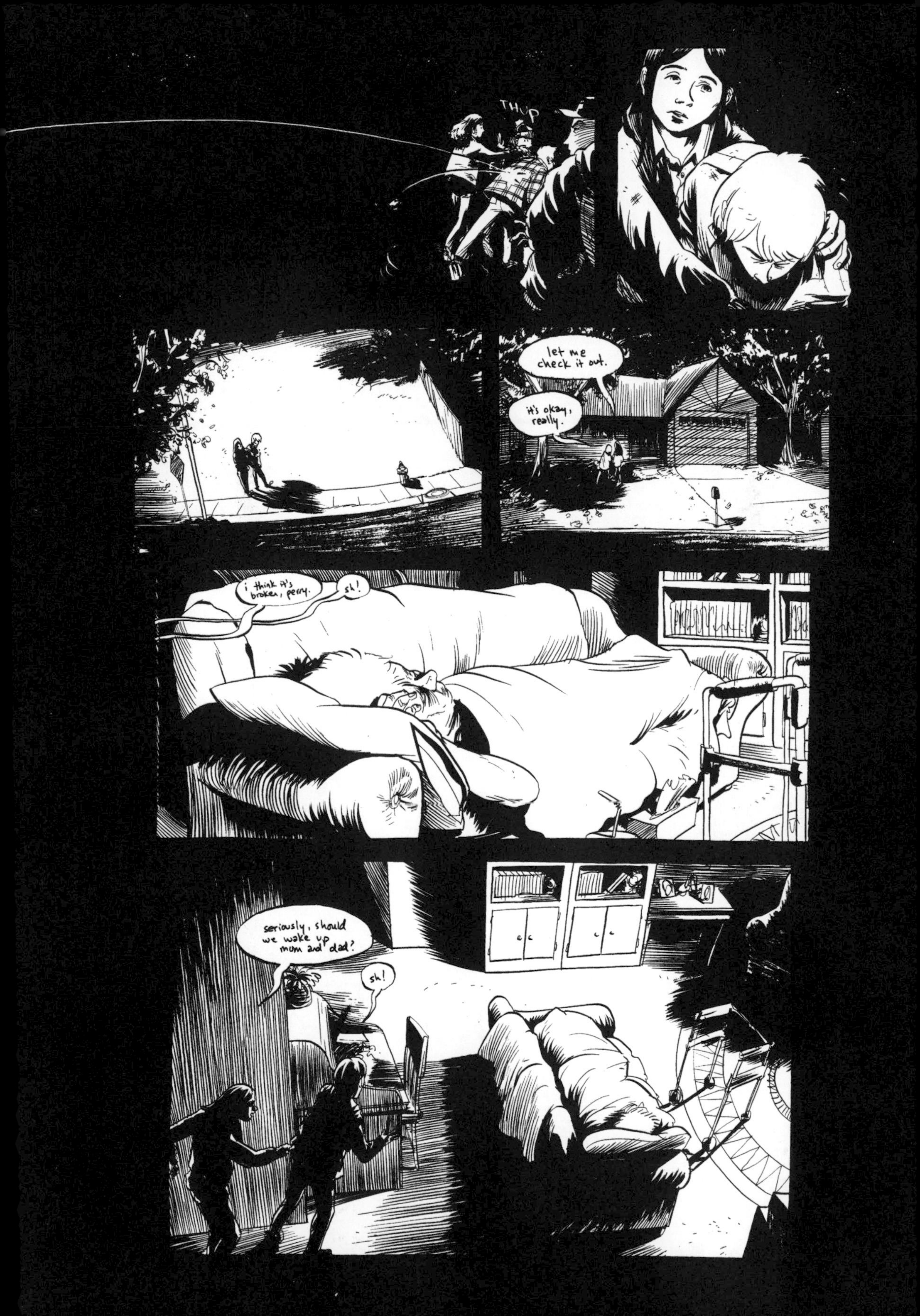
THUP
let me check it out.
it's okay, really.
i think it's broken, perry.
sh!
seriously, should we wake up mum and dad?
sh!

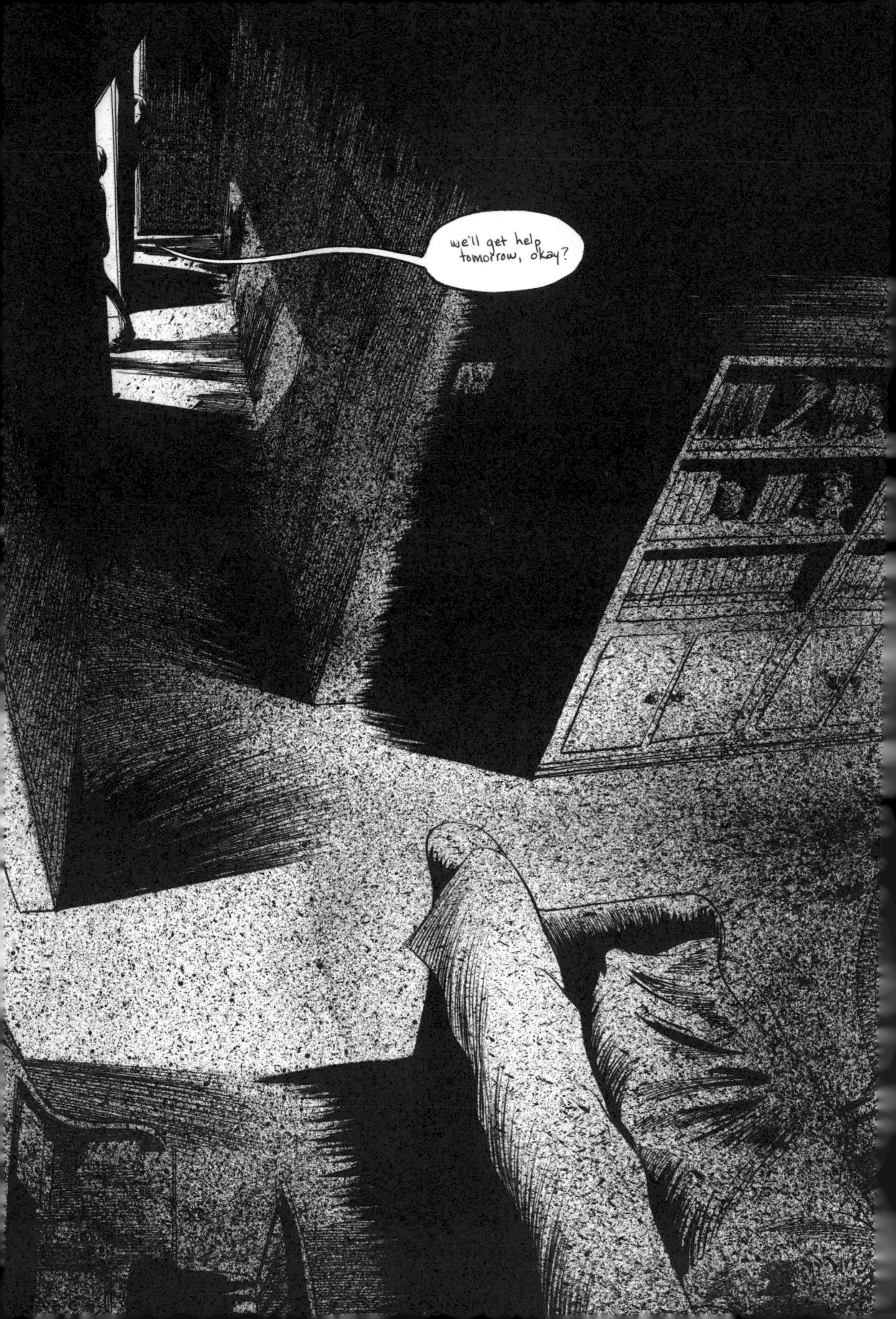
we'll get help tomorrow, okay?

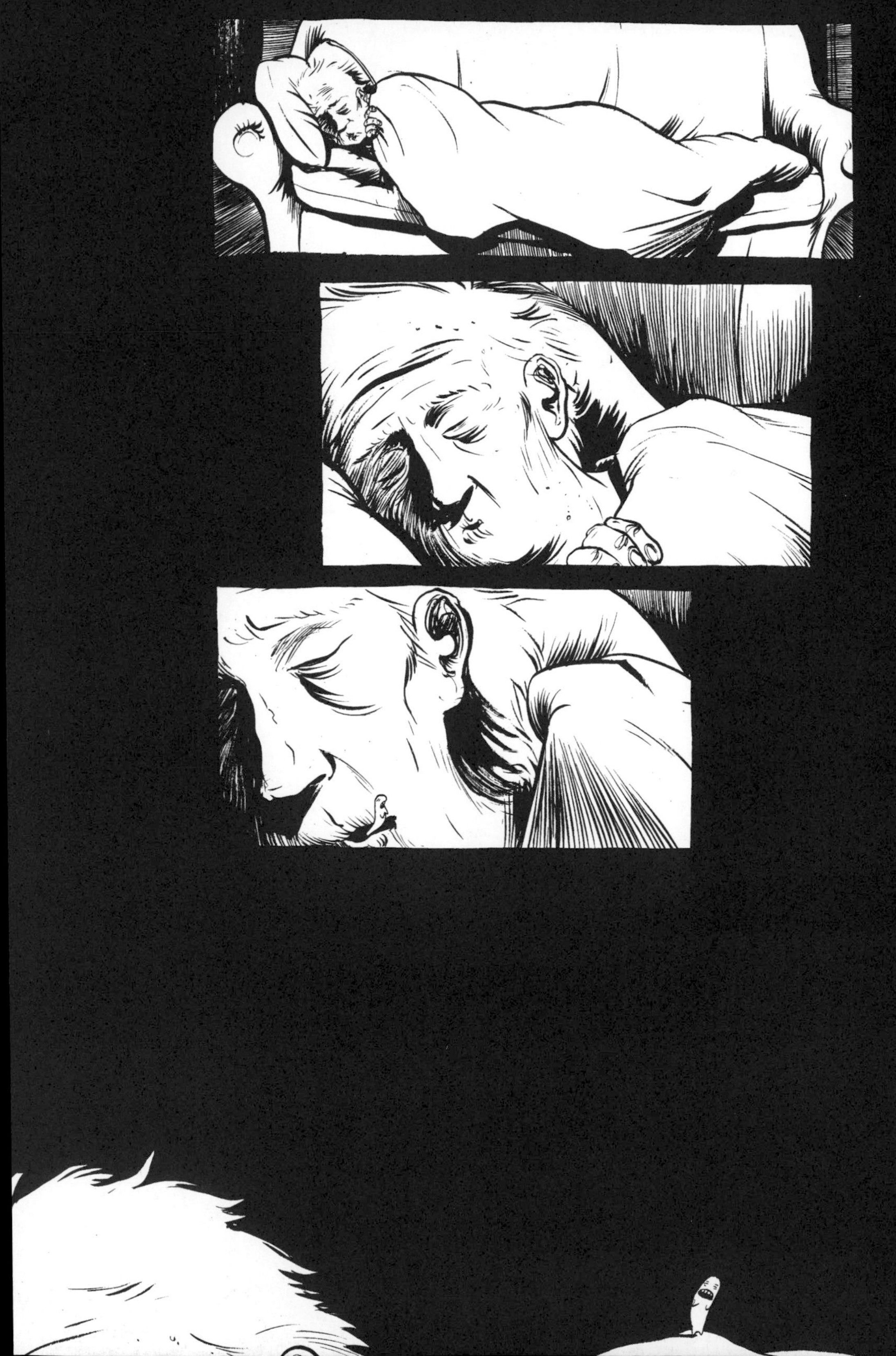

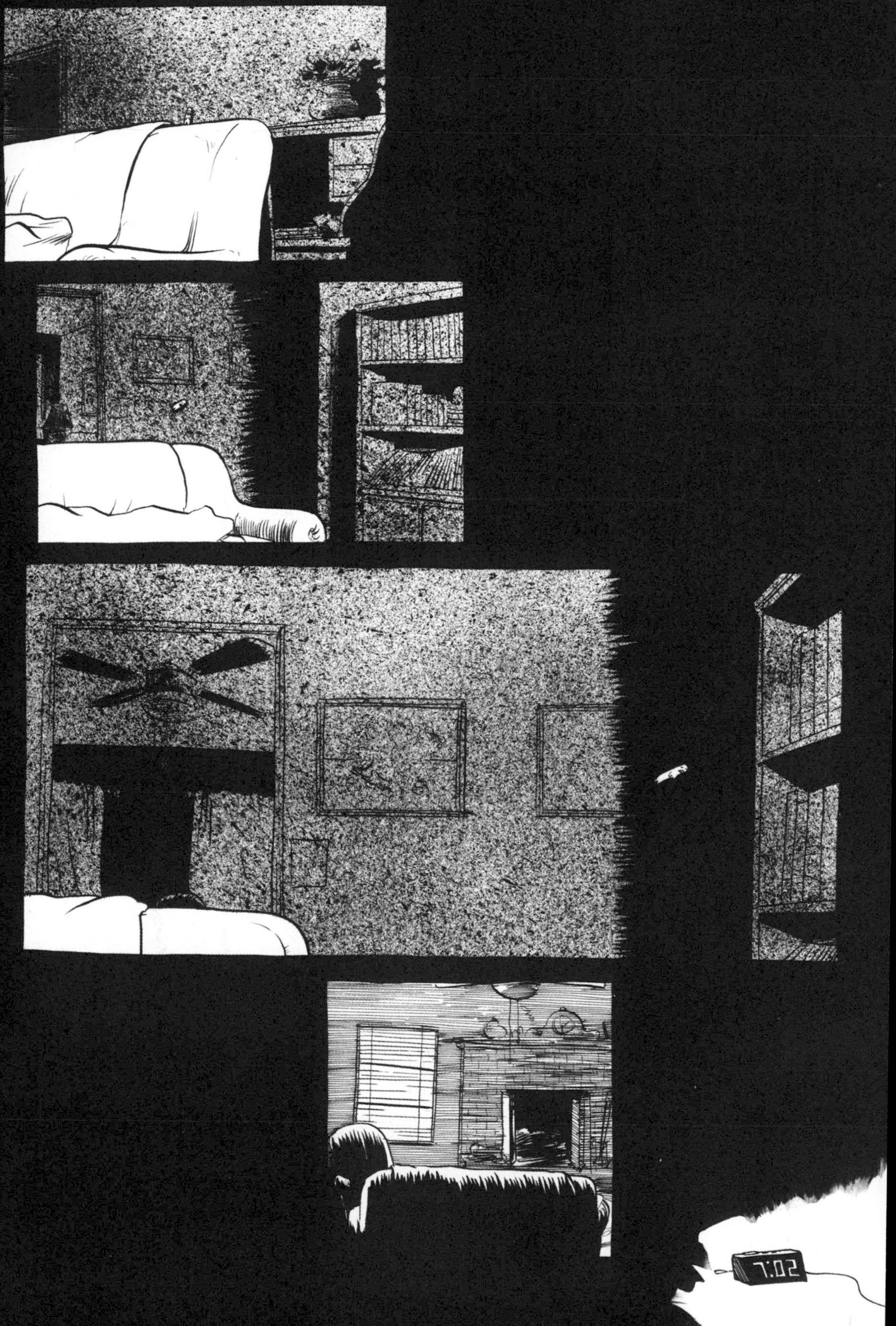
7:02

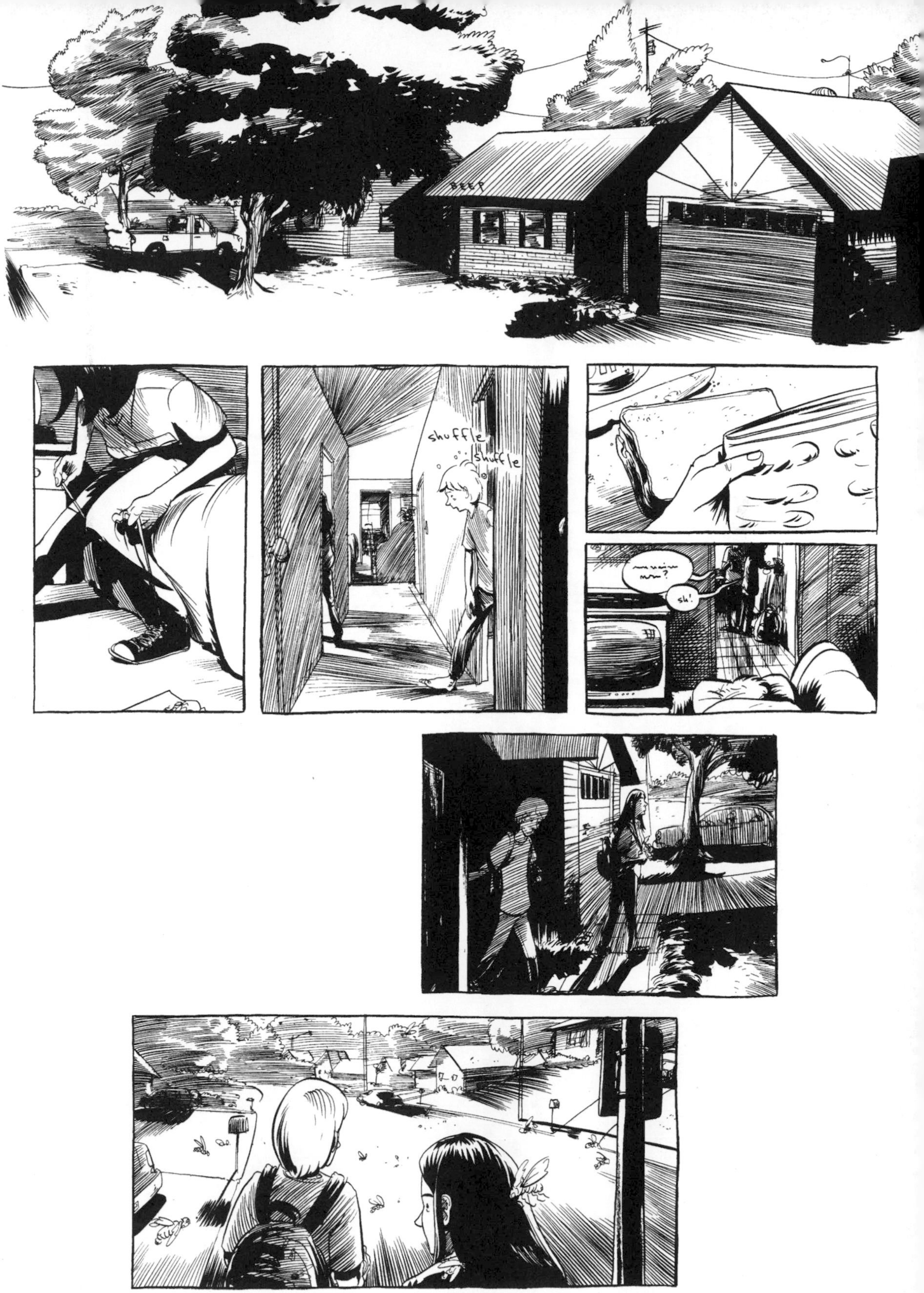
BEEP
shuffle
shuffle
sh!

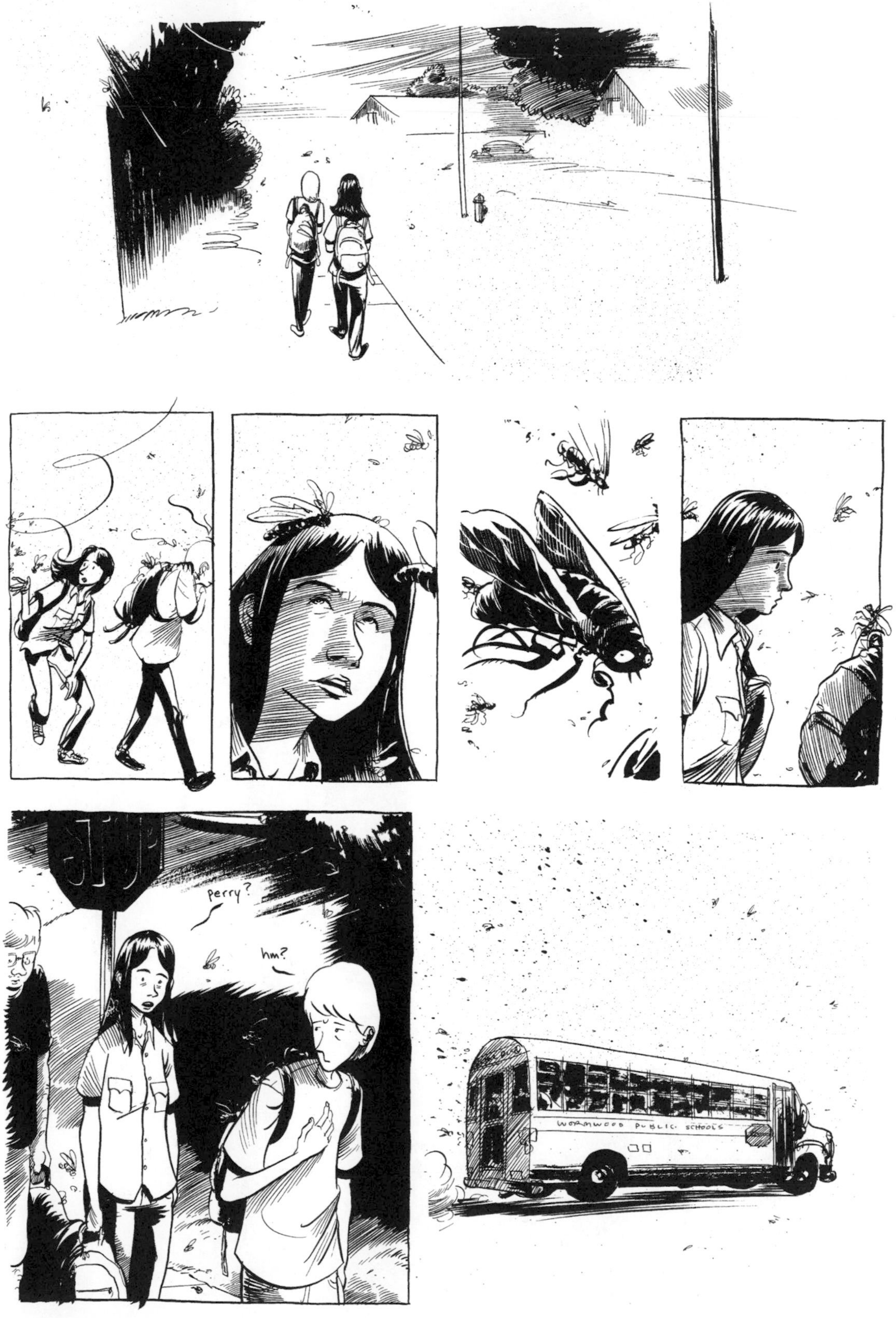
perry?
hm?
WORMWOOD PUBLIC SCHOOLS

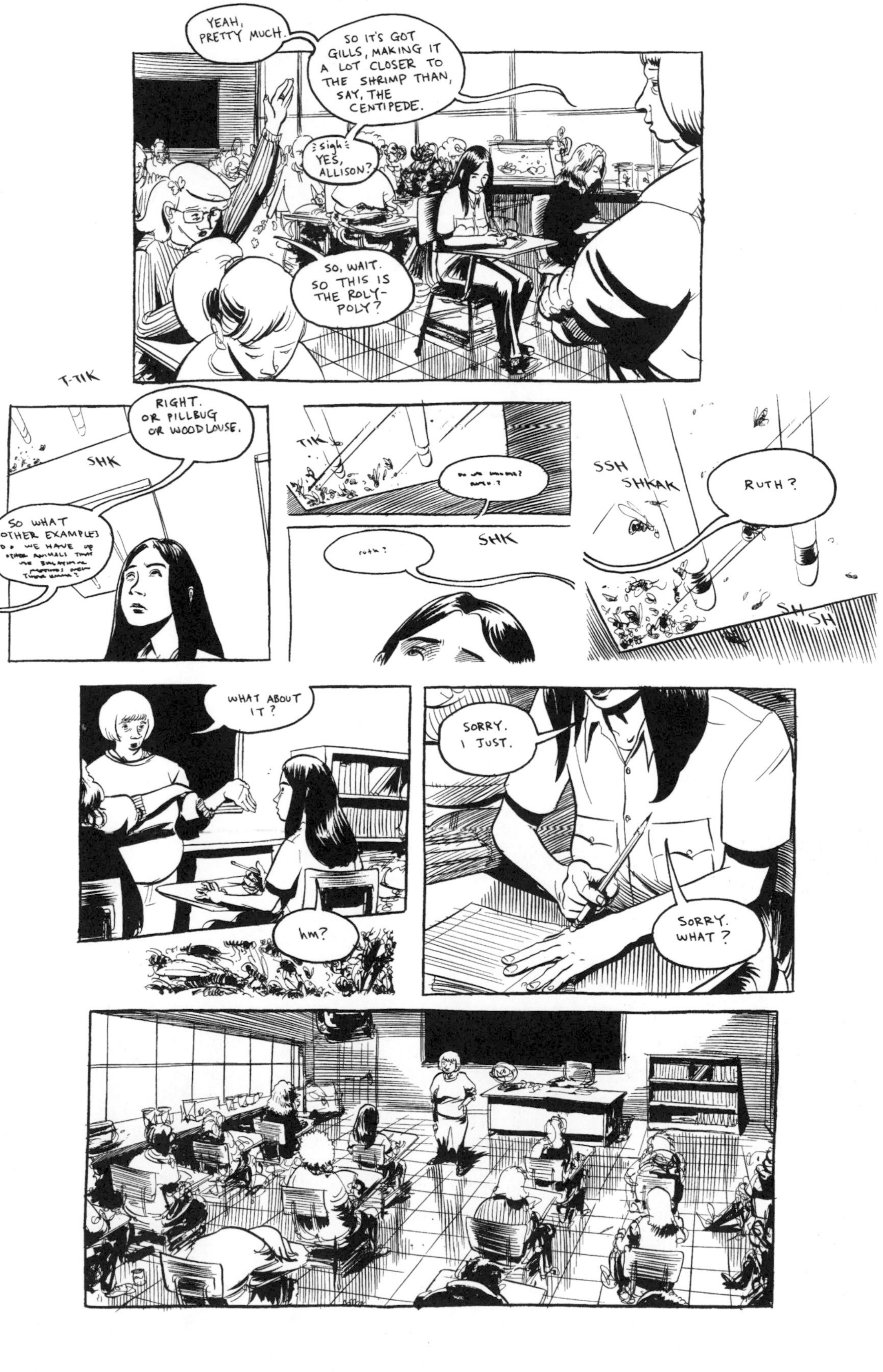
YEAH, PRETTY MUCH.
SO IT'S GOT GILLS, MAKING IT A LOT CLOSER TO THE SHRIMP THAN, SAY, THE CENTIPEDE.
sigh YES, ALLISON?
SO, WAIT. SO THIS IS THE ROLY-POLY?
T-TIK
RIGHT. OR PILLBUG OR WOODLOUSE.
SHK
SO WHAT OTHER EXAMPLES DO WE HAVE
TIK
ruth?
SHK
SSH
SHKAK
RUTH?
SH
SH
WHAT ABOUT IT?
hm?
SORRY. I JUST.
SORRY. WHAT?

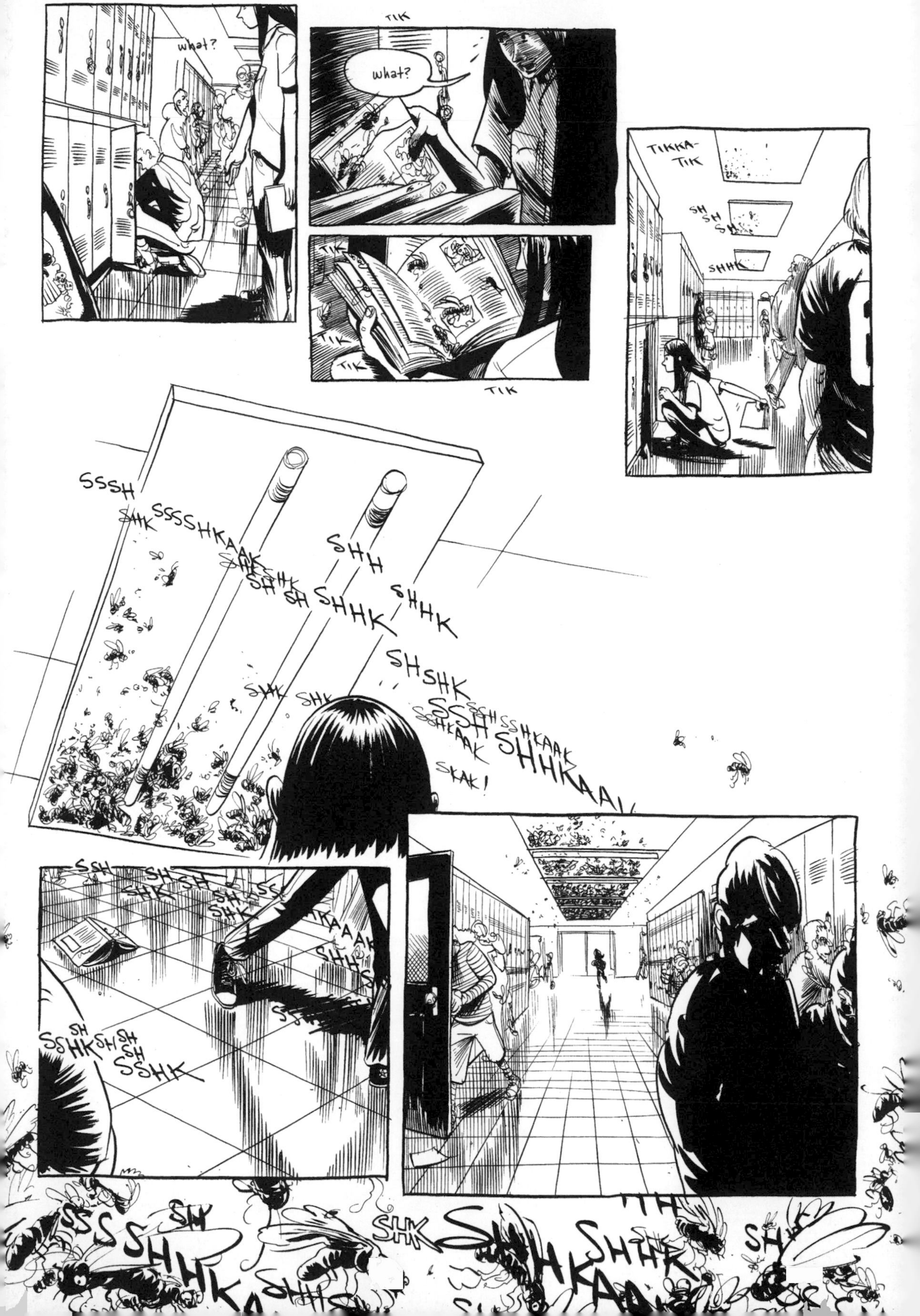
what?
TIK
what?
TIK
TIK
TIK
TIK
TIKKA-
TIK
SH
SH
SH
SHHK
SSSH
SHK
SSSSHKAAK
SH
SH SH
SHH
SHHK
SHHK
SHSHK
SHK
SHK
SSSH
SHKAAK
SHKAAK
SHHKAAA
SKAK!
SSH
SHK SH SH
SH
SHK
KAAAK
SHH
SH
SSHK SH SH
SH
SSHK
SSSHHKA
SHK
SHHKAA
SHHK
SH

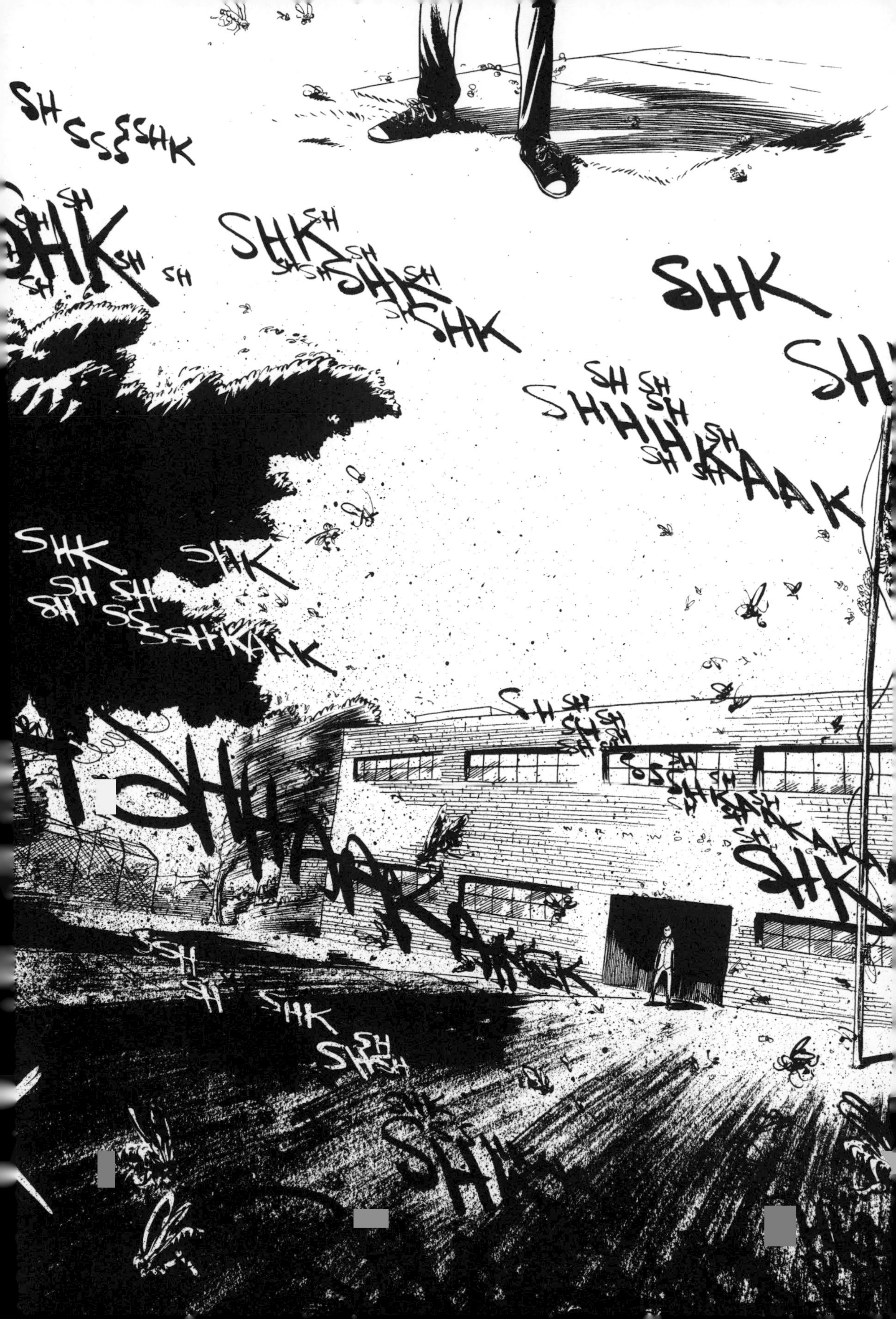

SHSSSSHK
SHK
SHK
SHK
SHK
SHHHKAAK
SHK
SHK
SSSHKAAK
SHK
SHK
SHK

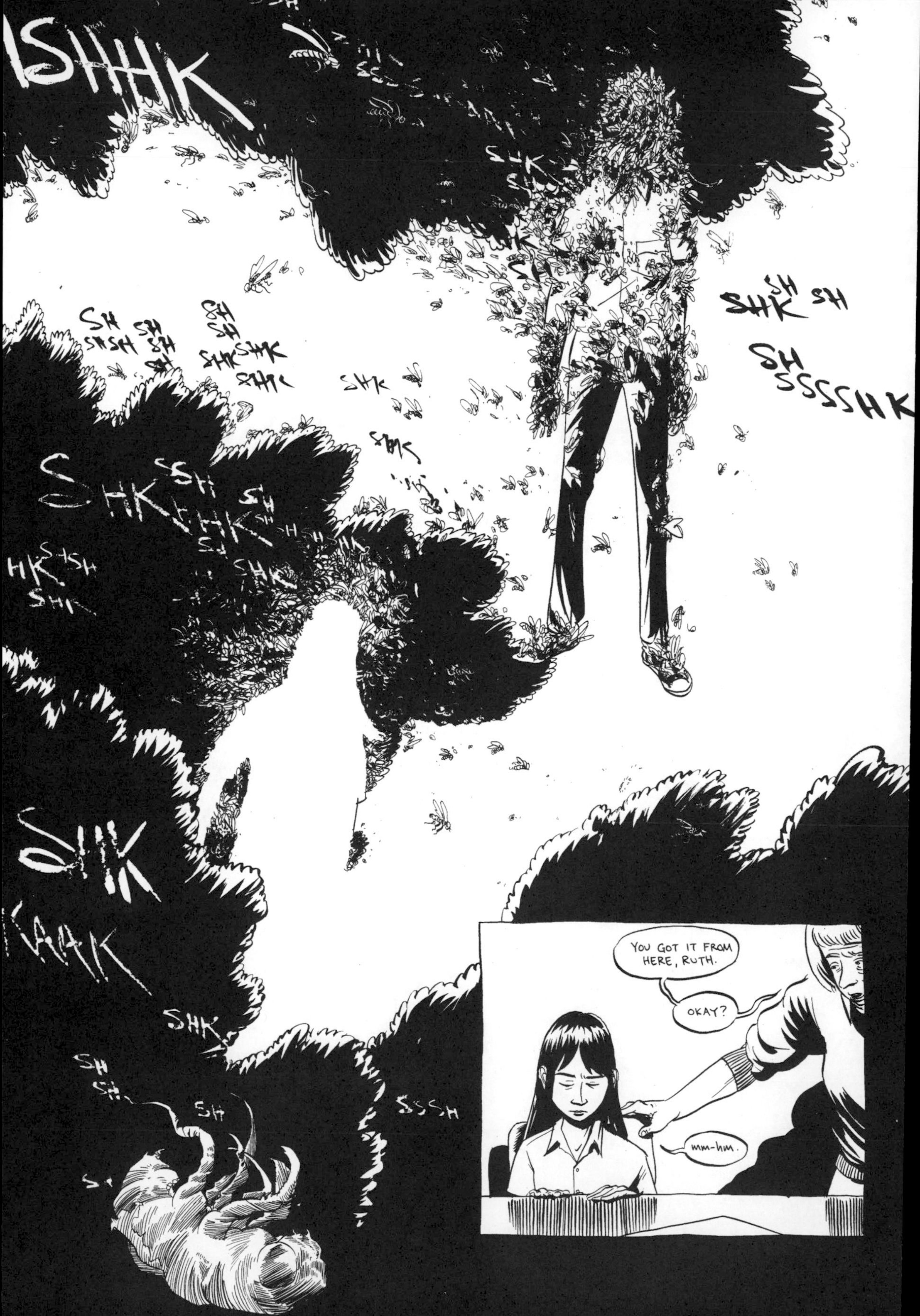
SHHK
SH SH SH
SHK SH SH
SH SSSSSHK
SHK
SHK
SHK
SHK
SSSH
SH
YOU GOT IT FROM HERE, RUTH.
OKAY?
mm-hm.

I'LL BE IN CLASS.
THANK YOU, COACH. NOW, IF YOU'LL EXCUSE US,
KLIK
RUTH.
FIRST, WE'RE GLAD THAT YOU SEEM TO BE OKAY, AND EXCEPT FOR ALL THE TARDIES YOU SEEM TO
WHO GAVE YOU THE DRUGS?
ahem
WHAT DID YOU TAKE AND HOW DID YOU GET IT?
RUTH! WAKE UP.
what?
OFFICER NICKEL AND I ARE HERE FOR YOUR SAFETY, RUTH.
WHO GAVE YOU THE DRUGS?
wh--
HELP US, RUTH.
i don't
RUTH! WE KNOW YOU CAME TO SCHOOL ON DRUGS!
LOOK AT YOU.
TELL US WHO GAVE YOU THE DAMN DRUGS.

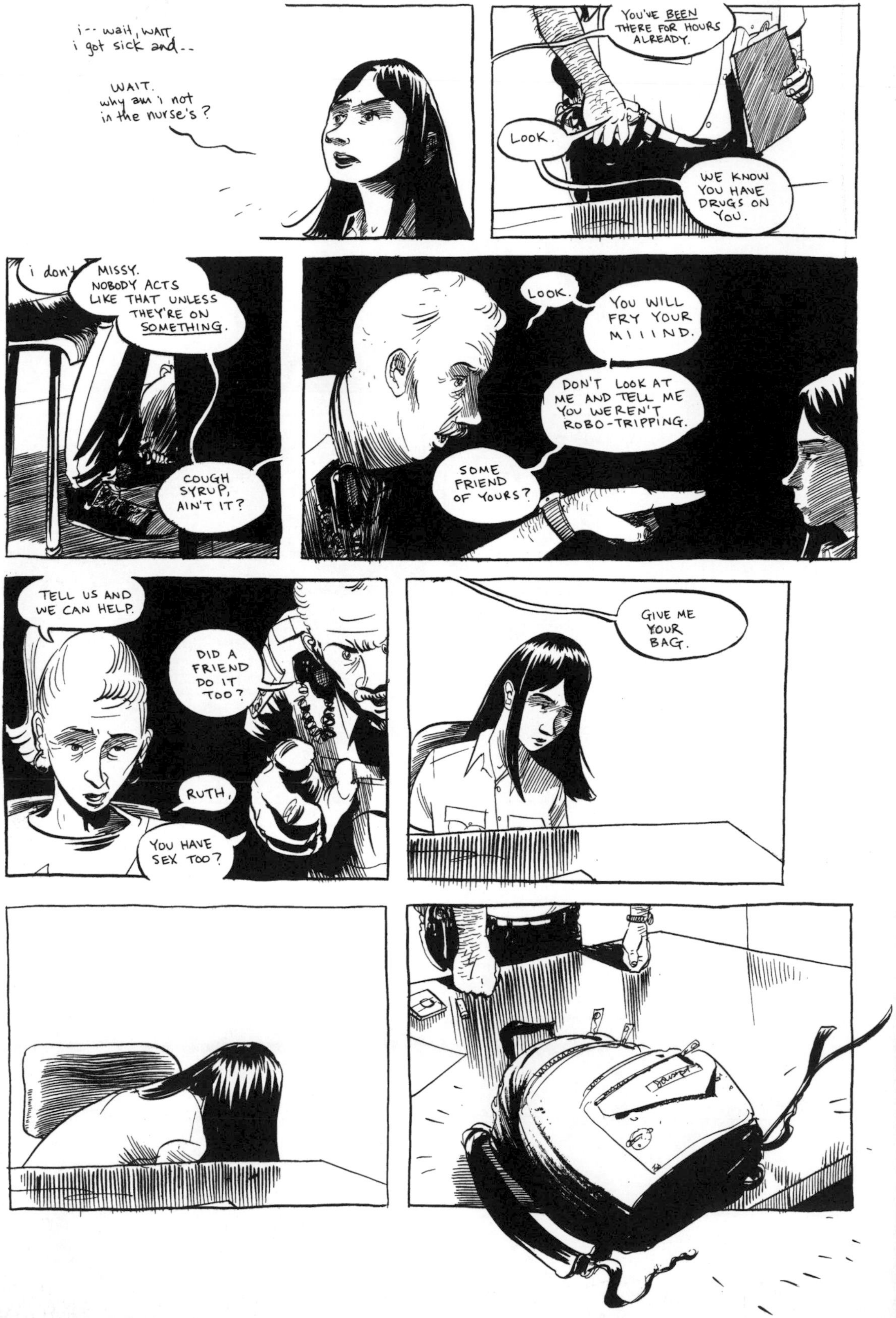
i-- wait, WAIT, i got sick and--
WAIT. why am i not in the nurse's?
YOU'VE BEEN THERE FOR HOURS ALREADY.
LOOK.
WE KNOW YOU HAVE DRUGS ON YOU.
i don't
MISSY. NOBODY ACTS LIKE THAT UNLESS THEY'RE ON SOMETHING.
COUGH SYRUP, AIN'T IT?
LOOK.
YOU WILL FRY YOUR MIIIND.
DON'T LOOK AT ME AND TELL ME YOU WEREN'T ROBO-TRIPPING.
SOME FRIEND OF YOURS?
TELL US AND WE CAN HELP.
DID A FRIEND DO IT TOO?
RUTH,
YOU HAVE SEX TOO?
GIVE ME YOUR BAG.

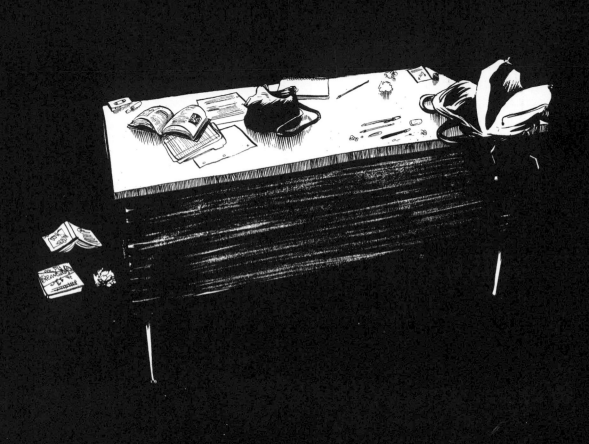

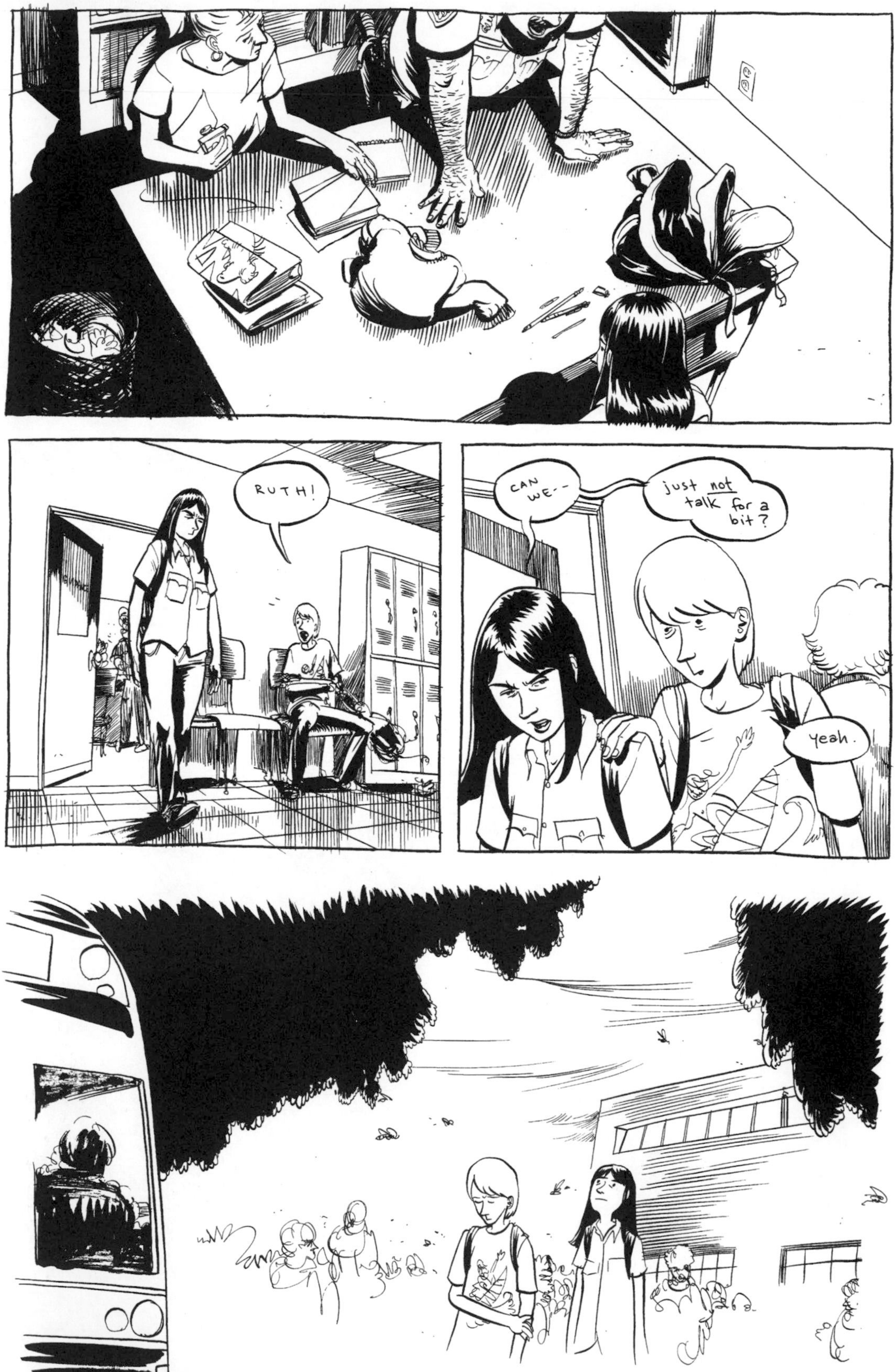
RUTH!
CAN WE--
just not talk for a bit?
yeah.

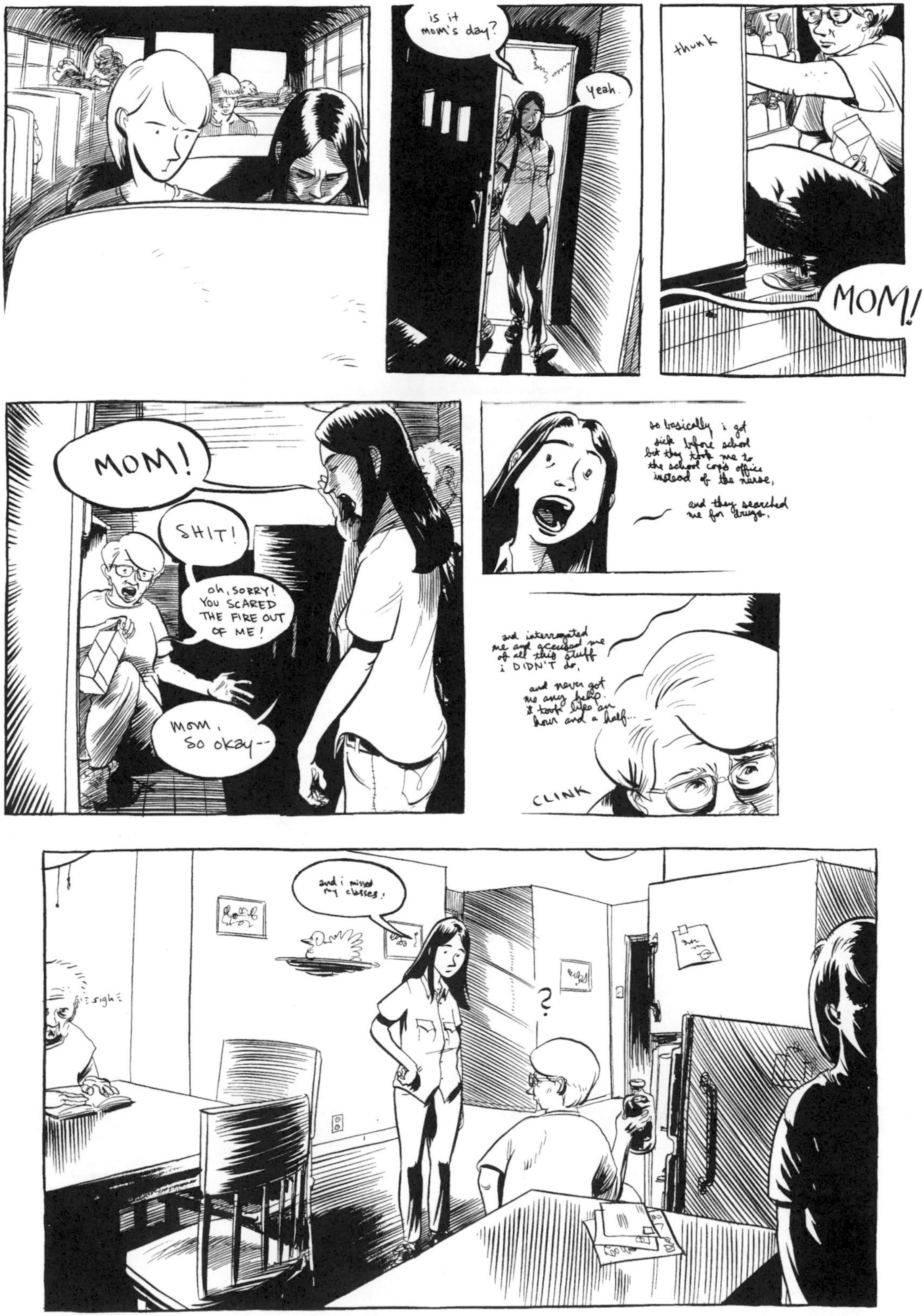

is it mom's day?
yeah.
thunk
MOM!
MOM!
SHIT!
oh, SORRY! YOU SCARED THE FIRE OUT OF ME!
mom, so okay--
so basically i got sick before school but they took me to the school cop's office instead of the nurse,
and they searched me for drugs.
and interrogated me and accused me of all this stuff i DIDN'T do,
and never got me any help. it took like an hour and a half...
CLINK
and i missed my classes!
sigh
?

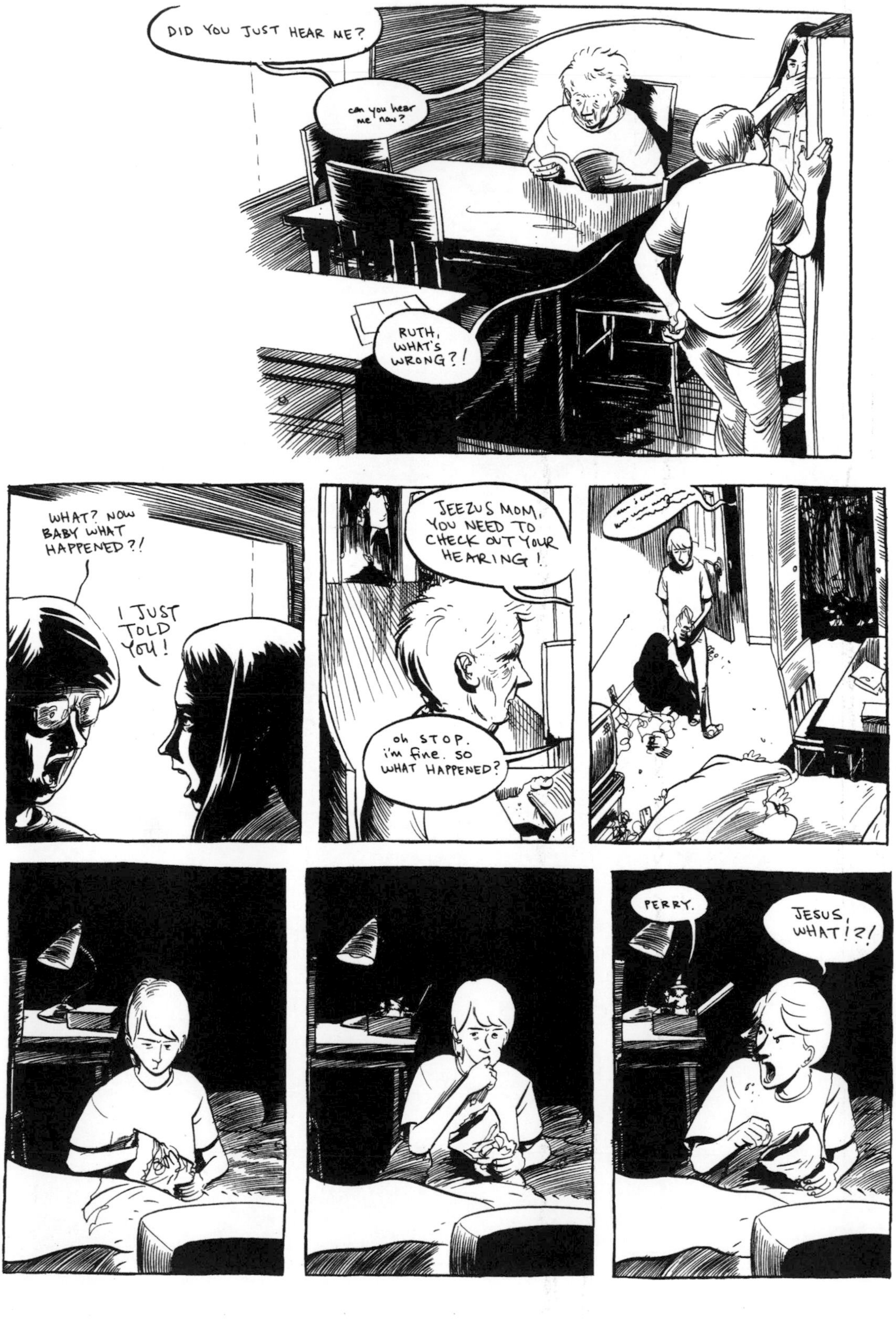
DID YOU JUST HEAR ME?
can you hear me now?
RUTH, WHAT'S WRONG?!
WHAT? NOW BABY WHAT HAPPENED?!
I JUST TOLD YOU!
JEEZUS MOM, YOU NEED TO CHECK OUT YOUR HEARING!
oh STOP. i'm fine. so WHAT HAPPENED?
PERRY.
JESUS, WHAT!?!

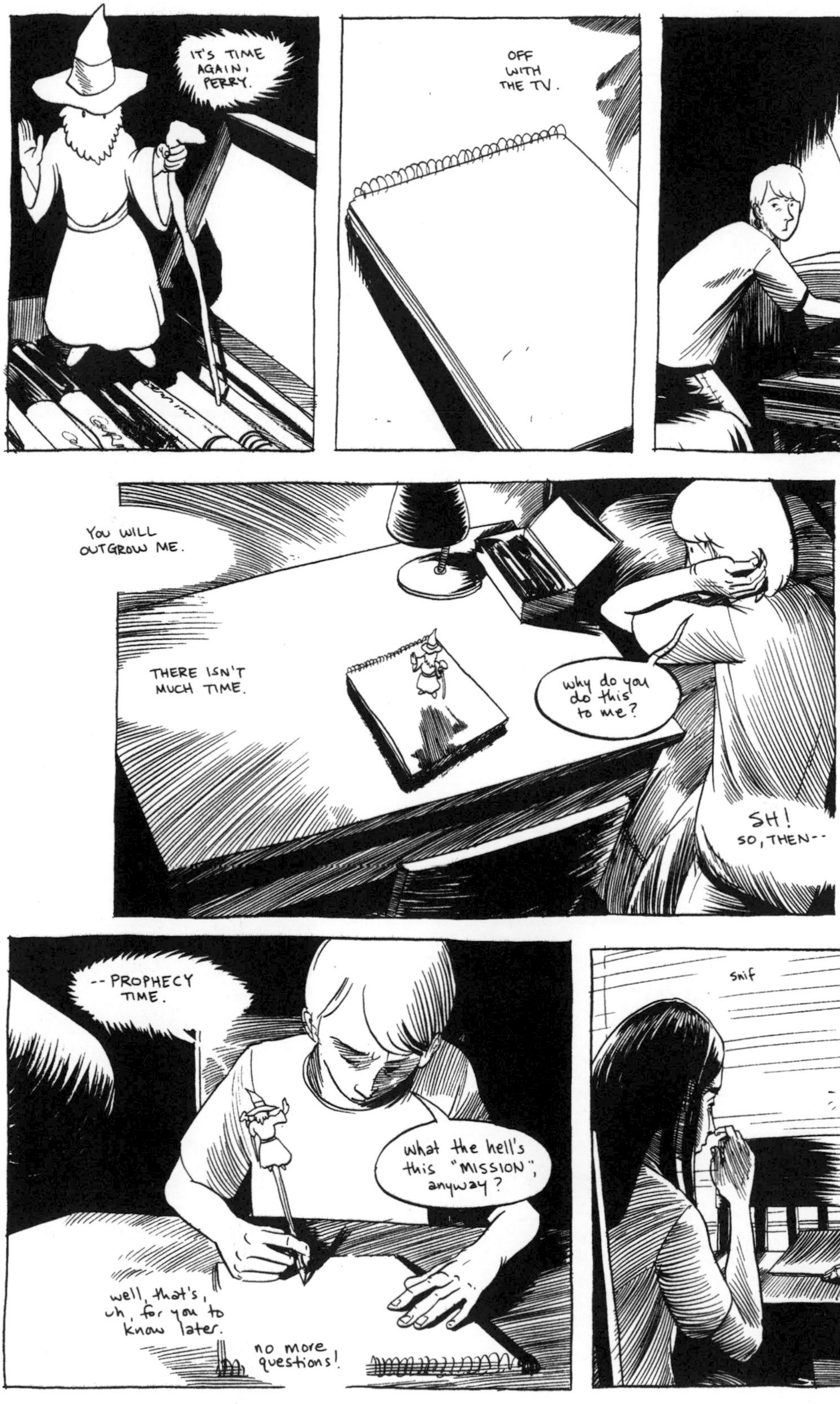

IT'S TIME AGAIN, PERRY.
OFF WITH THE TV.
YOU WILL OUTGROW ME.
THERE ISN'T MUCH TIME.
why do you do this to me?
SH! SO, THEN--
--PROPHECY TIME.
what the hell's this "MISSION", anyway?
well, that's, uh, for you to know later.
no more questions!
snif
ahem

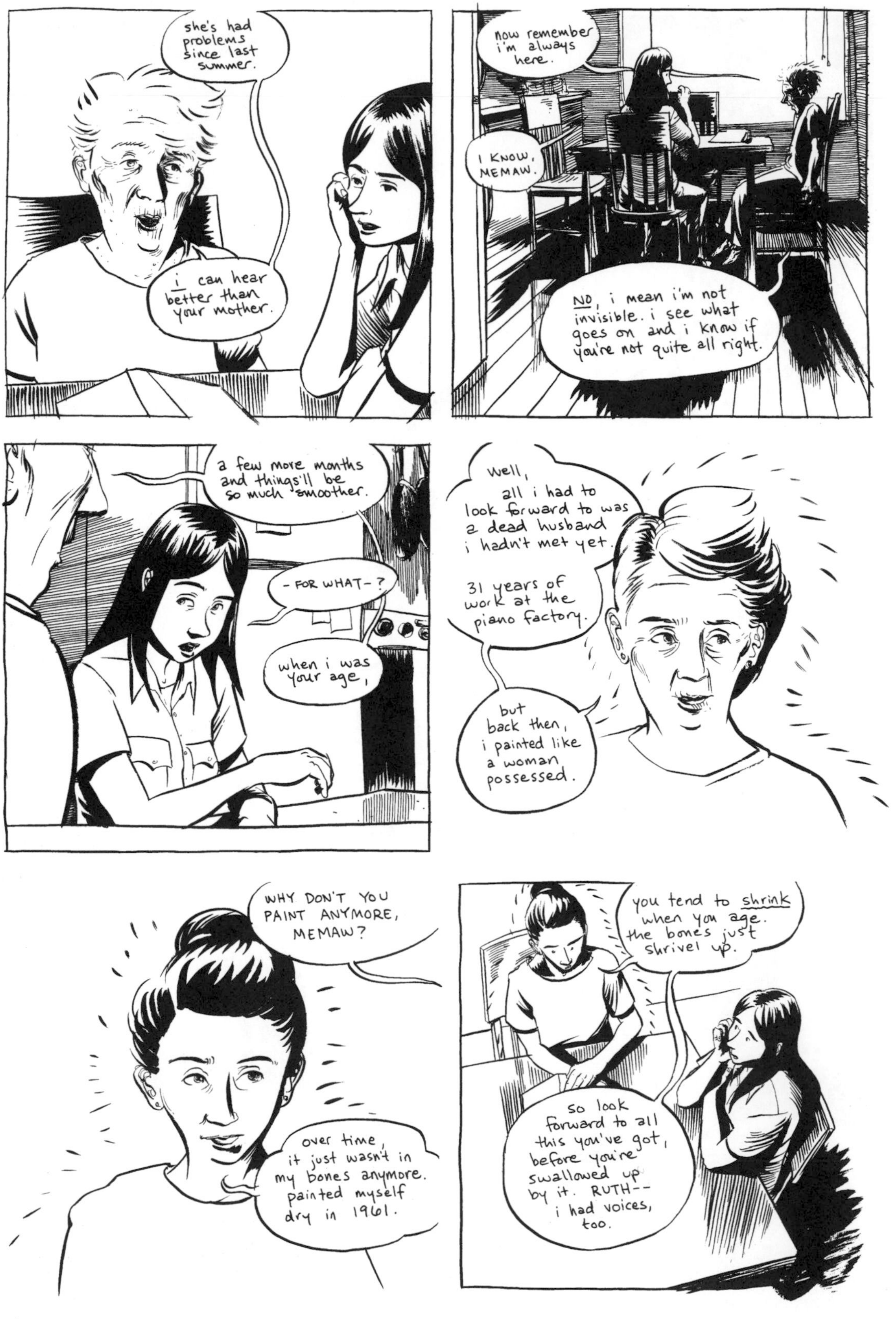
she's had problems since last summer.
i can hear better than your mother.
now remember i'm always here.
I KNOW, MEMAW.
NO, i mean i'm not invisible. i see what goes on and i know if you're not quite all right.
a few more months and things'll be so much smoother.
- FOR WHAT - ?
when i was your age,
well, all i had to look forward to was a dead husband i hadn't met yet.
31 years of work at the piano factory.
but back then, i painted like a woman possessed.
WHY DON'T YOU PAINT ANYMORE, MEMAW?
over time, it just wasn't in my bones anymore. painted myself dry in 1961.
you tend to shrink when you age. the bones just shrivel up.
so look forward to all this you've got, before you're swallowed up by it. RUTH-- i had voices, too.

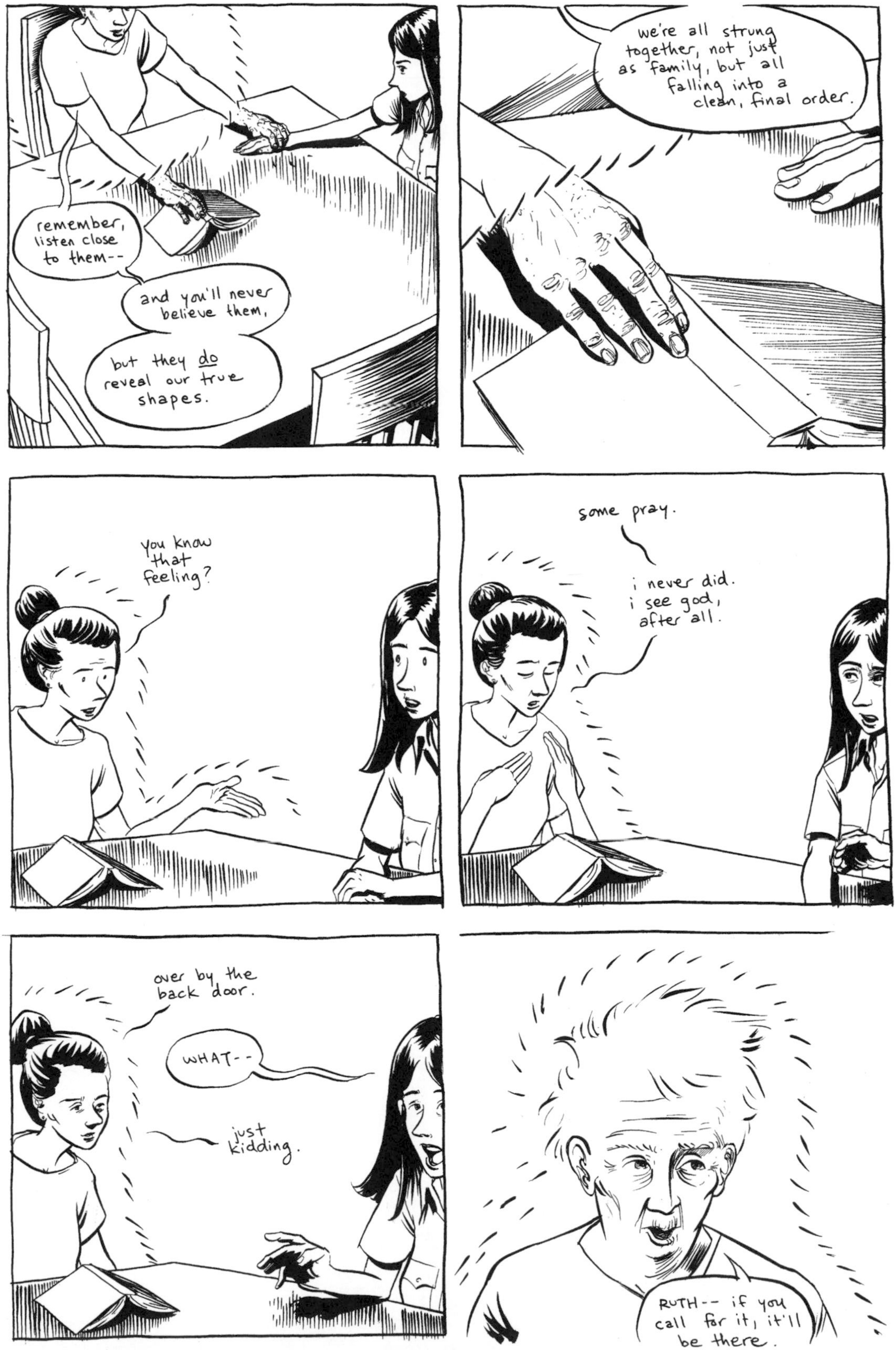
remember, listen close to them--
and you'll never believe them,
but they do reveal our true shapes.
we're all strung together, not just as family, but all falling into a clean, final order.
you know that feeling?
some pray.
i never did. i see god, after all.
over by the back door.
WHAT--
just kidding.
RUTH-- if you call for it, it'll be there.

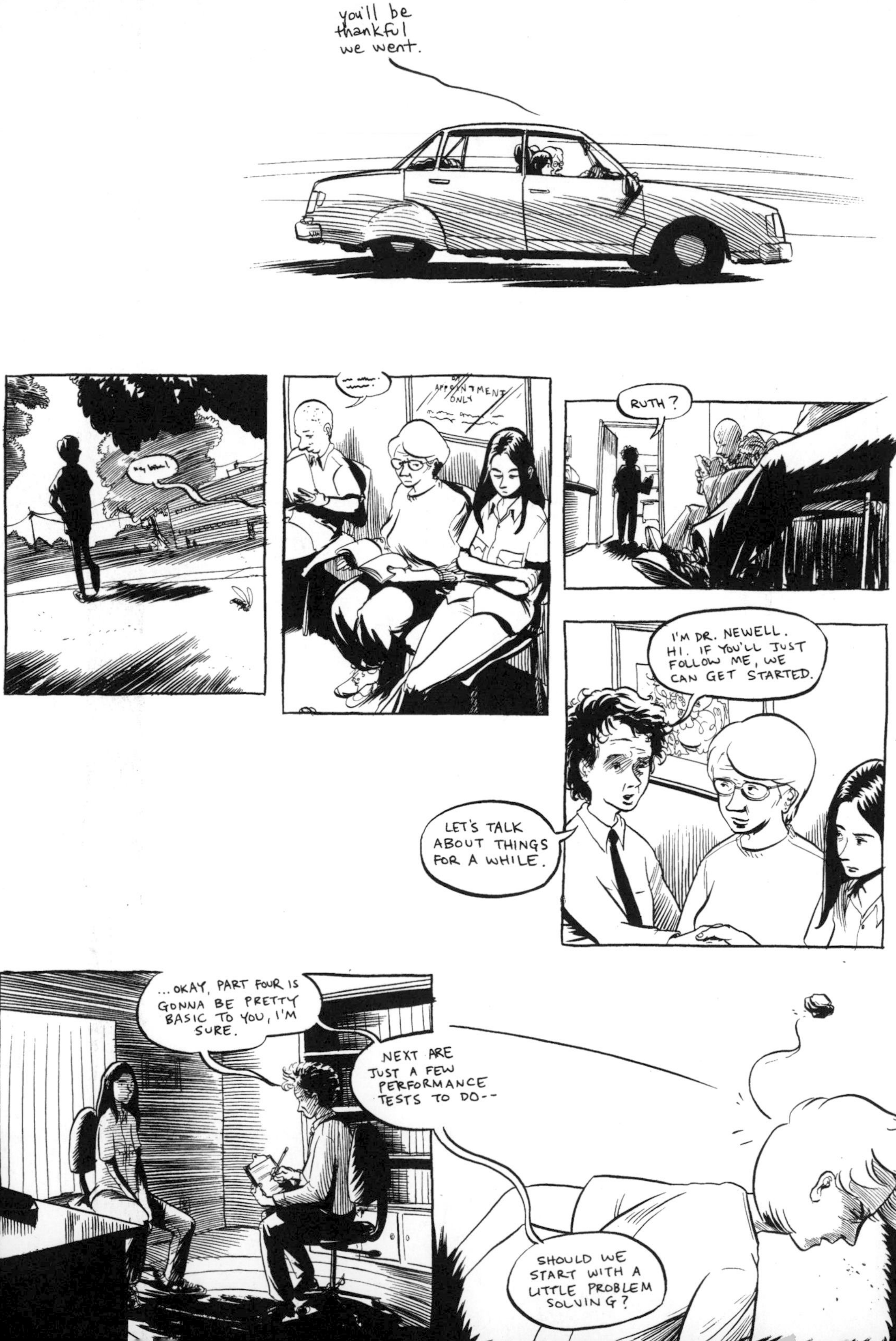
you'll be thankful we went.
APPOINTMENT ONLY
RUTH?
I'M DR. NEWELL. HI. IF YOU'LL JUST FOLLOW ME, WE CAN GET STARTED.
LET'S TALK ABOUT THINGS FOR A WHILE.
...OKAY, PART FOUR IS GONNA BE PRETTY BASIC TO YOU, I'M SURE.
NEXT ARE JUST A FEW PERFORMANCE TESTS TO DO--
SHOULD WE START WITH A LITTLE PROBLEM SOLVING?

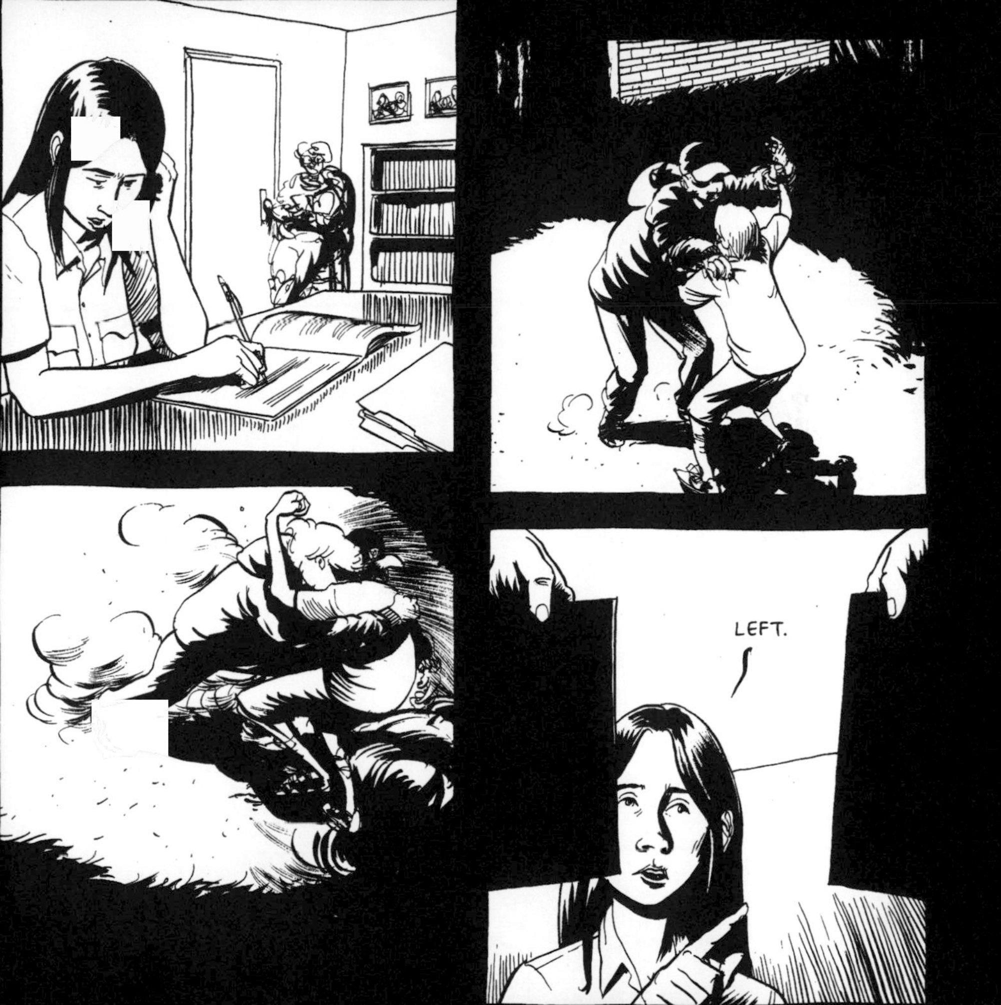
LEFT.

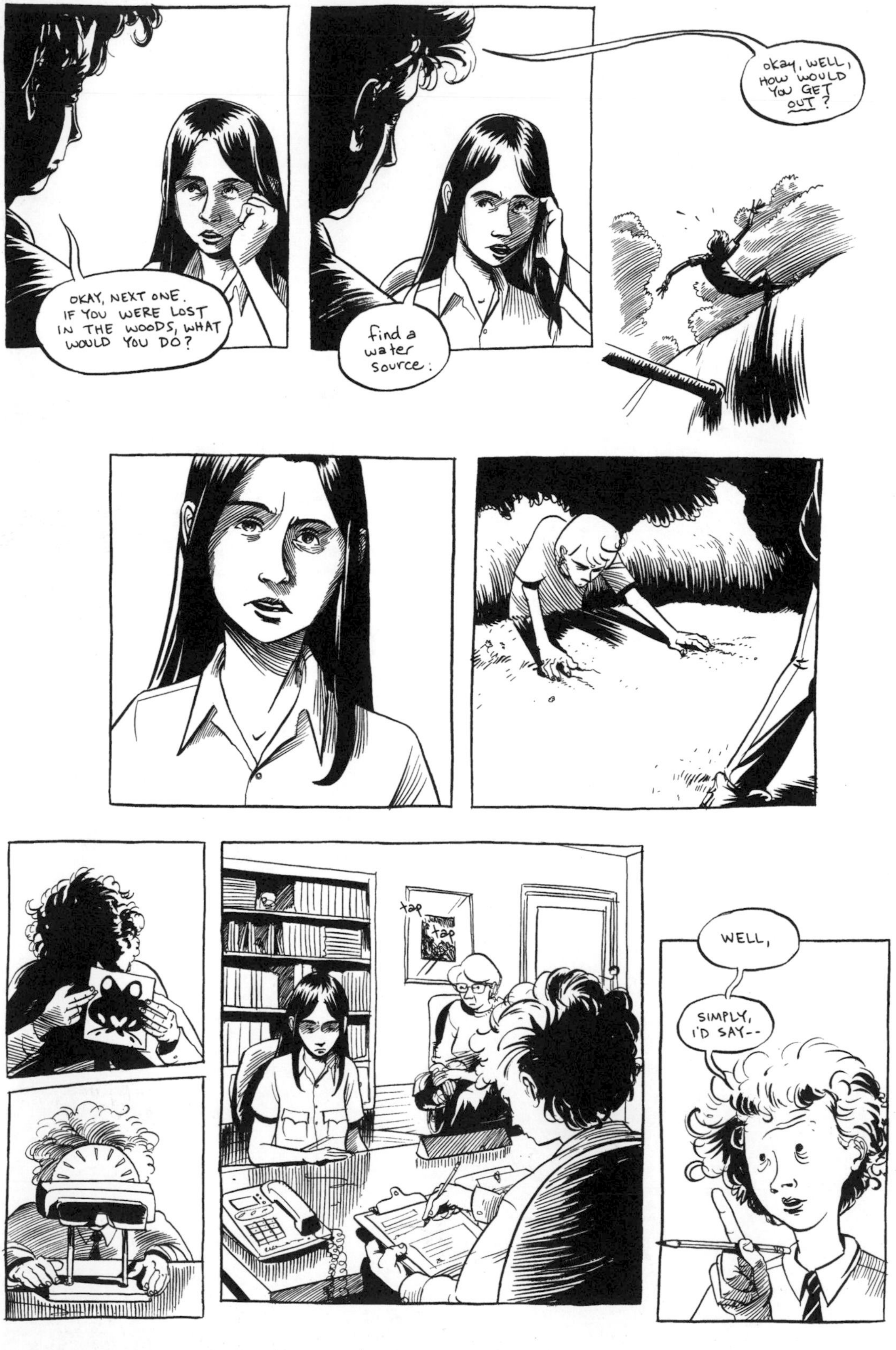
OKAY, NEXT ONE. IF YOU WERE LOST IN THE WOODS, WHAT WOULD YOU DO?
find a water source.
okay, WELL, HOW WOULD YOU GET OUT?
tap
tap
WELL,
SIMPLY, I'D SAY--

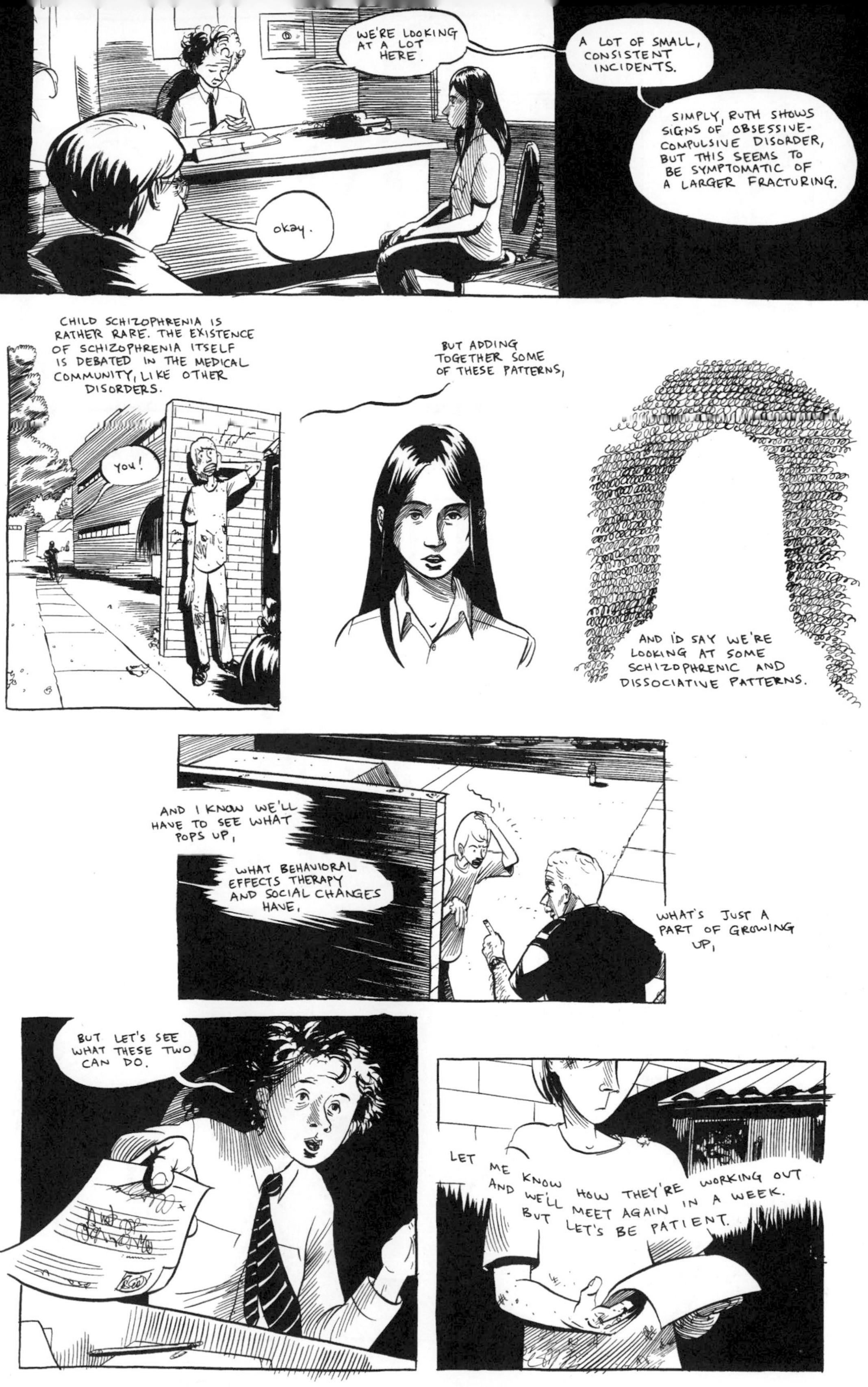
WE'RE LOOKING AT A LOT HERE.
A LOT OF SMALL, CONSISTENT INCIDENTS.
SIMPLY, RUTH SHOWS SIGNS OF OBSESSIVE-COMPULSIVE DISORDER, BUT THIS SEEMS TO BE SYMPTOMATIC OF A LARGER FRACTURING.
okay.
CHILD SCHIZOPHRENIA IS RATHER RARE. THE EXISTENCE OF SCHIZOPHRENIA ITSELF IS DEBATED IN THE MEDICAL COMMUNITY, LIKE OTHER DISORDERS.
YOU!
BUT ADDING TOGETHER SOME OF THESE PATTERNS,
AND I'D SAY WE'RE LOOKING AT SOME SCHIZOPHRENIC AND DISSOCIATIVE PATTERNS.
AND I KNOW WE'LL HAVE TO SEE WHAT POPS UP,
WHAT BEHAVIORAL EFFECTS THERAPY AND SOCIAL CHANGES HAVE,
WHAT'S JUST A PART OF GROWING UP,
BUT LET'S SEE WHAT THESE TWO CAN DO.
LET ME KNOW HOW THEY'RE WORKING OUT AND WE'LL MEET AGAIN IN A WEEK. BUT LET'S BE PATIENT.

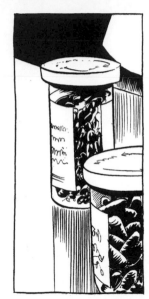

SLAM!

PERRY?

PERRY, WHAT HAPPENED TO YOU?!!

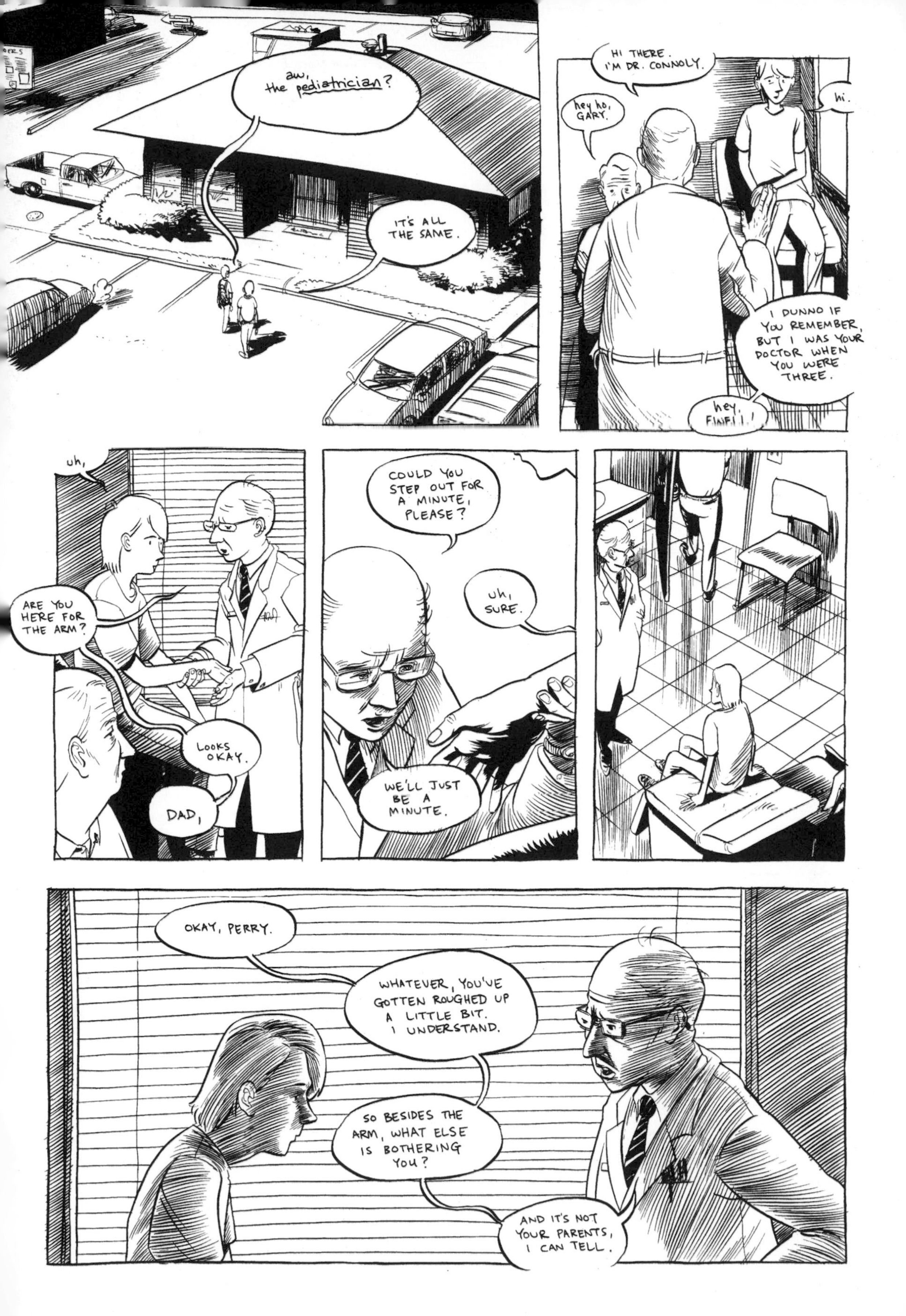
aw, the pediatrician?
IT'S ALL THE SAME.
HI THERE. I'M DR. CONNOLY.
hey ho, GARY.
hi.
I DUNNO IF YOU REMEMBER, BUT I WAS YOUR DOCTOR WHEN YOU WERE THREE.
hey, FINE!
uh,
ARE YOU HERE FOR THE ARM?
LOOKS OKAY.
DAD,
COULD YOU STEP OUT FOR A MINUTE, PLEASE?
uh, SURE.
WE'LL JUST BE A MINUTE.
OKAY, PERRY.
WHATEVER, YOU'VE GOTTEN ROUGHED UP A LITTLE BIT. I UNDERSTAND.
SO BESIDES THE ARM, WHAT ELSE IS BOTHERING YOU?
AND IT'S NOT YOUR PARENTS, I CAN TELL.

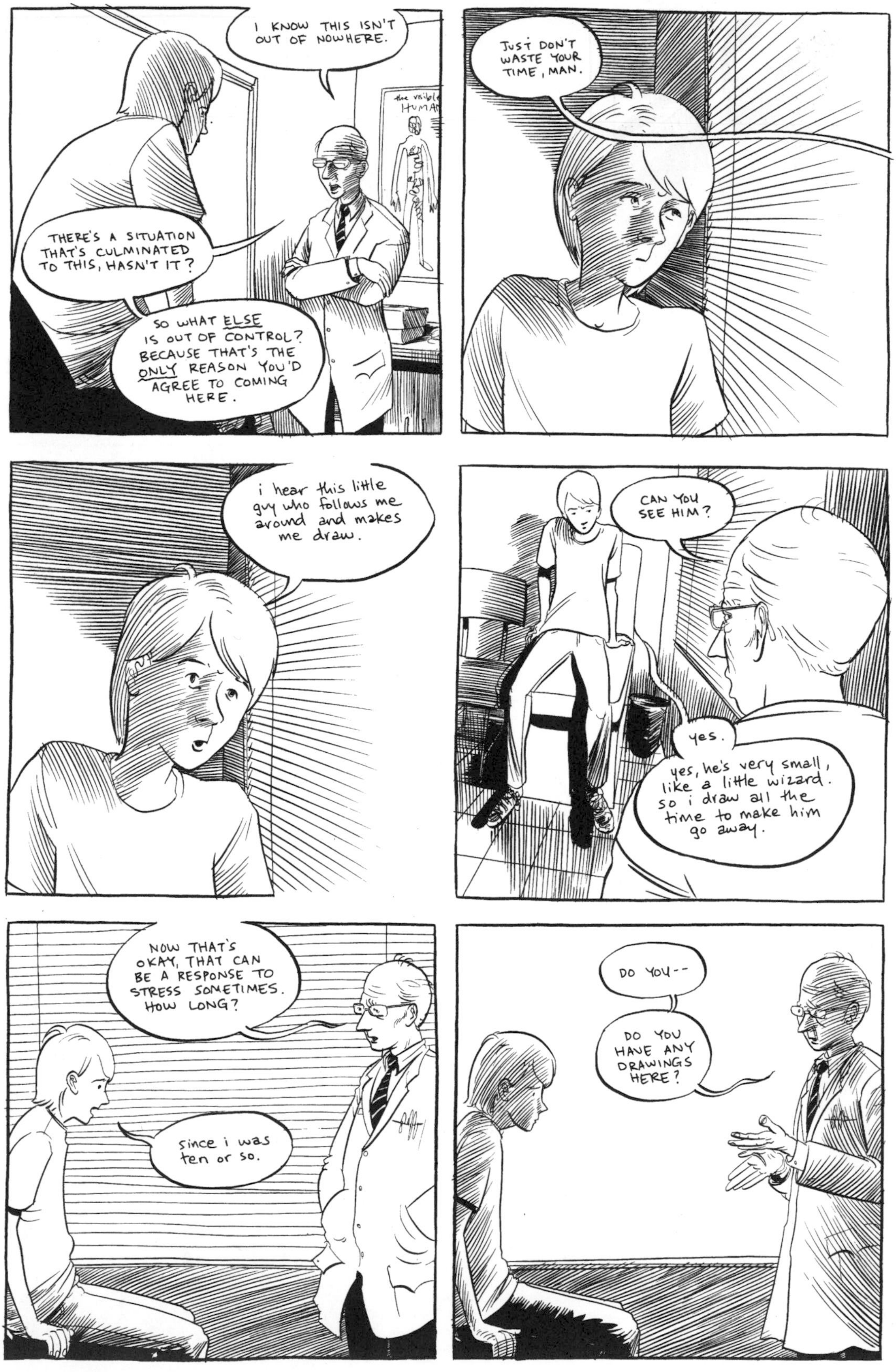
I KNOW THIS ISN'T OUT OF NOWHERE.
THERE'S A SITUATION THAT'S CULMINATED TO THIS, HASN'T IT?
SO WHAT ELSE IS OUT OF CONTROL? BECAUSE THAT'S THE ONLY REASON YOU'D AGREE TO COMING HERE.
JUST DON'T WASTE YOUR TIME, MAN.
i hear this little guy who follows me around and makes me draw.
CAN YOU SEE HIM?
yes.
yes, he's very small, like a little wizard. so i draw all the time to make him go away.
NOW THAT'S OKAY, THAT CAN BE A RESPONSE TO STRESS SOMETIMES. HOW LONG?
since i was ten or so.
DO YOU--
DO YOU HAVE ANY DRAWINGS HERE?

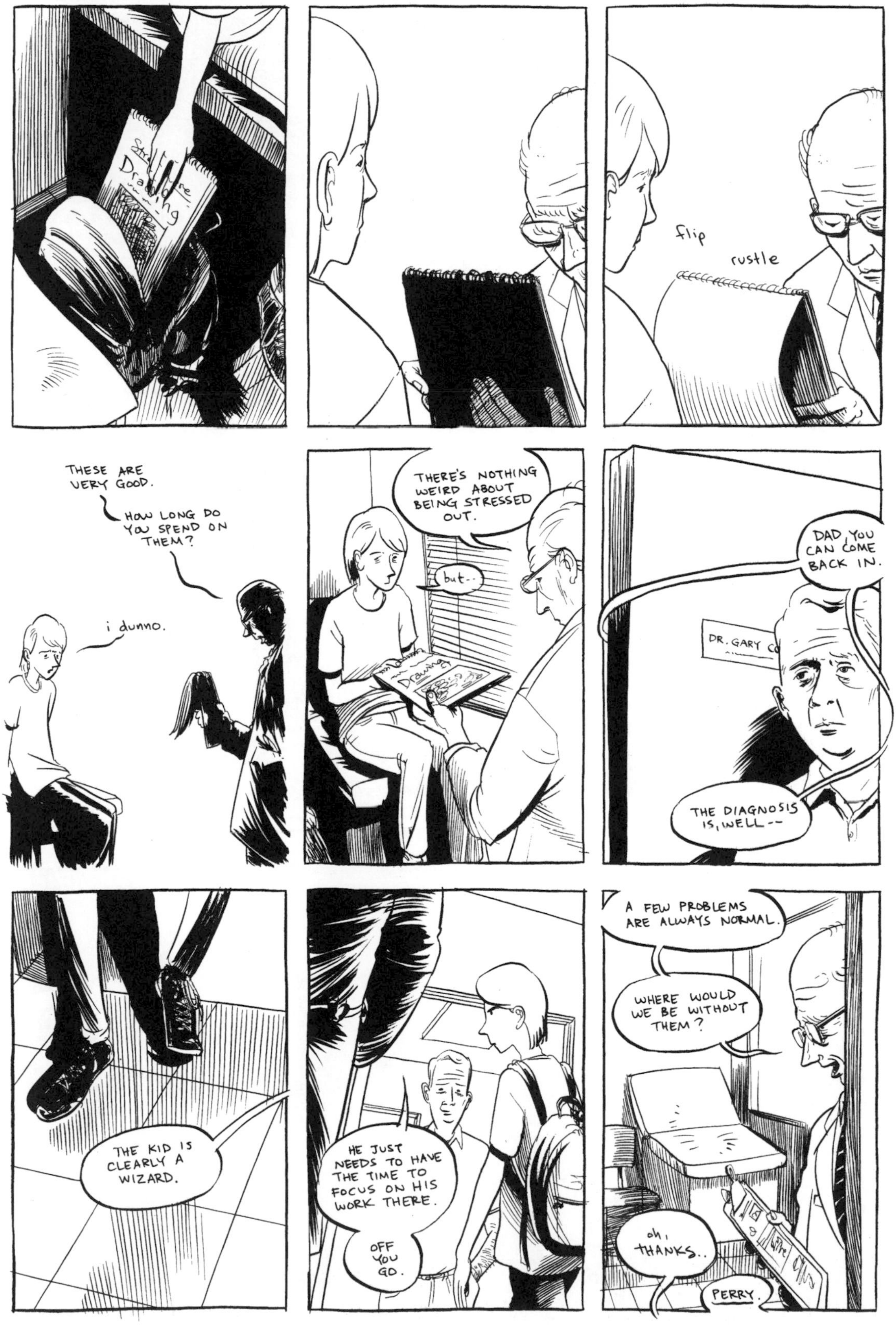
flip
rustle
THESE ARE VERY GOOD.
HOW LONG DO YOU SPEND ON THEM?
i dunno.
THERE'S NOTHING WEIRD ABOUT BEING STRESSED OUT.
but..
DAD, YOU CAN COME BACK IN.
DR. GARY C
THE DIAGNOSIS IS, WELL --
THE KID IS CLEARLY A WIZARD.
HE JUST NEEDS TO HAVE THE TIME TO FOCUS ON HIS WORK THERE.
OFF YOU GO.
A FEW PROBLEMS ARE ALWAYS NORMAL.
WHERE WOULD WE BE WITHOUT THEM?
oh, THANKS..
PERRY.

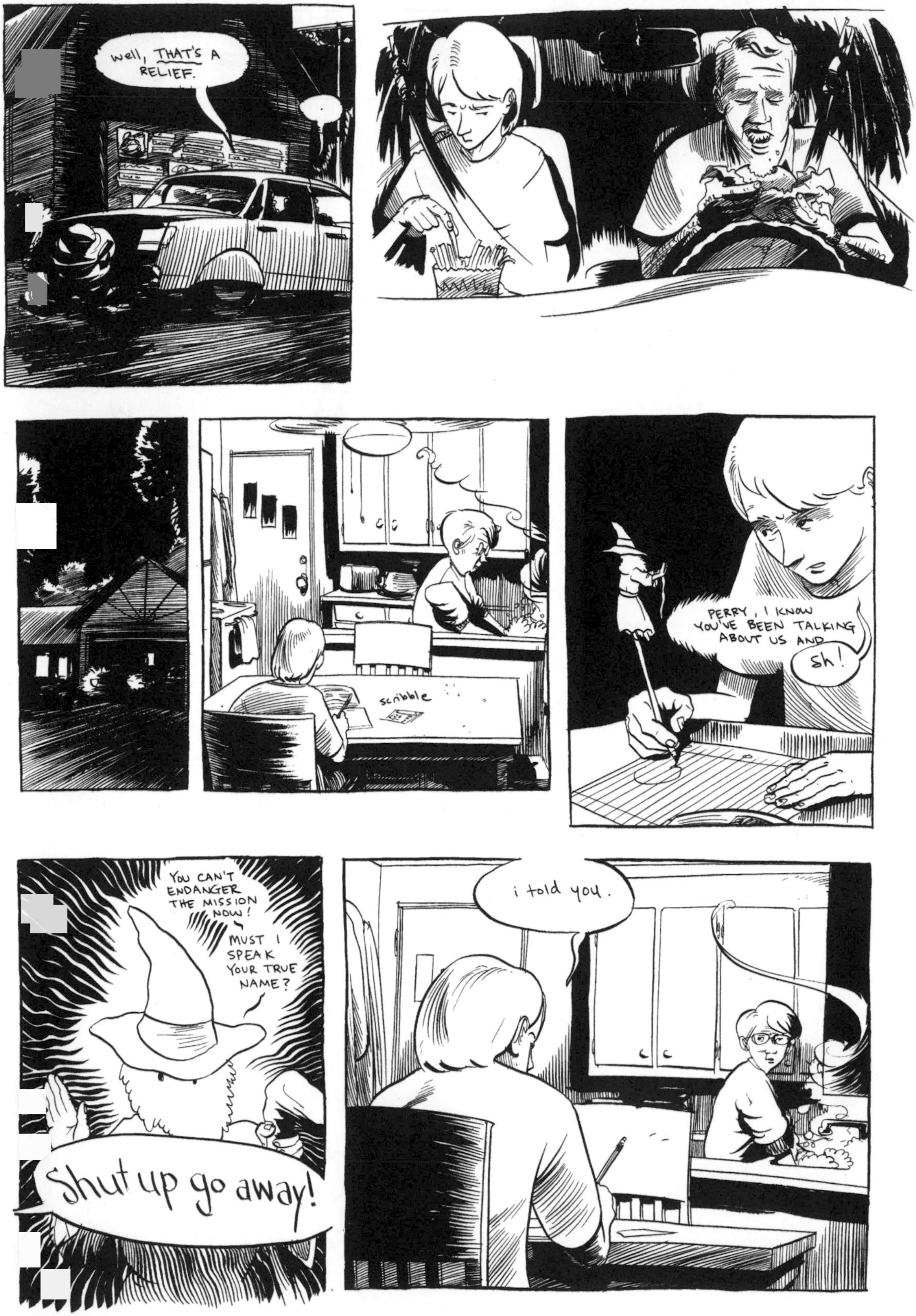
well, THAT'S A RELIEF.
PERRY, I KNOW YOU'VE BEEN TALKING ABOUT US AND
sh!
YOU CAN'T ENDANGER THE MISSION NOW!
MUST I SPEAK YOUR TRUE NAME?
Shut up go away!
i told you.

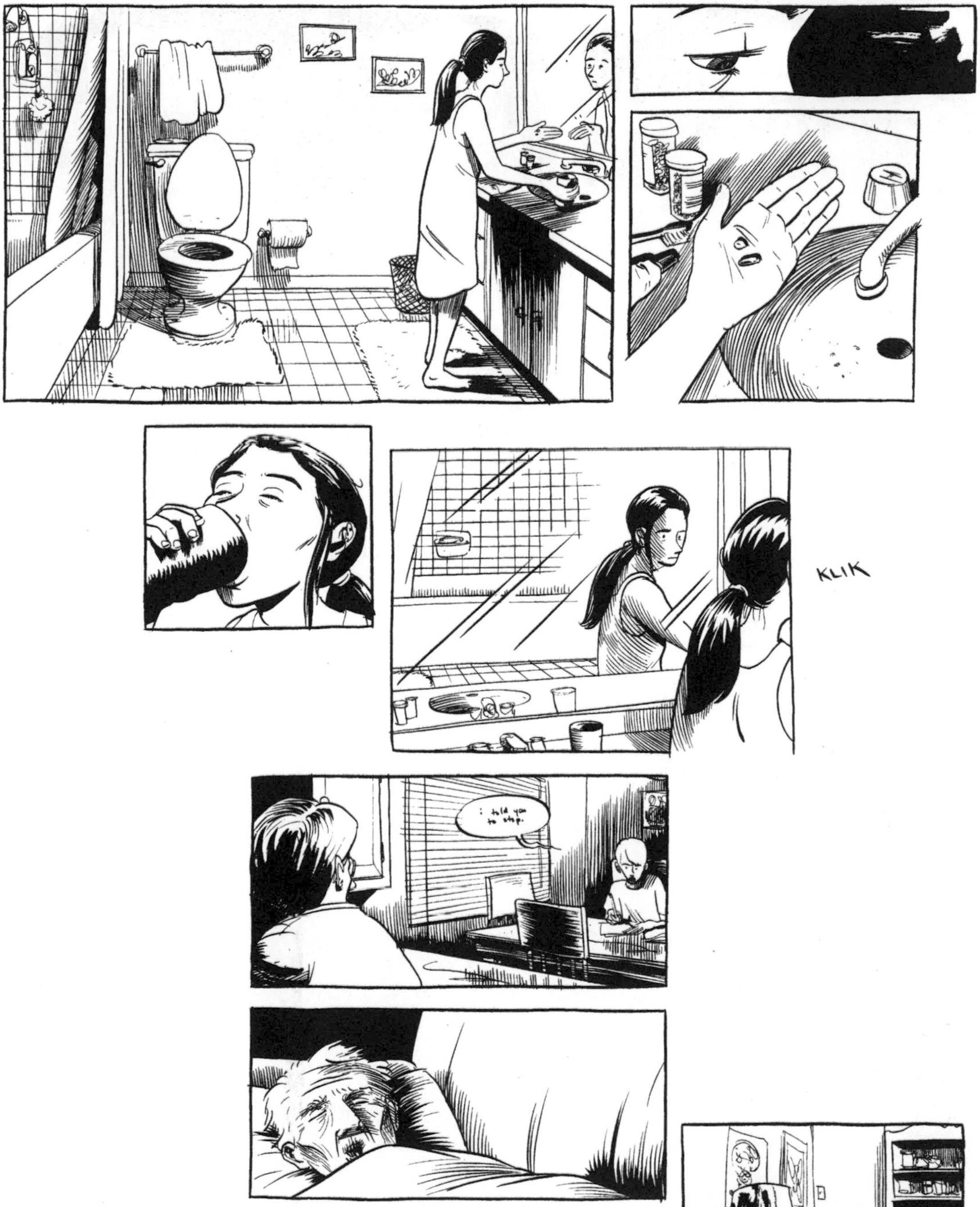
KLIK
i told you to stop.

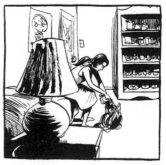

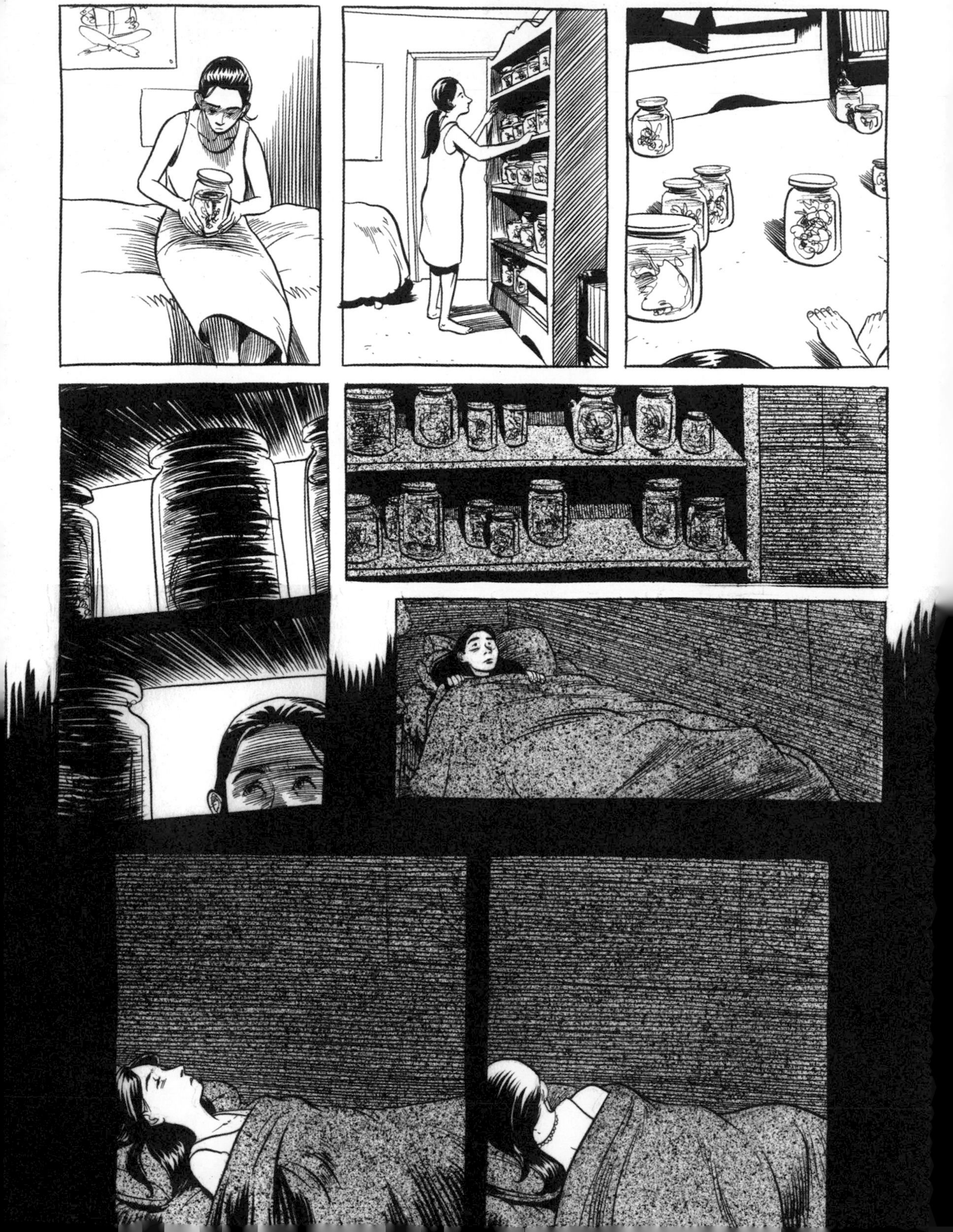

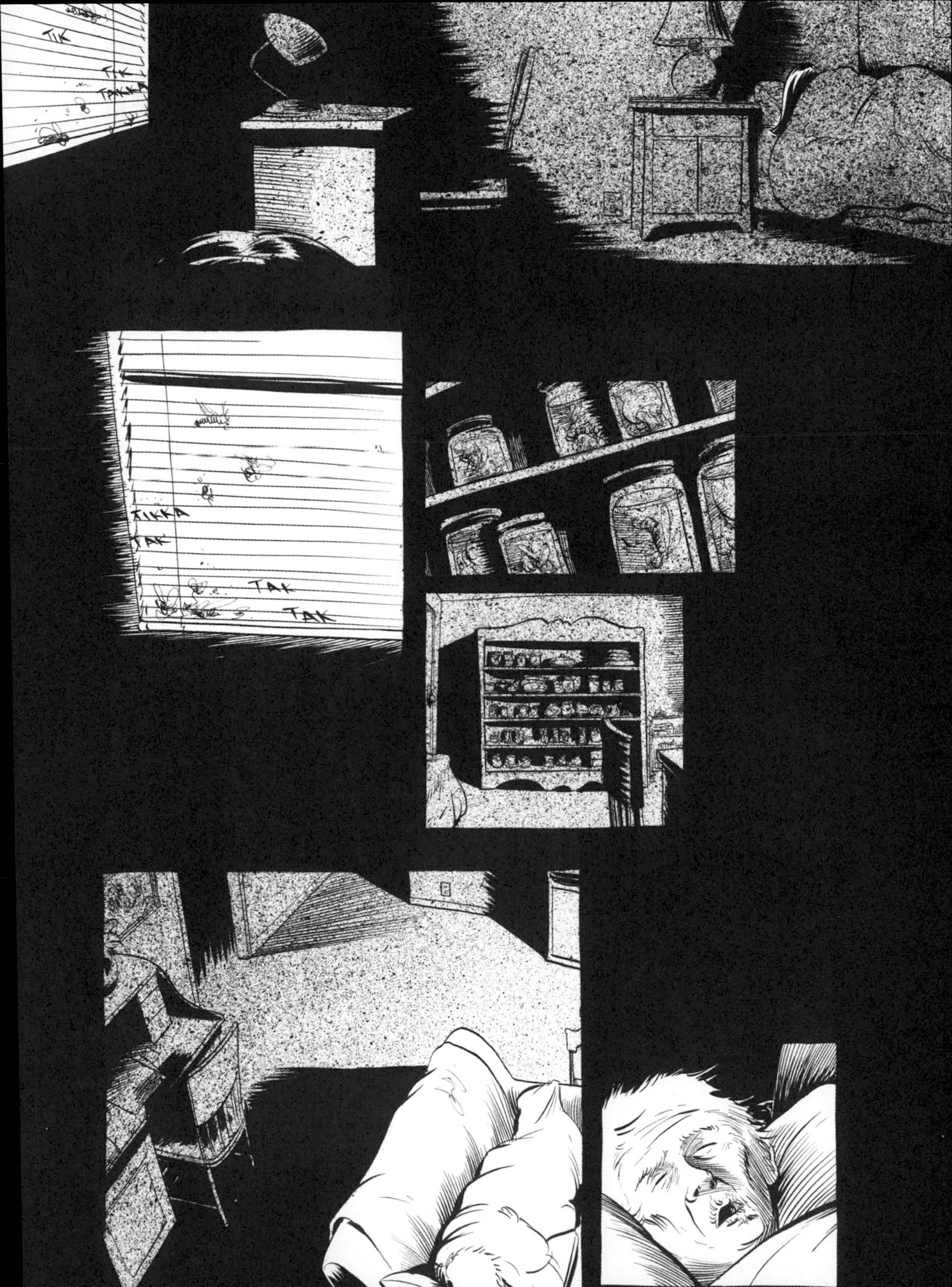
TIK
TIK
TAKKA
TIKKA
TAK
TAK
TAK

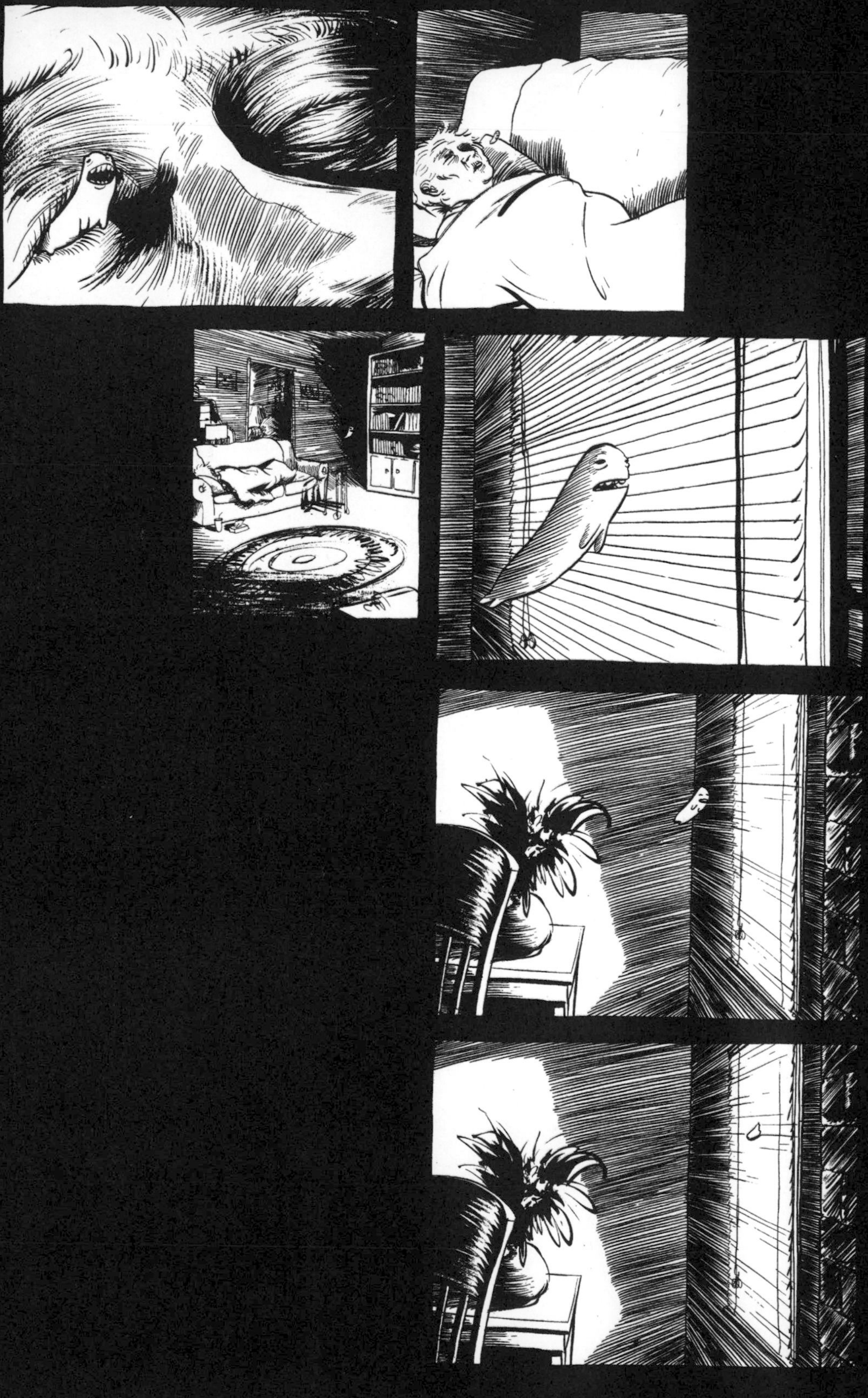

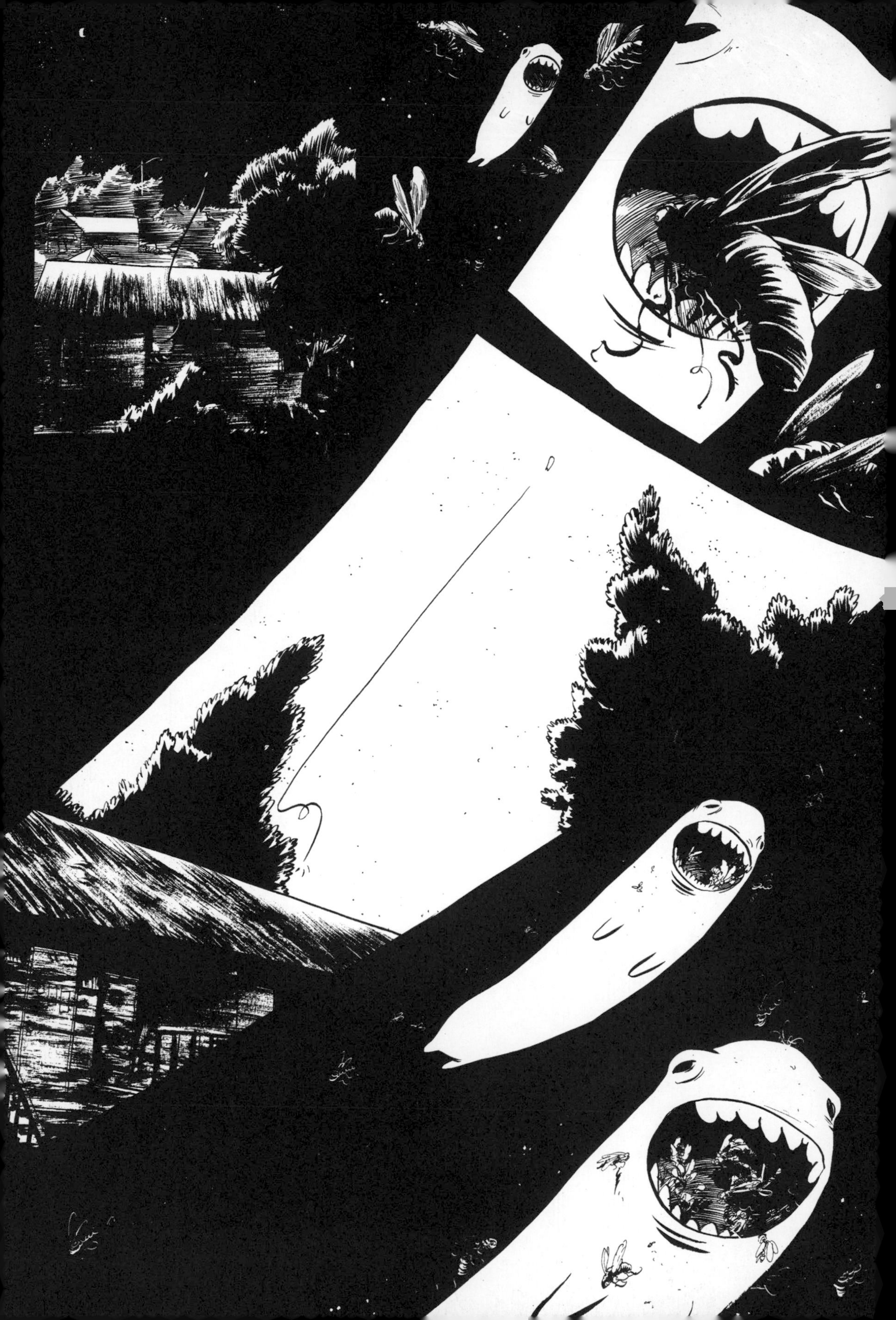

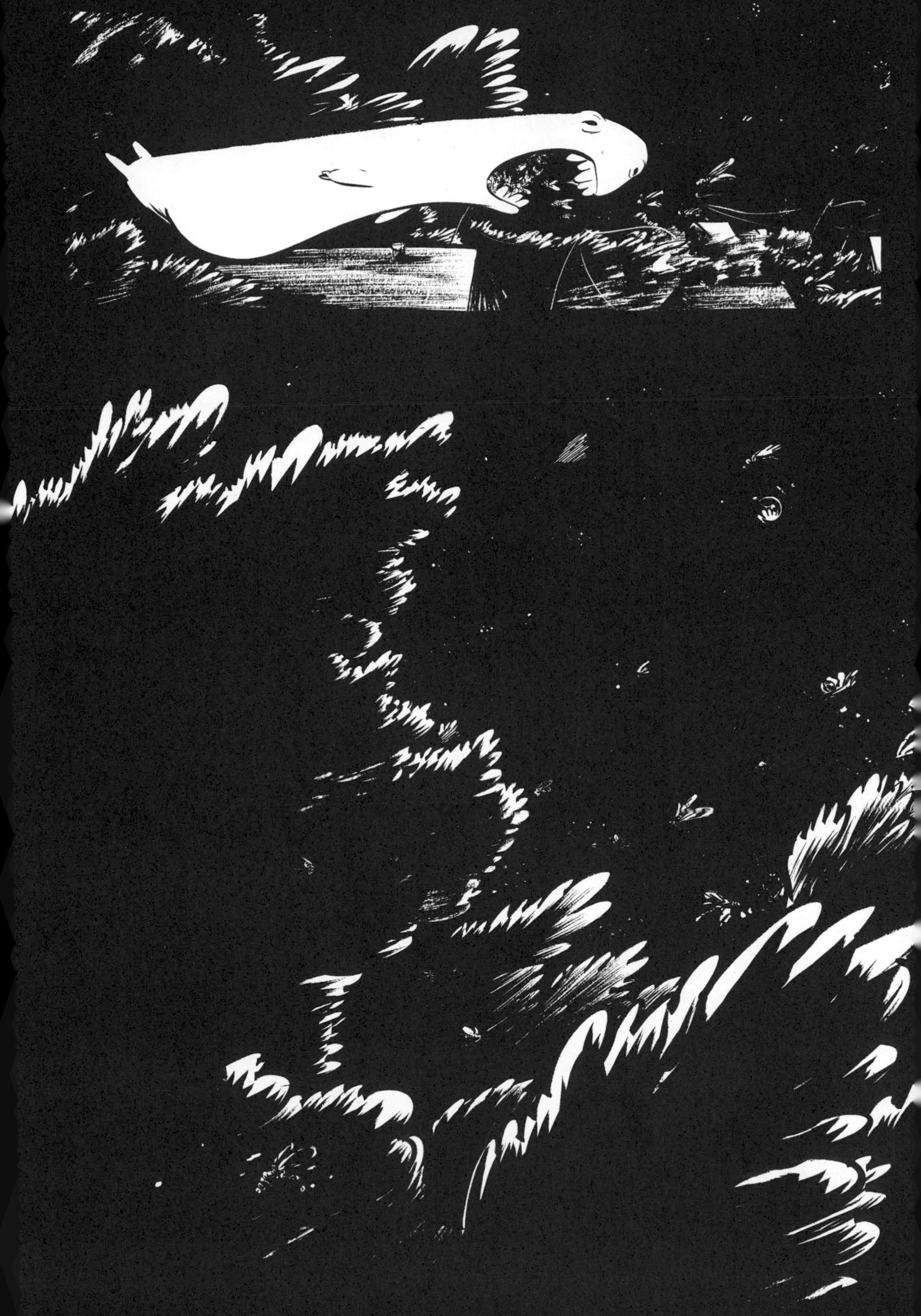

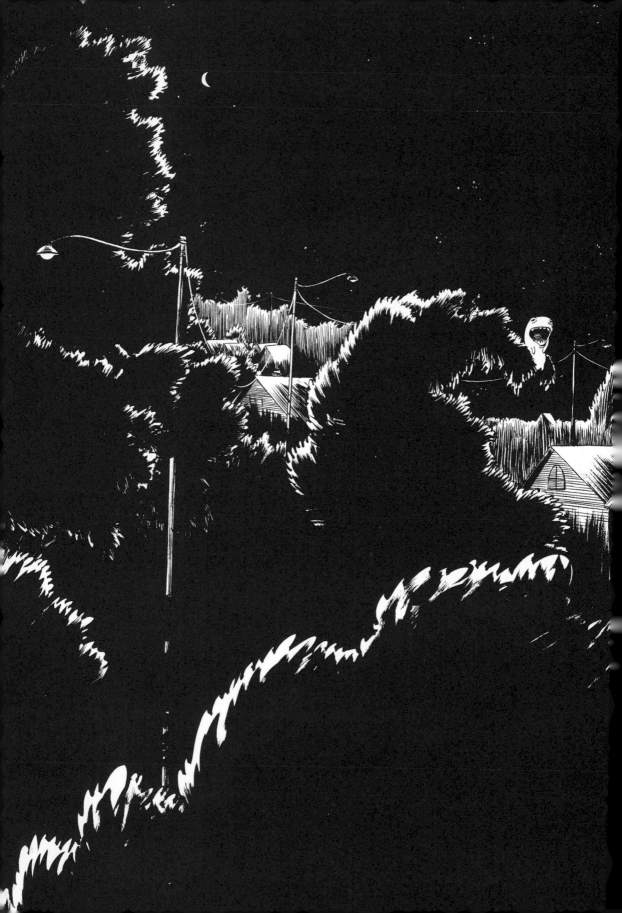

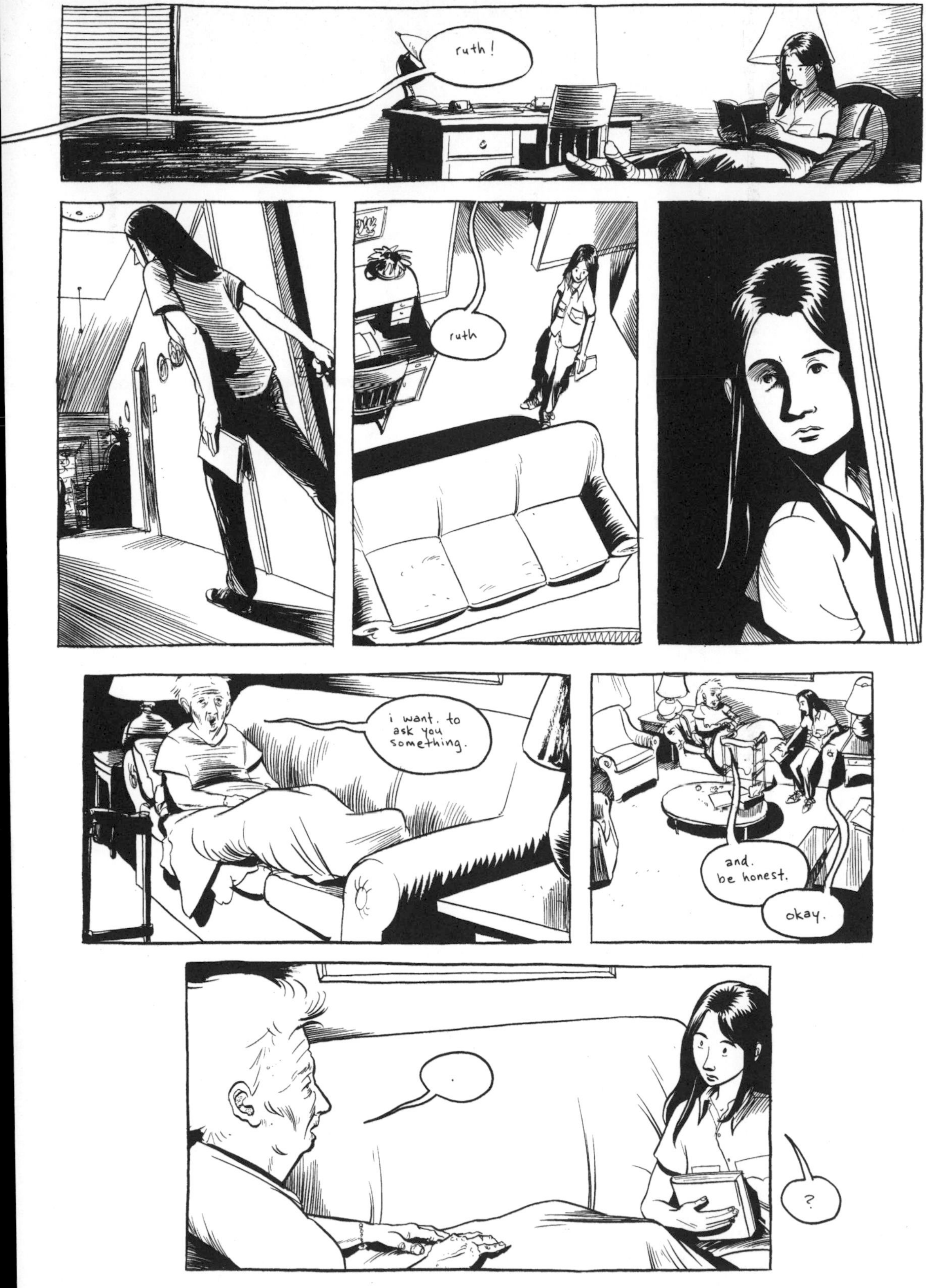
ruth!
ruth
i want. to ask you something.
and. be honest.
okay.
.
?

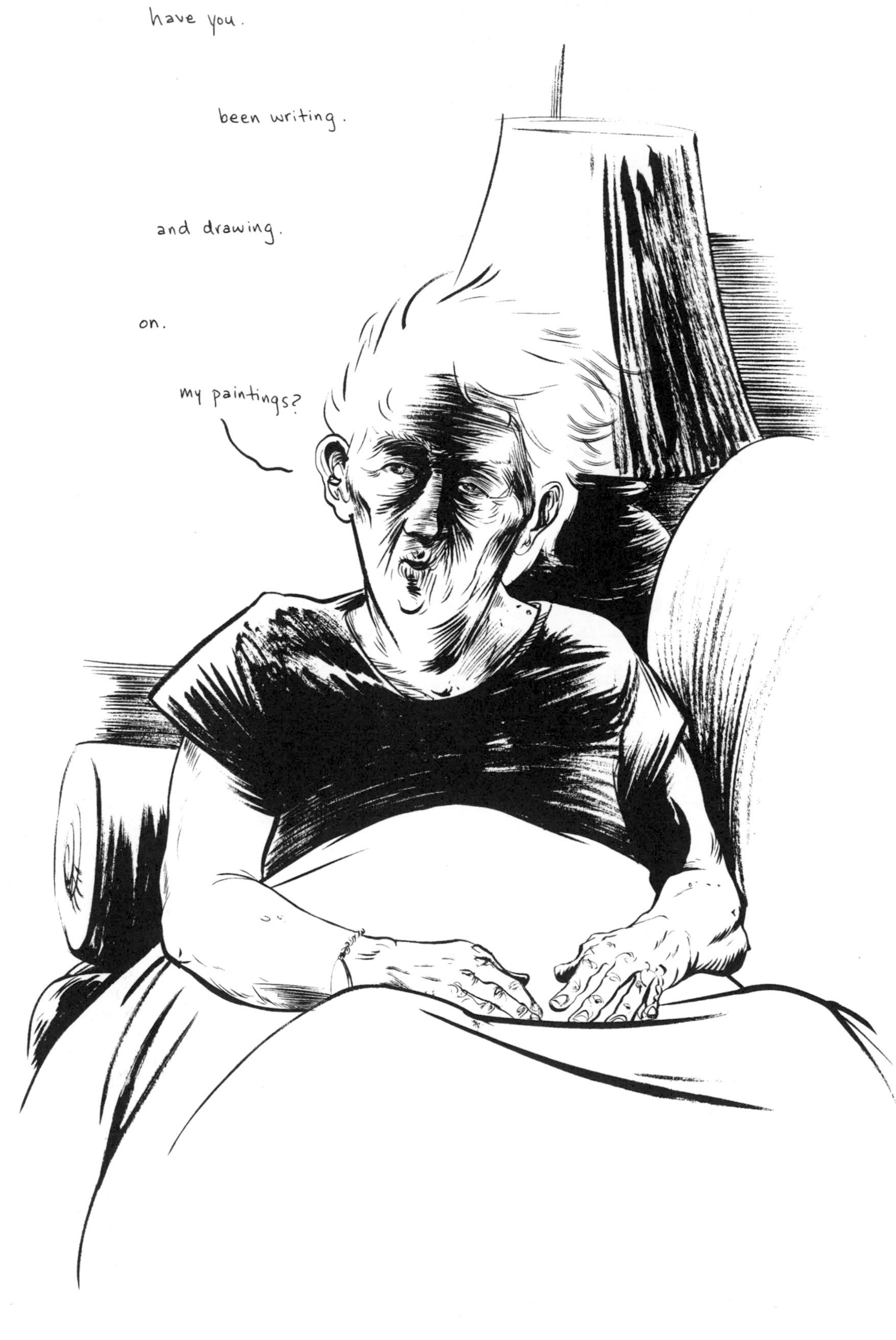
have you.
been writing.
and drawing.
on.
my paintings?

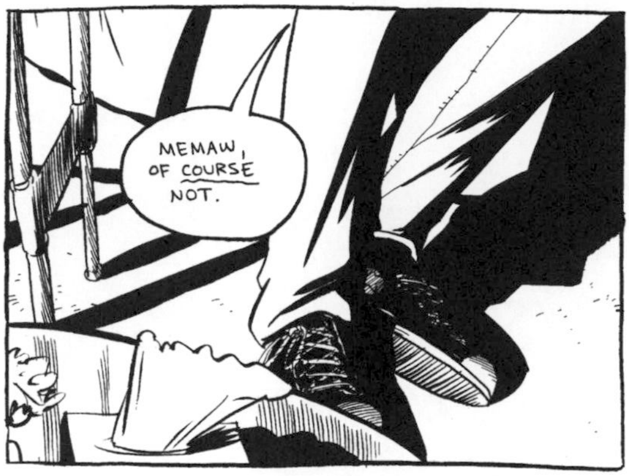
MEMAW, OF COURSE NOT.

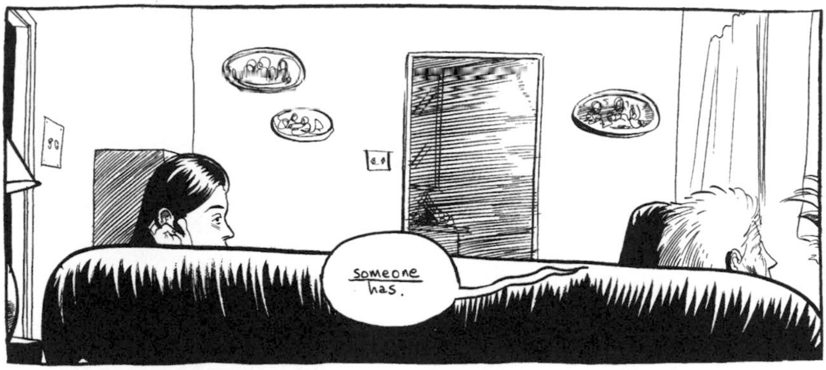
someone has.

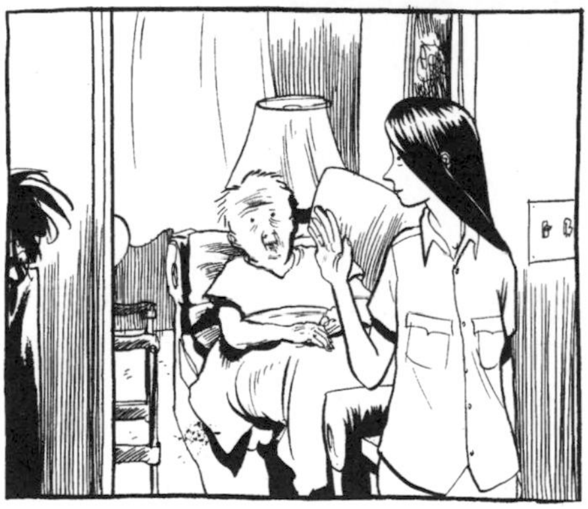

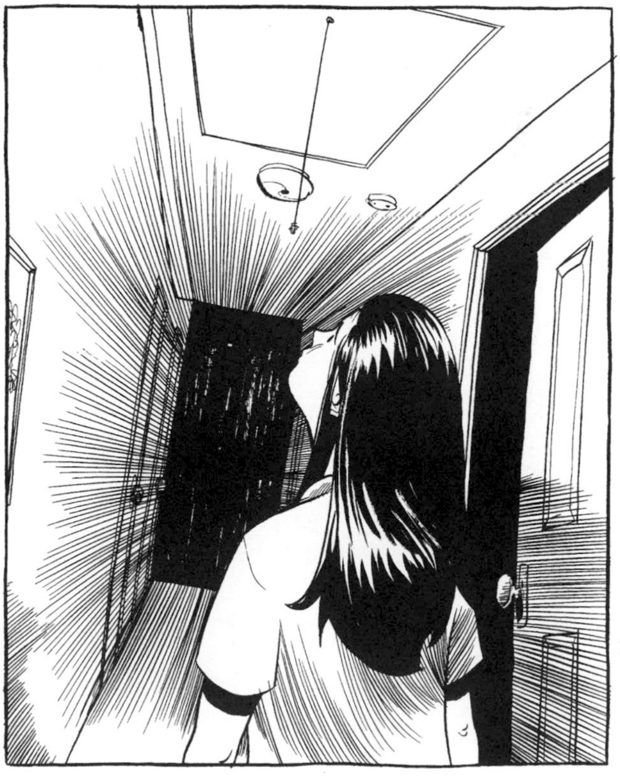

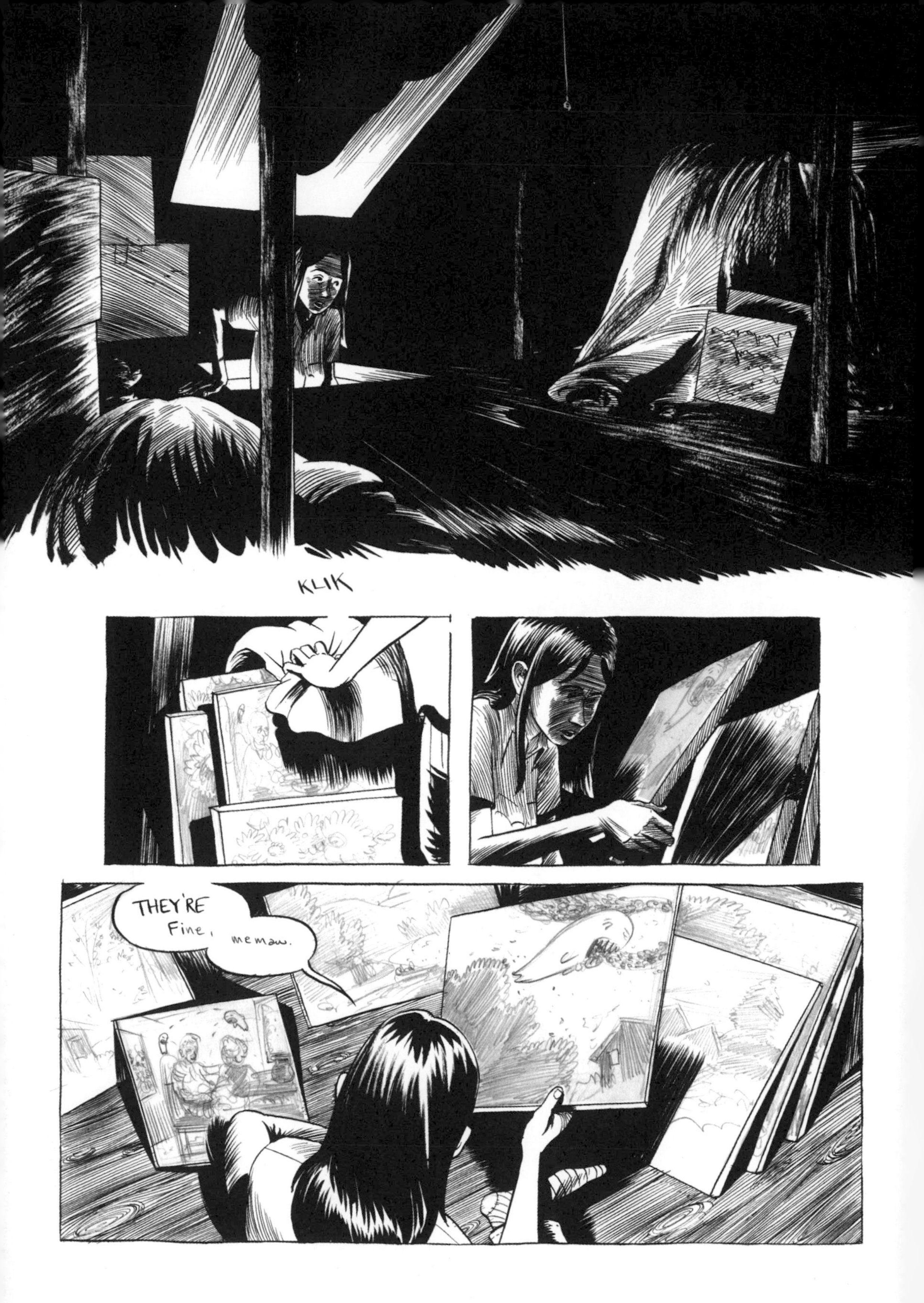
KLIK
THEY'RE Fine, memaw.

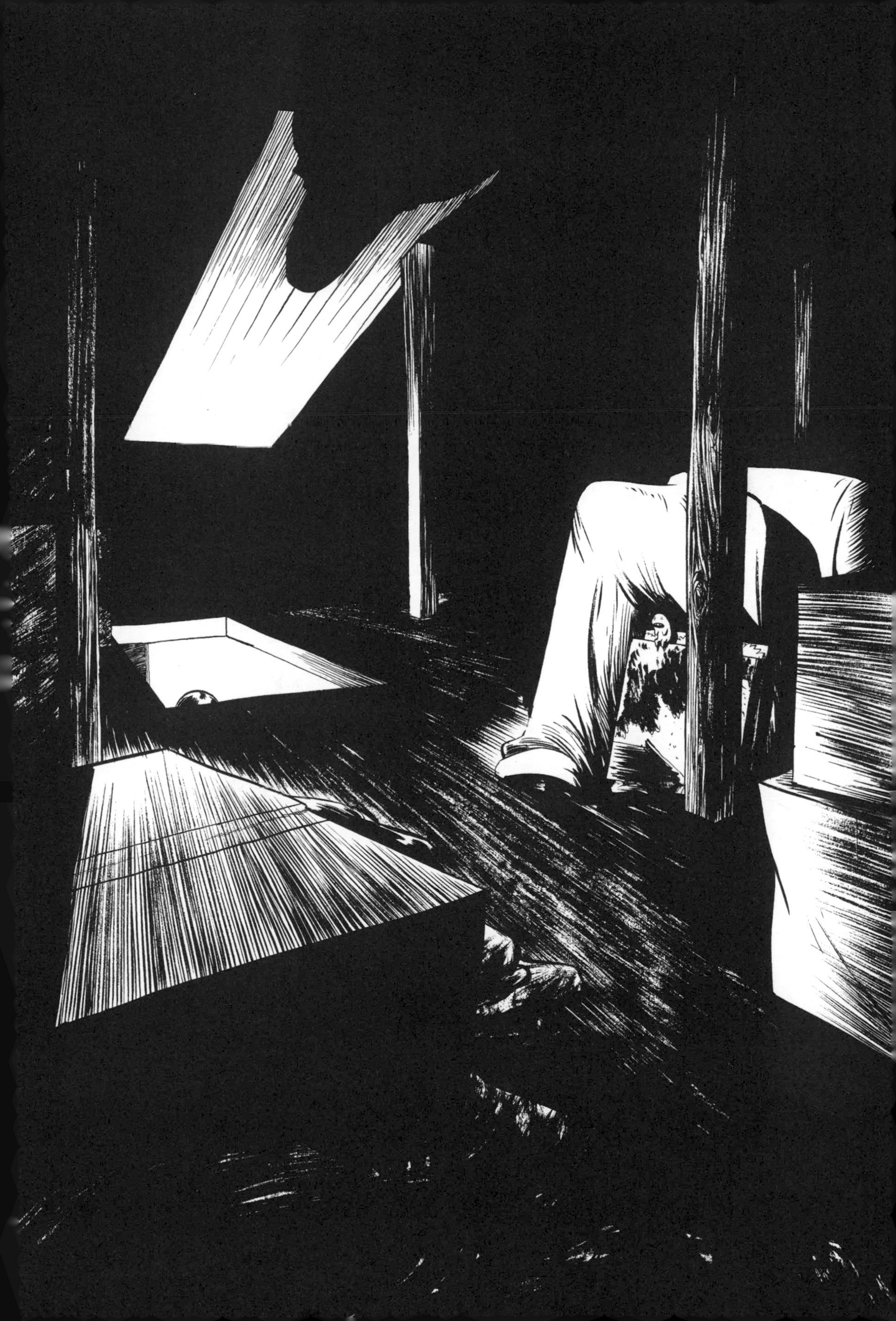

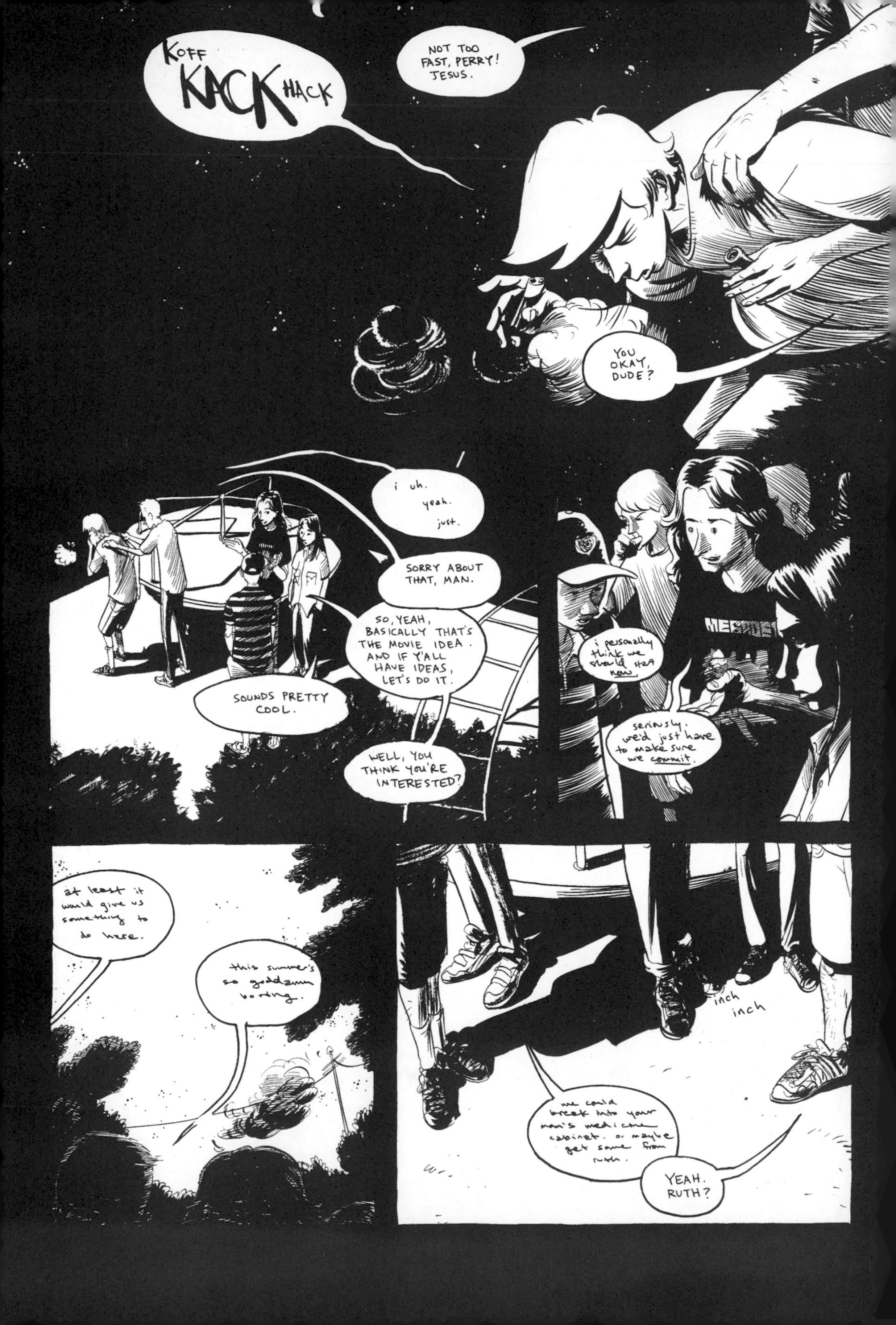
KOFF KACK HACK
NOT TOO FAST, PERRY! JESUS.
YOU OKAY, DUDE?
i uh. yeah. just.
SORRY ABOUT THAT, MAN.
SO, YEAH, BASICALLY THAT'S THE MOVIE IDEA. AND IF Y'ALL HAVE IDEAS, LET'S DO IT.
SOUNDS PRETTY COOL.
WELL, YOU THINK YOU'RE INTERESTED?
i personally think we should start now.
seriously. we'd just have to make sure we commit.
at least it would give us something to do here.
this summer's so goddamn boring.
inch inch
we could break into your mom's medicine cabinet. or maybe get some from ruth.
YEAH. RUTH?

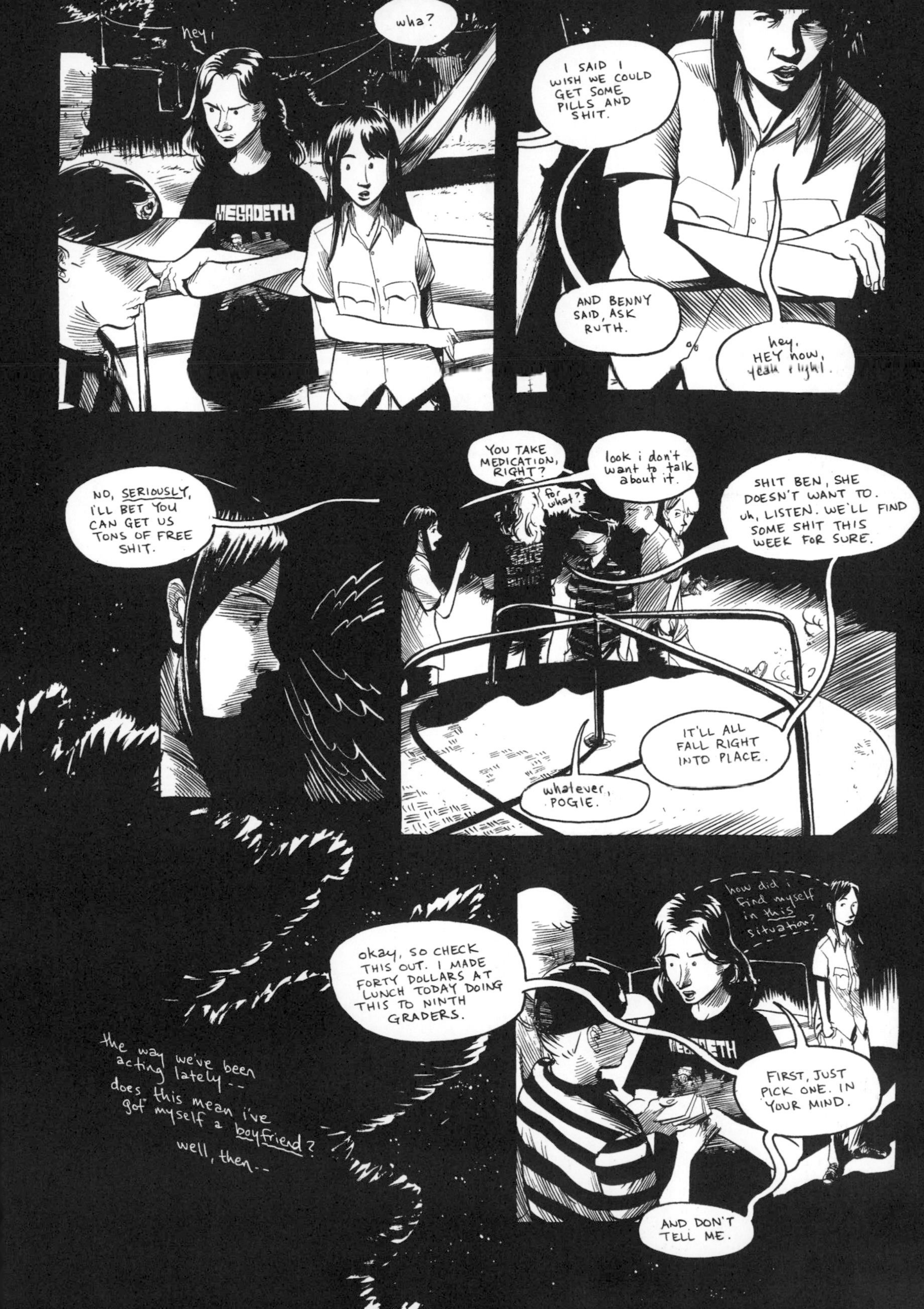
hey,
wha?
I SAID I WISH WE COULD GET SOME PILLS AND SHIT.
AND BENNY SAID, ASK RUTH.
hey. HEY now, yeah right.
NO, SERIOUSLY, I'LL BET YOU CAN GET US TONS OF FREE SHIT.
YOU TAKE MEDICATION, RIGHT?
for what?
look i don't want to talk about it.
SHIT BEN, SHE DOESN'T WANT TO. uh, LISTEN. WE'LL FIND SOME SHIT THIS WEEK FOR SURE.
IT'LL ALL FALL RIGHT INTO PLACE.
whatever, POGIE.
the way we've been acting lately--
does this mean i've got myself a boyfriend?
well, then--
okay, SO CHECK THIS OUT. I MADE FORTY DOLLARS AT LUNCH TODAY DOING THIS TO NINTH GRADERS.
how did i find myself in this situation?
FIRST, JUST PICK ONE. IN YOUR MIND.
AND DON'T TELL ME.

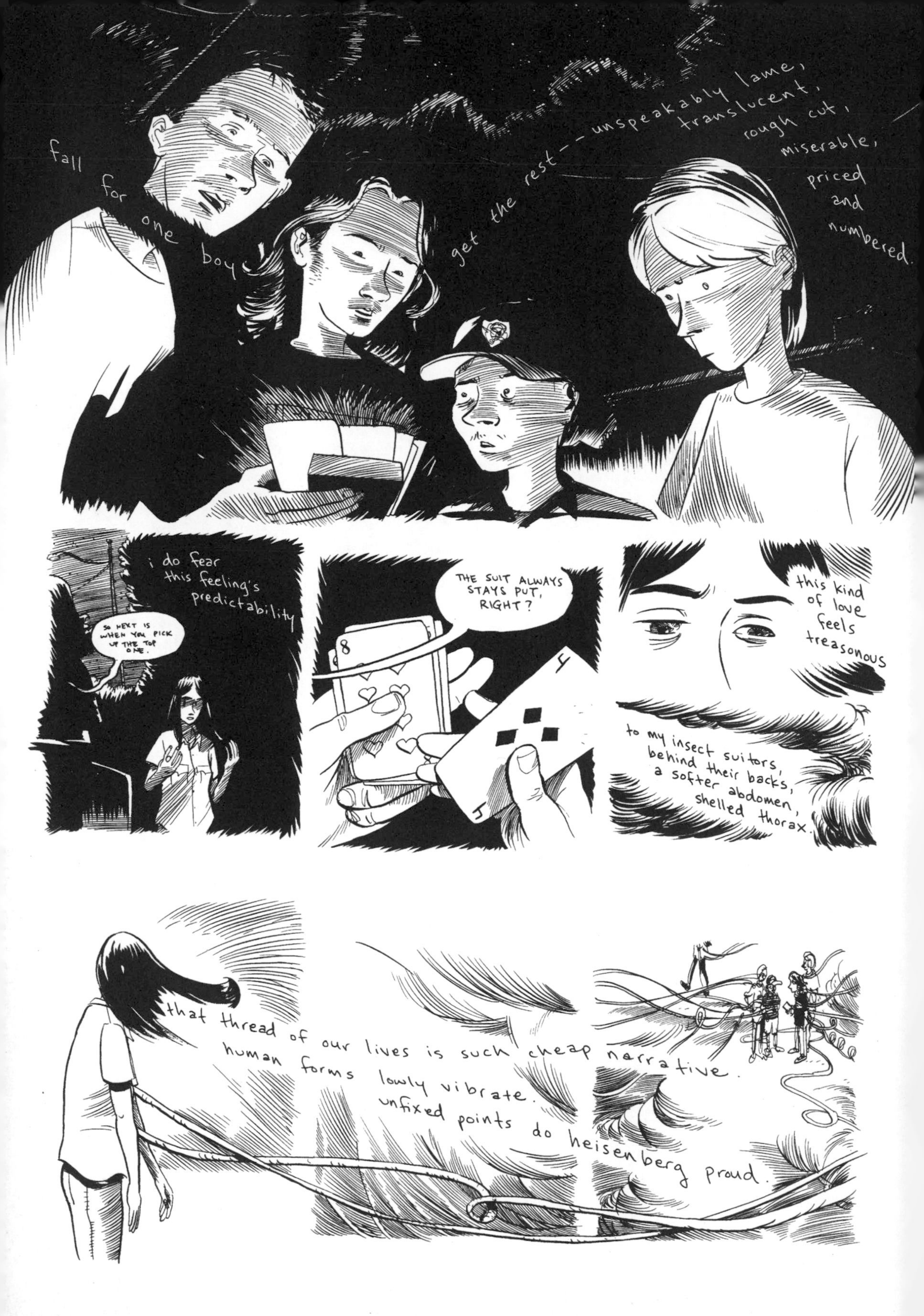
fall for one boy get the rest-- unspeakably lame, translucent, rough cut, miserable, priced and numbered.
i do fear this feeling's predictability
SO NEXT IS WHEN YOU PICK UP THE TOP ONE.
THE SUIT ALWAYS STAYS PUT, RIGHT?
this kind of love feels treasonous
to my insect suitors, behind their backs, a softer abdomen, shelled thorax.
that thread of our lives is such cheap narrative.
human forms lowly vibrate.
unfixed points do heisenberg proud.

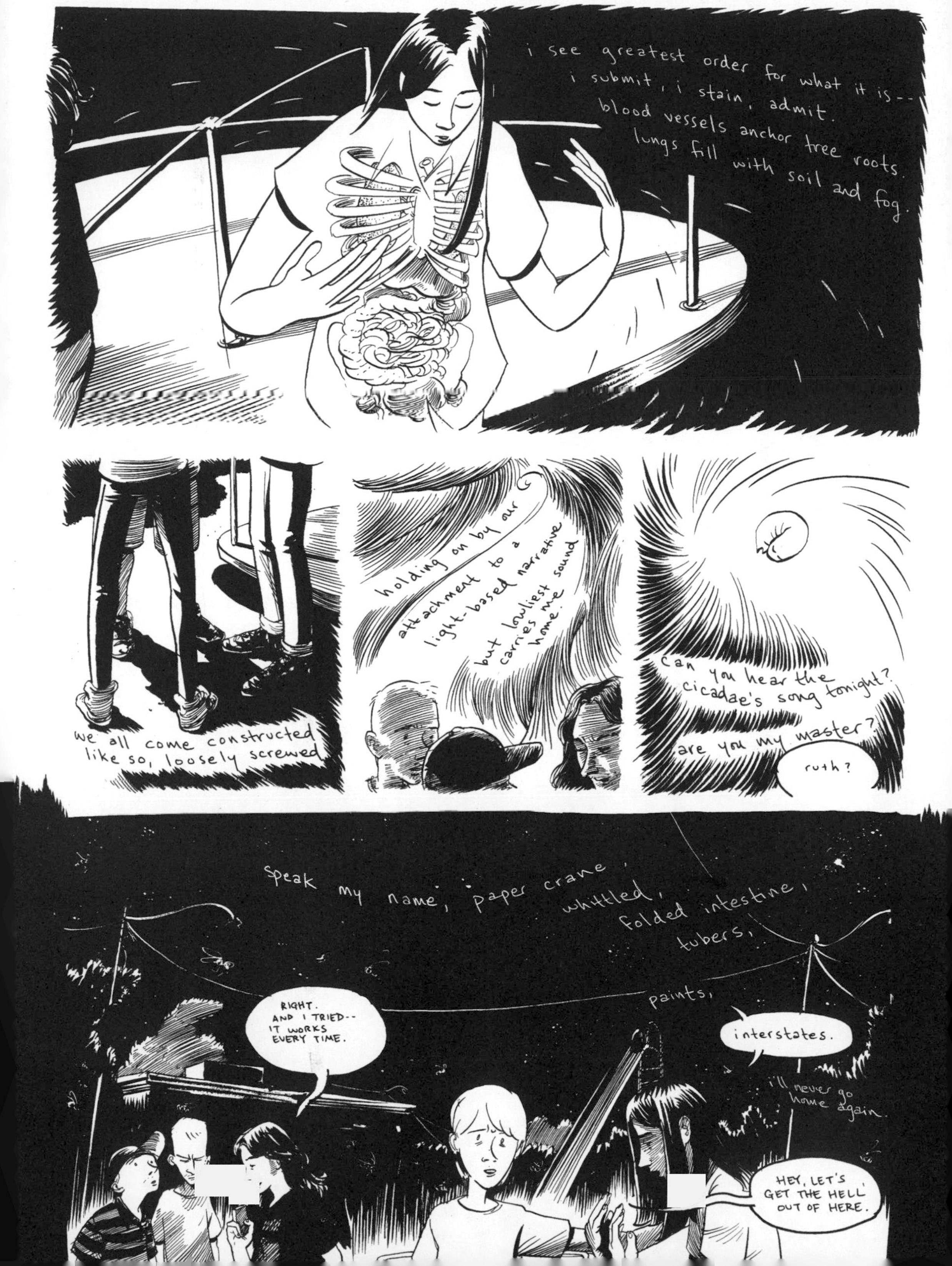
i see greatest order for what it is--
i submit, i stain, admit.
blood vessels anchor tree roots.
lungs fill with soil and fog.
we all come constructed
like so, loosely screwed
holding on by our attachment to a light-based narrative
but lowliest sound carries me home.
can you hear the cicadae's song tonight?
are you my master?
ruth?
speak my name, paper crane, whittled, folded intestine, tubers,
RIGHT. AND I TRIED-- IT WORKS EVERY TIME.
paints,
interstates.
i'll never go home again.
HEY, LET'S GET THE HELL OUT OF HERE.

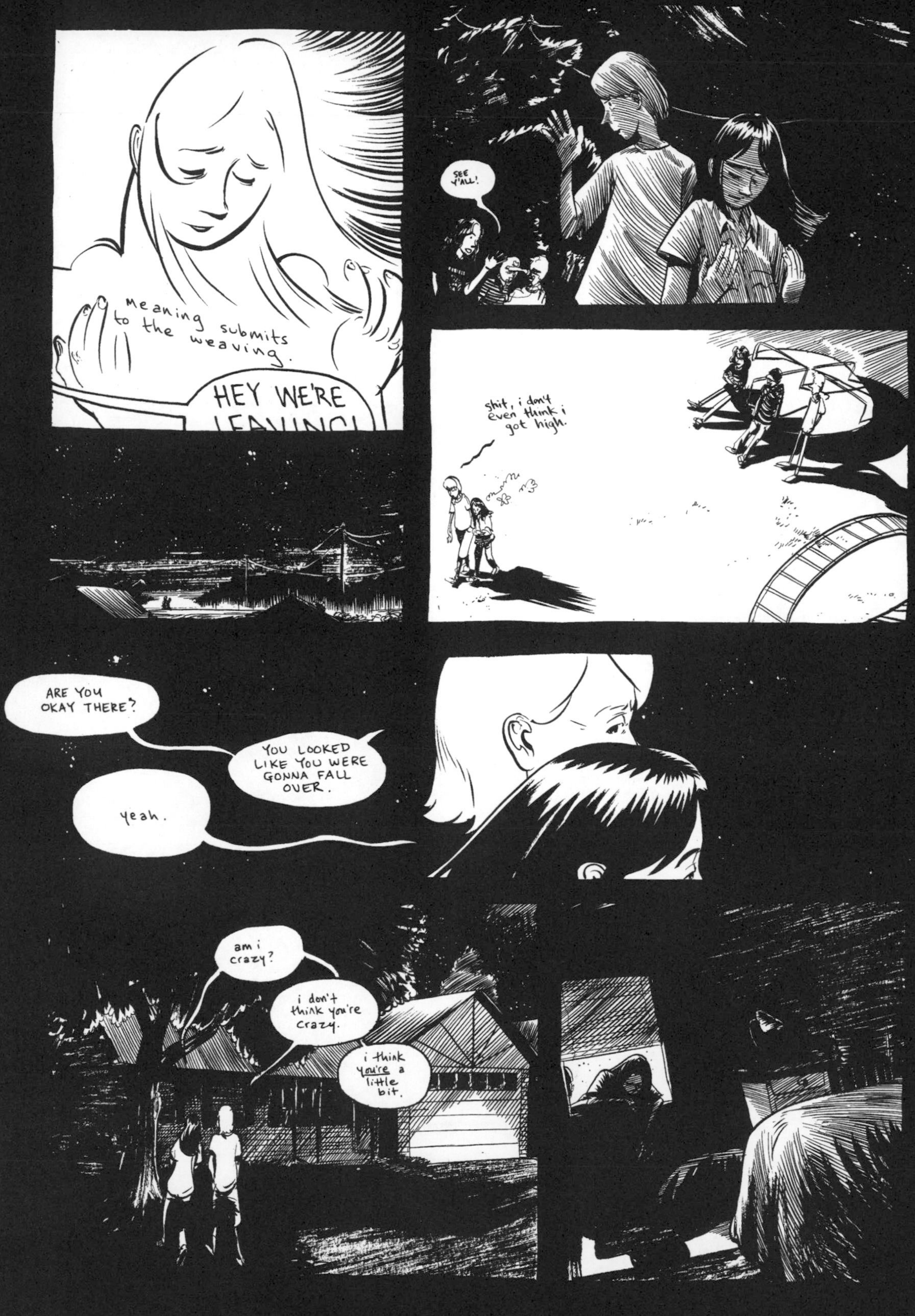
meaning submits to the weaving.
HEY WE'RE LEAVING!
SEE Y'ALL!
shit, i don't even think i got high.
ARE YOU OKAY THERE?
YOU LOOKED LIKE YOU WERE GONNA FALL OVER.
yeah.
am i crazy?
i don't think you're crazy.
i think you're a little bit.

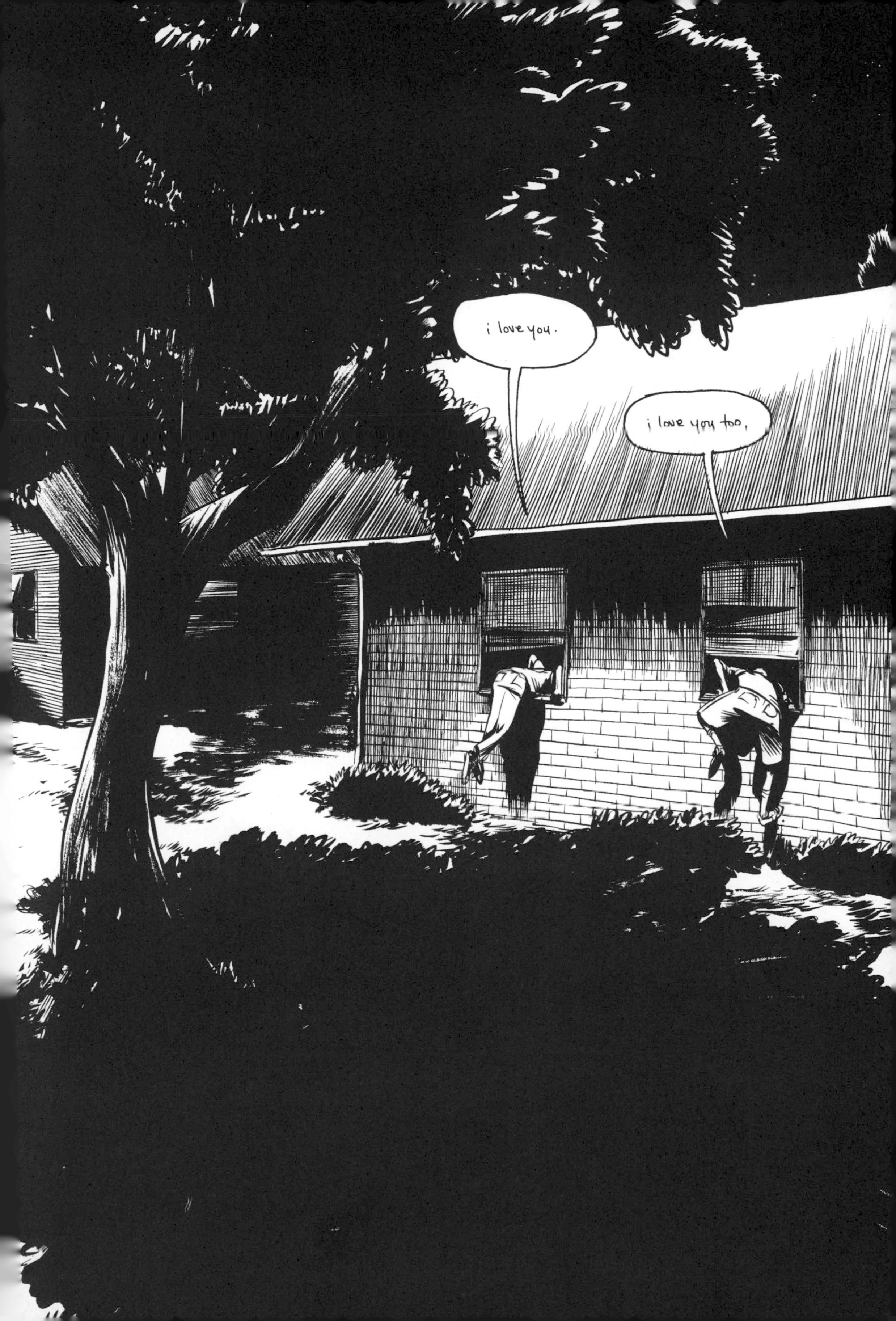
i love you.
i love you too,

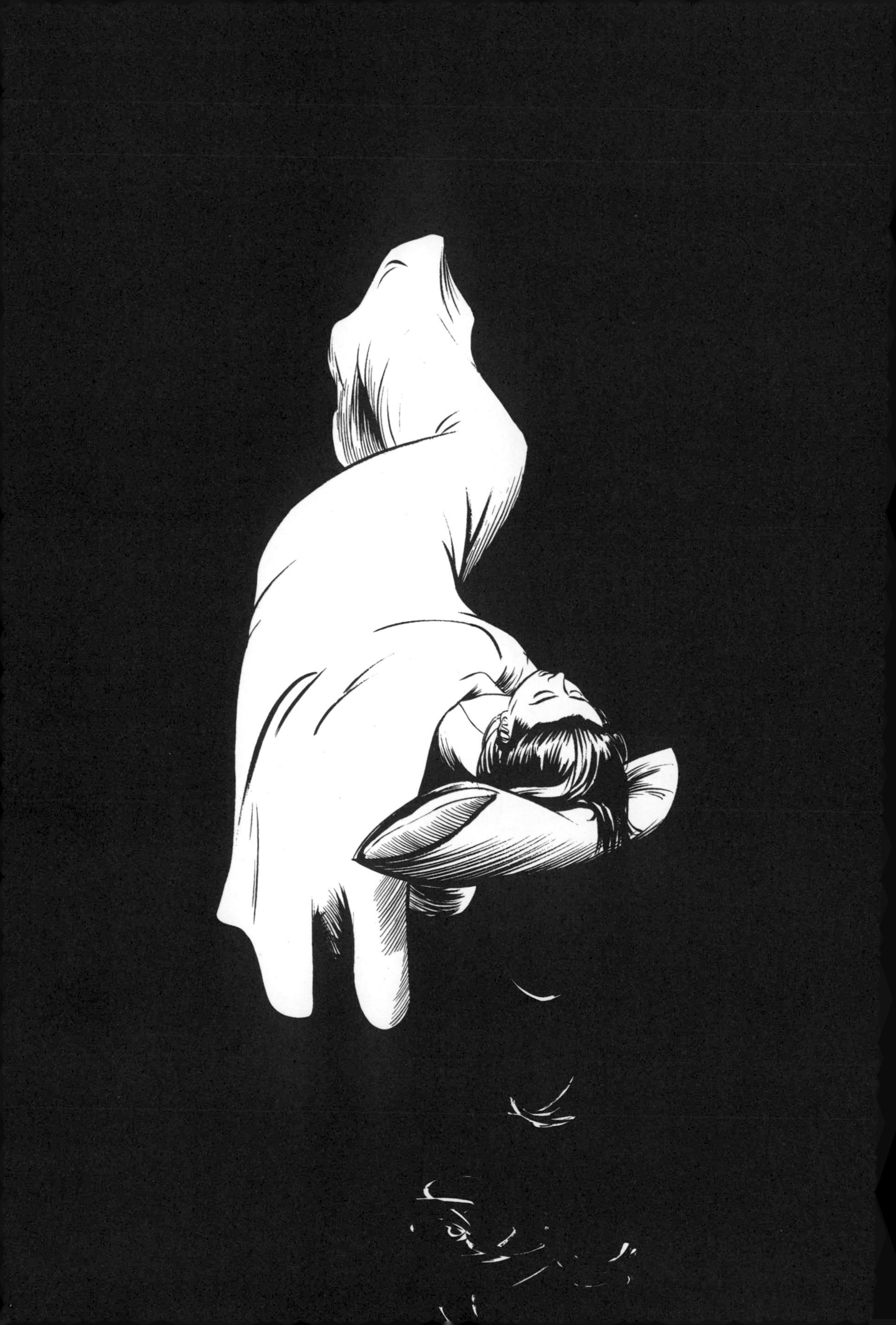

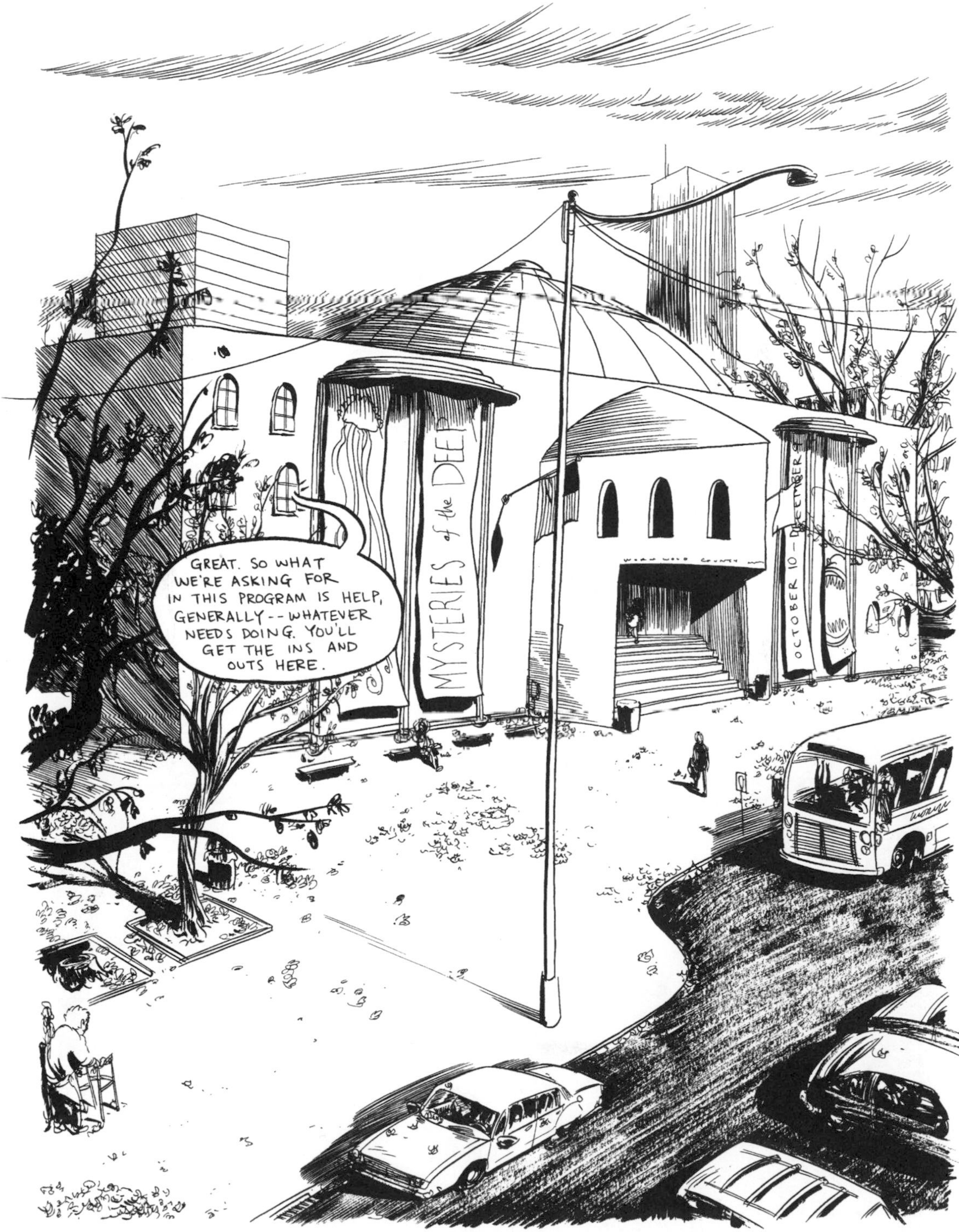
GREAT. SO WHAT WE'RE ASKING FOR IN THIS PROGRAM IS HELP, GENERALLY -- WHATEVER NEEDS DOING. YOU'LL GET THE INS AND OUTS HERE.
MYSTERIES of the DEE
OCTOBER 10 -

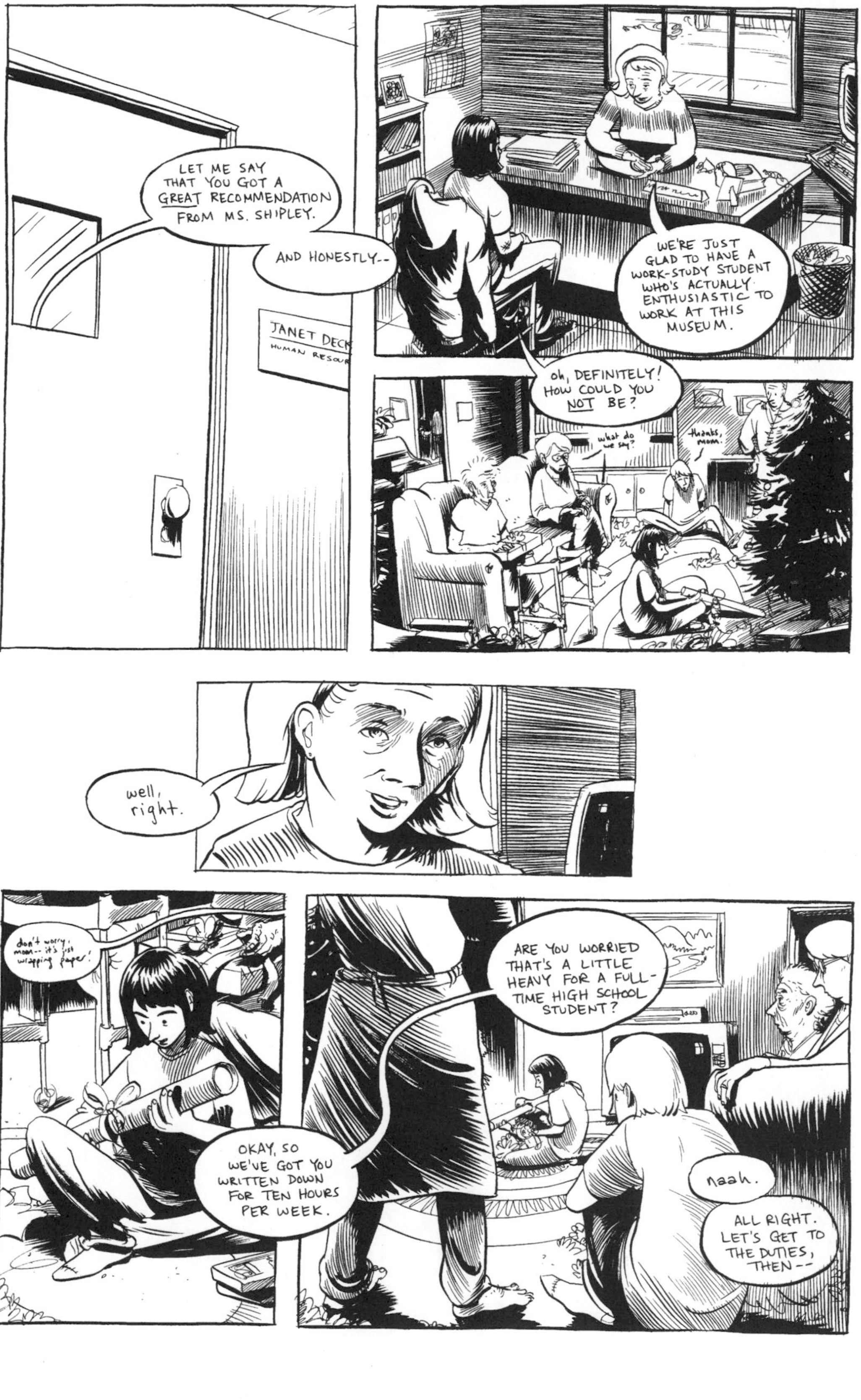

LET ME SAY THAT YOU GOT A GREAT RECOMMENDATION FROM MS. SHIPLEY.
AND HONESTLY--
JANET DECK
HUMAN RESOUR
WE'RE JUST GLAD TO HAVE A WORK-STUDY STUDENT WHO'S ACTUALLY ENTHUSIASTIC TO WORK AT THIS MUSEUM.
oh, DEFINITELY! HOW COULD YOU NOT BE?
what do we say?
thanks, mom.
well, right.
don't worry, mom-- it's just wrapping paper!
ARE YOU WORRIED THAT'S A LITTLE HEAVY FOR A FULL-TIME HIGH SCHOOL STUDENT?
OKAY, SO WE'VE GOT YOU WRITTEN DOWN FOR TEN HOURS PER WEEK.
naah.
ALL RIGHT. LET'S GET TO THE DUTIES, THEN--

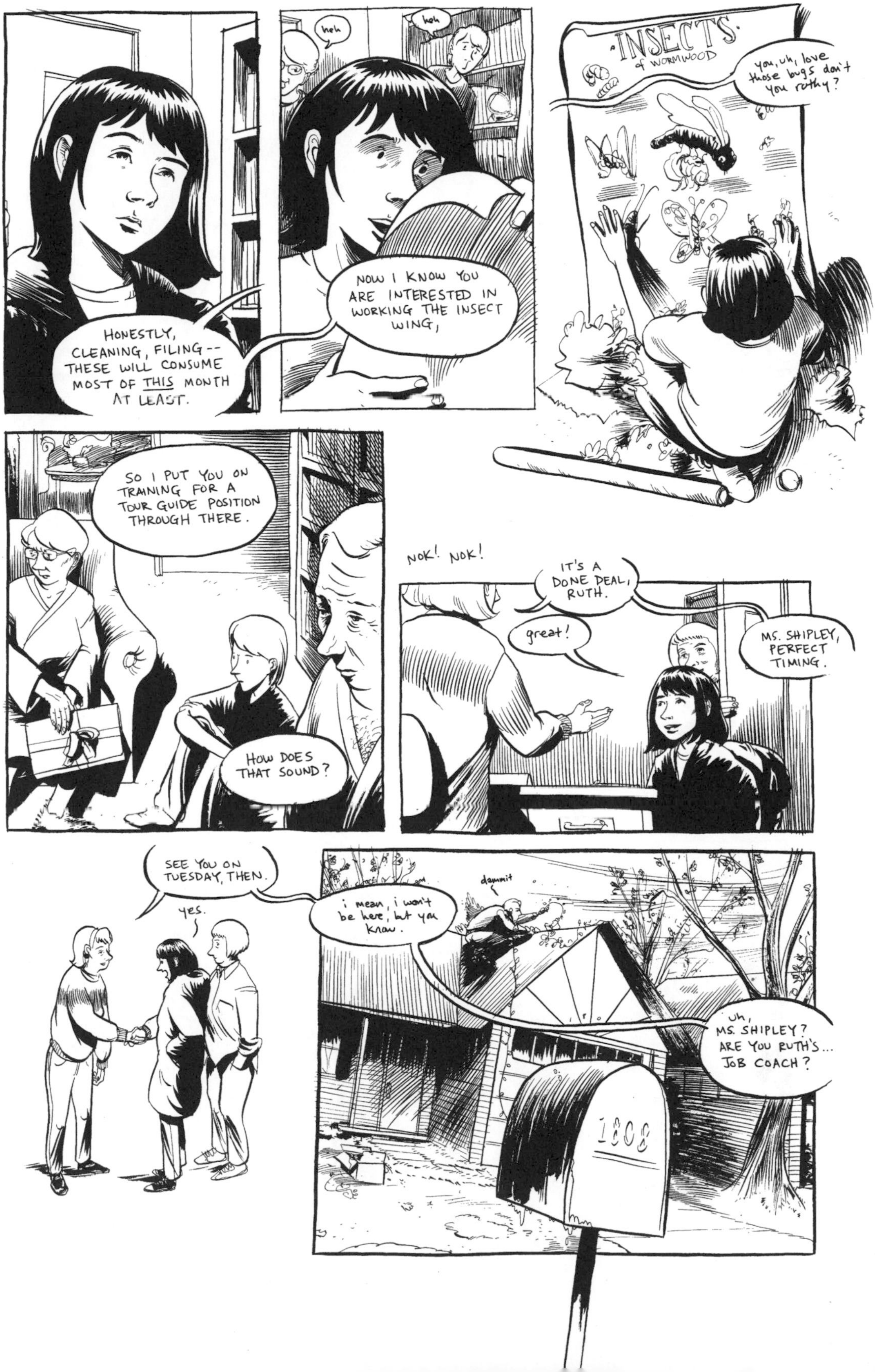
HONESTLY, CLEANING, FILING-- THESE WILL CONSUME MOST OF THIS MONTH AT LEAST.
heh
heh
NOW I KNOW YOU ARE INTERESTED IN WORKING THE INSECT WING,
INSECTS of WORMWOOD
You, uh, love those bugs don't you ruthy?
SO I PUT YOU ON TRAINING FOR A TOUR GUIDE POSITION THROUGH THERE.
HOW DOES THAT SOUND?
NOK! NOK!
IT'S A DONE DEAL, RUTH.
great!
MS. SHIPLEY, PERFECT TIMING.
SEE YOU ON TUESDAY, THEN.
yes.
i mean, i won't be here, but you know.
dammit
uh, MS. SHIPLEY? ARE YOU RUTH'S... JOB COACH?
1808

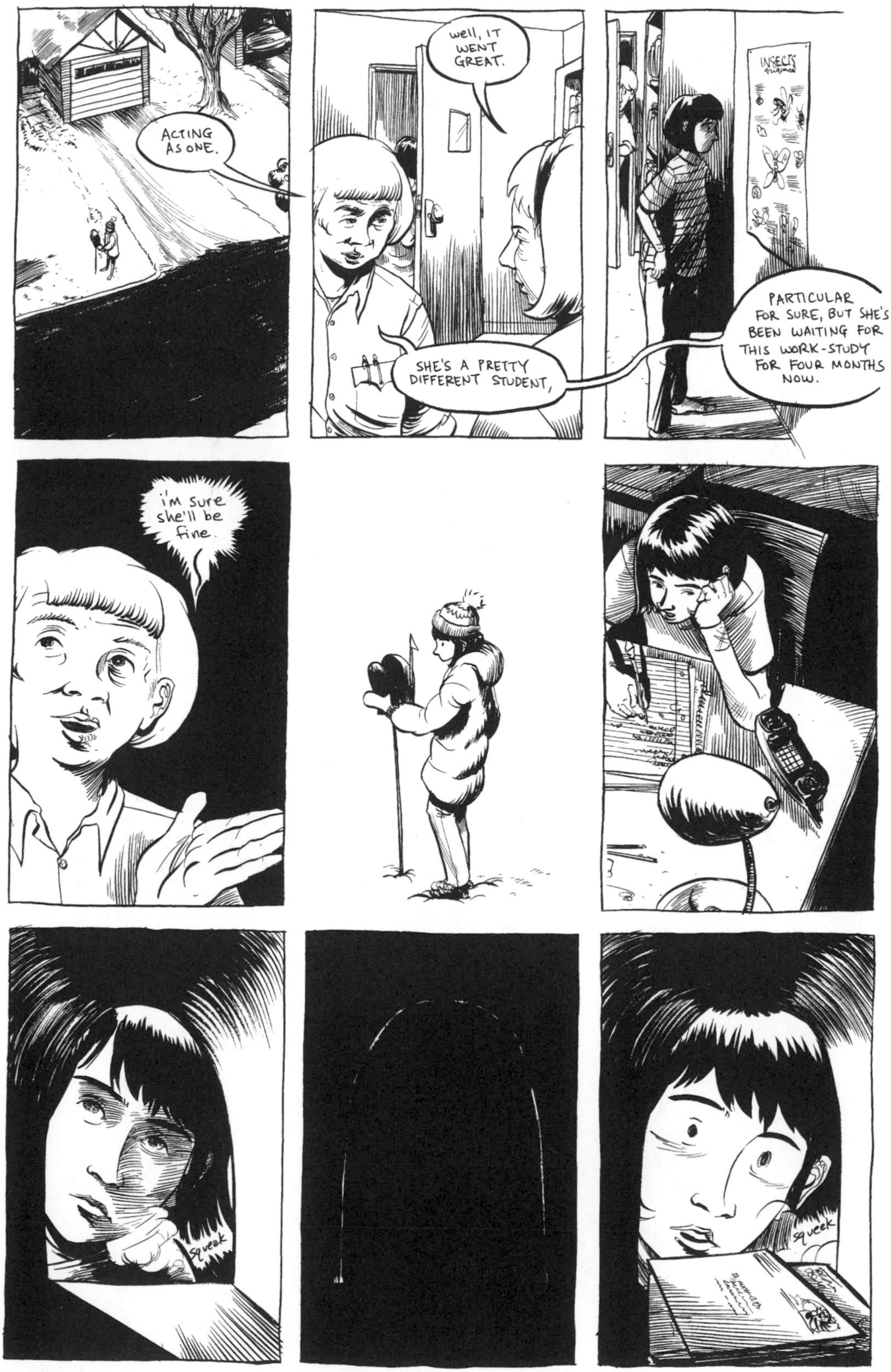
ACTING AS ONE.
well, IT WENT GREAT.
SHE'S A PRETTY DIFFERENT STUDENT,
PARTICULAR FOR SURE, BUT SHE'S BEEN WAITING FOR THIS WORK-STUDY FOR FOUR MONTHS NOW.
INSECTS
i'm sure she'll be fine.
squeek
squeek

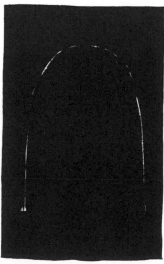

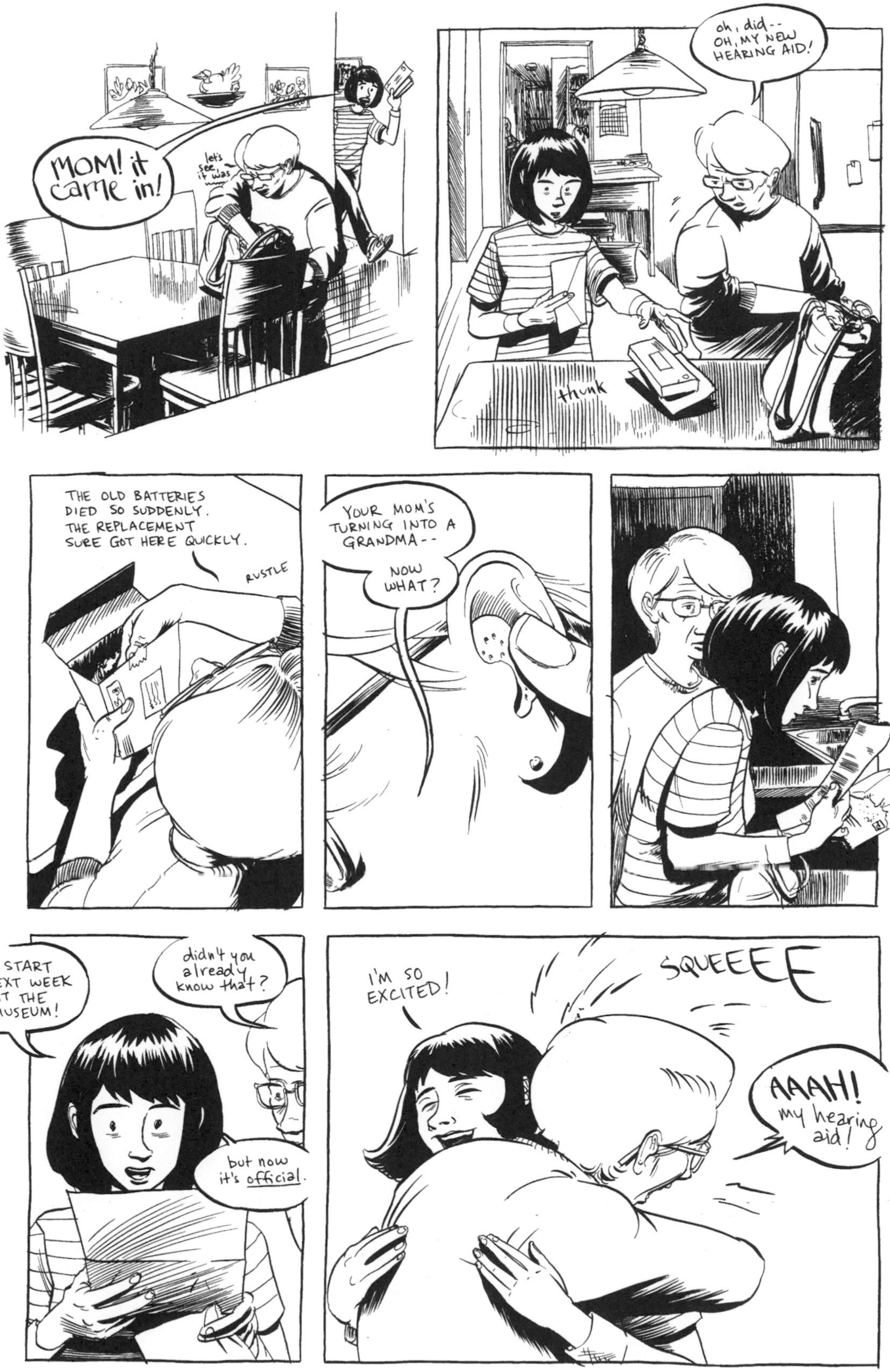
MOM! it came in!
let's see, it was
oh, did-- OH, MY NEW HEARING AID!
thunk
THE OLD BATTERIES DIED SO SUDDENLY. THE REPLACEMENT SURE GOT HERE QUICKLY.
RUSTLE
YOUR MOM'S TURNING INTO A GRANDMA--
NOW WHAT?
I START NEXT WEEK AT THE MUSEUM!
didn't you already know that?
but now it's official.
I'M SO EXCITED!
SQUEEEE
AAAH! my hearing aid!

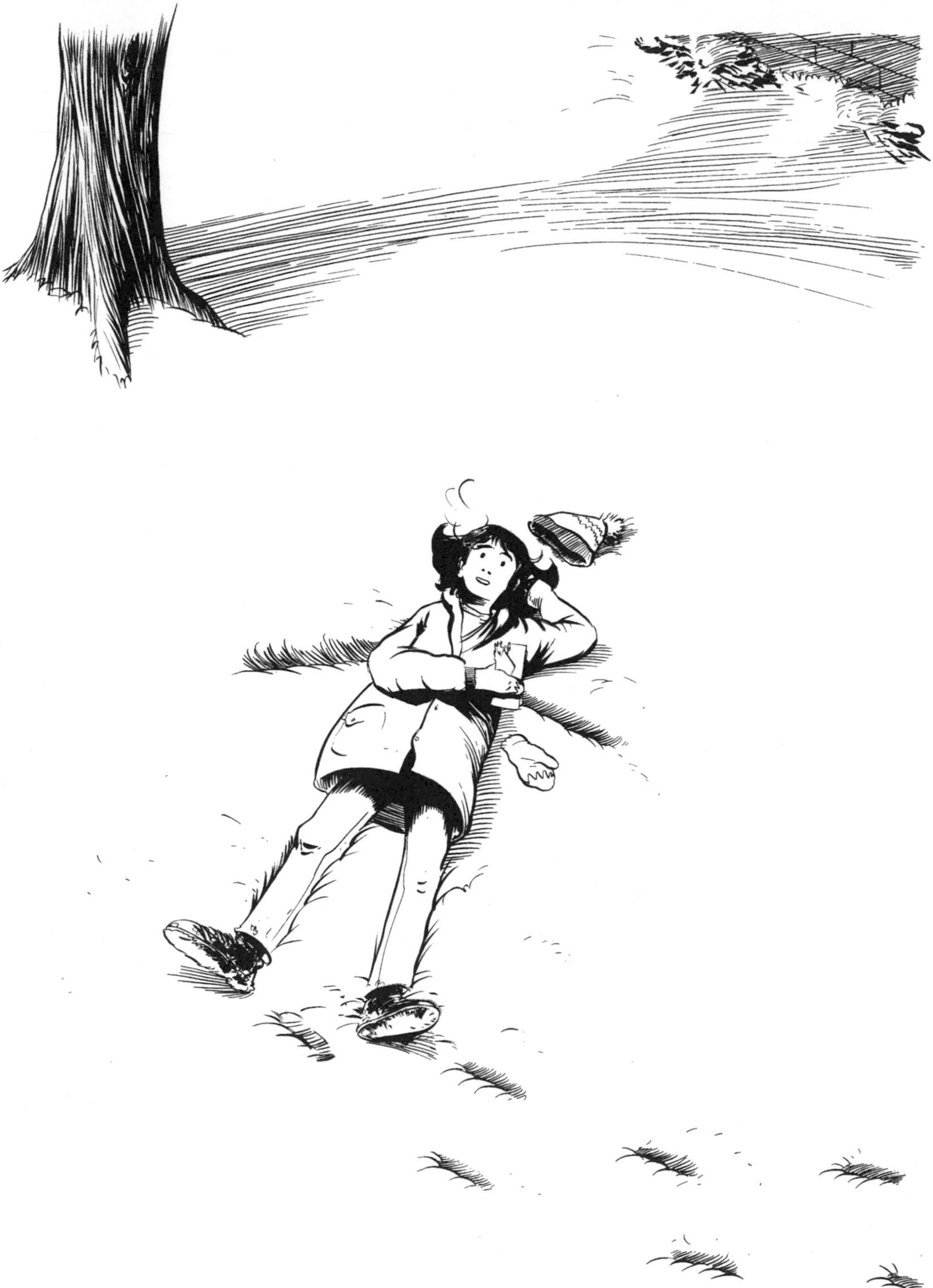

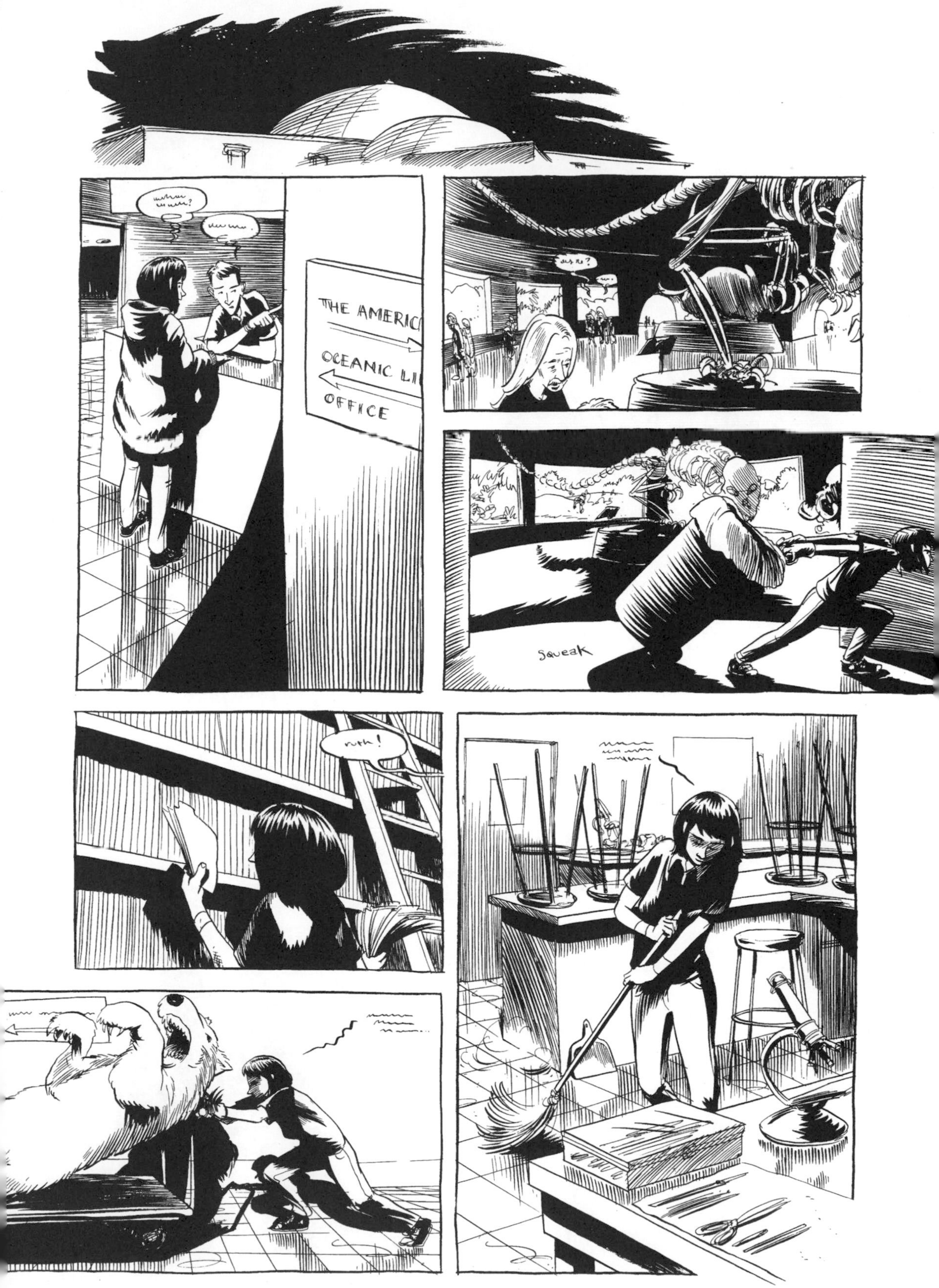

THE AMERIC
OCEANIC LI
OFFICE
SQUEAK

TIK TIK TIK

RRRRIINNNNG

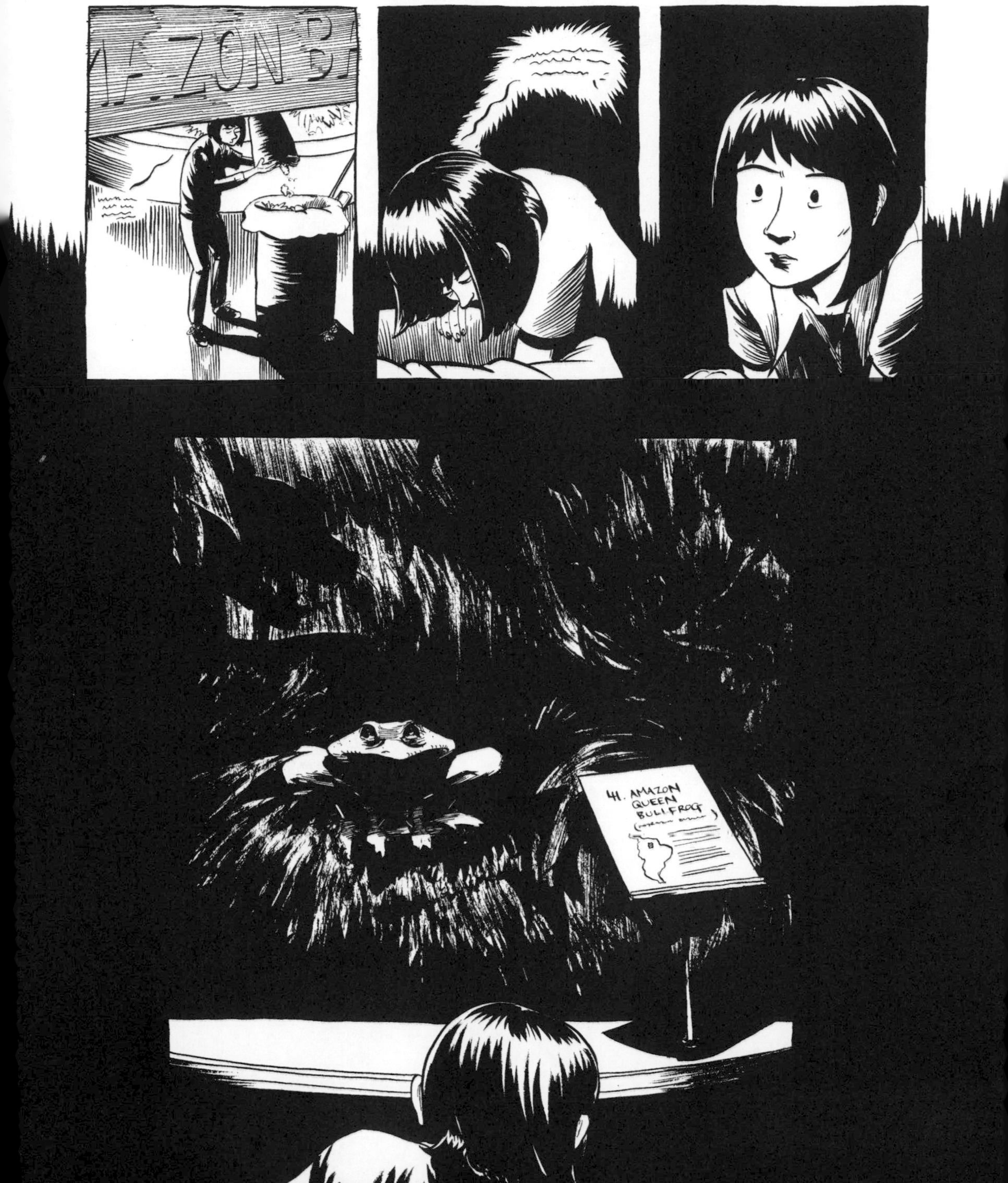
41. AMAZON
QUEEN
BULLFROG

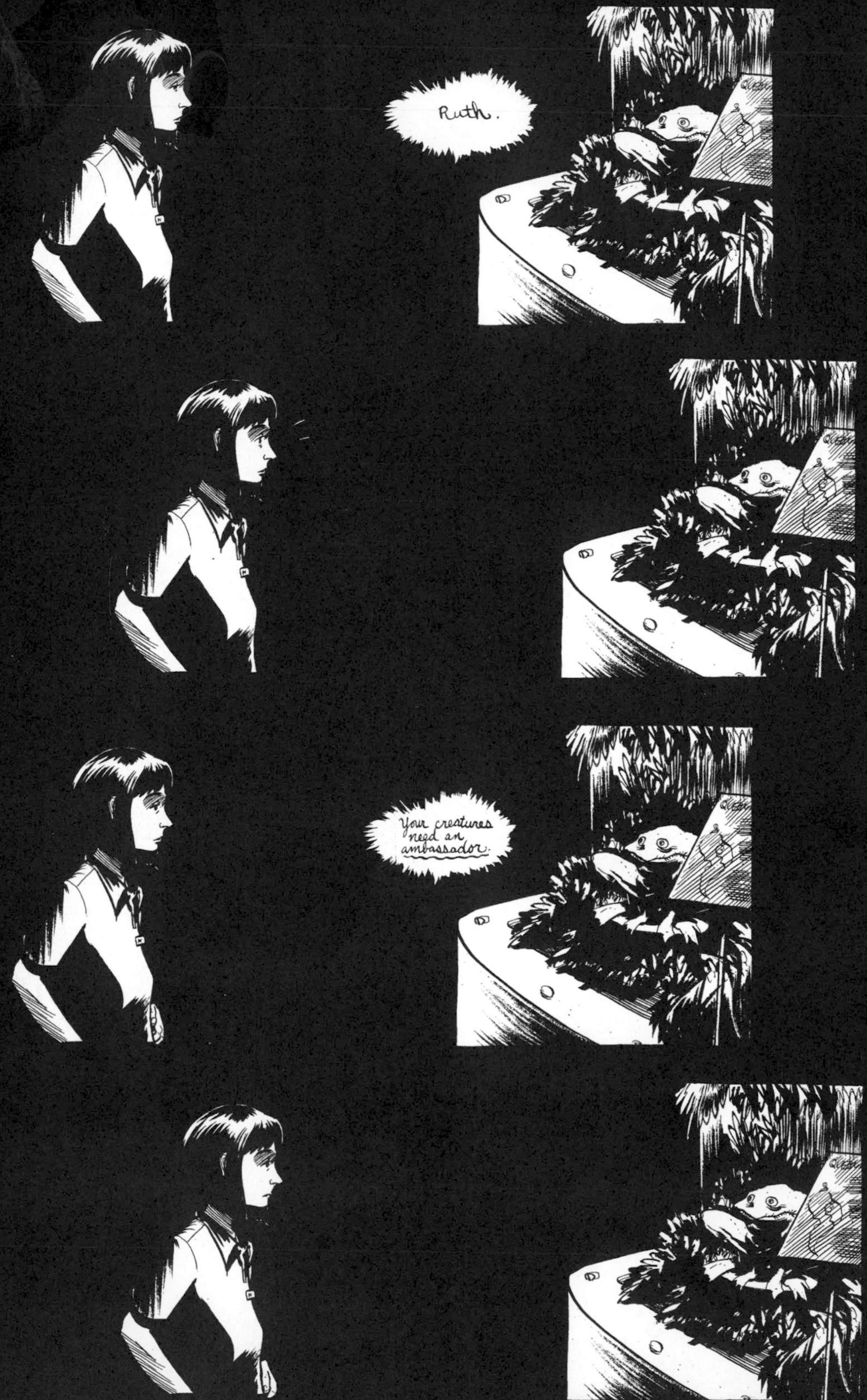
Ruth.
Your creatures need an ambassador.

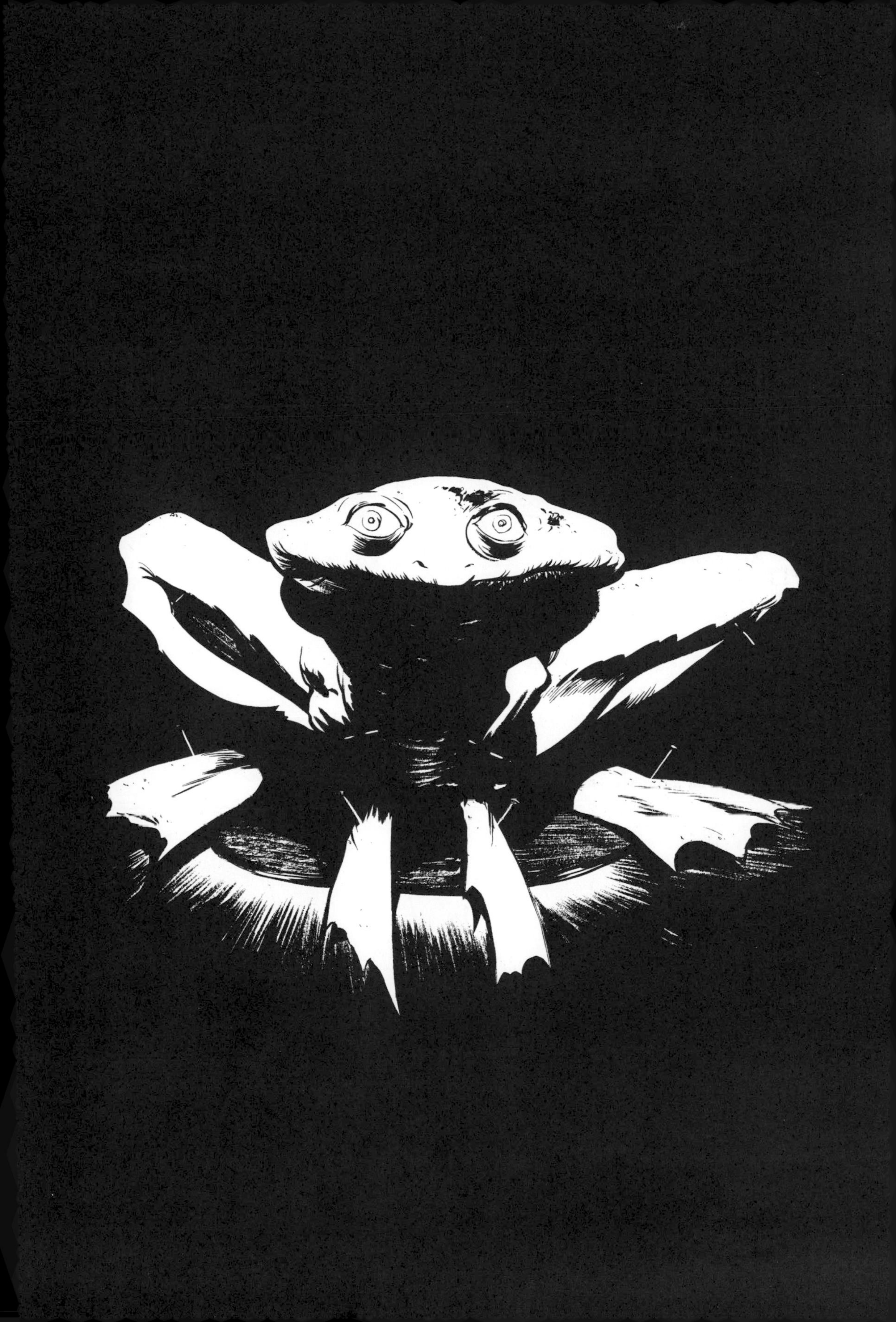

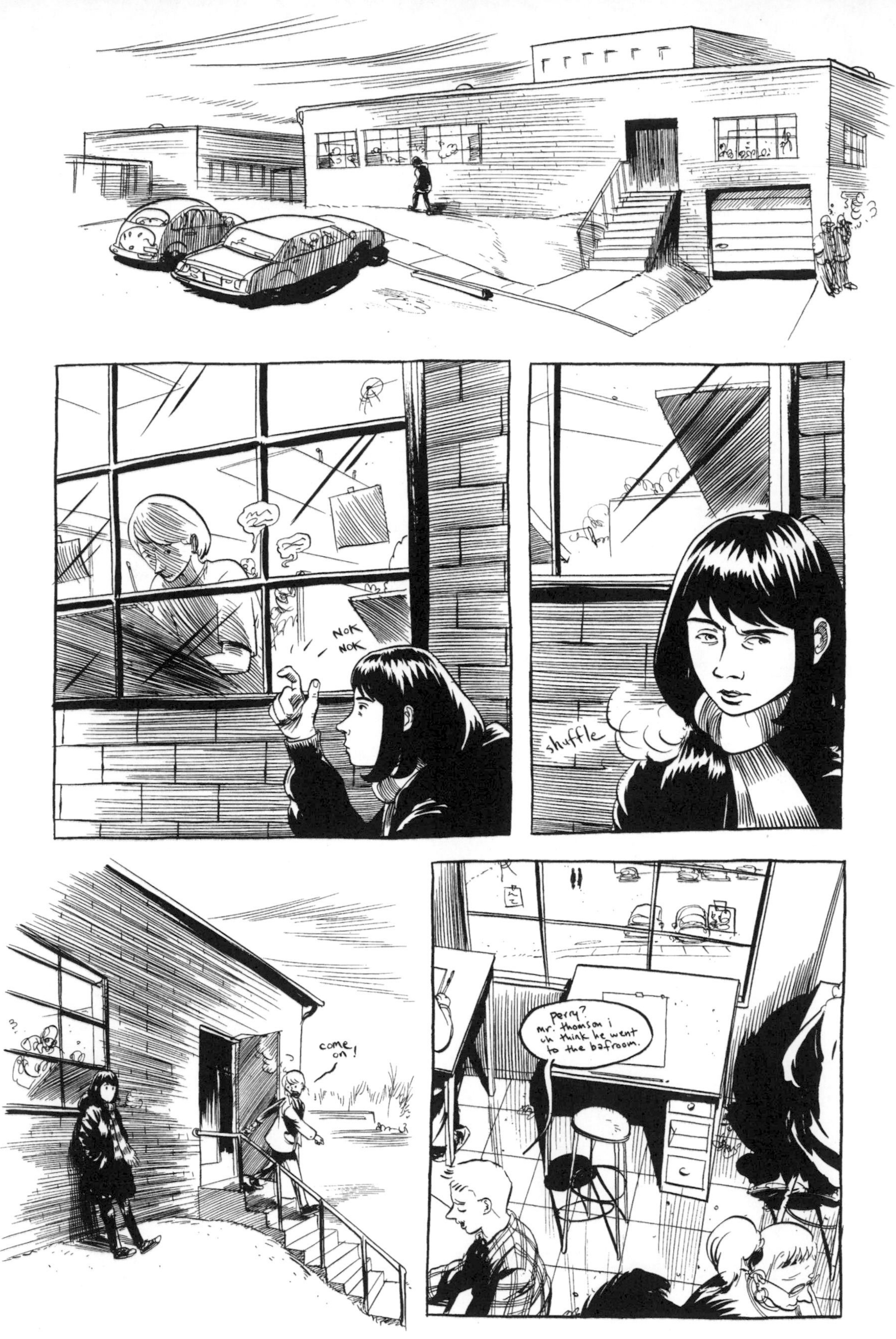
NOK
NOK
shuffle
come on!
perry? mr. thomson i uh think he went to the bafroom.

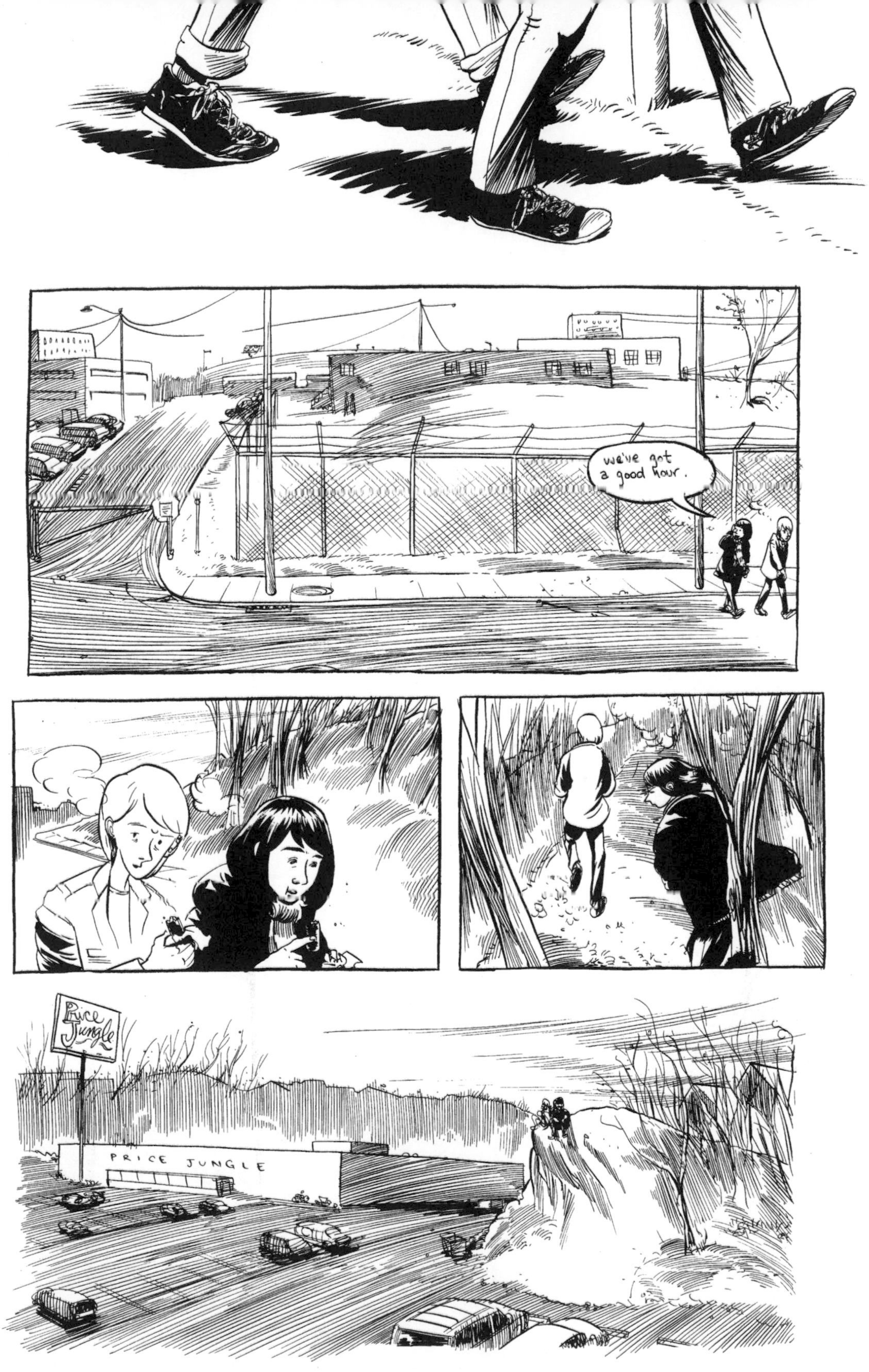
we've got a good hour.
Price Jungle
PRICE JUNGLE

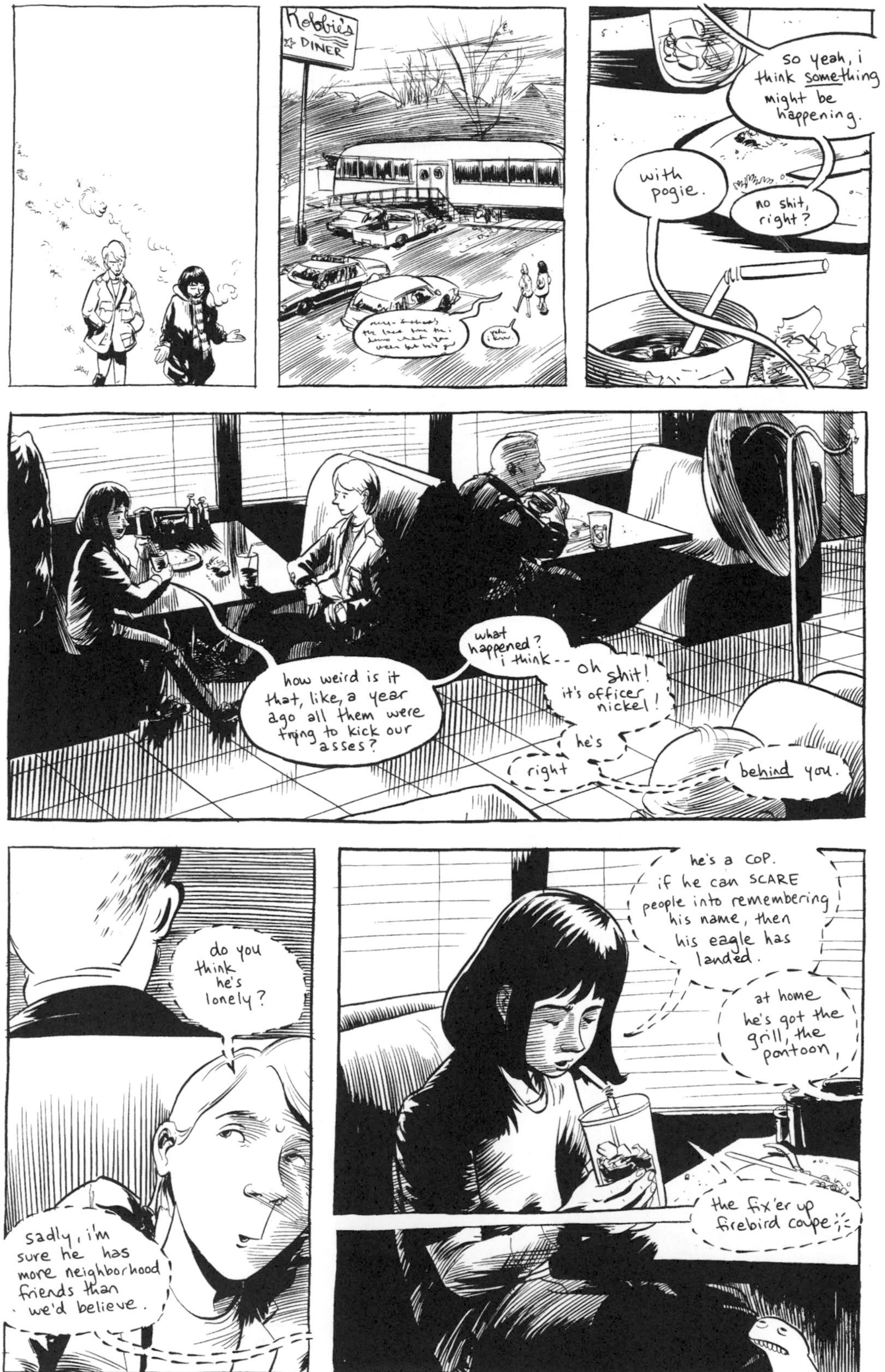

Robbie's DINER
so yeah, i think something might be happening.
with pogie.
no shit, right?
how weird is it that, like, a year ago all them were trying to kick our asses?
what happened? i think--
oh shit! it's officer nickel!
he's right behind you.
do you think he's lonely?
sadly, i'm sure he has more neighborhood friends than we'd believe.
he's a cop. if he can SCARE people into remembering his name, then his eagle has landed.
at home he's got the grill, the pontoon,
the fix'er up firebird coupe.

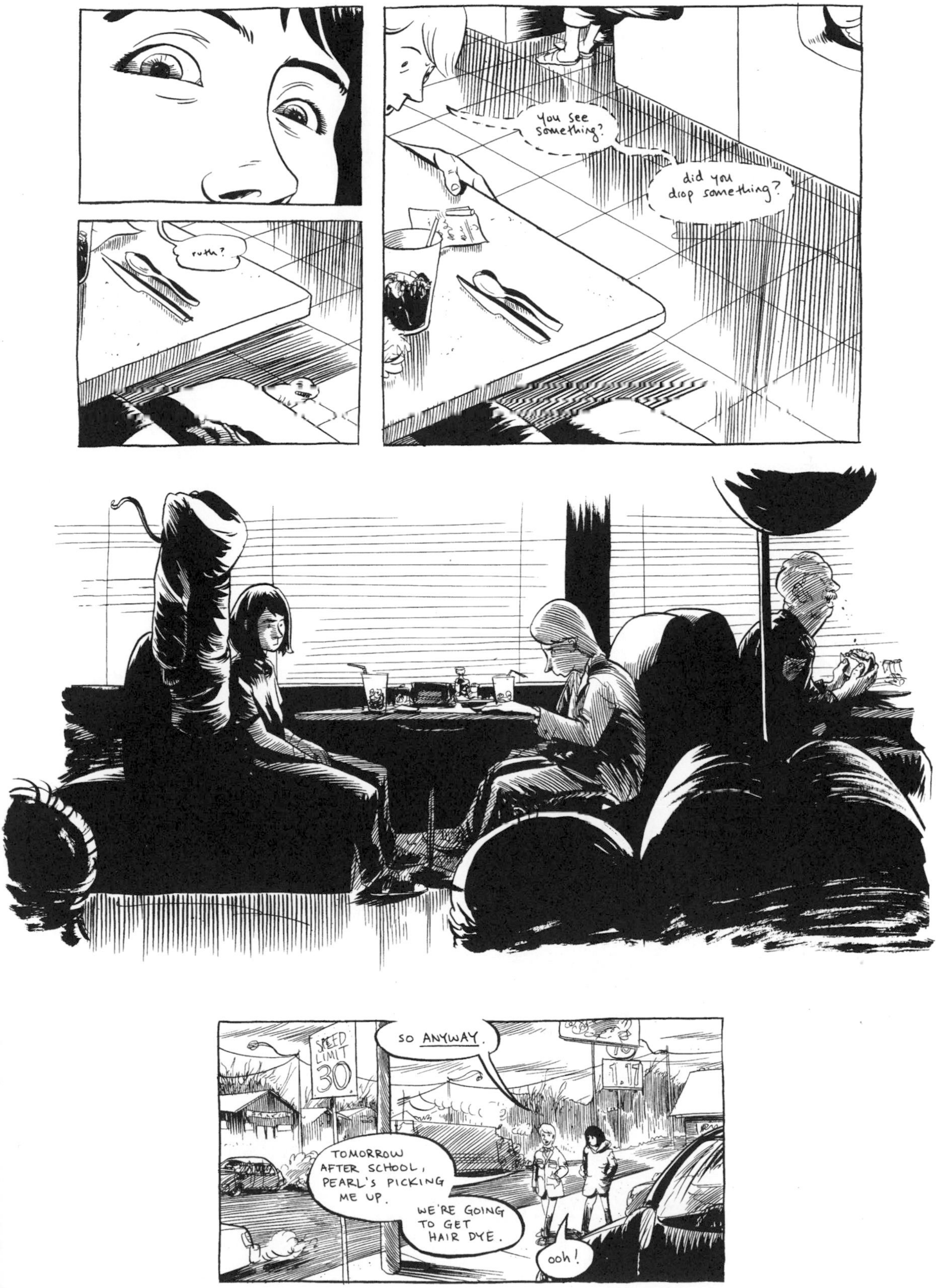
ruth?
you see something?
did you drop something?
SO ANYWAY.
SPEED LIMIT 30
TOMORROW AFTER SCHOOL, PEARL'S PICKING ME UP.
WE'RE GOING TO GET HAIR DYE.
ooh!

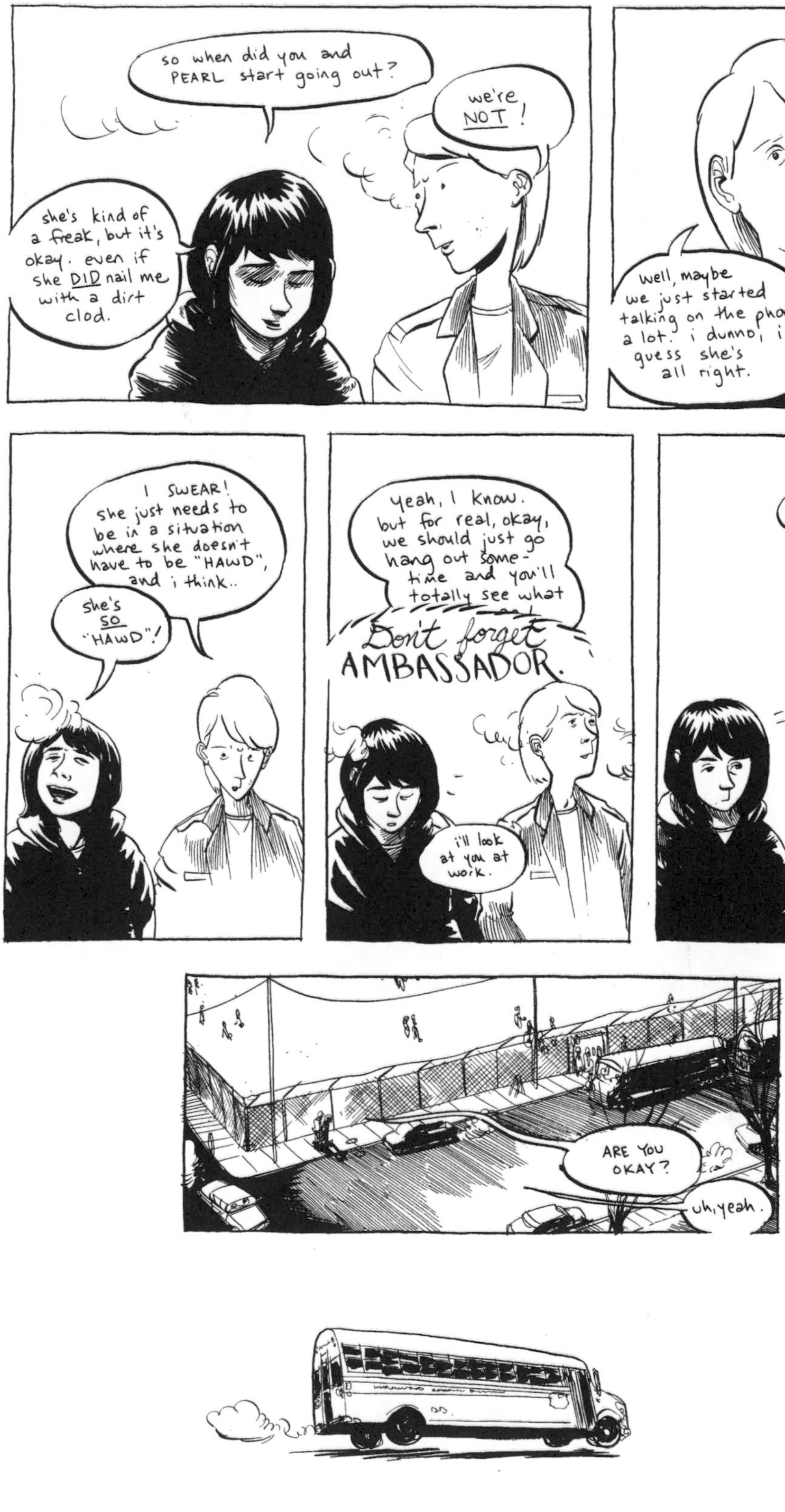
so when did you and PEARL start going out?
we're NOT!
she's kind of a freak, but it's okay. even if she DID nail me with a dirt clod.
just don't hide it!
well, maybe we just started talking on the phone a lot. i dunno, i guess she's all right.
I SWEAR! she just needs to be in a situation where she doesn't have to be "HAWD", and i think..
she's SO "HAWD"!
Yeah, I know. but for real, okay, we should just go hang out sometime and you'll totally see what
Don't forget AMBASSADOR.
i'll look at you at work.
?
ARE YOU OKAY?
uh, yeah.

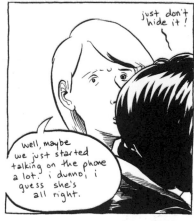

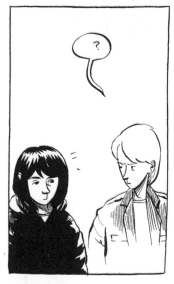

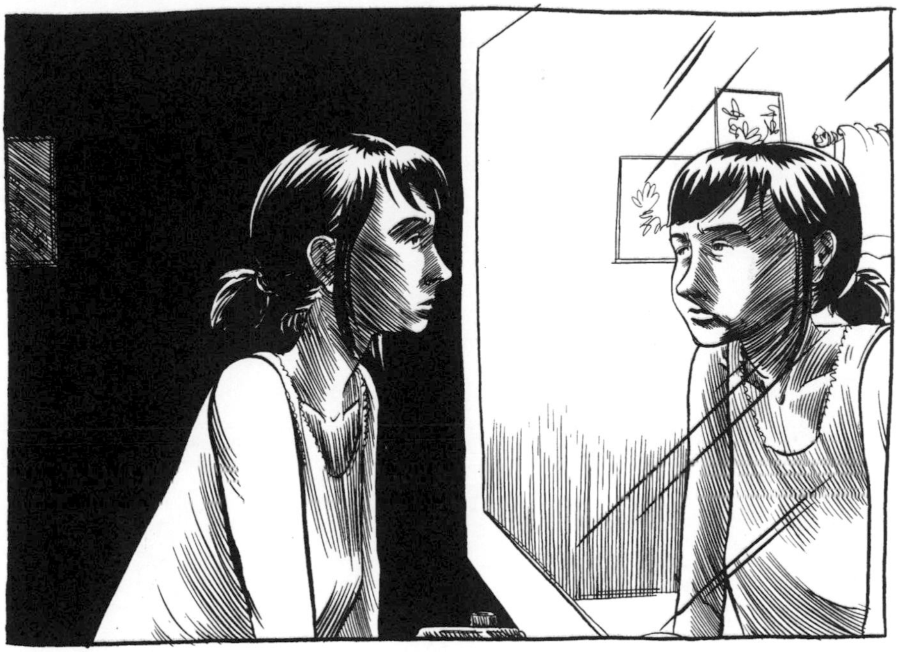

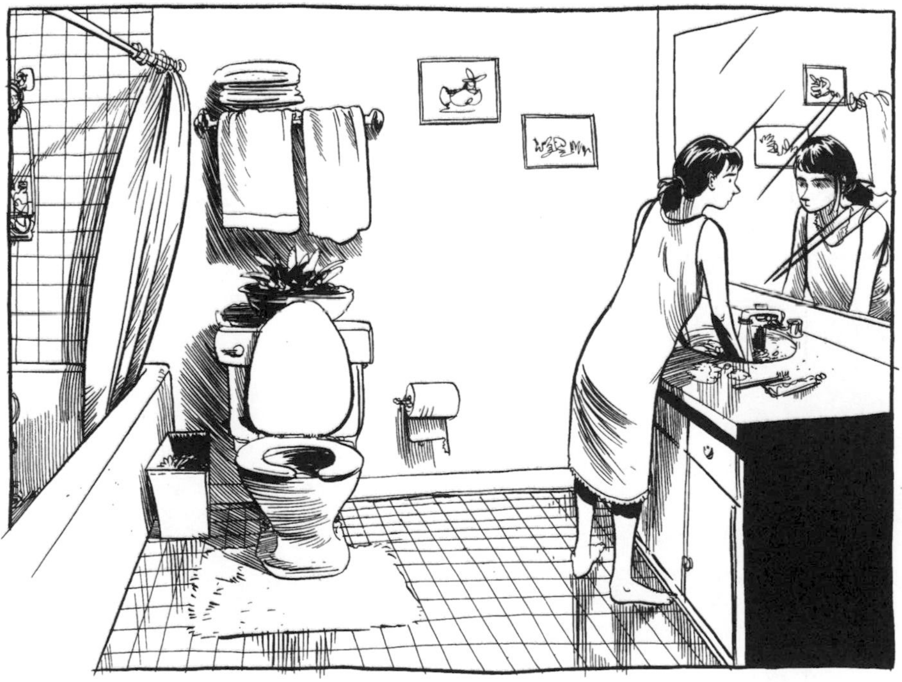

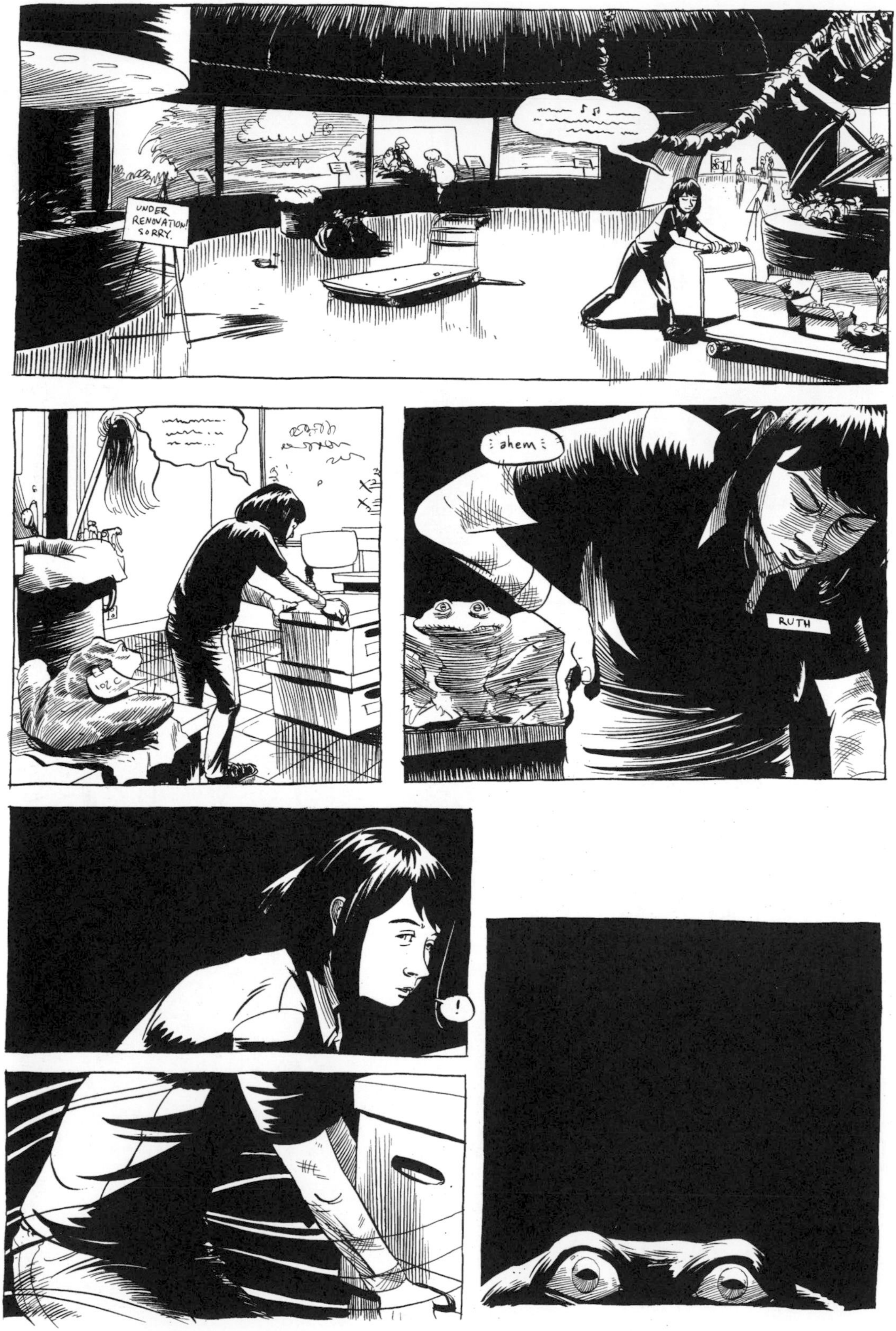
UNDER RENOVATION! SORRY.
ahem
RUTH
!

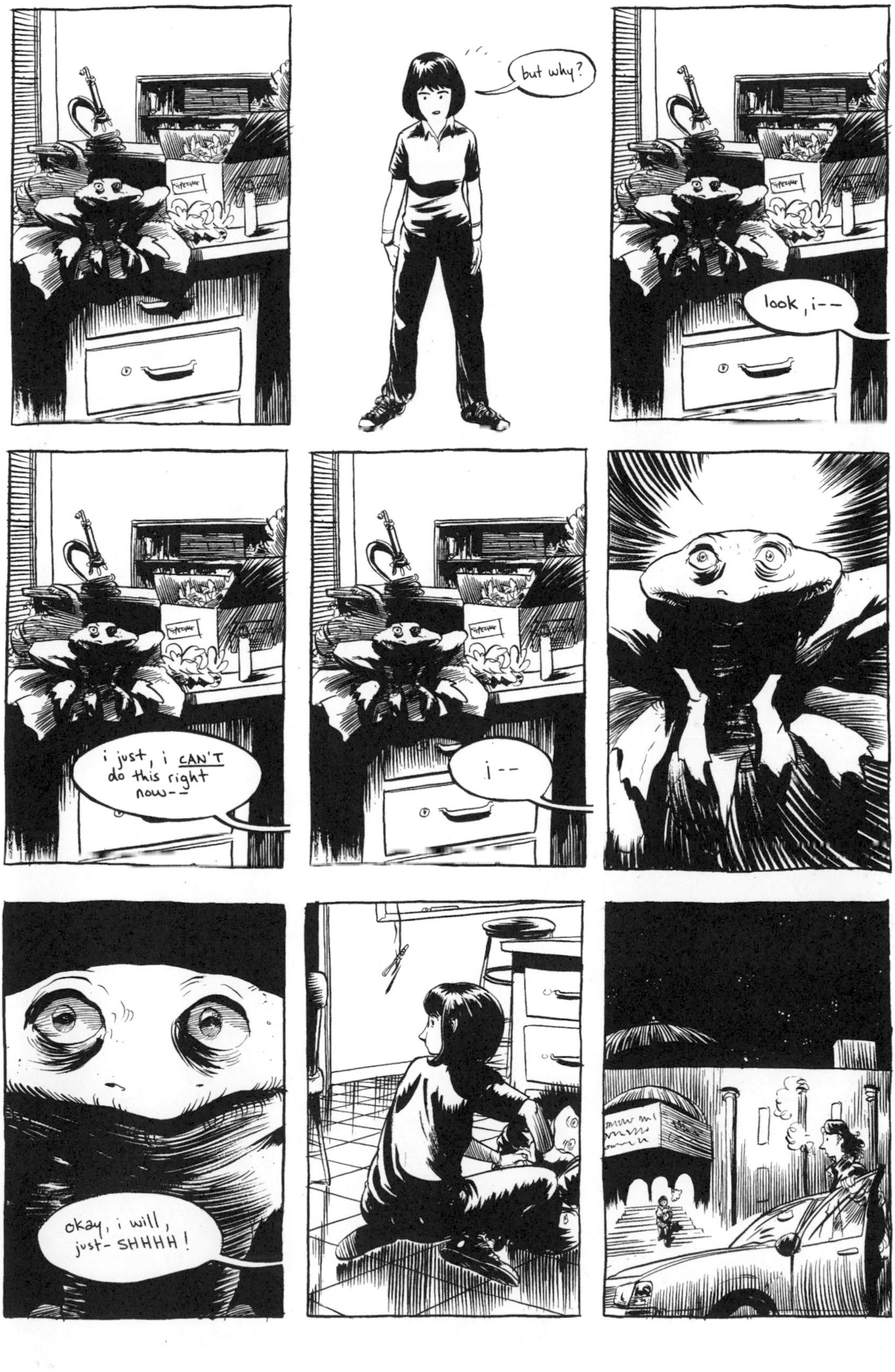

but why?
look, i--
i just, i CAN'T do this right now--
i--
okay, i will, just- SHHHH!

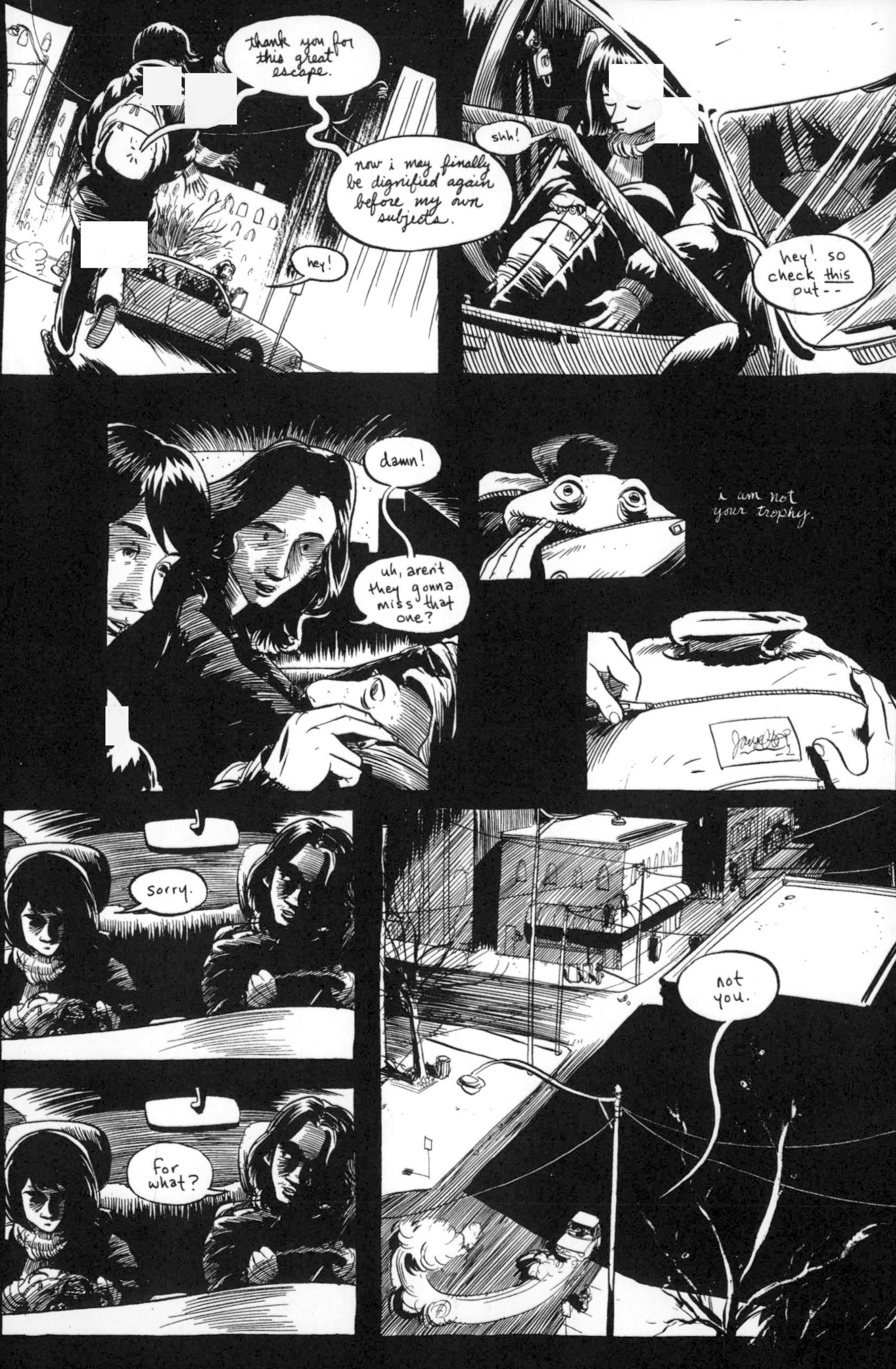
thank you for this great escape.
now i may finally be dignified again before my own subjects.
hey!
shh!
hey! so check this out--
damn!
uh, aren't they gonna miss that one?
i am not your trophy.
sorry.
for what?
not you.

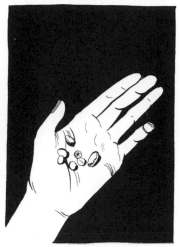

perry?

yeah?

um,

there's a problem.

there's an extra pill in my meds that i don't take.

You take six, right?

Yeah.

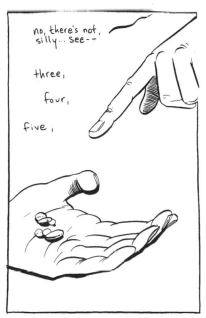

no, there's not, silly... see--

three,

four,

five,

six.

what?

there's seven pills, here, in my hand.

do you not see this one?

--i--

i ... don't--

SIIIIIKE!!

and YOU believed me, didn't you?

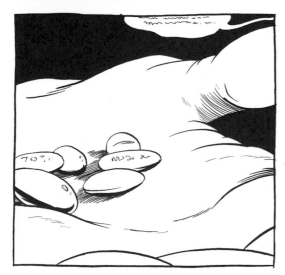

wait, hold on, i should take these--
what?
huh?

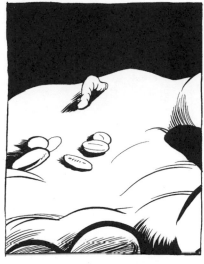

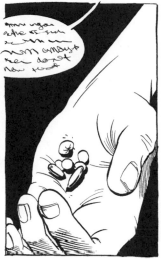

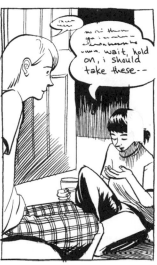

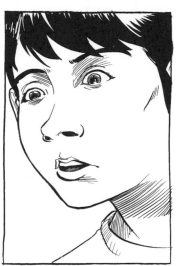

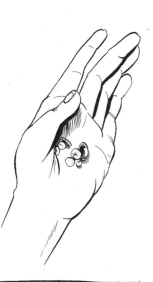

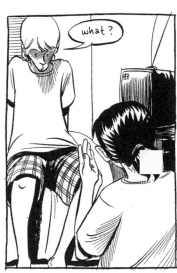

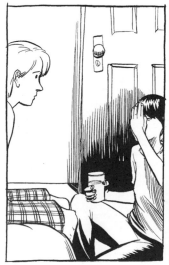

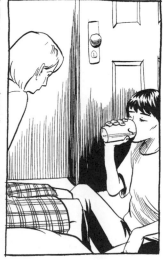

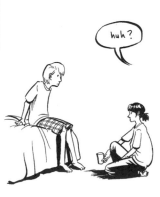

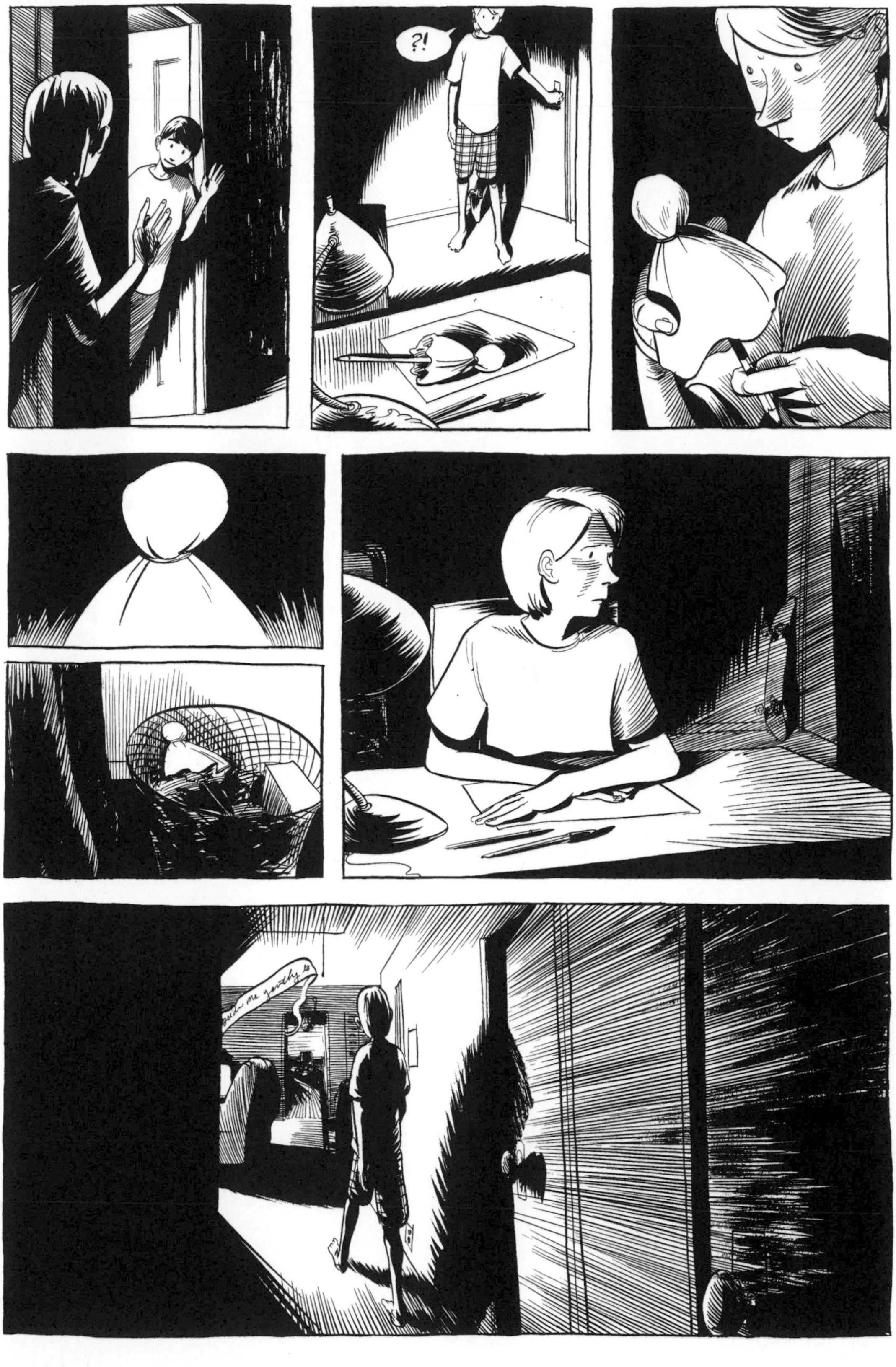
?!
me gently to

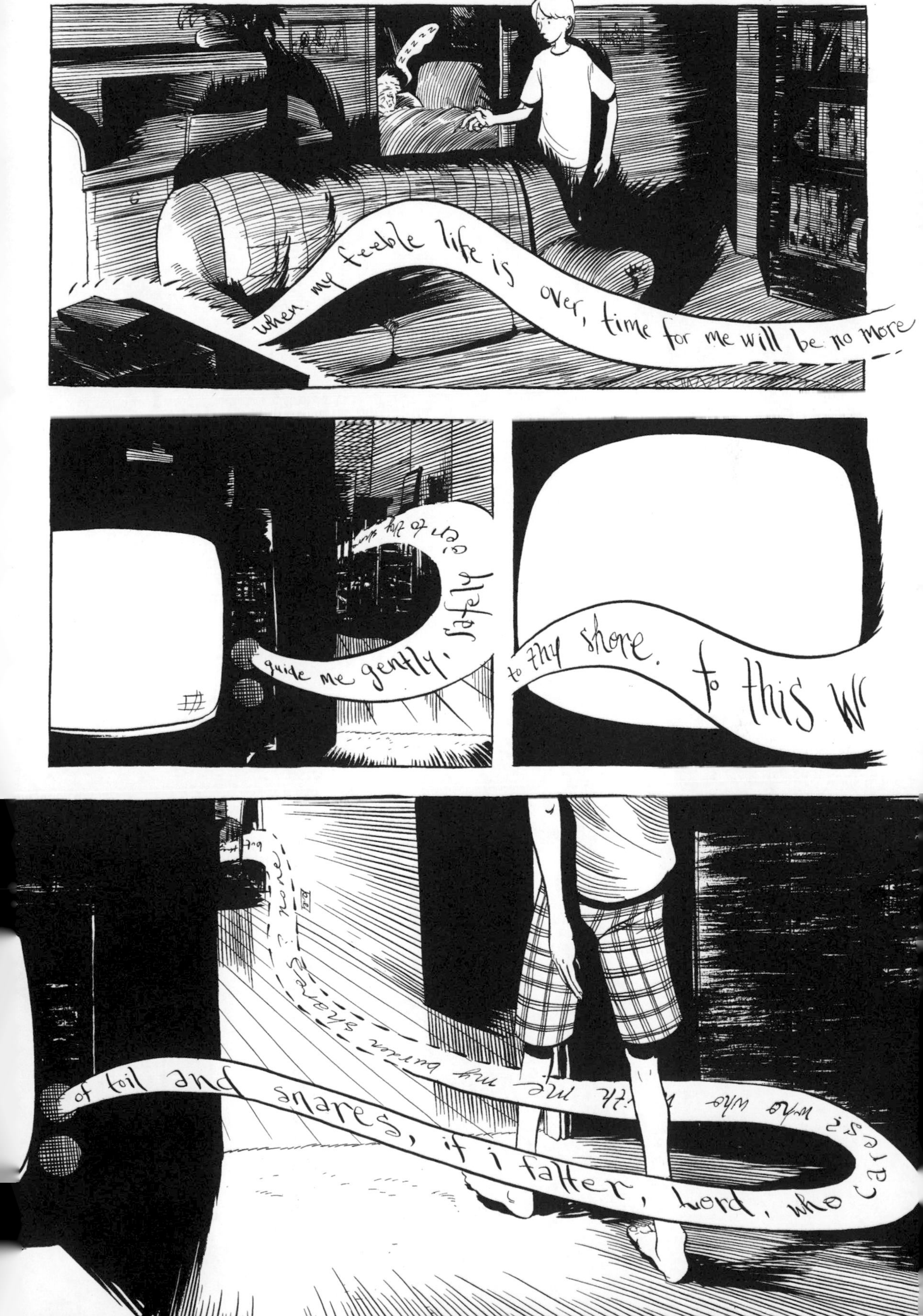

zzzz
when my feeble life is over, time for me will be no more
guide me gently, safely o'er to thy shore
to thy shore.
to this w
of toil and snares, if i falter, lord, who cares? who with me my burden shares? none

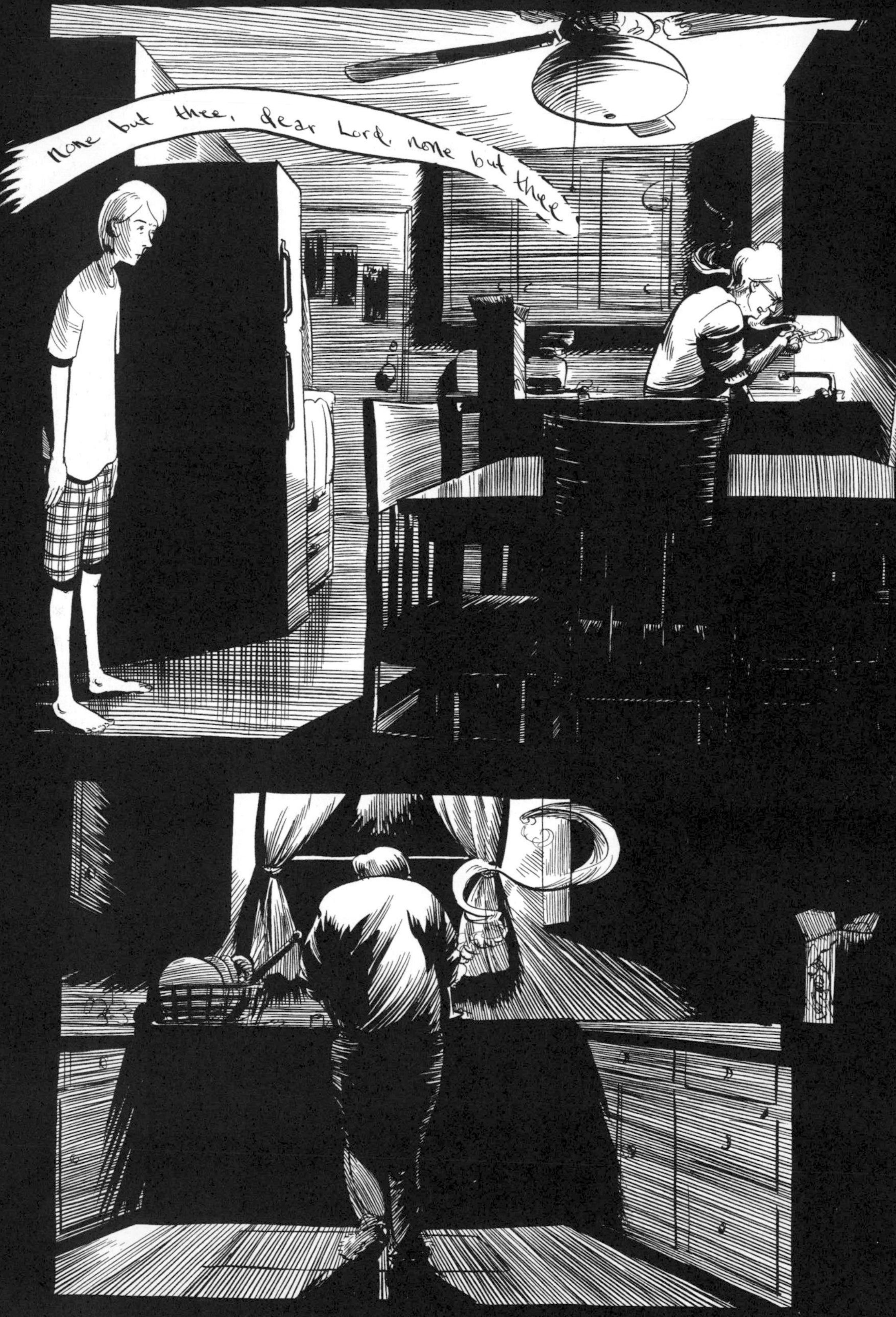
None but thee, dear Lord, none but thee

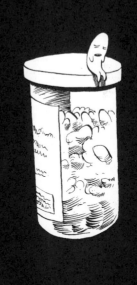

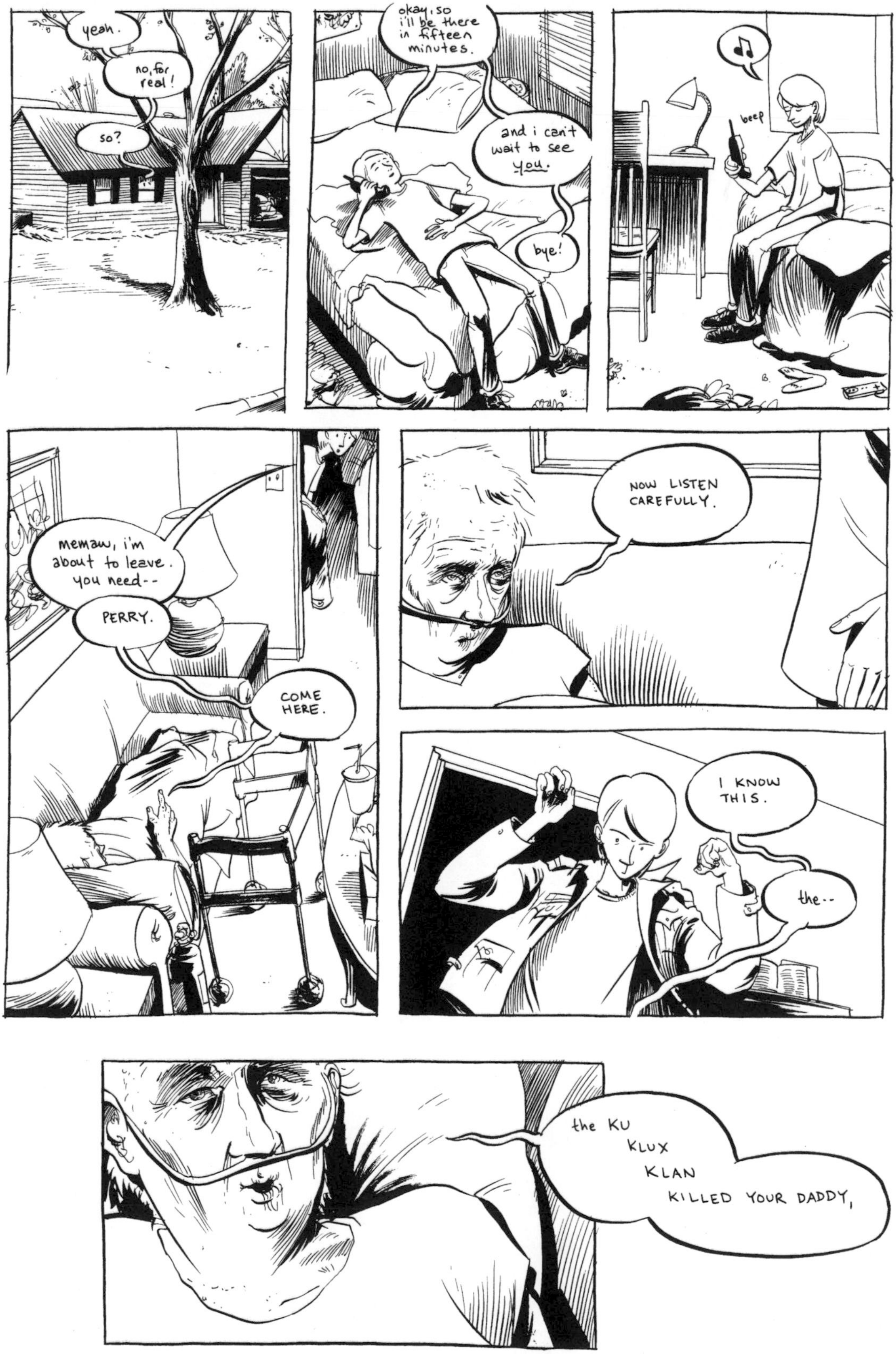
yeah.
no, for real!
so?
okay, so i'll be there in fifteen minutes.
and i can't wait to see you.
bye!
♫
beep
memaw, i'm about to leave. you need--
PERRY.
COME HERE.
NOW LISTEN CAREFULLY.
I KNOW THIS.
the--
the KU KLUX KLAN KILLED YOUR DADDY,

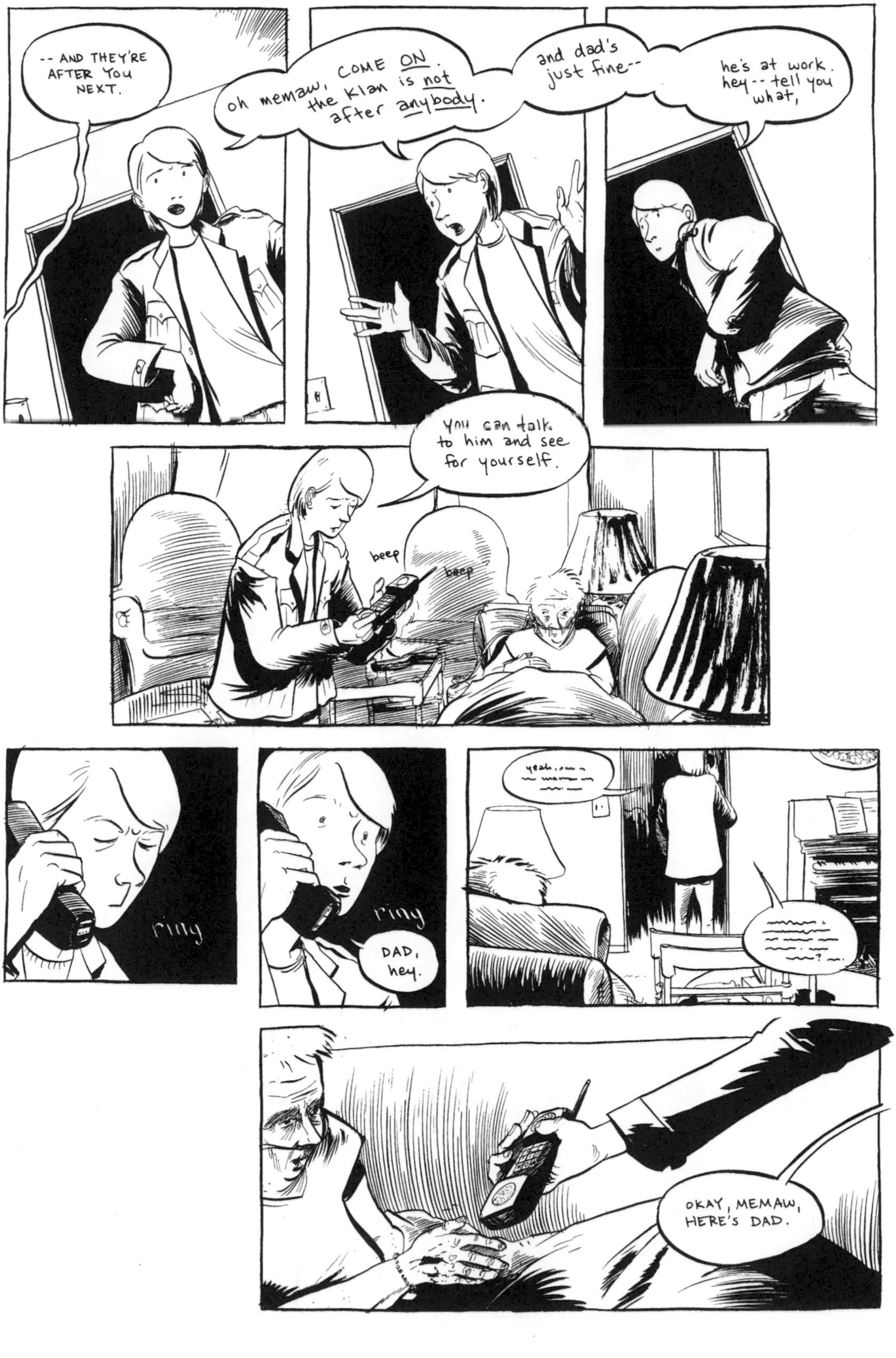
-- AND THEY'RE AFTER YOU NEXT.
oh memaw, COME ON. the klan is not after anybody.
and dad's just fine--
he's at work. hey -- tell you what,
you can talk to him and see for yourself.
beep
beep
ring
ring
DAD, hey.
OKAY, MEMAW, HERE'S DAD.

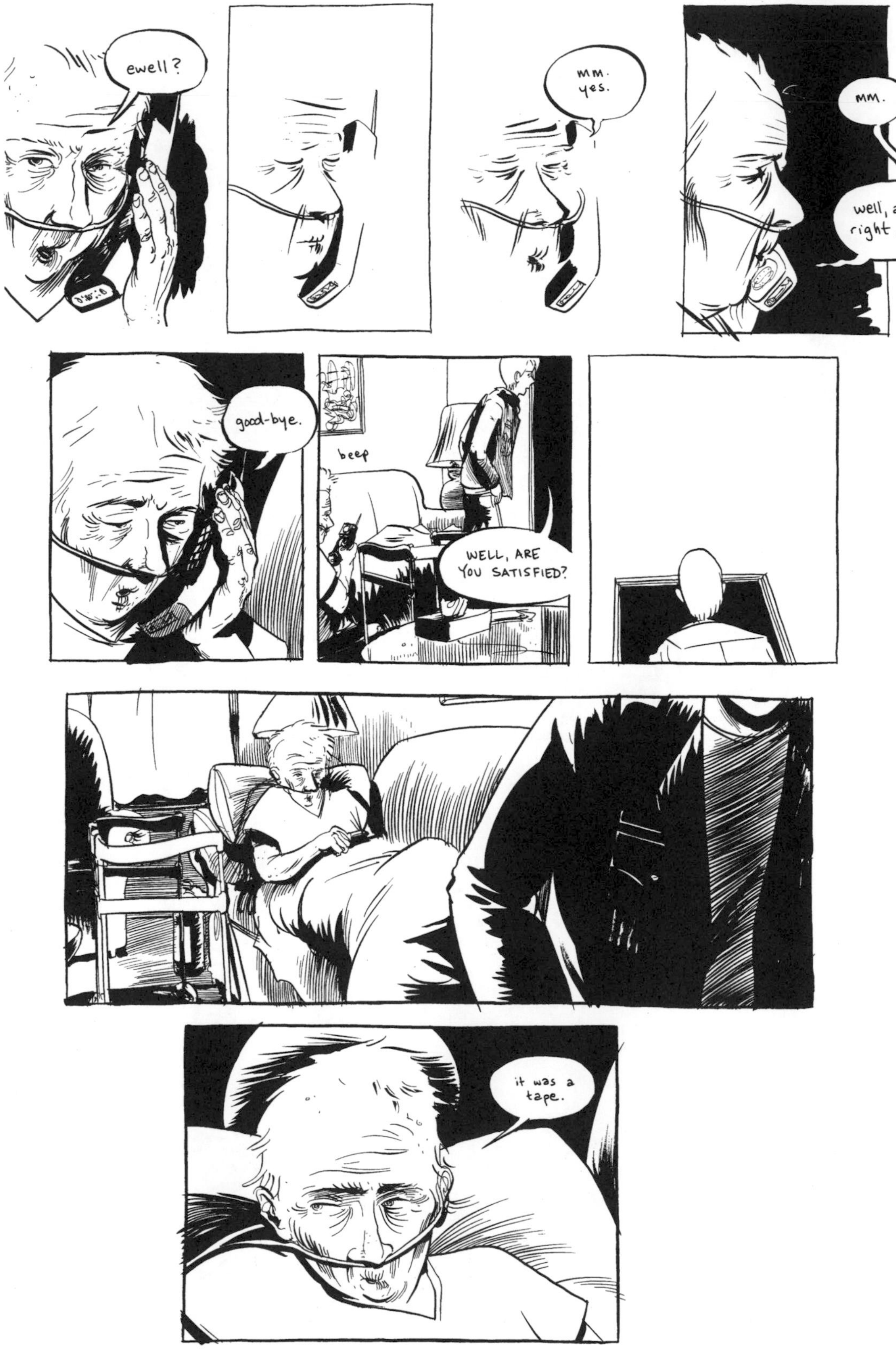
ewell?
mm. yes.
mm.
well, all right, dear.
good-bye.
beep
WELL, ARE YOU SATISFIED?
it was a tape.

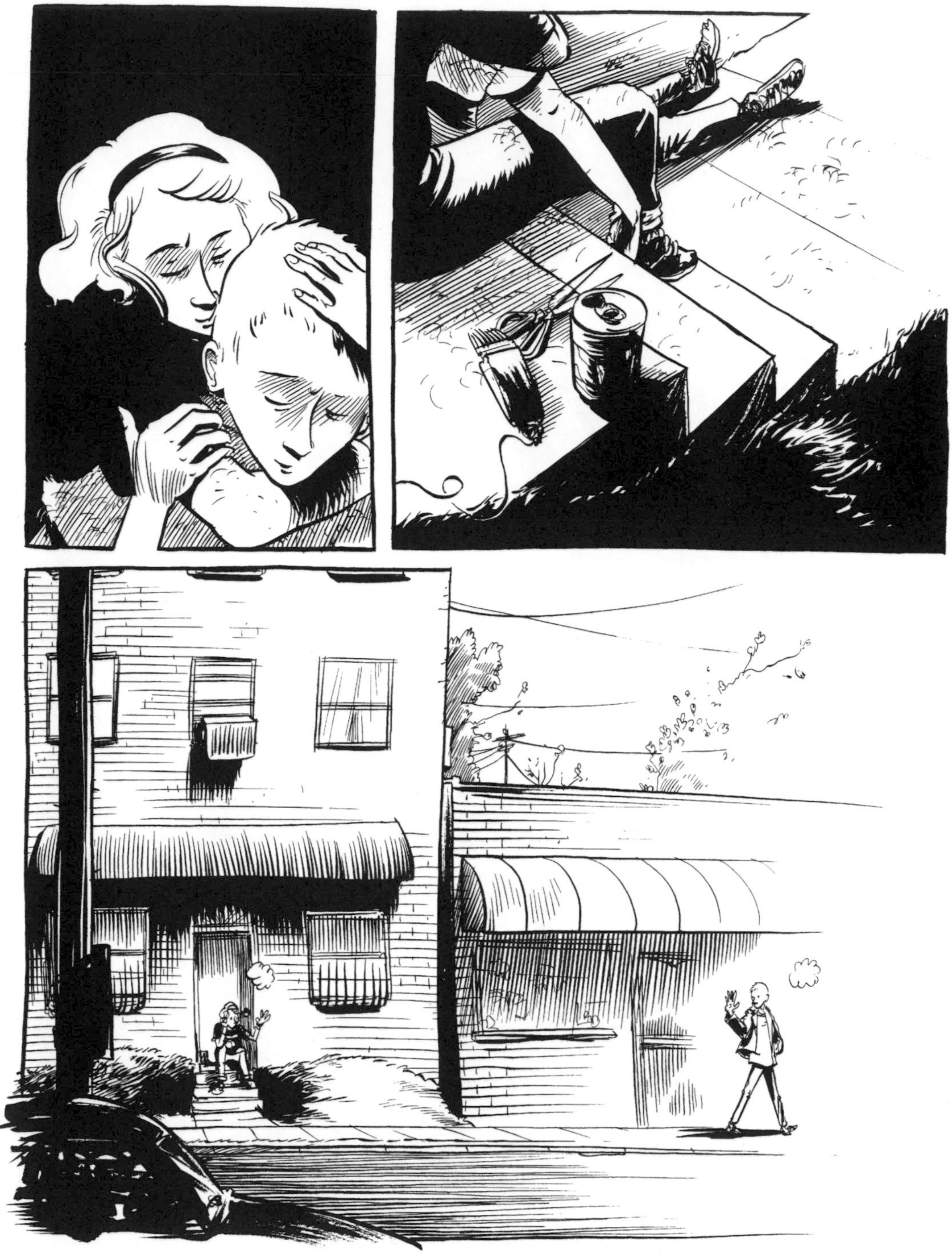

ART STUF
ART

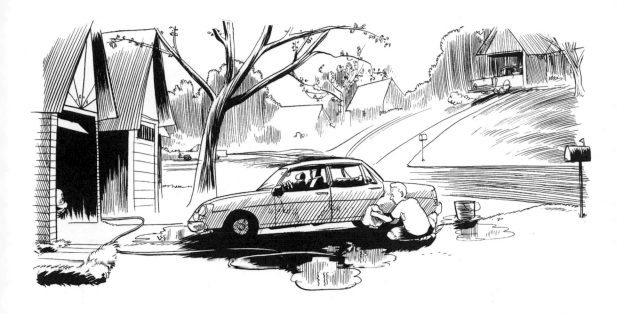

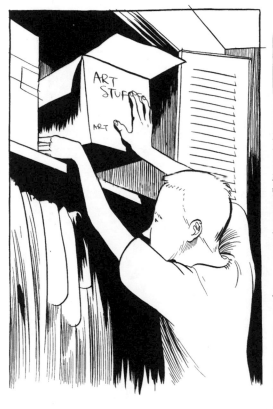

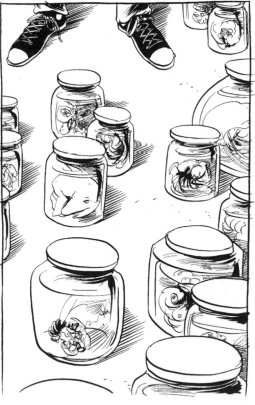

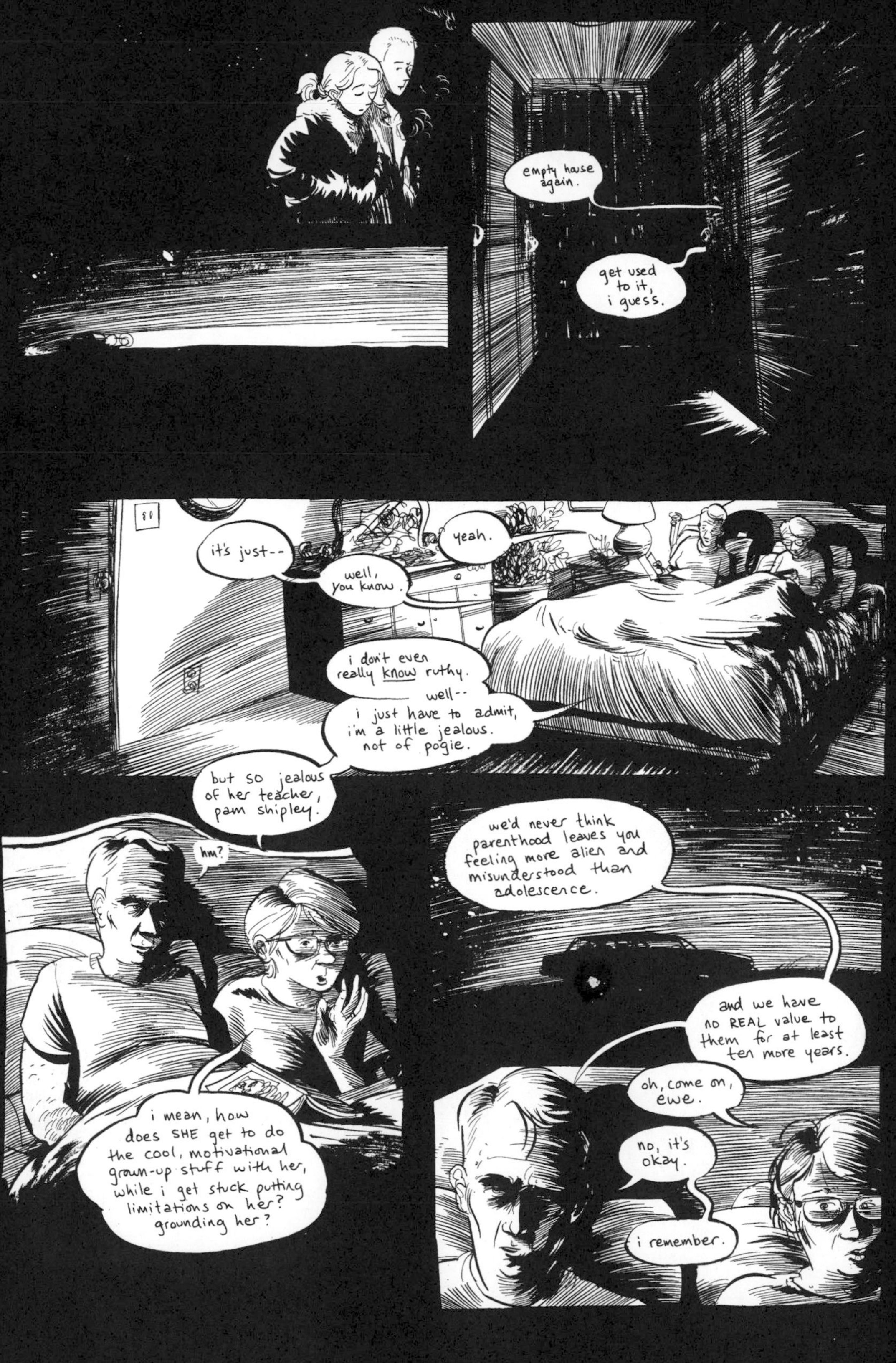
empty house again.
get used to it, i guess.
it's just--
well, you know.
yeah.
i don't even really know ruthy.
well-- i just have to admit, i'm a little jealous. not of pogie.
but so jealous of her teacher, pam shipley.
hm?
i mean, how does SHE get to do the cool, motivational grown-up stuff with her, while i get stuck putting limitations on her? grounding her?
we'd never think parenthood leaves you feeling more alien and misunderstood than adolescence.
and we have no REAL value to them for at least ten more years.
oh, come on, ewe.
no, it's okay.
i remember.

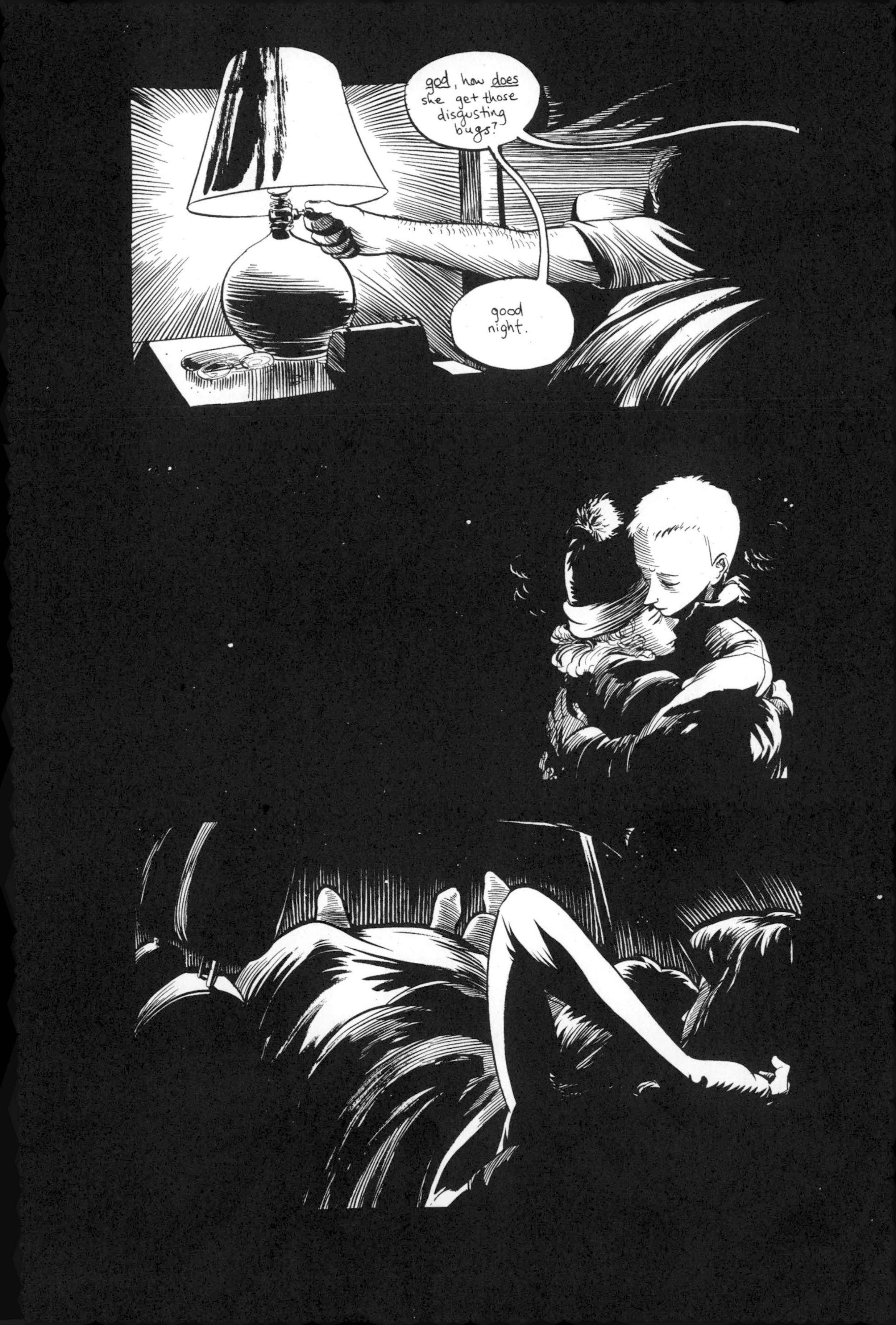
god, how does she get those disgusting bugs?
good night.

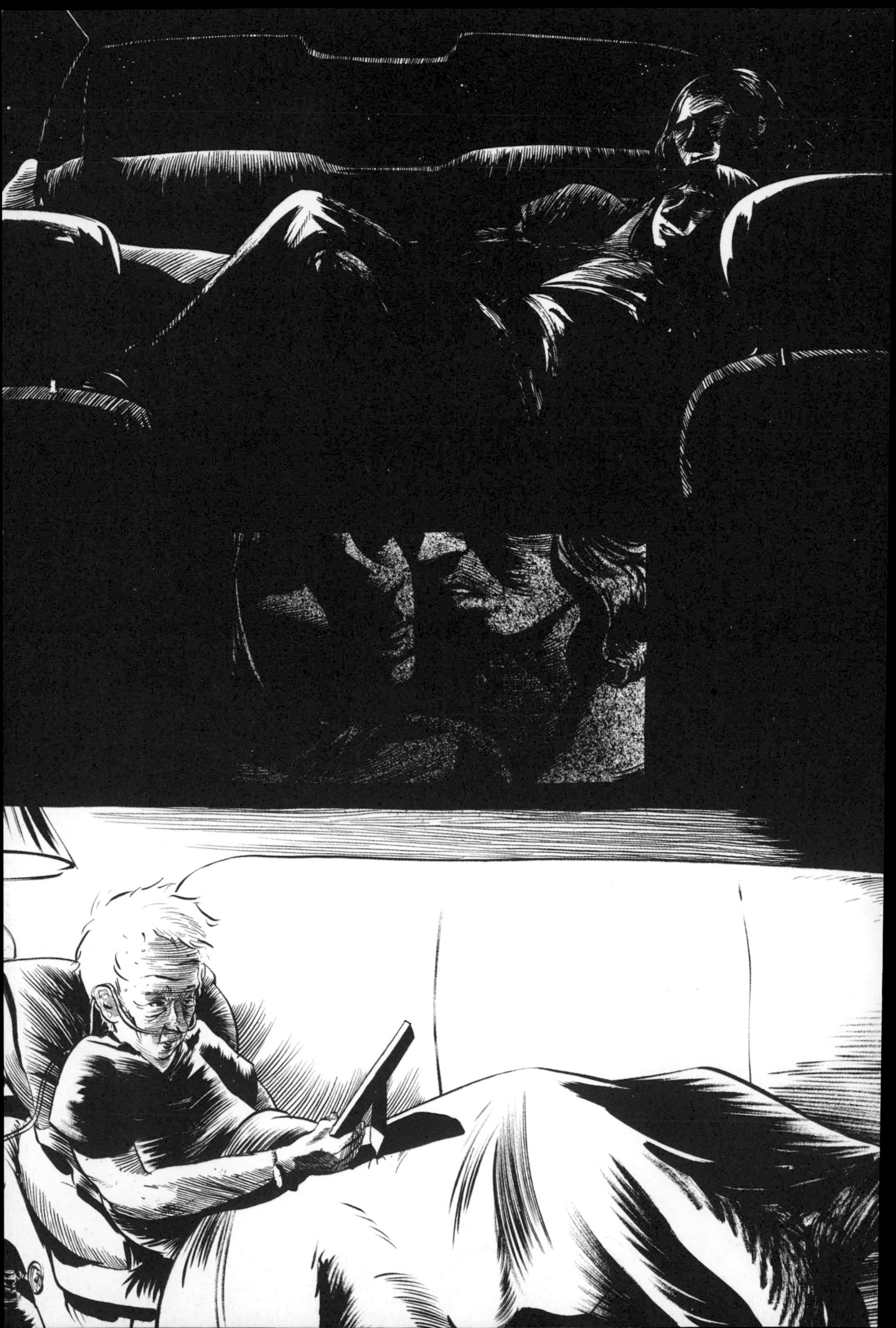

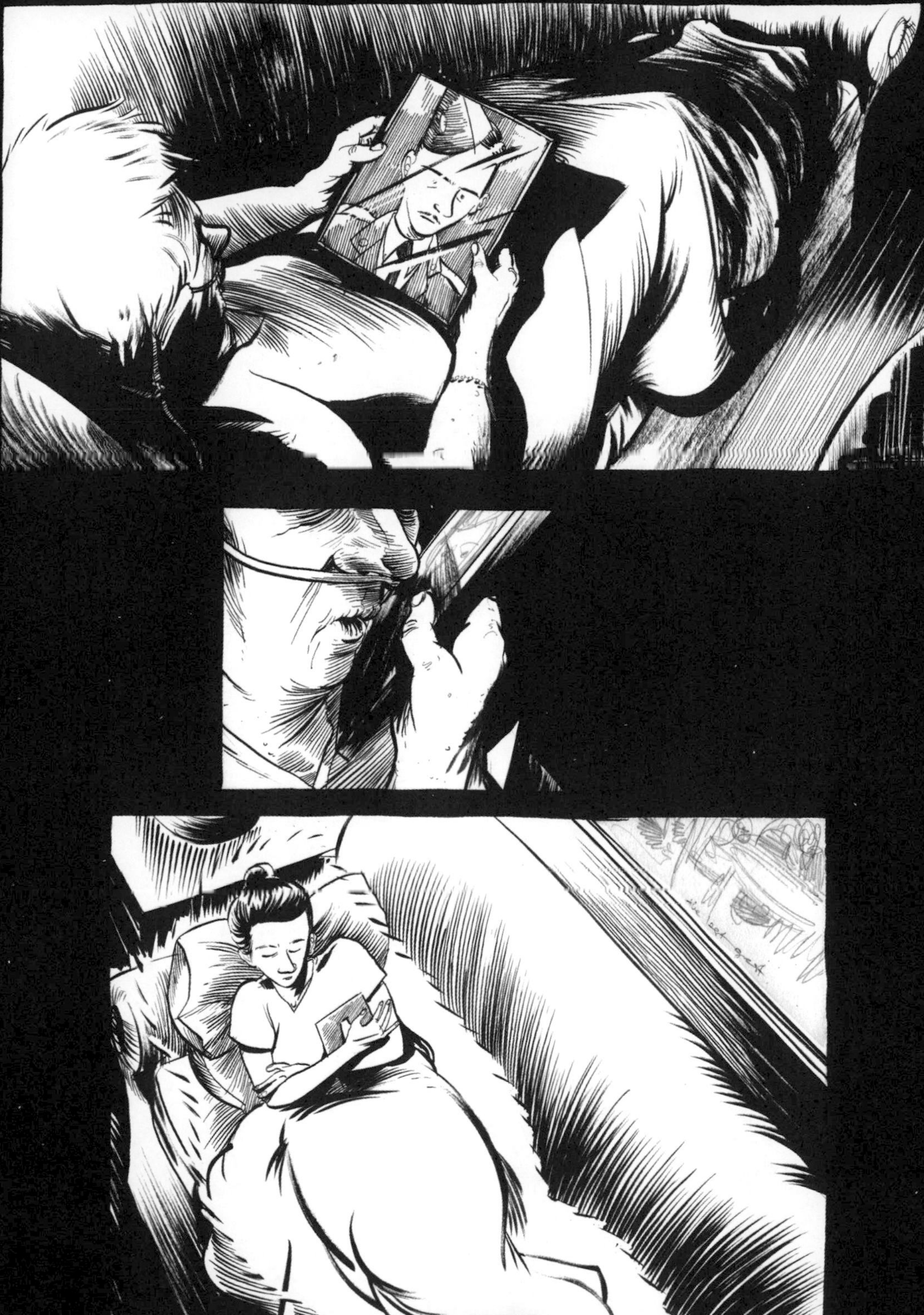

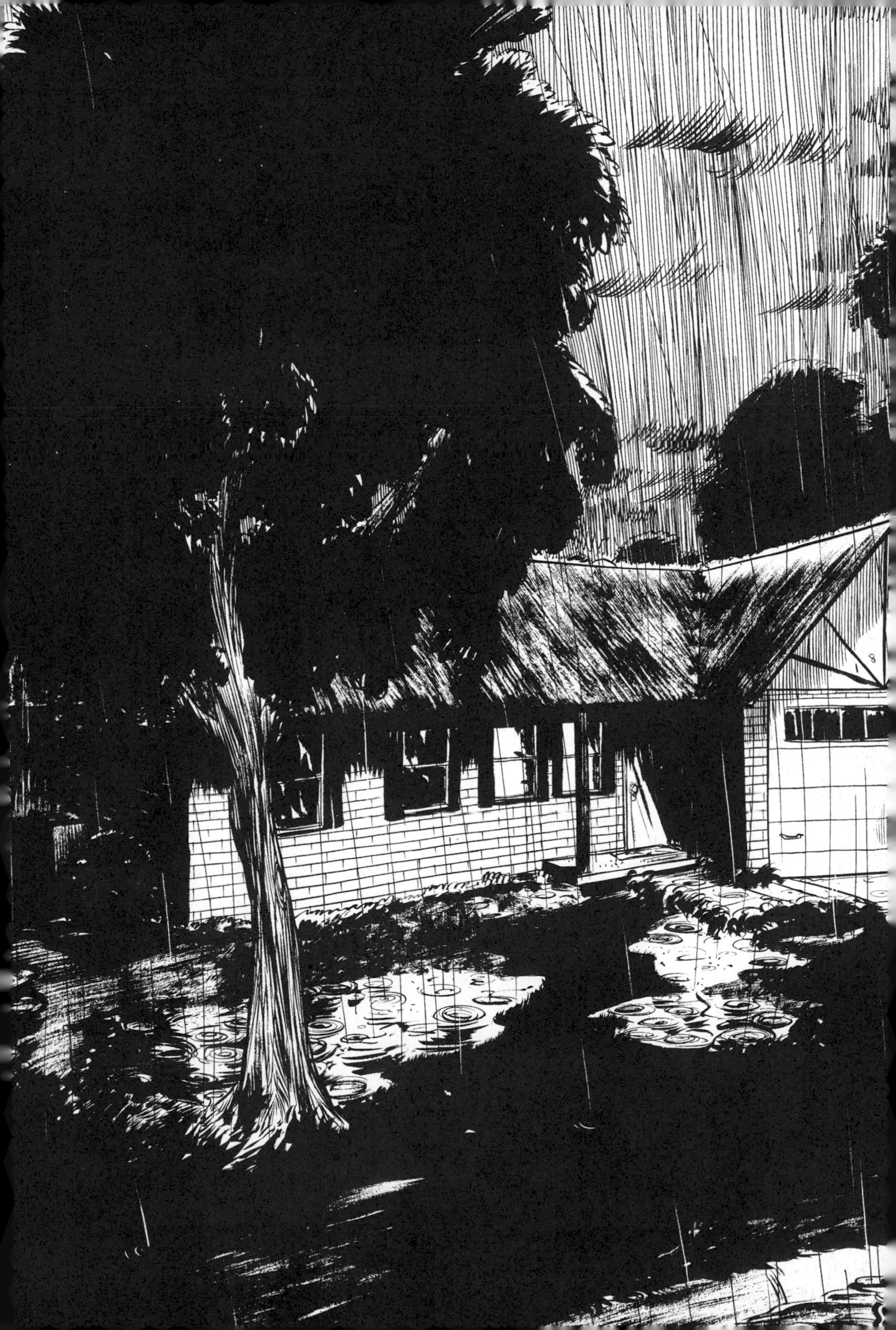

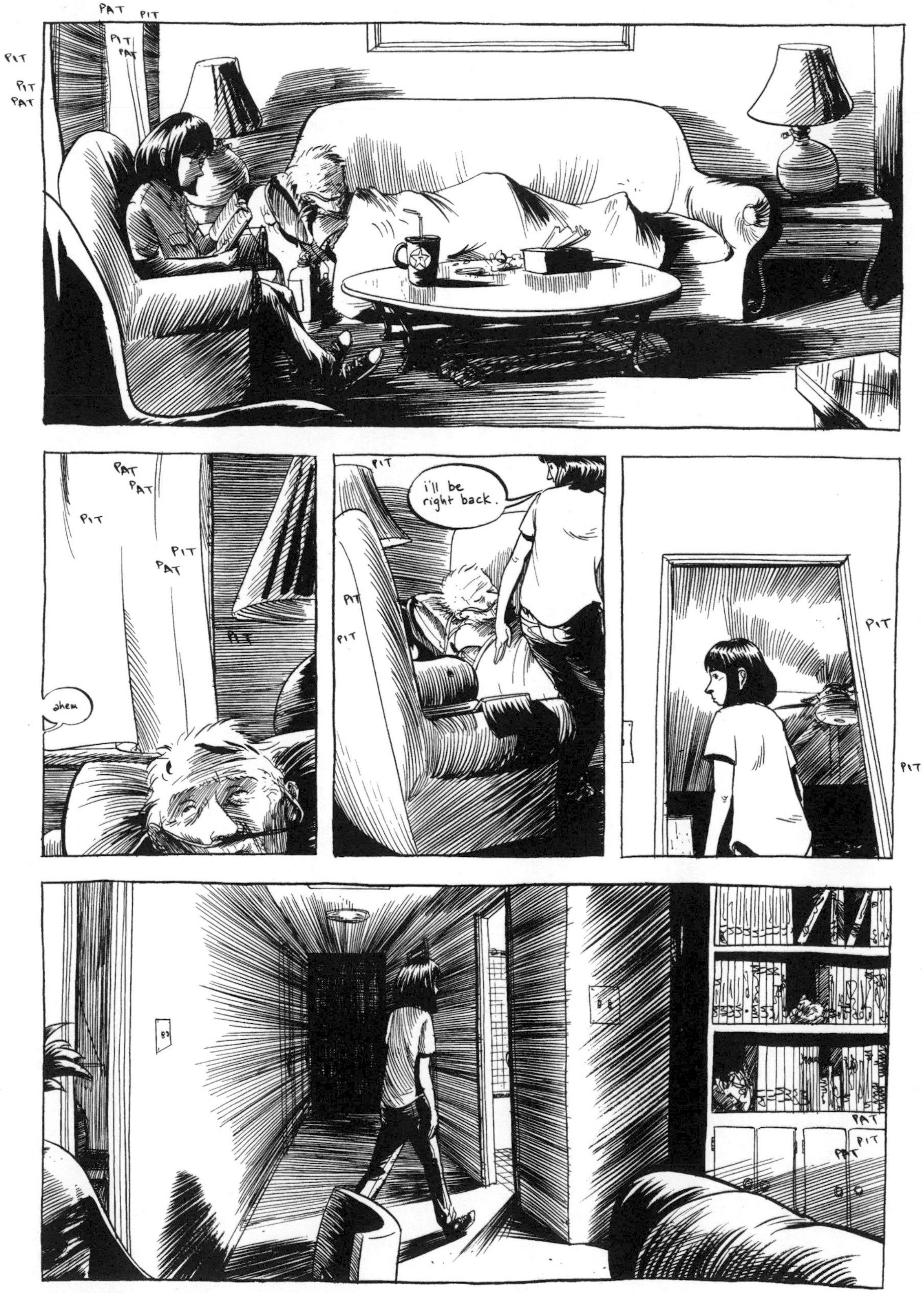
PAT PIT
PIT PAT
PIT
PIT PAT
PAT PAT
PIT
PIT PAT
ahem
PIT
i'll be right back.
PIT
PIT
PIT
PIT
PAT
PIT
PAT

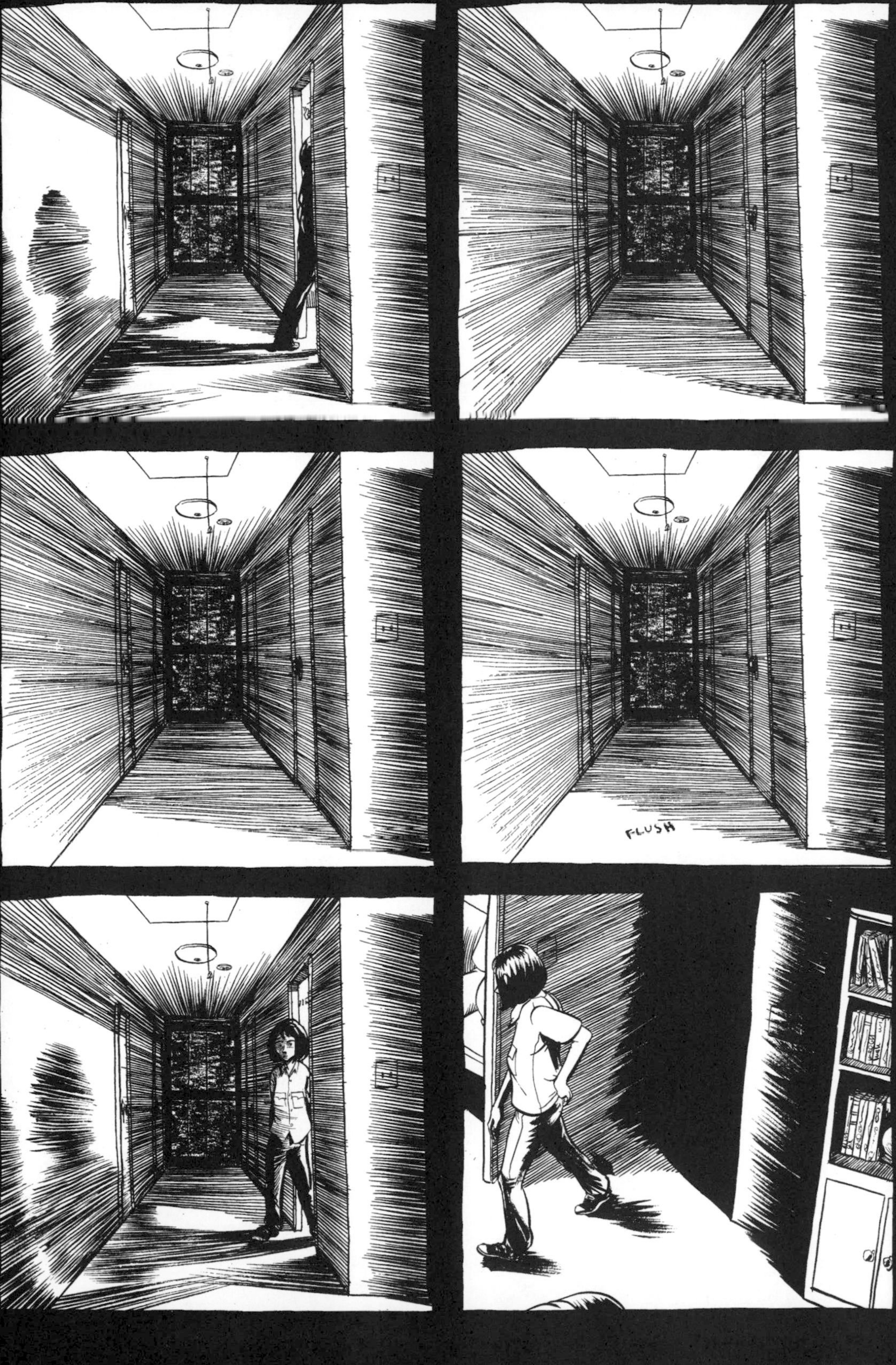
FLUSH

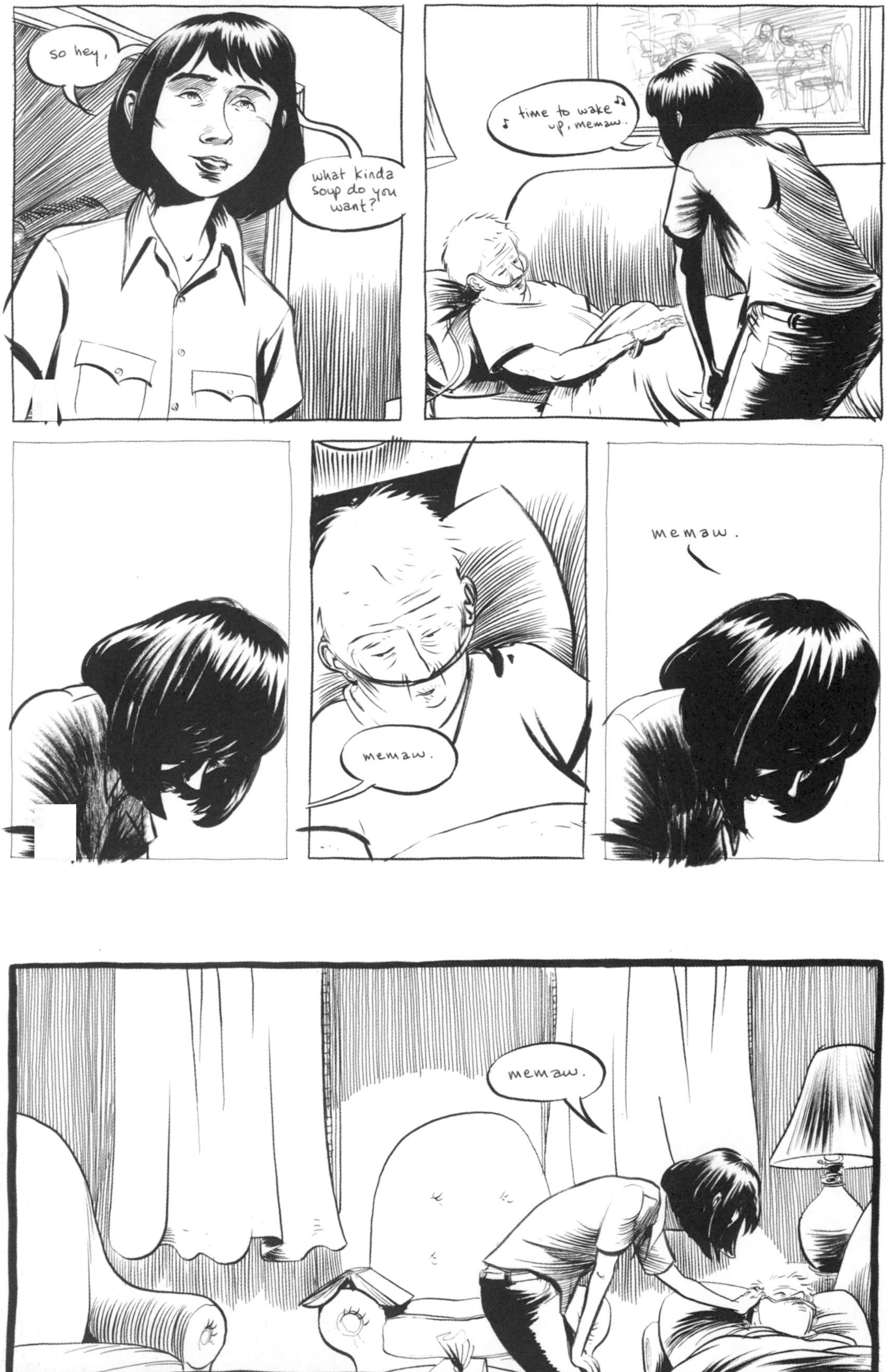
so hey,
what kinda soup do you want?
♪ time to wake up, memaw. ♫
memaw.
memaw.
memaw.

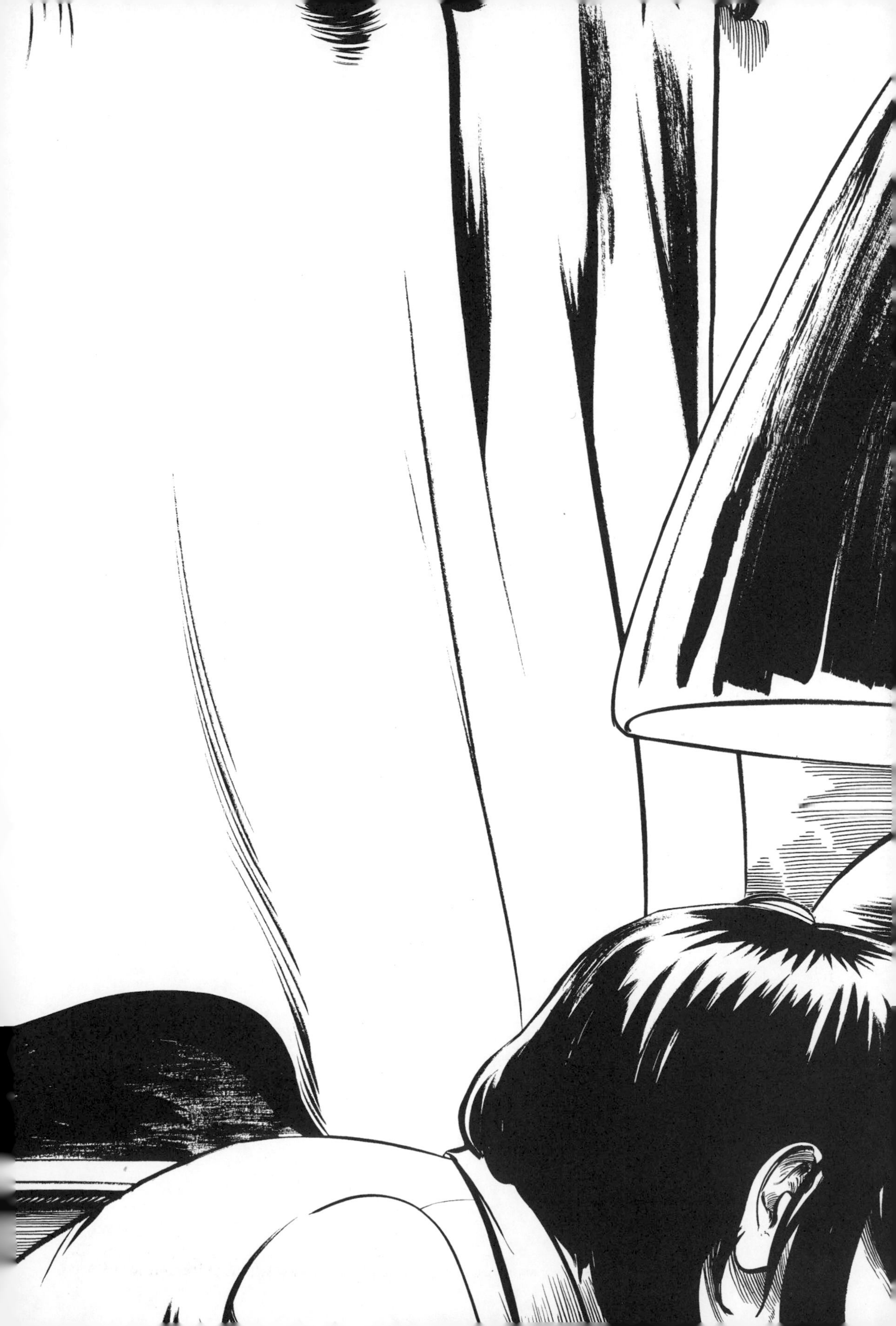

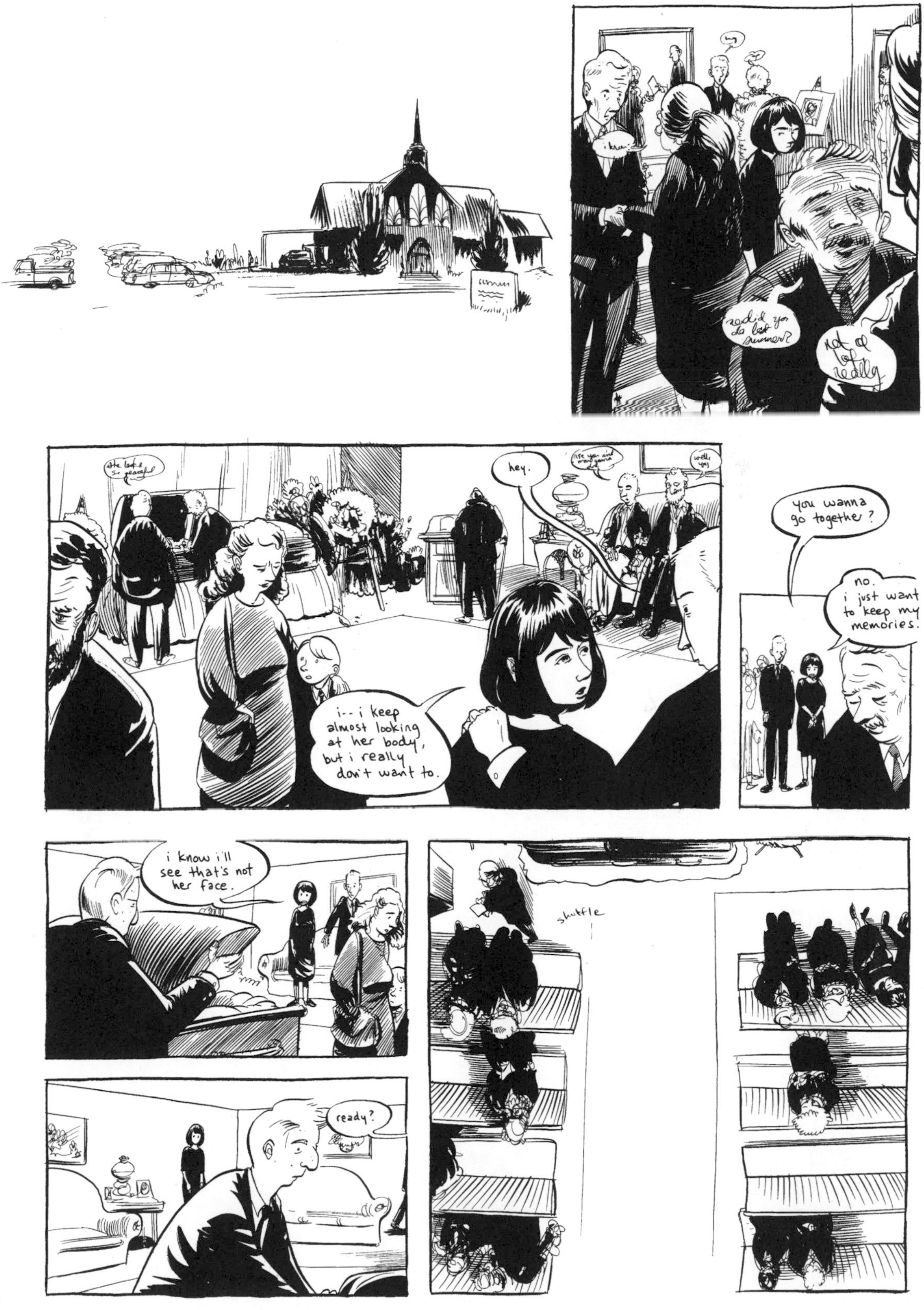
hey.
i-- i keep almost looking at her body, but i really don't want to.
you wanna go together?
no. i just want to keep my memories.
i know i'll see that's not her face.
shuffle
ready?

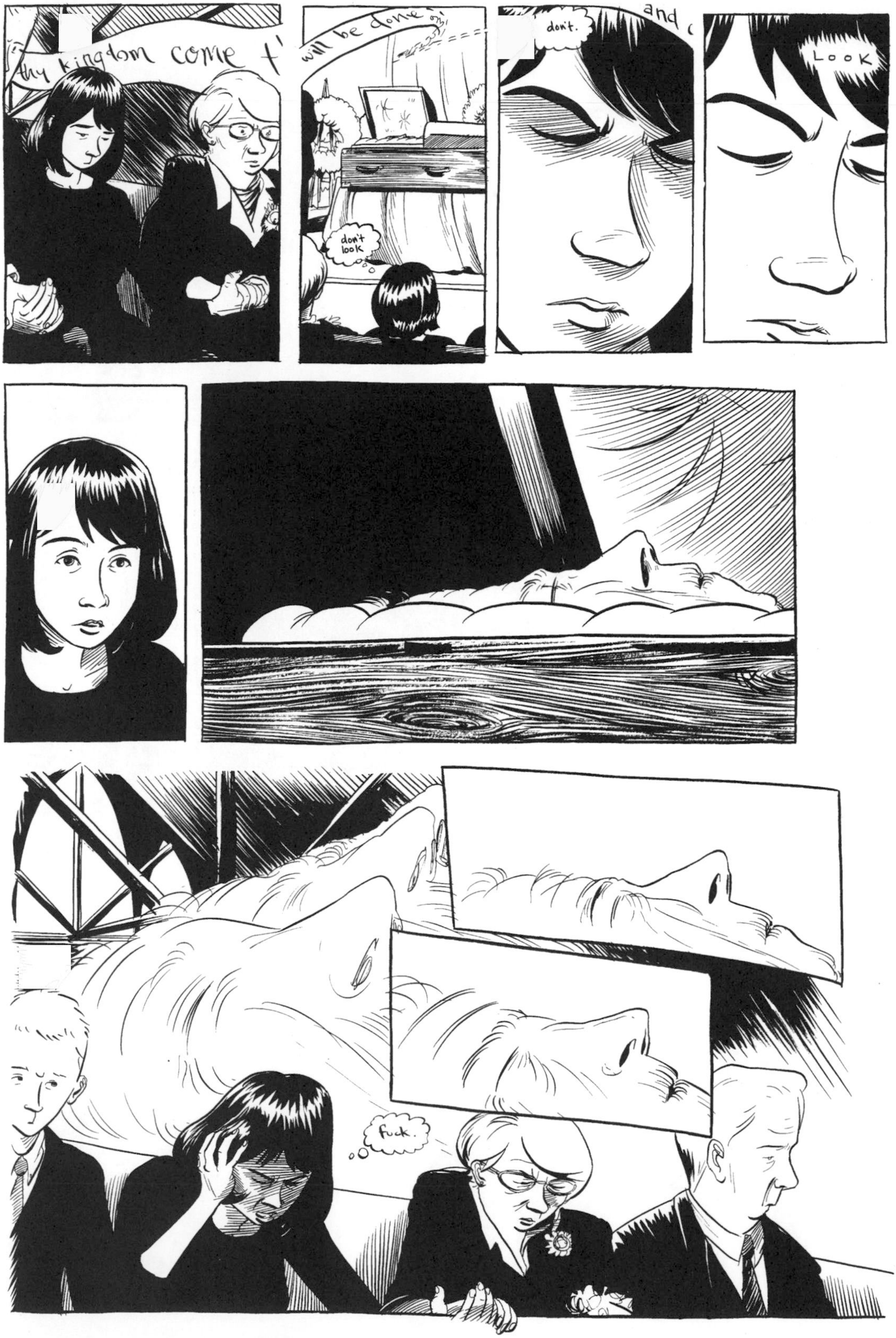
thy kingdom come t'
will be done
don't look
don't.
and
LOOK
fuck.

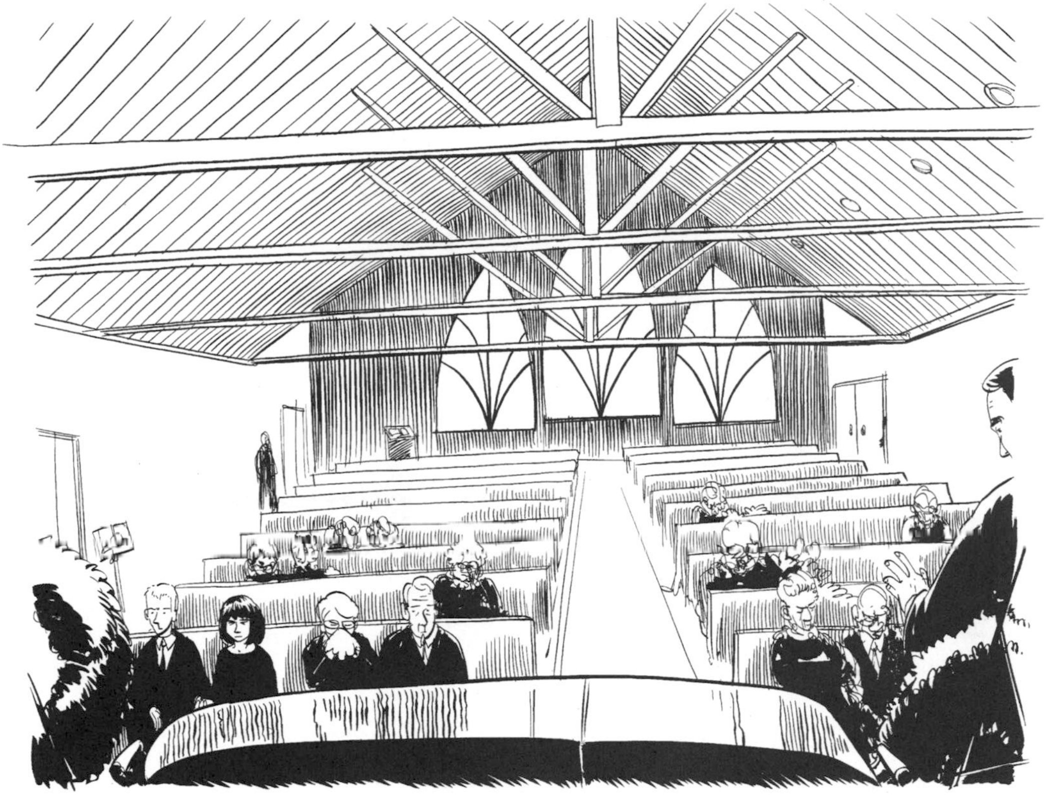

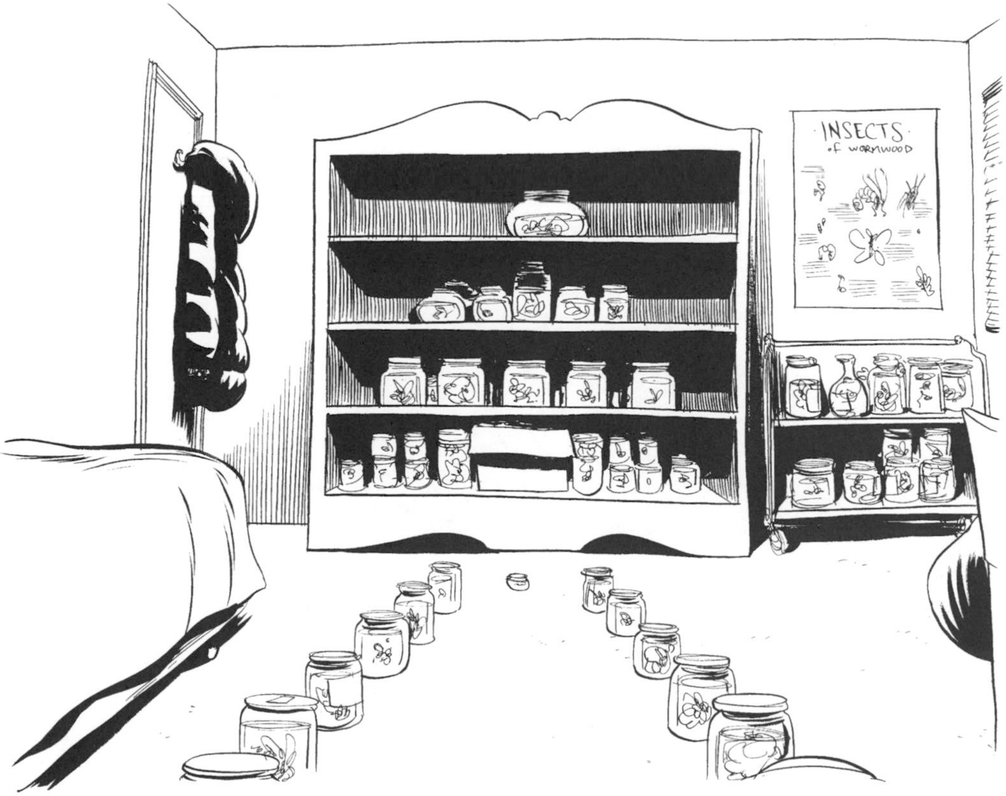
INSECTS
of WORMWOOD

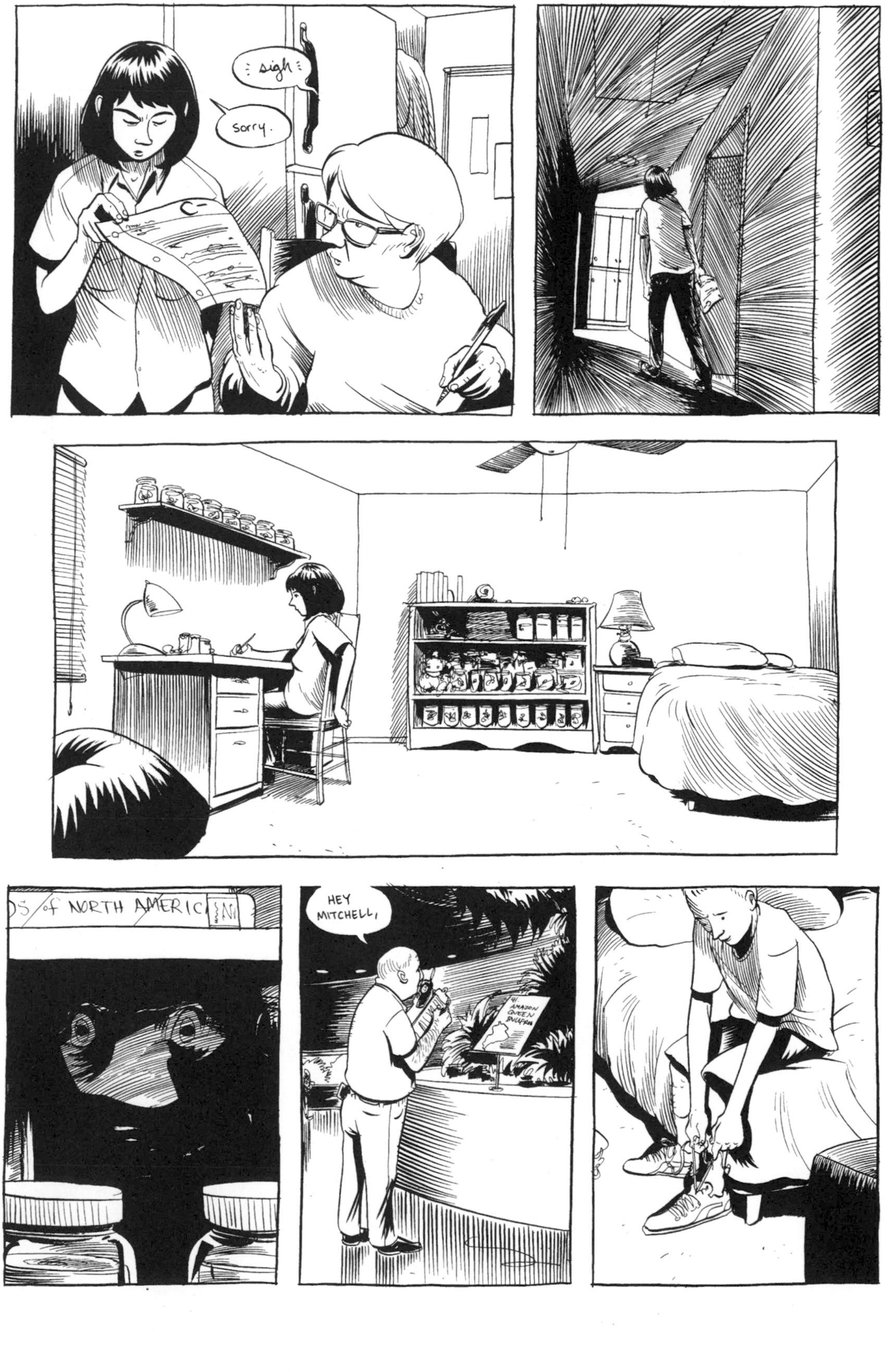
sigh
sorry.
C-
S of NORTH AMERIC
HEY MITCHELL,
41. AMAZON QUEEN BULLFROG

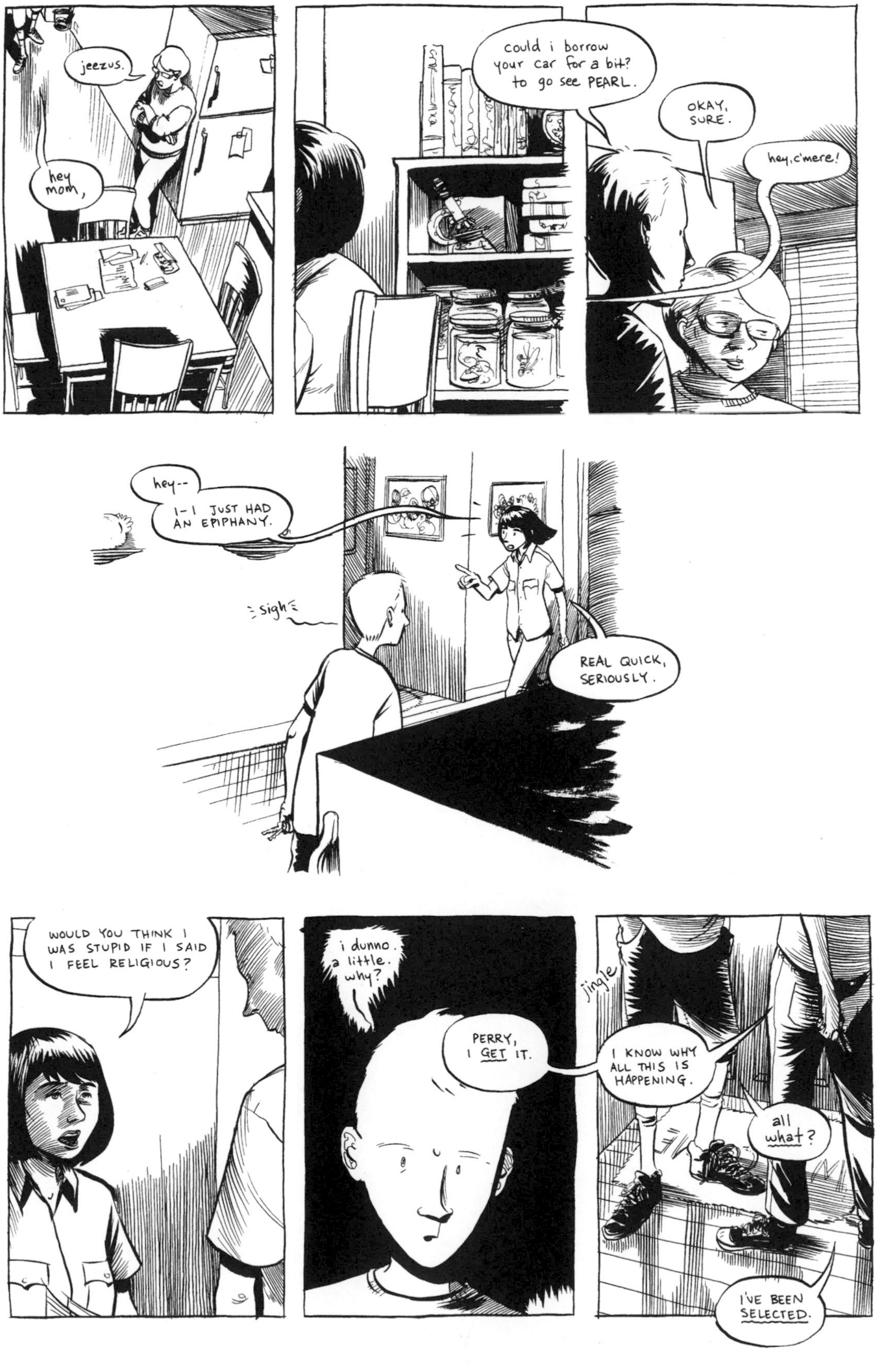

jeezus.
hey mom,
could i borrow your car for a bit? to go see PEARL.
OKAY, SURE.
hey, c'mere!
hey--
I-I JUST HAD AN EPIPHANY.
sigh
REAL QUICK, SERIOUSLY.
WOULD YOU THINK I WAS STUPID IF I SAID I FEEL RELIGIOUS?
i dunno. a little. why?
PERRY, I GET IT.
I KNOW WHY ALL THIS IS HAPPENING.
jingle
all what?
I'VE BEEN SELECTED.

YOU'VE BEEN SELECTED?

THAT FROG IS MY KEEPER.

?

OKAY, LOOK--

SO THIS THING OF MINE, THIS DISABILITY OR WHATEVER--I'VE UNRAVELED IT.

YES, I'M CONSUMED BY ORDER, RIGHTNESS.

I REALIZE NOW THAT I KNOW A SUPREME ORDER. WHEN I GIVE IN TO IT, I CHANNEL IT.

AND WHEN I CHANNEL IT, ONLY THEN DO I FIND PEACE.

≈SIGH≈ RIGHT, YOU TALK ABOUT THIS ALL THE TIME.

SORRY! jeezus.

EXCUSE ME FOR BEING CONFUSED. I'M TRYING TO TELL YOU SOMETHING--IT'S NOT THAT IT'S SO TOUGH TO LIVE WITH IT ALL--

BUT WHY FIGHT IT JUST TO SEEM A LITTLE MORE ACCEPTABLE TO PEOPLE?

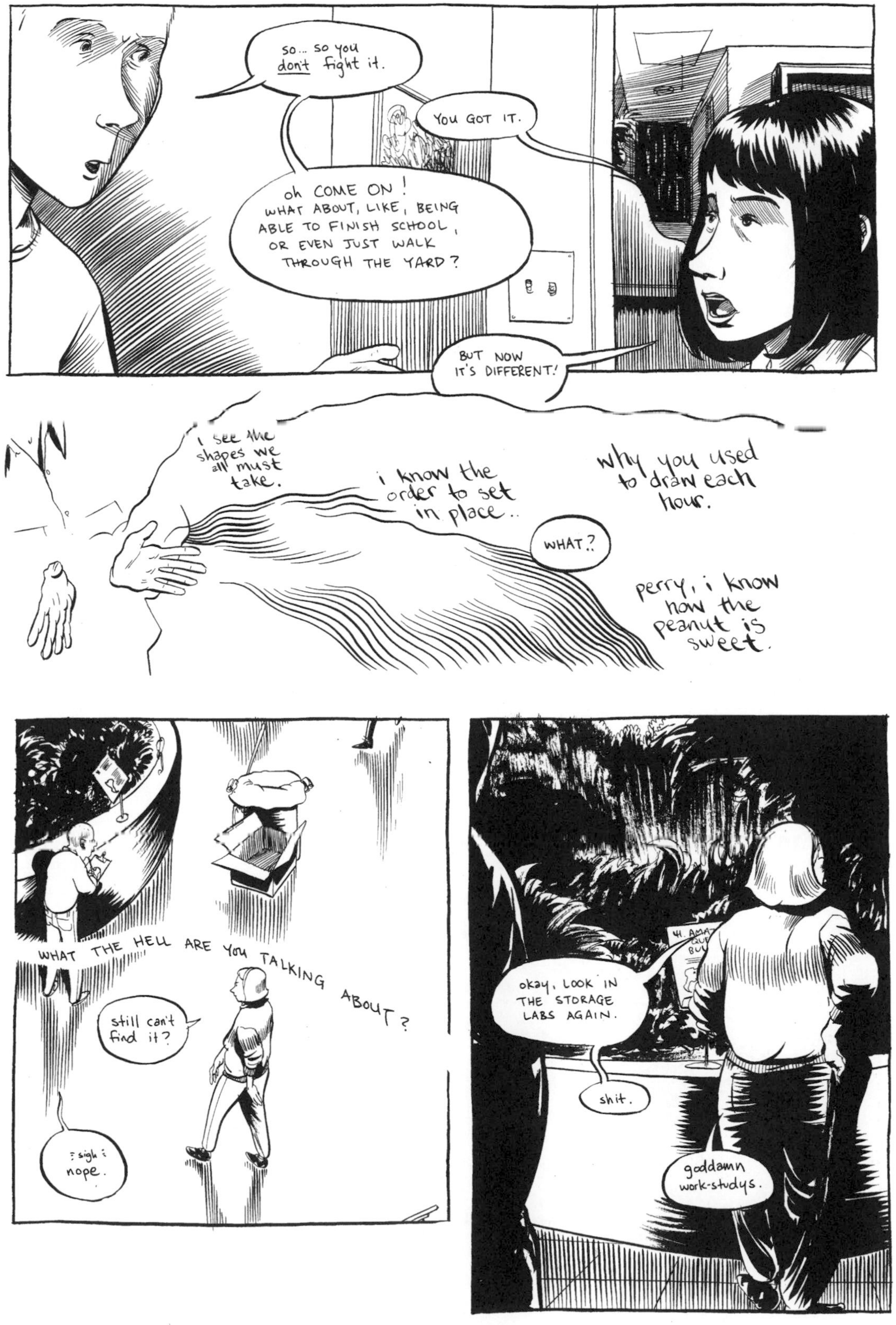
so... so you don't fight it.
You GOT IT.
oh COME ON! WHAT ABOUT, LIKE, BEING ABLE TO FINISH SCHOOL, OR EVEN JUST WALK THROUGH THE YARD?
BUT NOW IT'S DIFFERENT!
i see the shapes we all must take.
i know the order to set in place..
why you used to draw each hour.
WHAT?
perry, i know how the peanut is sweet.
WHAT THE HELL ARE YOU TALKING ABOUT?
still can't find it?
: sigh : nope.
okay, LOOK IN THE STORAGE LABS AGAIN.
shit.
goddamn work-studys.

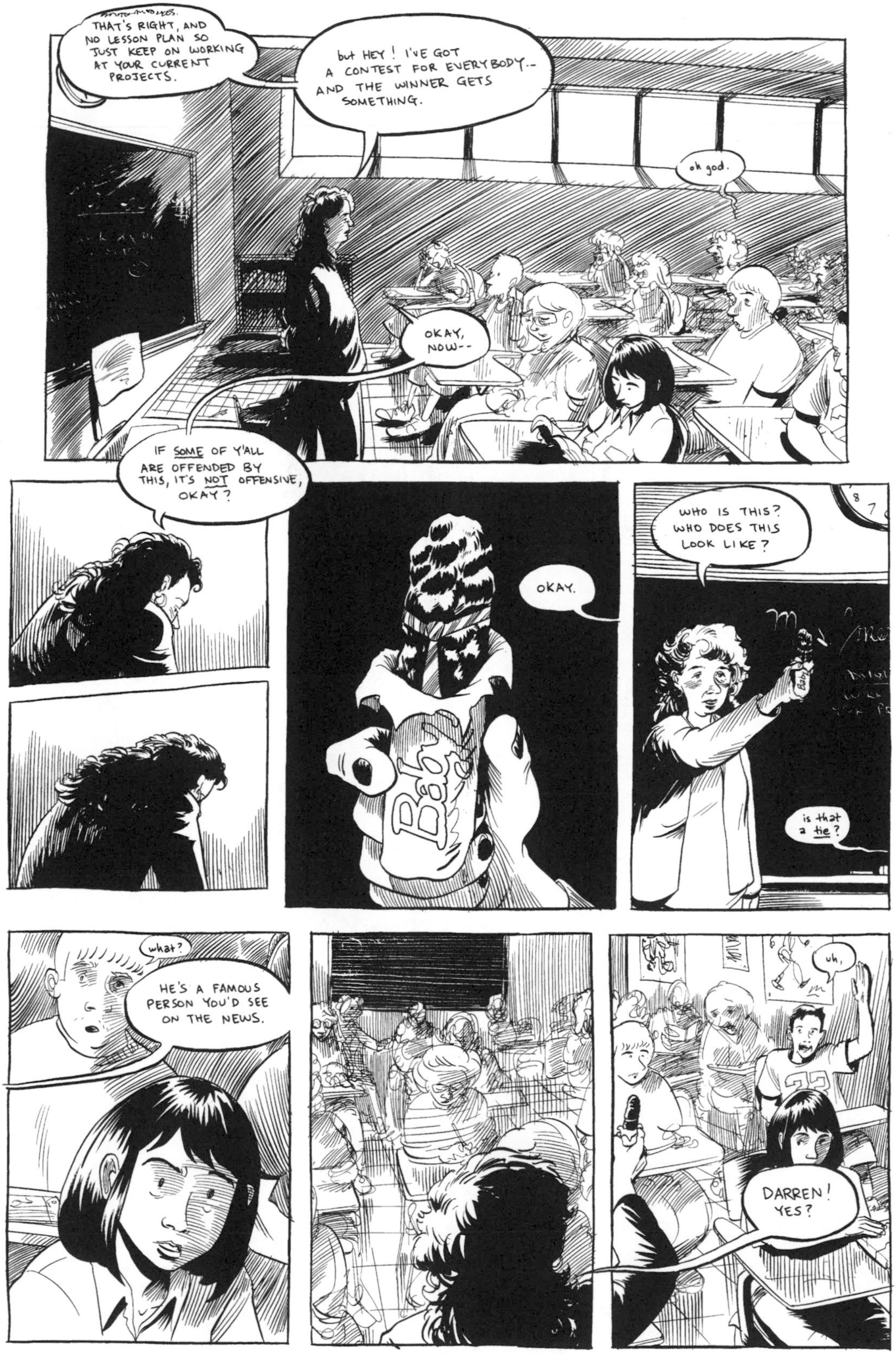
THAT'S RIGHT, AND NO LESSON PLAN SO JUST KEEP ON WORKING AT YOUR CURRENT PROJECTS.
but HEY ! I'VE GOT A CONTEST FOR EVERYBODY.- AND THE WINNER GETS SOMETHING.
oh god.
OKAY, NOW--
IF SOME OF Y'ALL ARE OFFENDED BY THIS, IT'S NOT OFFENSIVE, OKAY ?
OKAY.
Baby
WHO IS THIS? WHO DOES THIS LOOK LIKE ?
is that a tie ?
what?
HE'S A FAMOUS PERSON YOU'D SEE ON THE NEWS.
uh,
DARREN ! YES ?

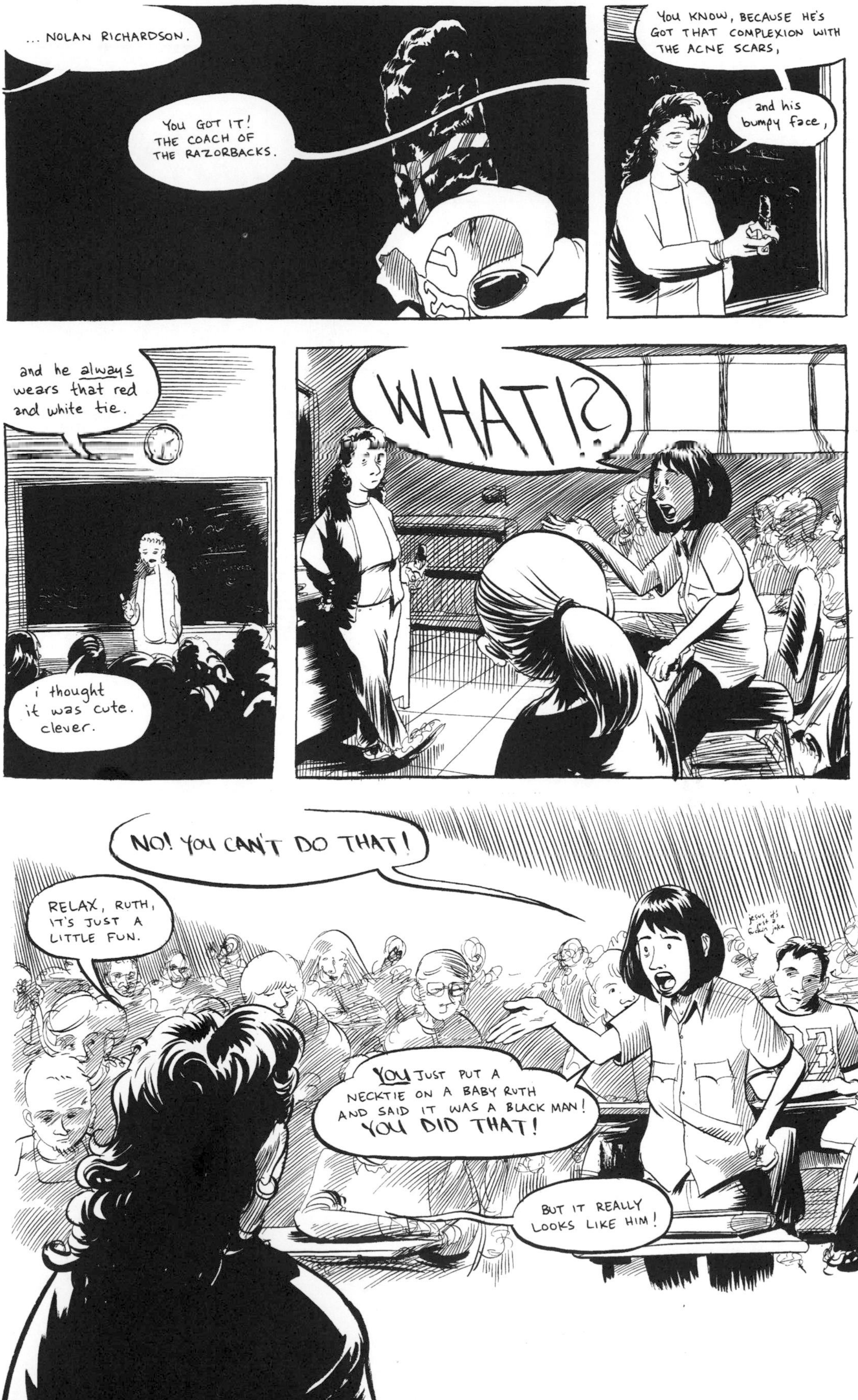
... NOLAN RICHARDSON.
YOU GOT IT! THE COACH OF THE RAZORBACKS.
YOU KNOW, BECAUSE HE'S GOT THAT COMPLEXION WITH THE ACNE SCARS,
and his bumpy face,
and he always wears that red and white tie.
i thought it was cute. clever.
WHAT!?
NO! YOU CAN'T DO THAT!
RELAX, RUTH, IT'S JUST A LITTLE FUN.
jesus it's just a fuckin joke
YOU JUST PUT A NECKTIE ON A BABY RUTH AND SAID IT WAS A BLACK MAN! YOU DID THAT!
BUT IT REALLY LOOKS LIKE HIM!

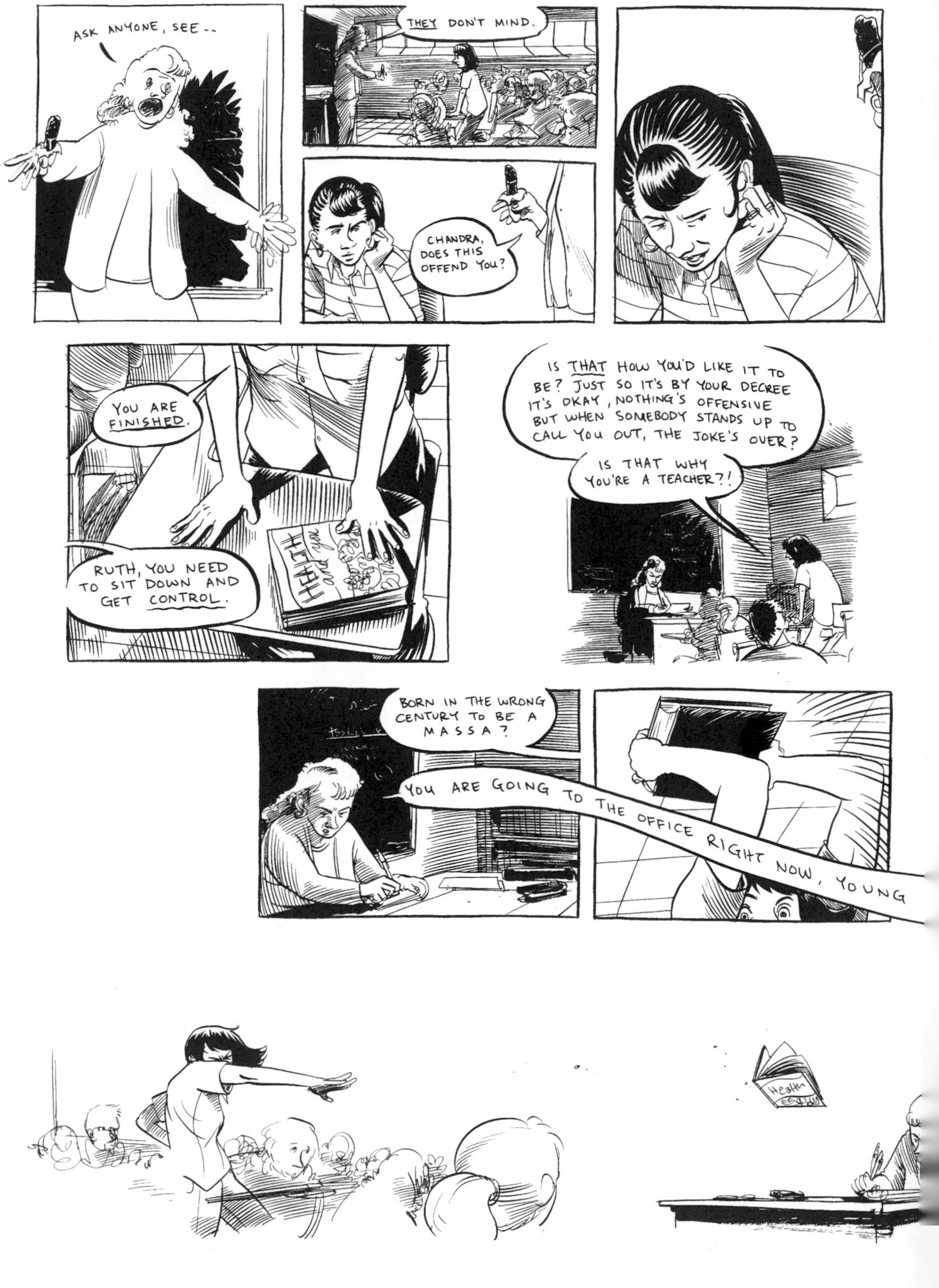
ASK ANYONE, SEE --
THEY DON'T MIND.
CHANDRA, DOES THIS OFFEND YOU?
YOU ARE FINISHED.
RUTH, YOU NEED TO SIT DOWN AND GET CONTROL.
HEALTH and you
IS THAT HOW YOU'D LIKE IT TO BE? JUST SO IT'S BY YOUR DECREE IT'S OKAY, NOTHING'S OFFENSIVE BUT WHEN SOMEBODY STANDS UP TO CALL YOU OUT, THE JOKE'S OVER?
IS THAT WHY YOU'RE A TEACHER?!
BORN IN THE WRONG CENTURY TO BE A MASSA?
YOU ARE GOING TO THE OFFICE RIGHT NOW, YOUNG
Health

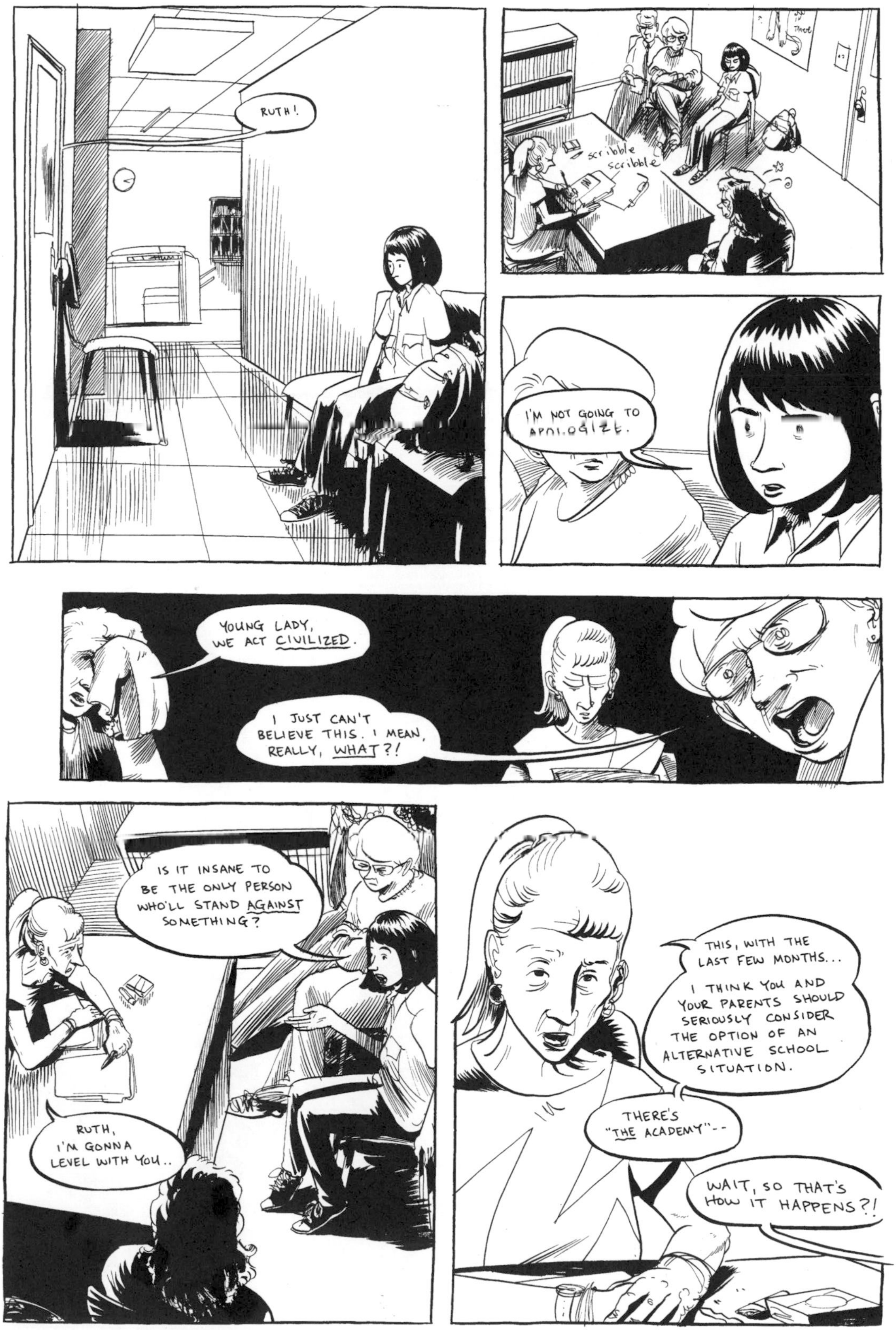
RUTH!
scribble
scribble
I'M NOT GOING TO APOLOGIZE.
YOUNG LADY, WE ACT CIVILIZED.
I JUST CAN'T BELIEVE THIS. I MEAN, REALLY, WHAT?!
IS IT INSANE TO BE THE ONLY PERSON WHO'LL STAND AGAINST SOMETHING?
RUTH, I'M GONNA LEVEL WITH YOU..
THIS, WITH THE LAST FEW MONTHS...
I THINK YOU AND YOUR PARENTS SHOULD SERIOUSLY CONSIDER THE OPTION OF AN ALTERNATIVE SCHOOL SITUATION.
THERE'S "THE ACADEMY"--
WAIT, SO THAT'S HOW IT HAPPENS?!

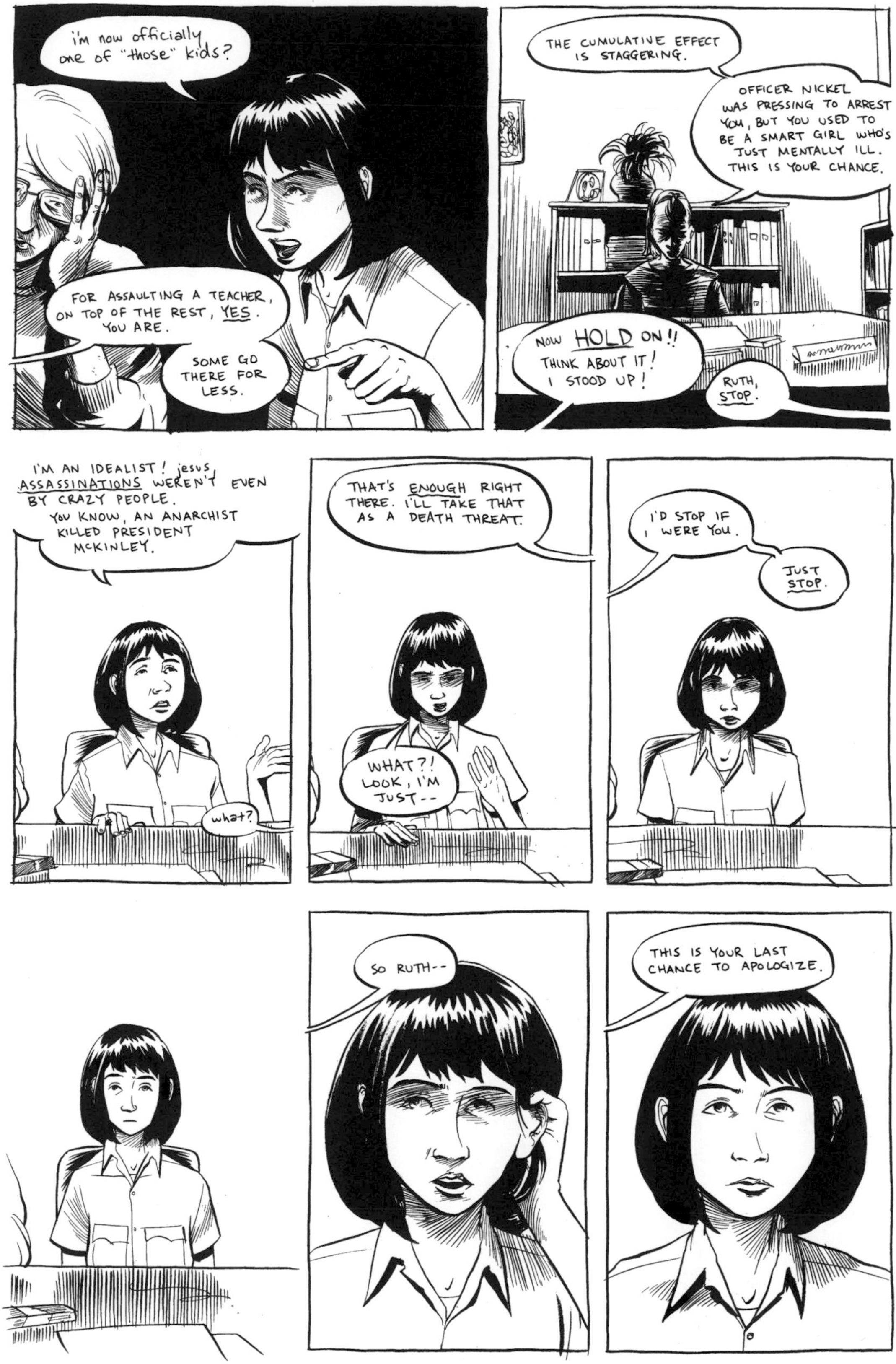
i'm now officially one of "those" kids?
FOR ASSAULTING A TEACHER, ON TOP OF THE REST, YES. YOU ARE.
SOME GO THERE FOR LESS.
THE CUMULATIVE EFFECT IS STAGGERING.
OFFICER NICKEL WAS PRESSING TO ARREST YOU, BUT YOU USED TO BE A SMART GIRL WHO'S JUST MENTALLY ILL. THIS IS YOUR CHANCE.
NOW HOLD ON!! THINK ABOUT IT! I STOOD UP!
RUTH, STOP.
I'M AN IDEALIST! jesus, ASSASSINATIONS WEREN'T EVEN BY CRAZY PEOPLE. YOU KNOW, AN ANARCHIST KILLED PRESIDENT McKINLEY.
what?
THAT'S ENOUGH RIGHT THERE. I'LL TAKE THAT AS A DEATH THREAT.
WHAT?! LOOK, I'M JUST--
I'D STOP IF I WERE YOU.
JUST STOP.
SO RUTH--
THIS IS YOUR LAST CHANCE TO APOLOGIZE.

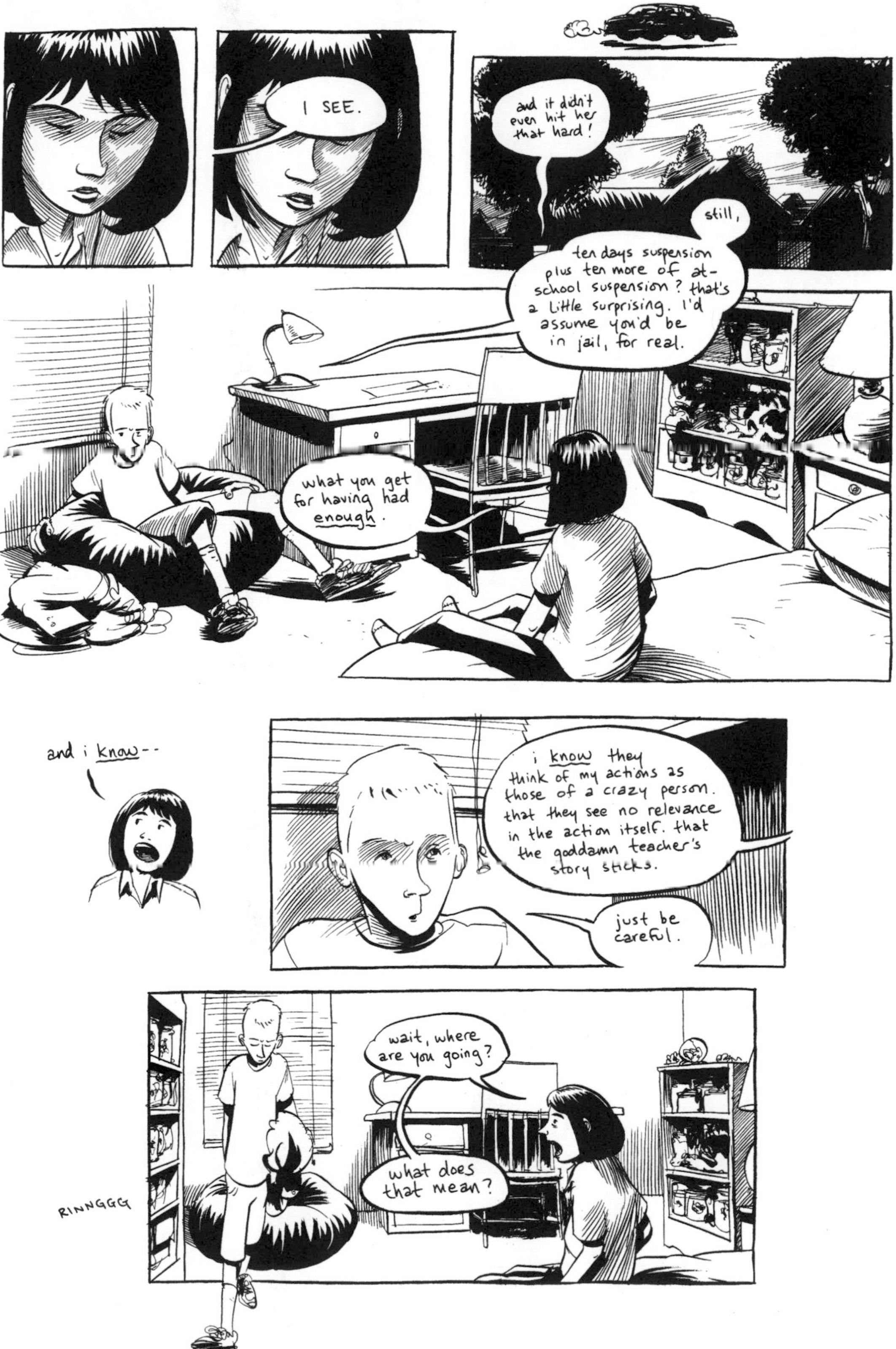
I SEE.
and it didn't even hit her that hard!
still,
ten days suspension plus ten more of at-school suspension? that's a little surprising. I'd assume you'd be in jail, for real.
what you get for having had enough.
and i know--
i know they think of my actions as those of a crazy person. that they see no relevance in the action itself. that the goddamn teacher's story sticks.
just be careful.
wait, where are you going?
what does that mean?
RINNGGG

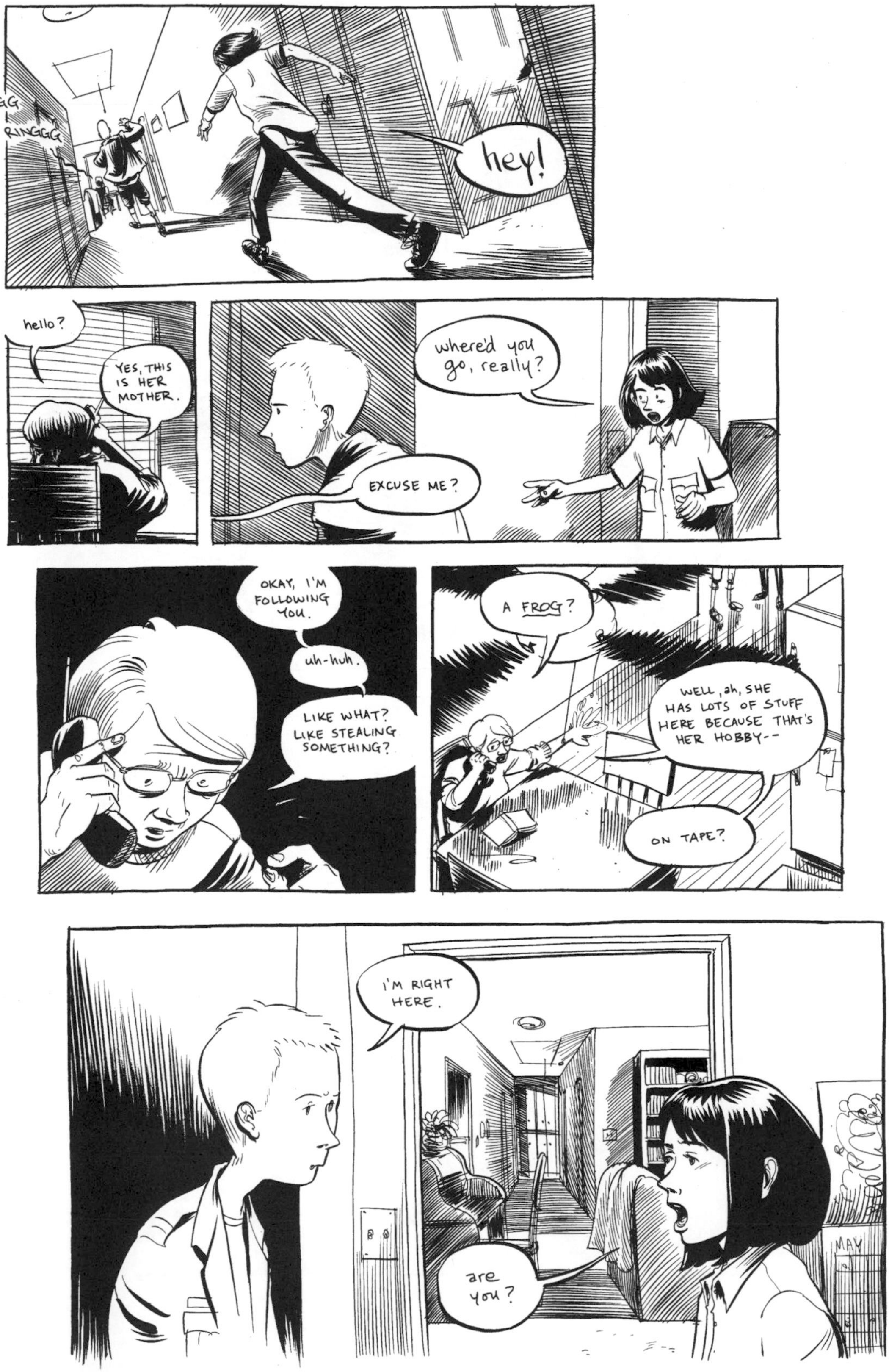
RINGGG
RINGGG
hey!
hello?
YES, THIS IS HER MOTHER.
where'd you go, really?
EXCUSE ME?
OKAY, I'M FOLLOWING YOU.
uh-huh.
LIKE WHAT? LIKE STEALING SOMETHING?
A FROG?
WELL, ah, SHE HAS LOTS OF STUFF HERE BECAUSE THAT'S HER HOBBY--
ON TAPE?
I'M RIGHT HERE.
are you?
MAY

SHOULD-- SHOULD I GET HER?
YES. BYE.
RUTH!!!
YOU AR
IN SOM
DEEP
NOW

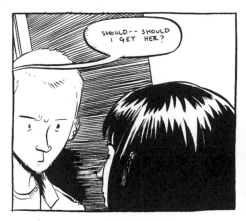

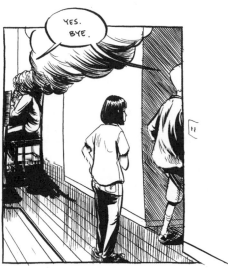

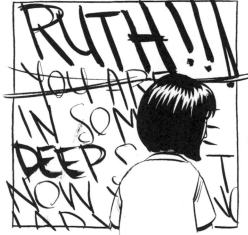

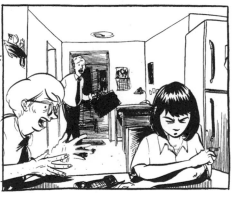

DEANNA PEAZAL
COUNSELLOR

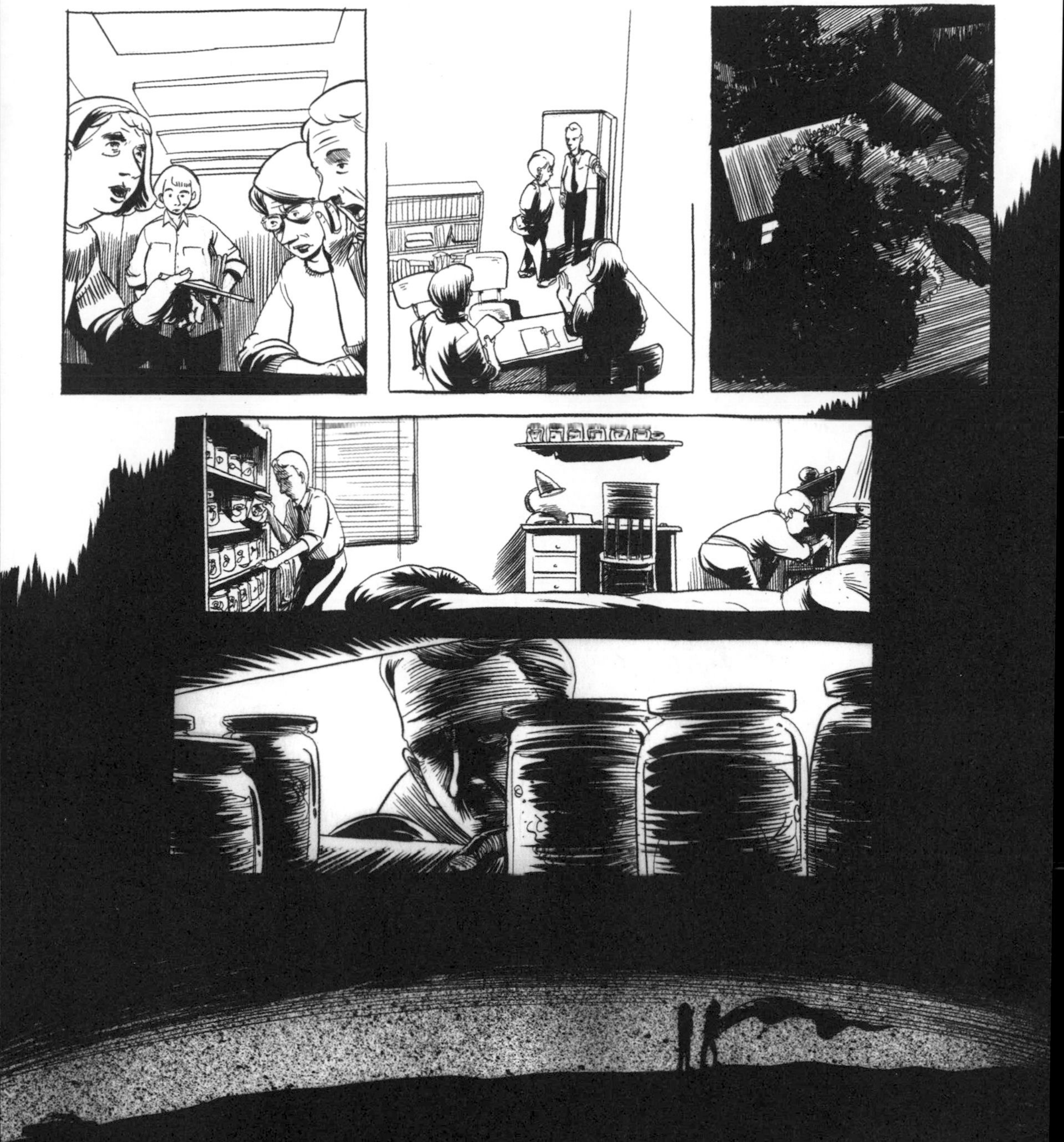

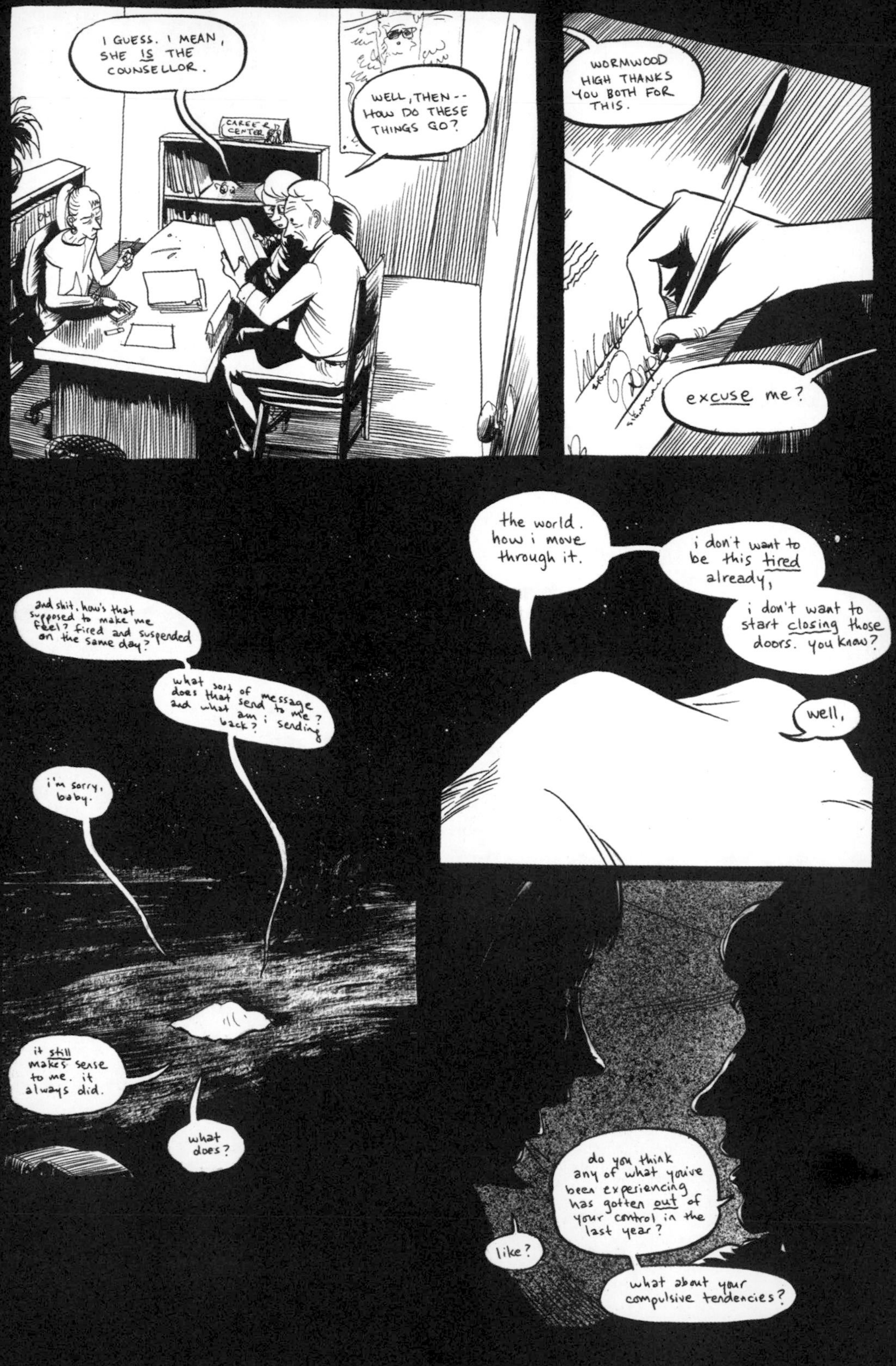
I GUESS. I MEAN, SHE IS THE COUNSELLOR.
CAREER CENTER
WELL, THEN-- HOW DO THESE THINGS GO?
WORMWOOD HIGH THANKS YOU BOTH FOR THIS.
excuse me?
the world. how i move through it.
i don't want to be this tired already,
i don't want to start closing those doors. you know?
well,
and shit, how's that supposed to make me feel? fired and suspended on the same day?
what sort of message does that send to me? and what am i sending back?
i'm sorry, baby.
it still makes sense to me. it always did.
what does?
do you think any of what you've been experiencing has gotten out of your control in the last year?
like?
what about your compulsive tendencies?

it's -- it's not a big deal.
just what i like to do.
do you like it? or do you obey it?

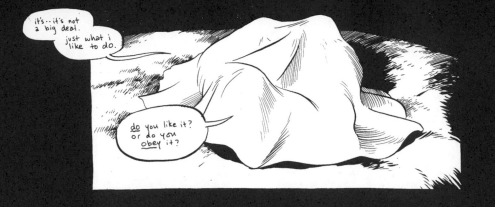

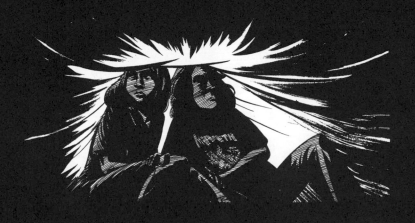

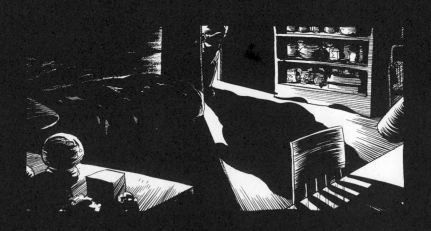

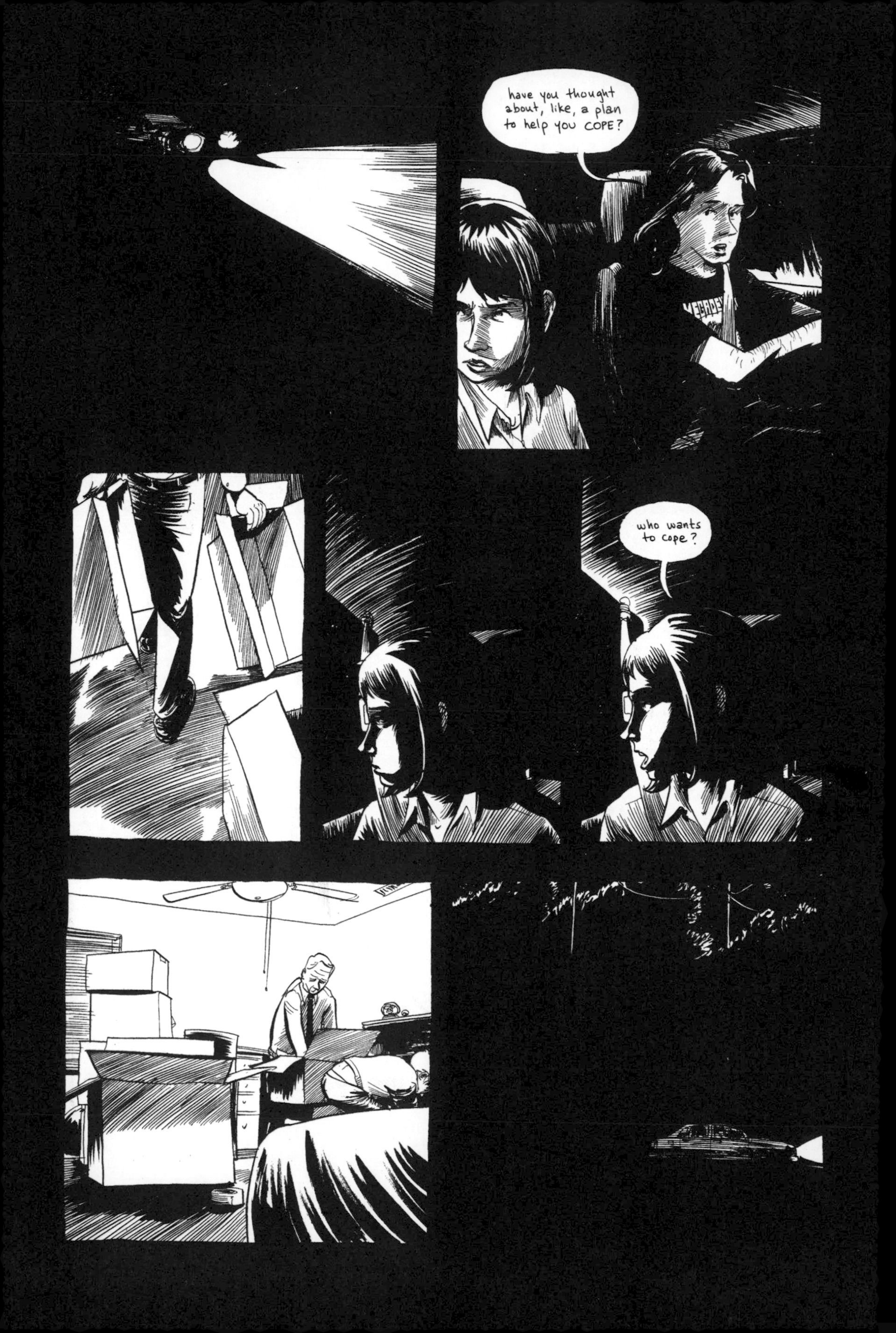
have you thought about, like, a plan to help you COPE?
who wants to cope?

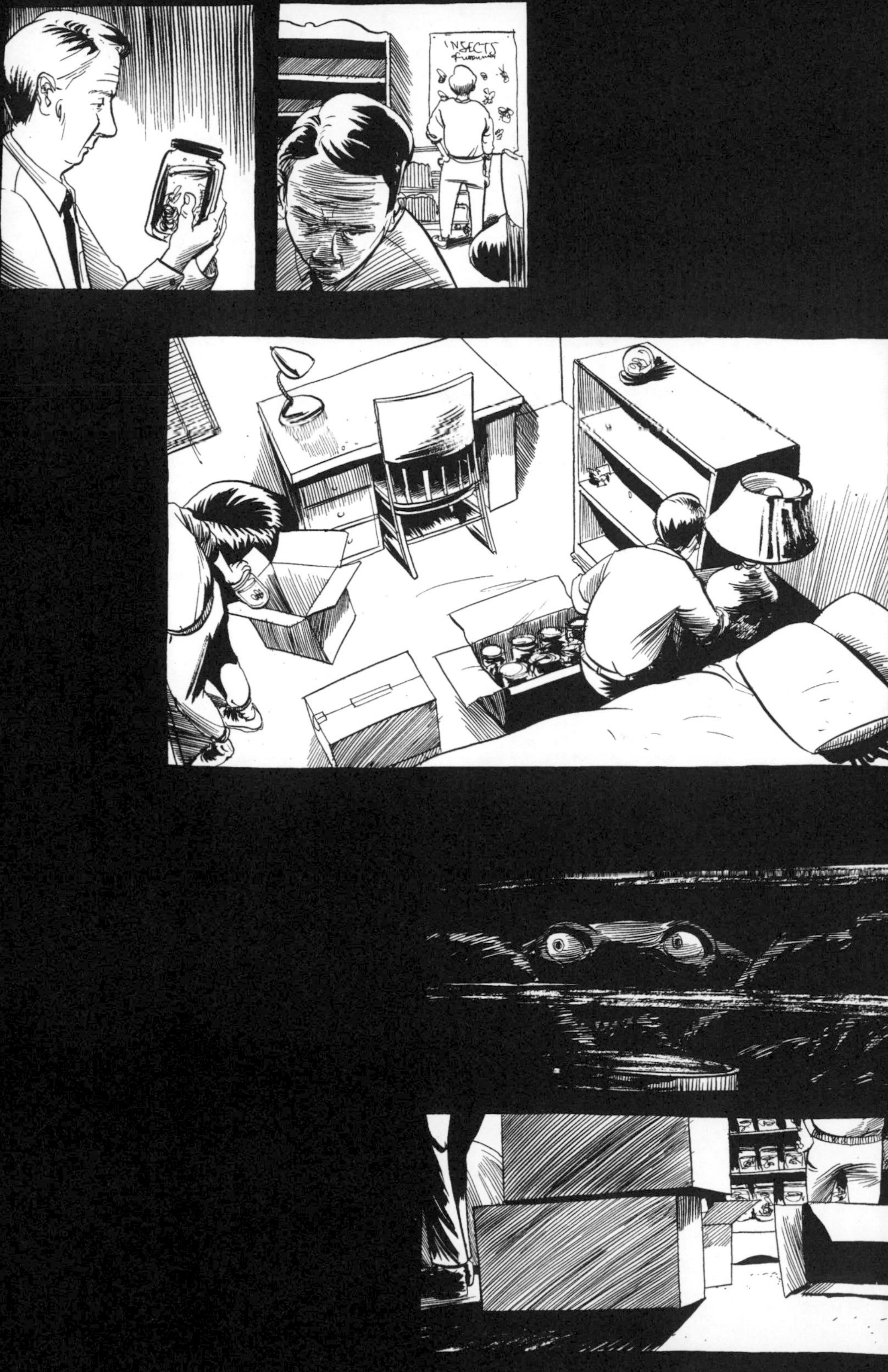
INSECTS

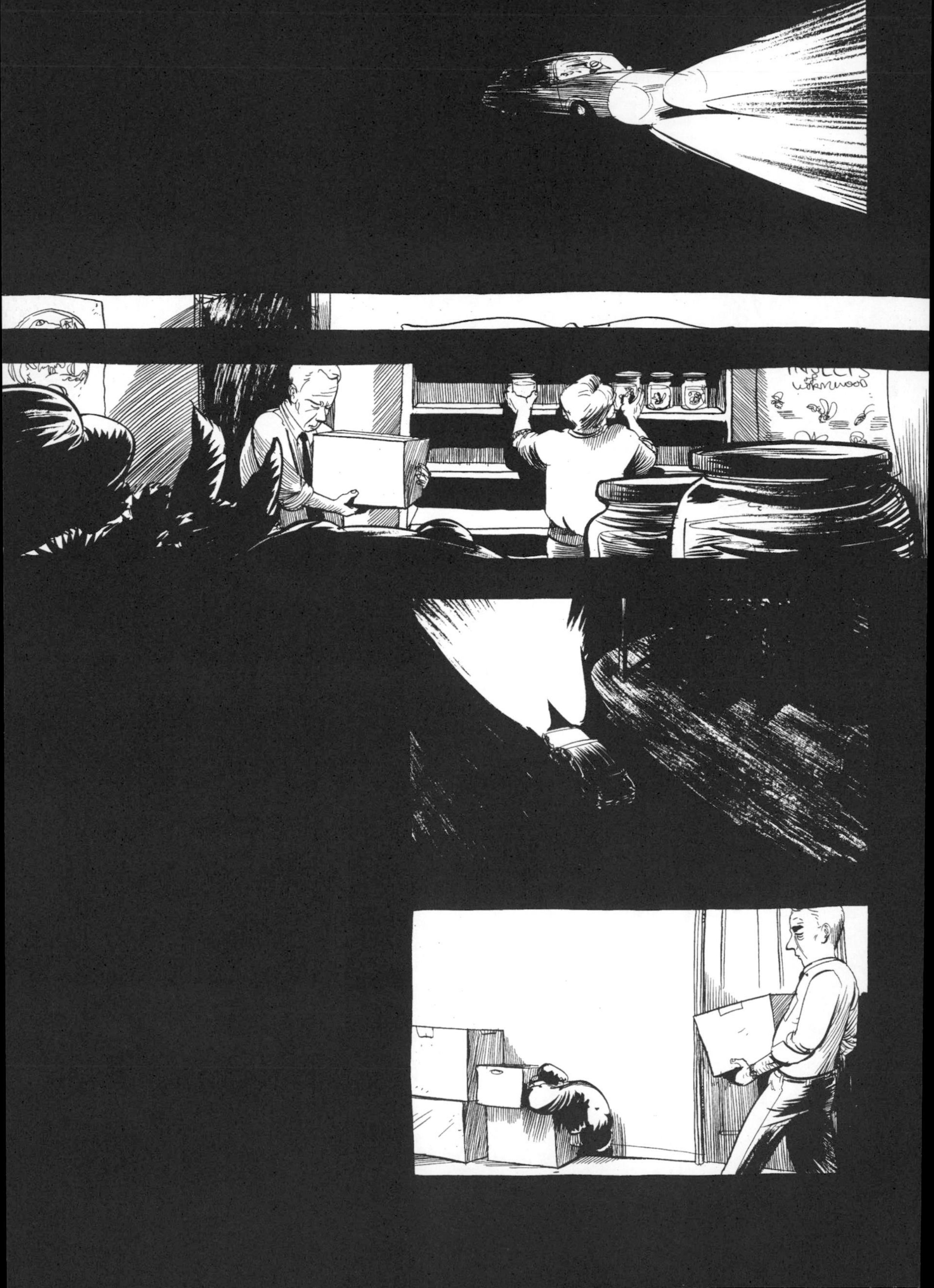

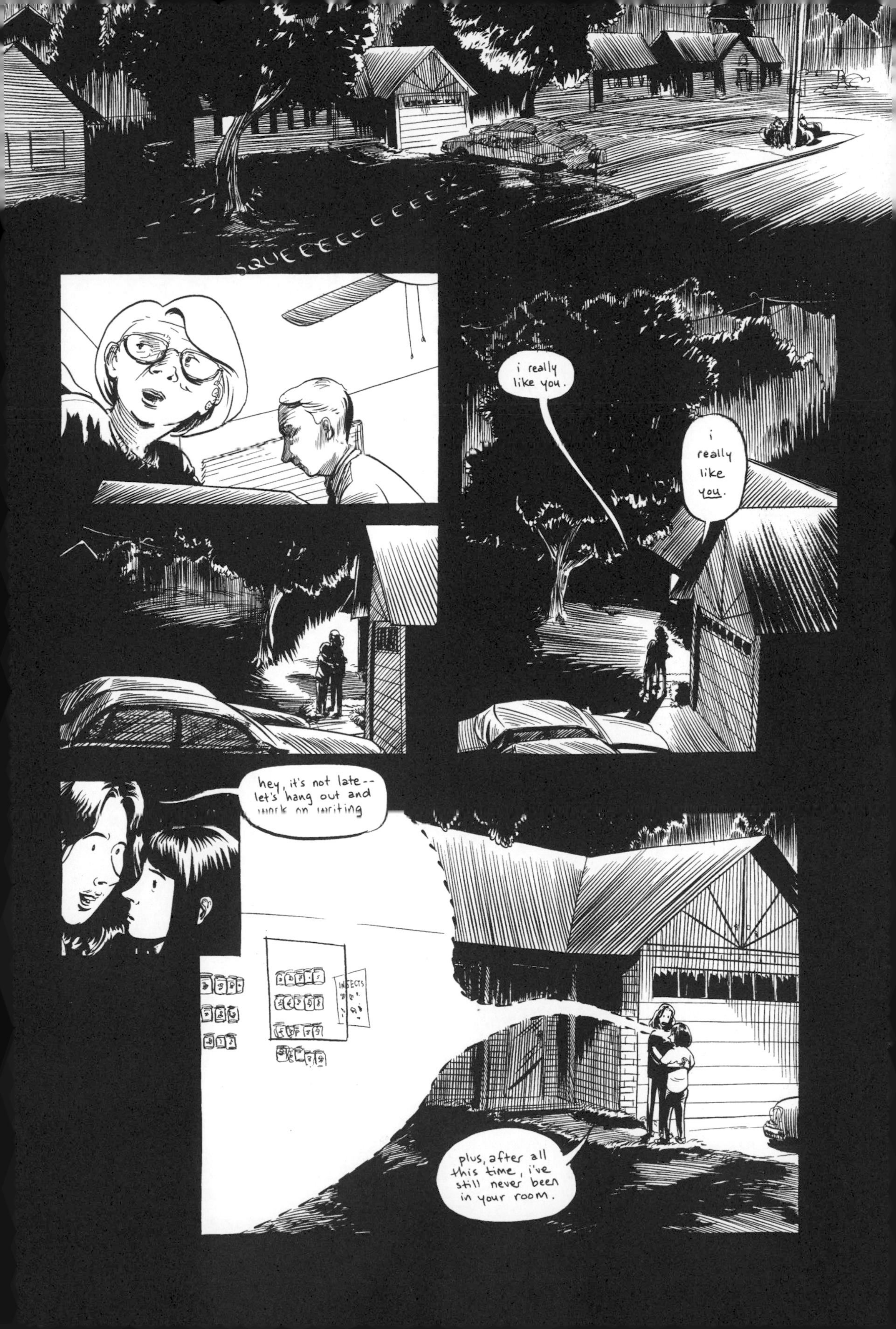
SQUEEEEEEEEEEE*
i really like you.
i really like you.
hey, it's not late-- let's hang out and work on writing
INSECTS
plus, after all this time, i've still never been in your room.

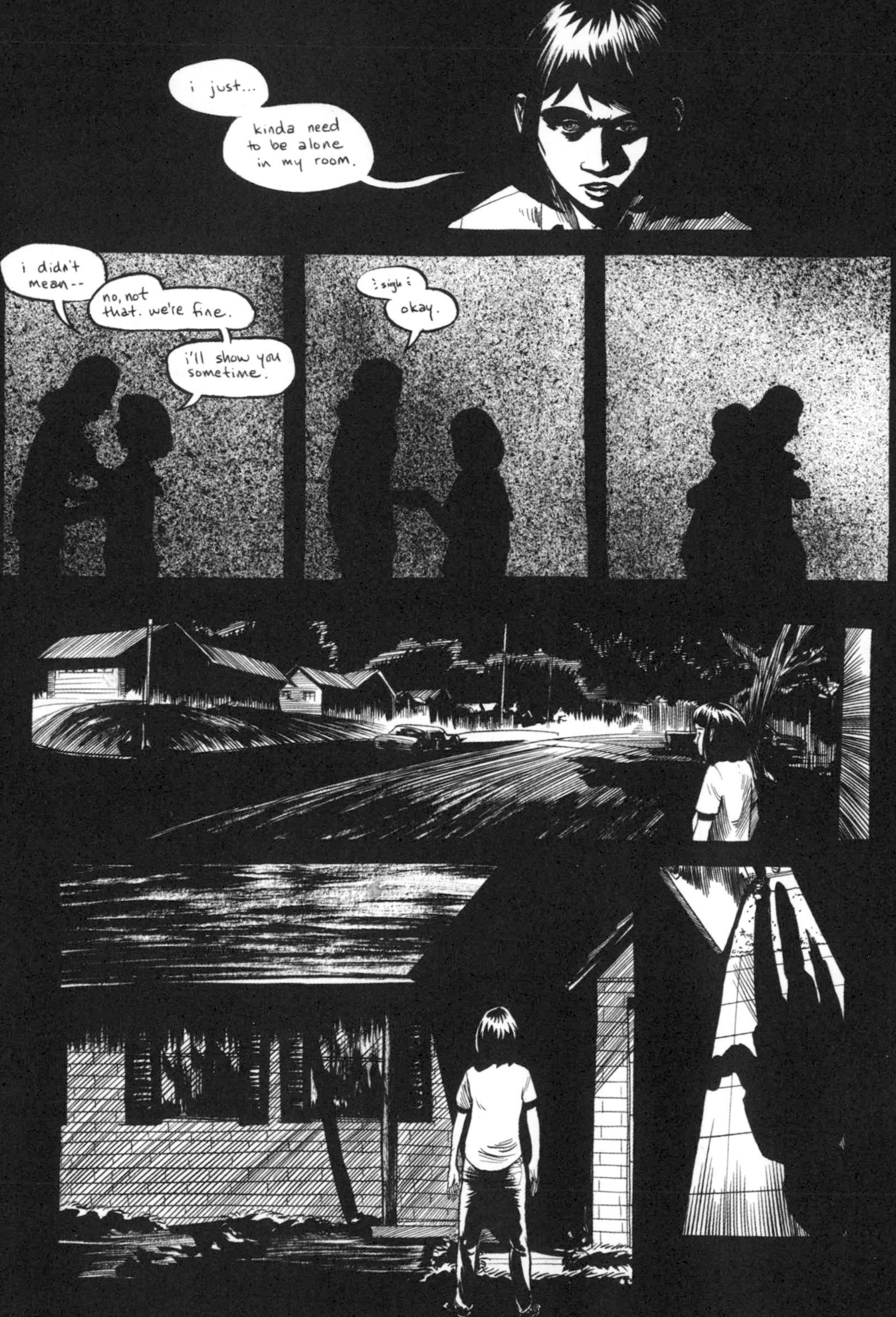
i just...
kinda need to be alone in my room.
i didn't mean--
no, not that. we're fine.
i'll show you sometime.
:sigh:
okay.

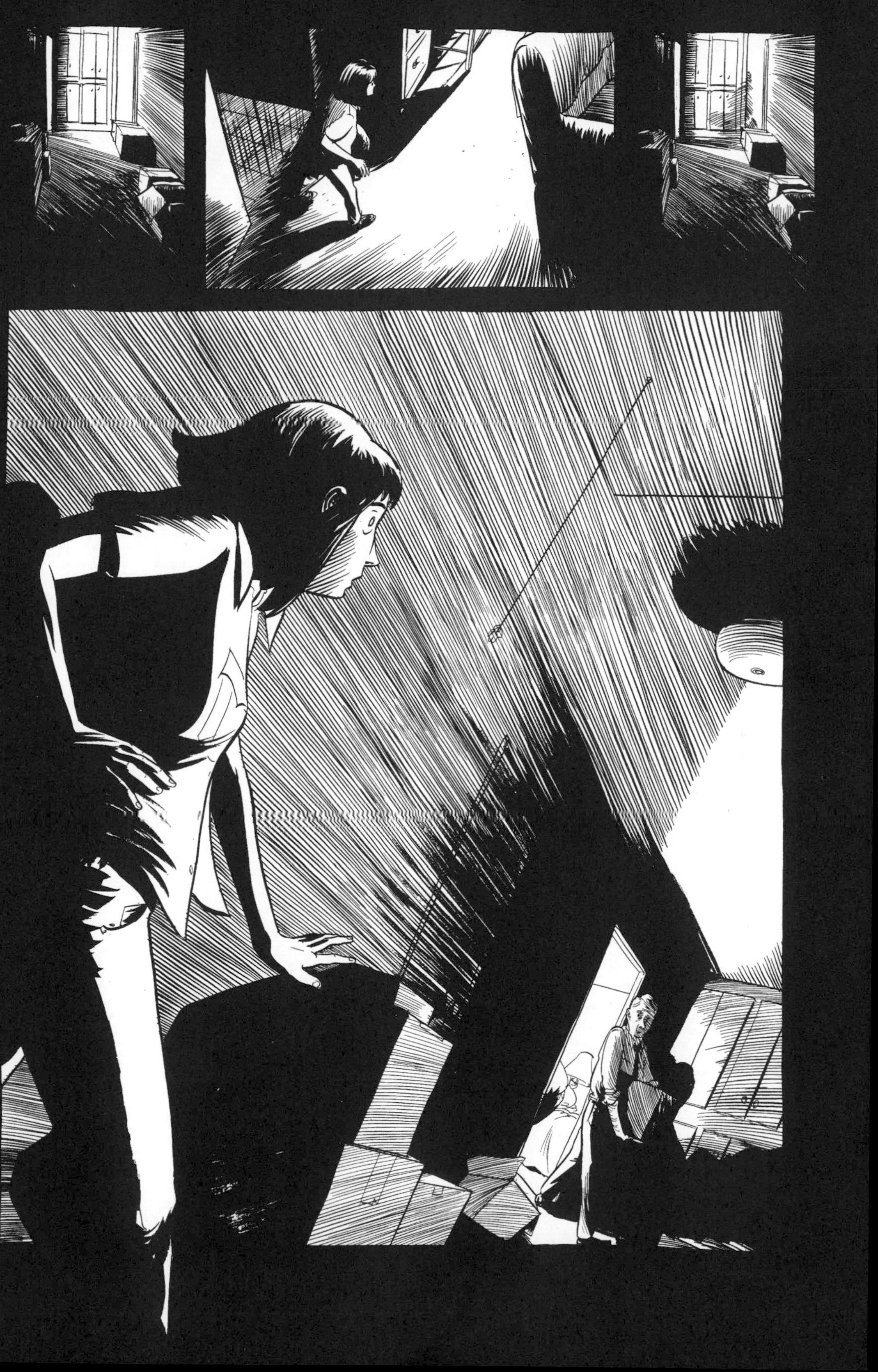

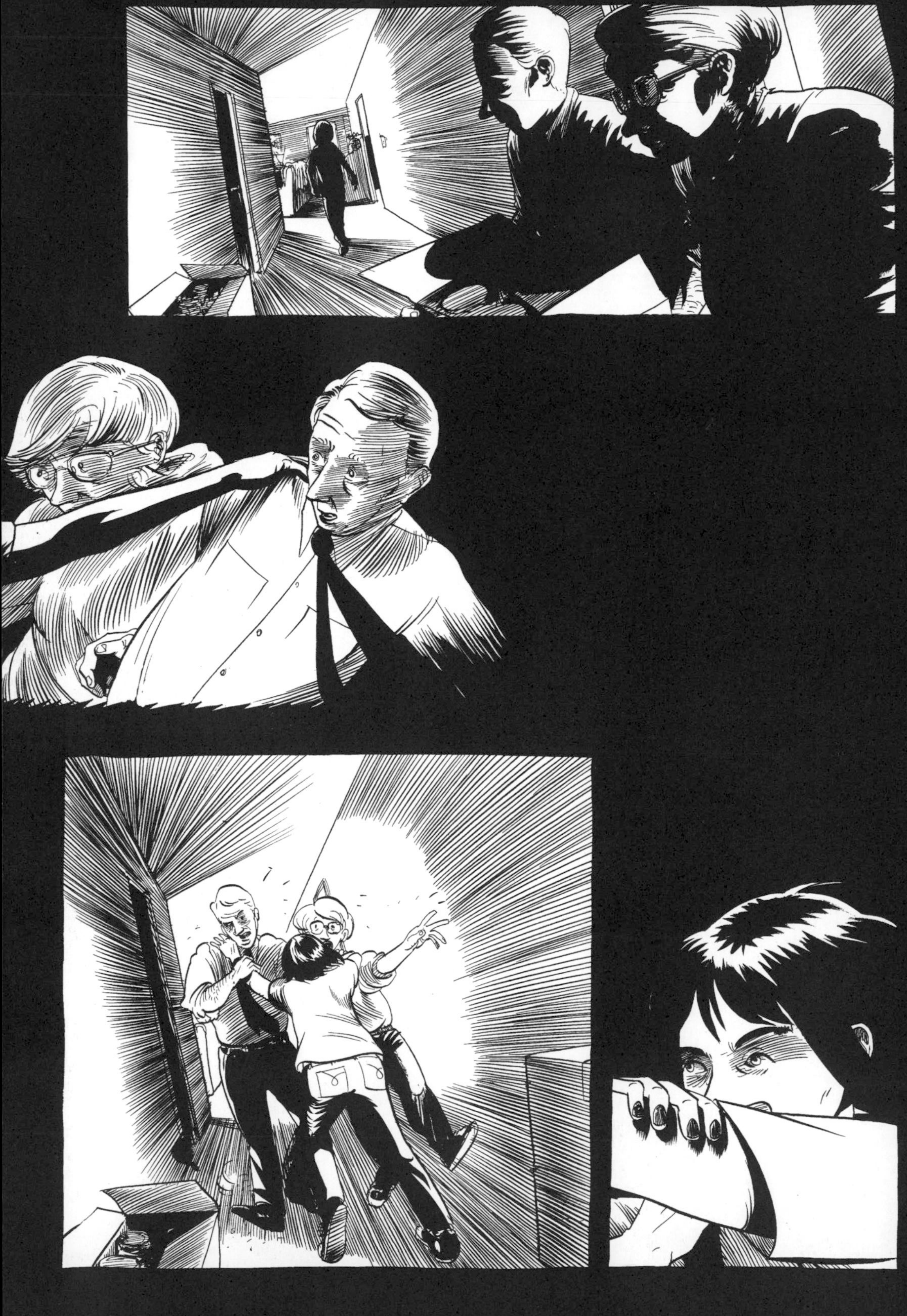

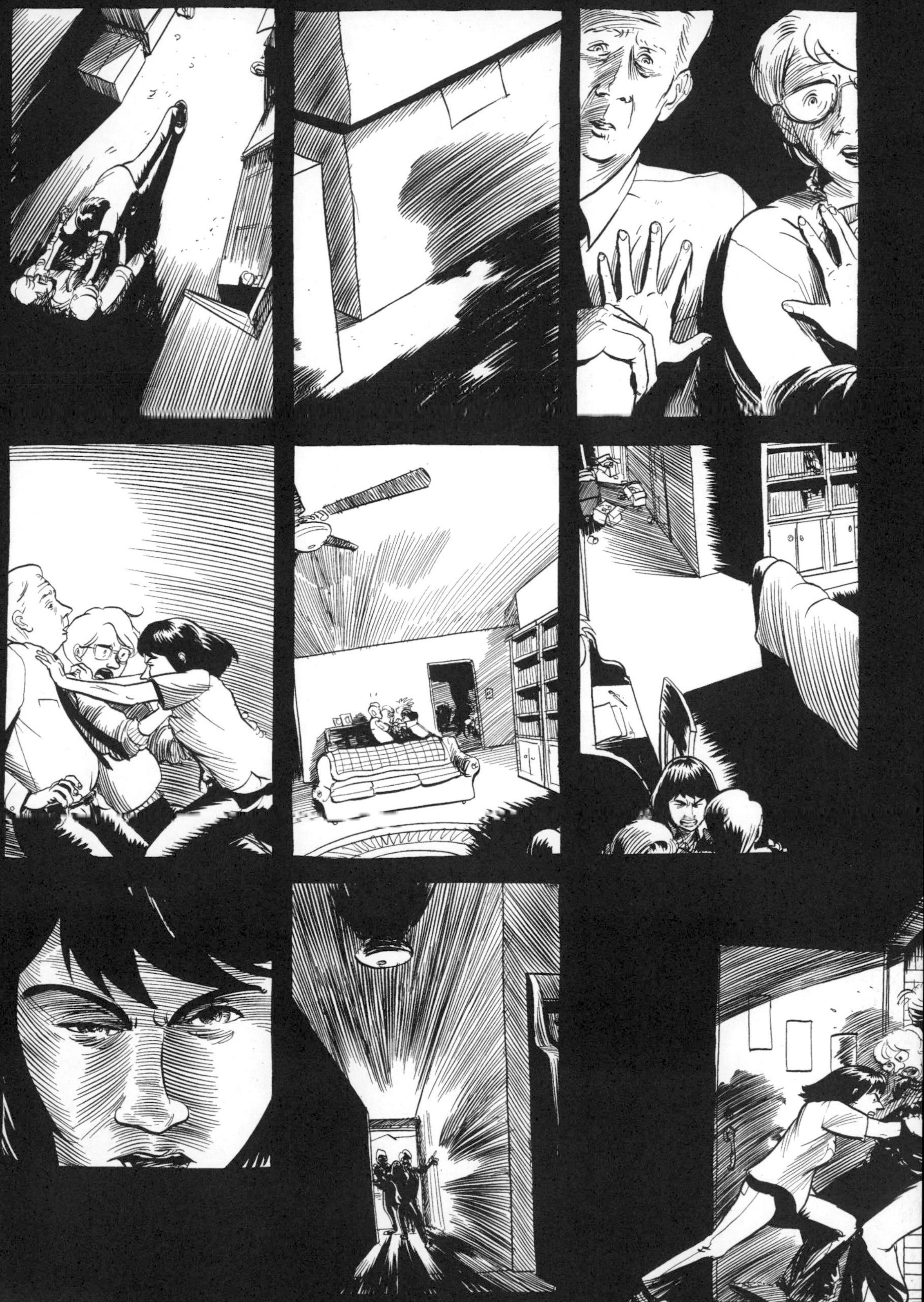

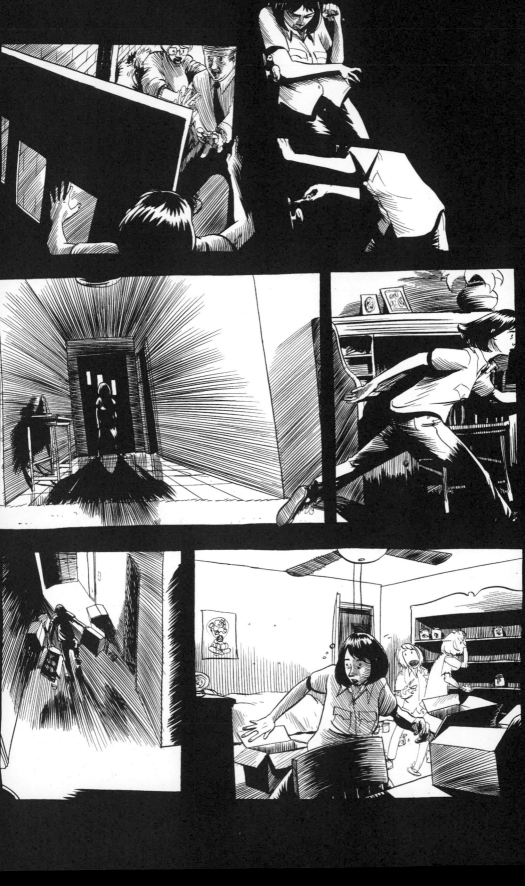

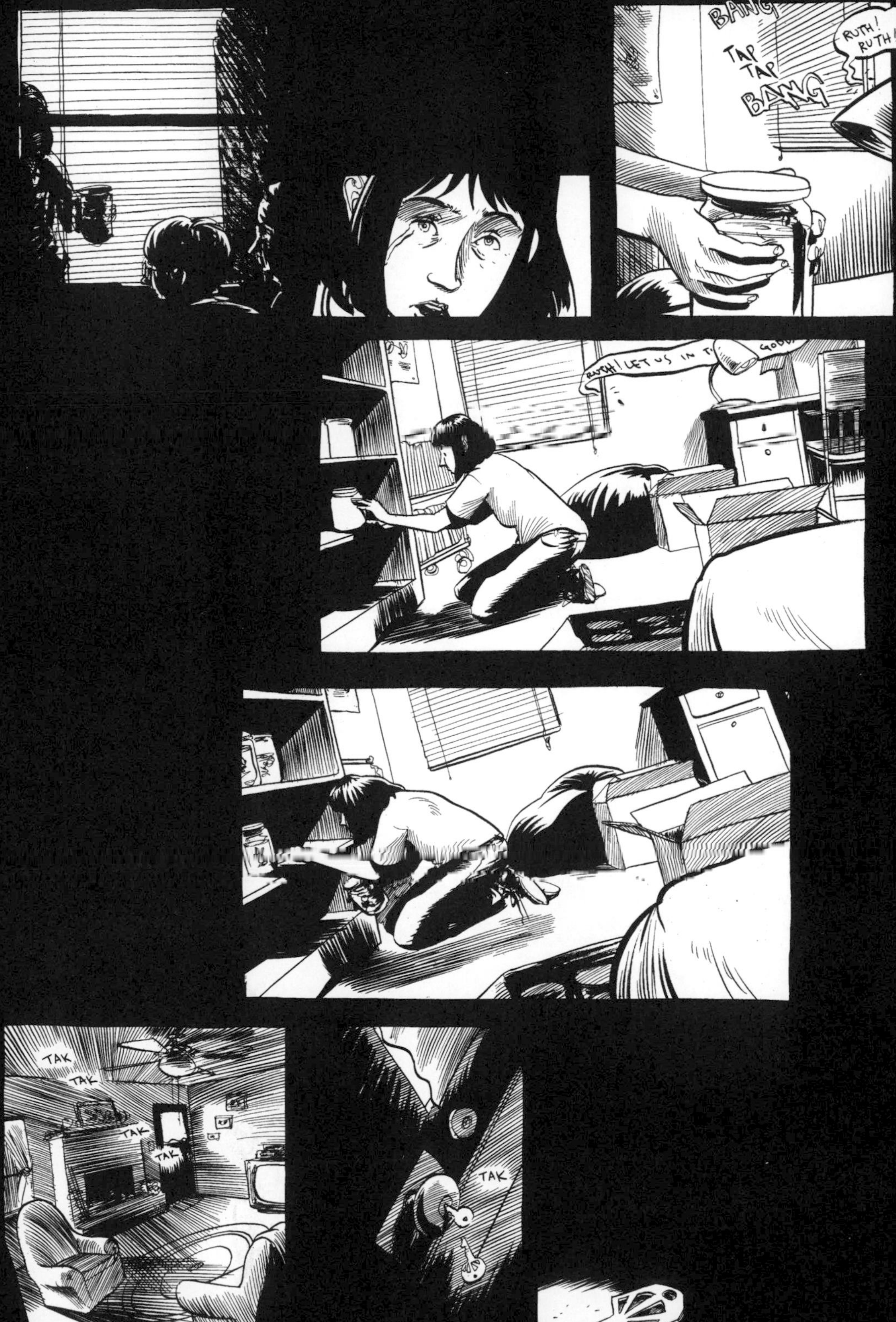
BANG
TAP TAP
BANG
RUTH! RUTH!!
RUTH! LET US IN
TAK
TAK
TAK
TAK
TAK

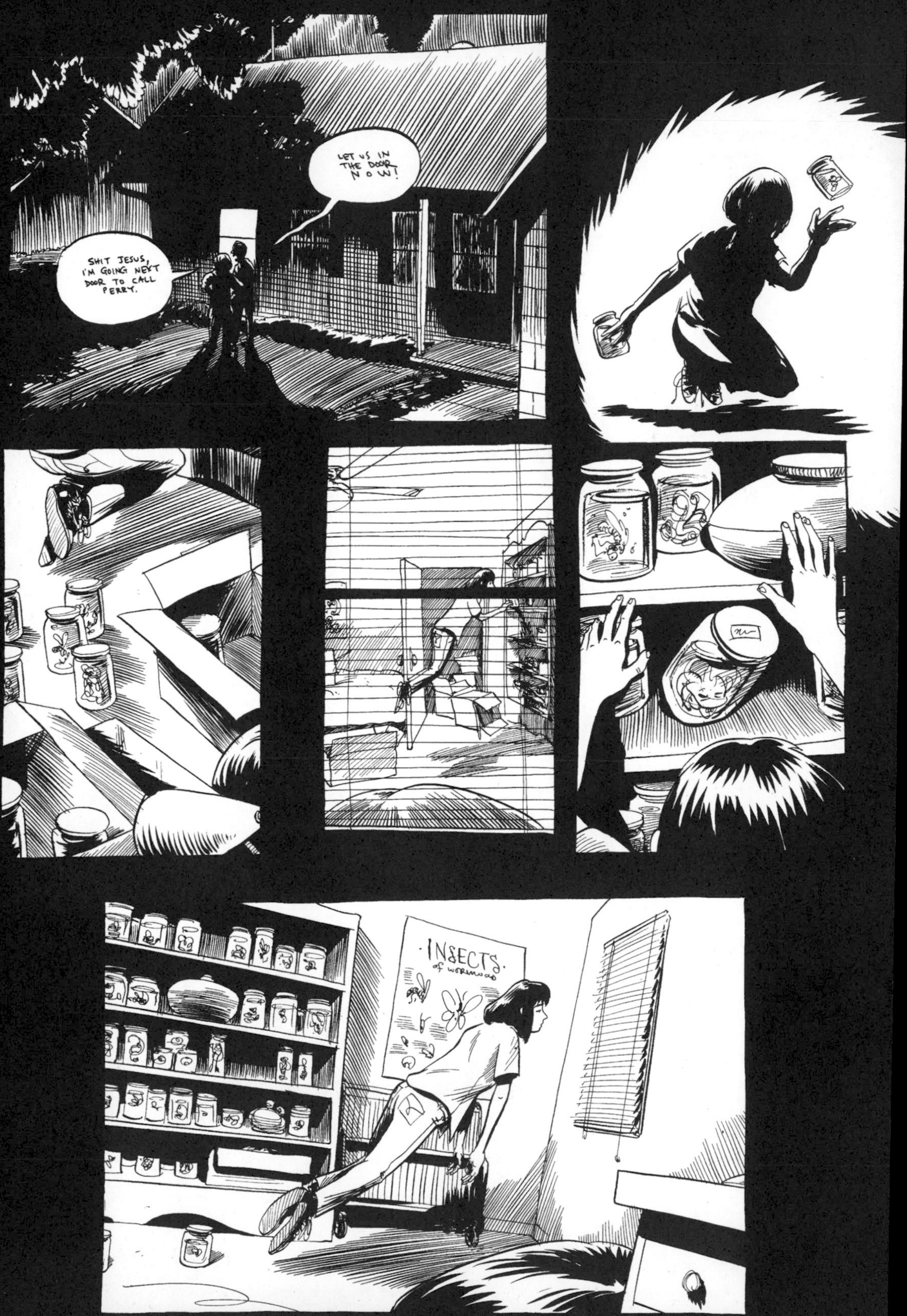
LET US IN THE DOOR NOW!
SHIT JESUS, I'M GOING NEXT DOOR TO CALL PERRY.
INSECTS
of wormwood

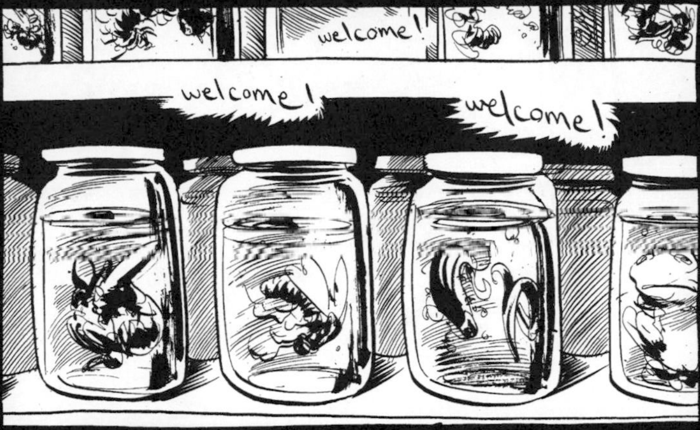
welcome!
welcome!
welcome!

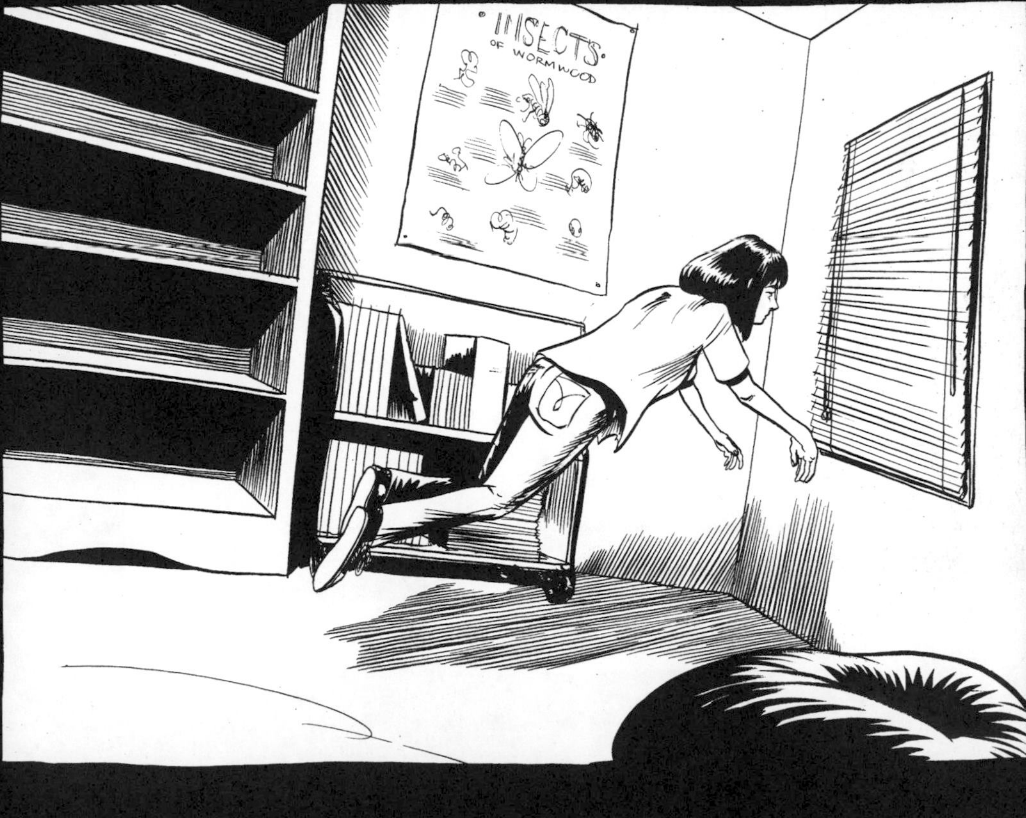
INSECTS
OF WORMWOOD

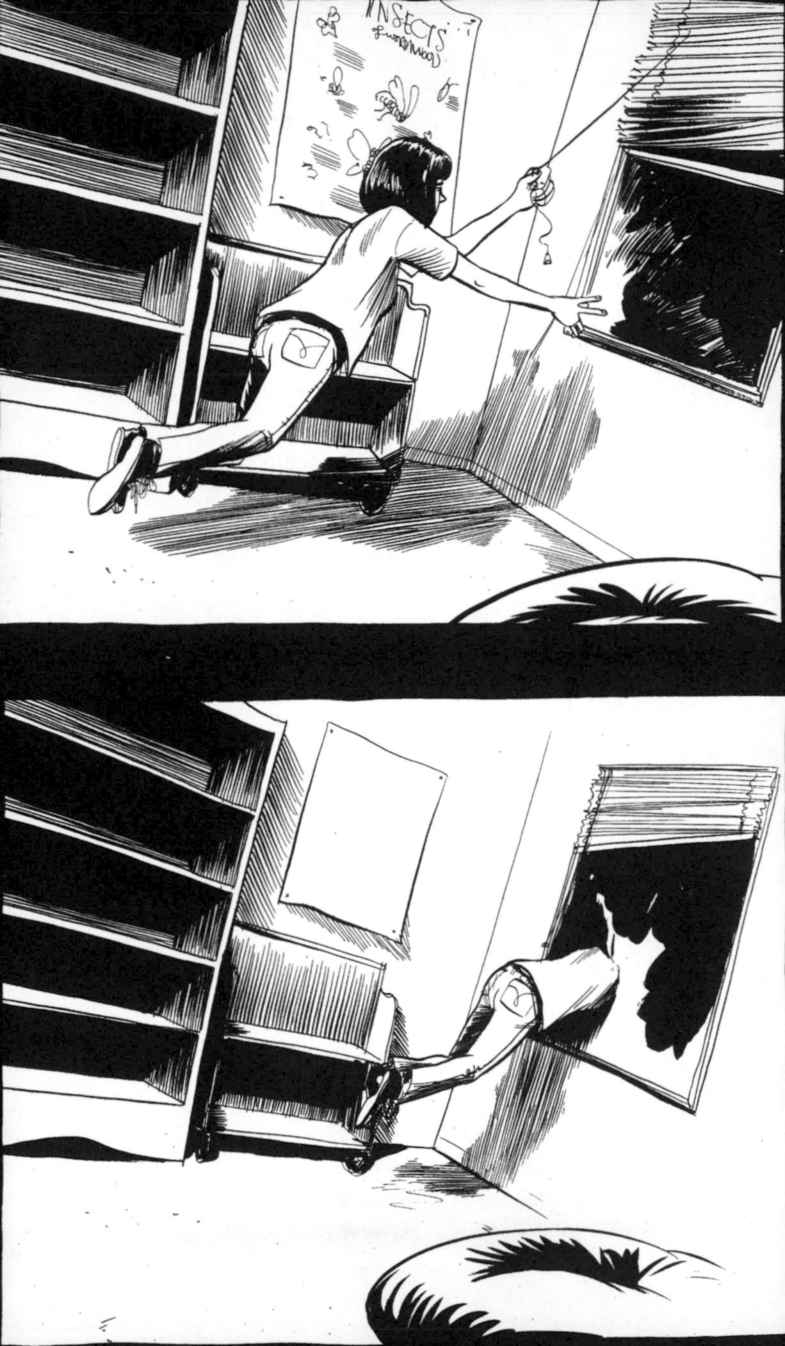
INSECTS

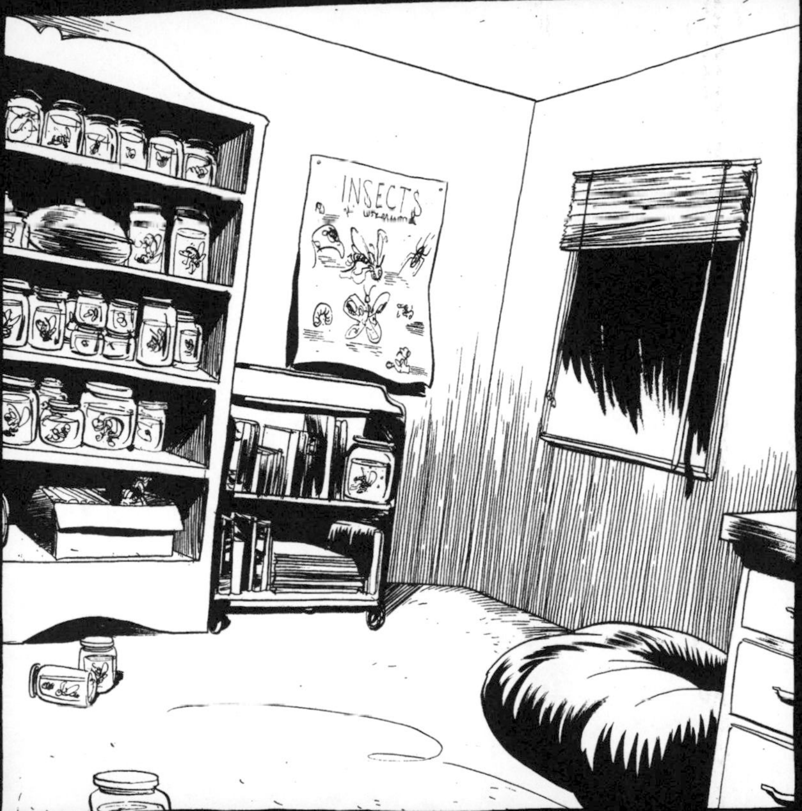
INSECTS

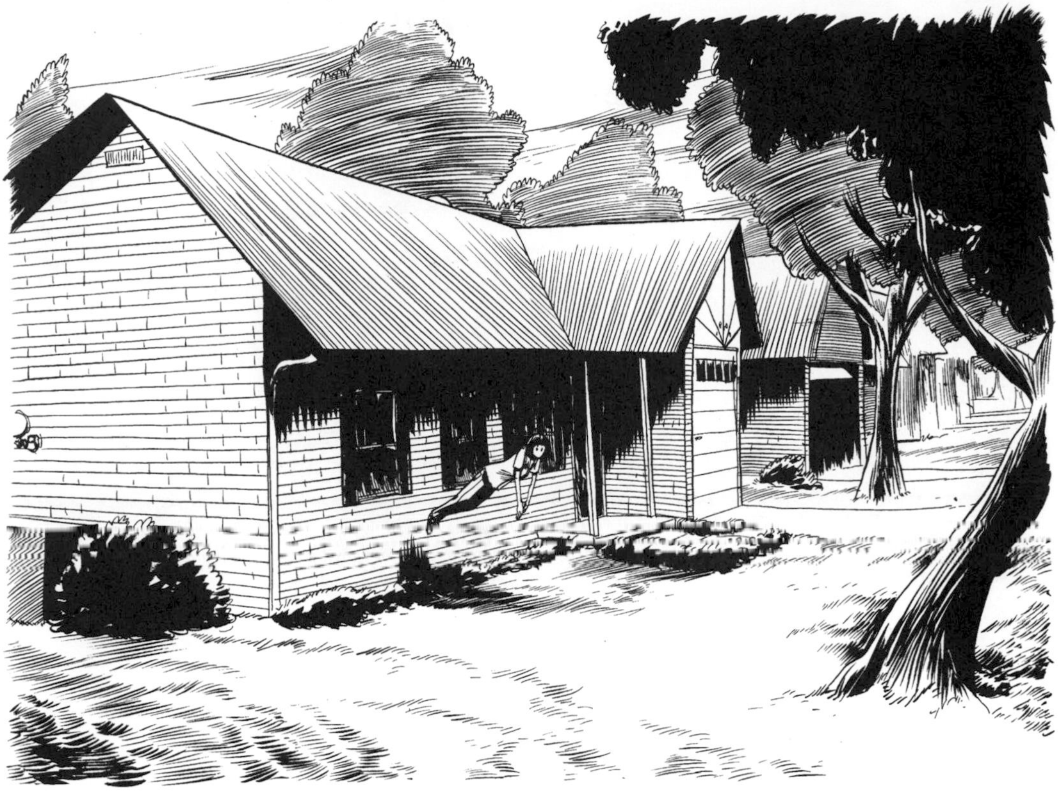

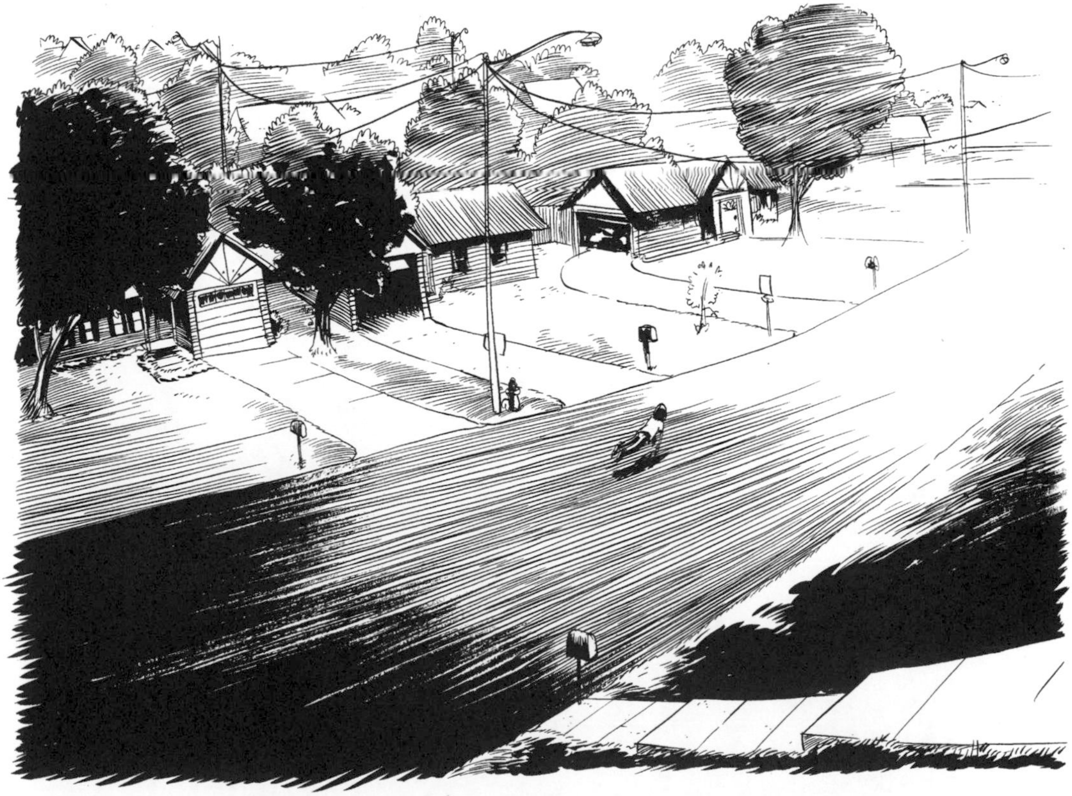

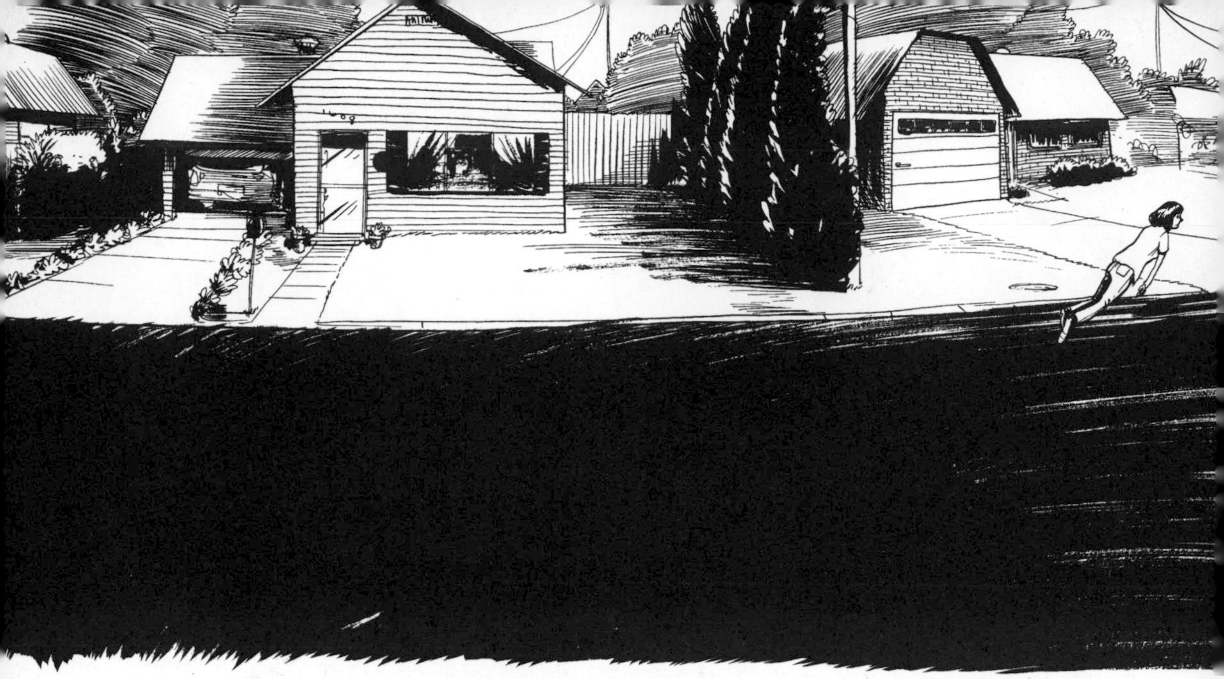

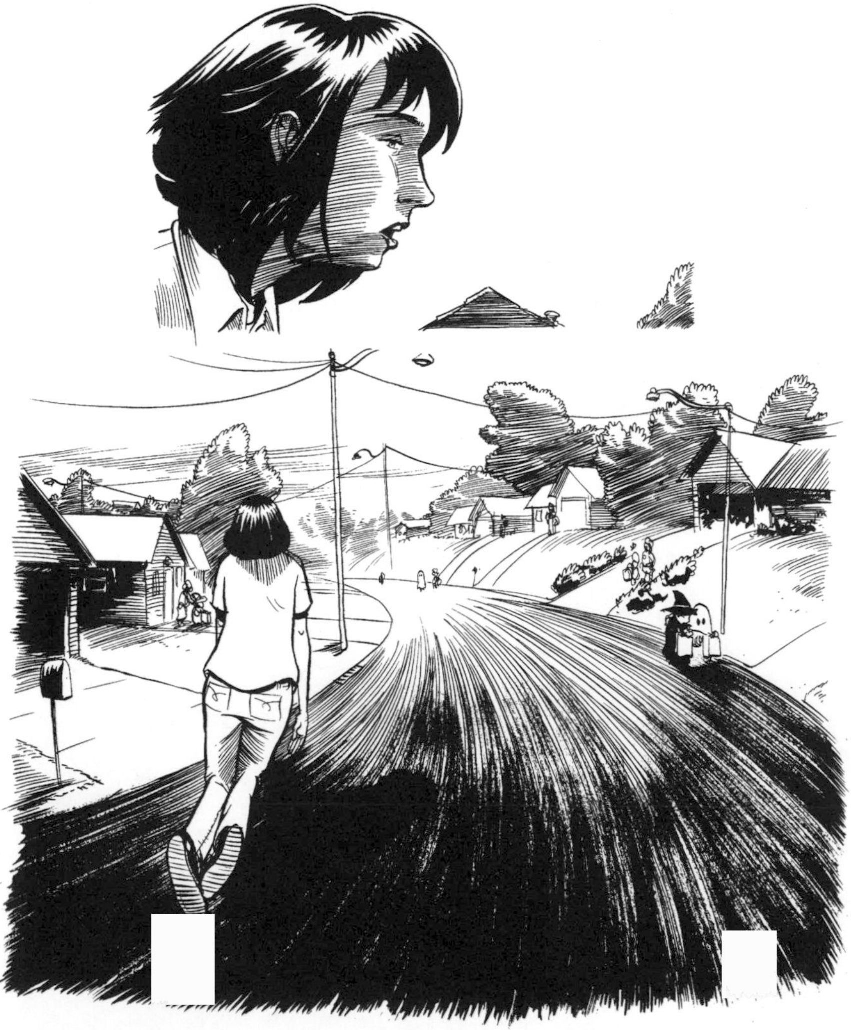

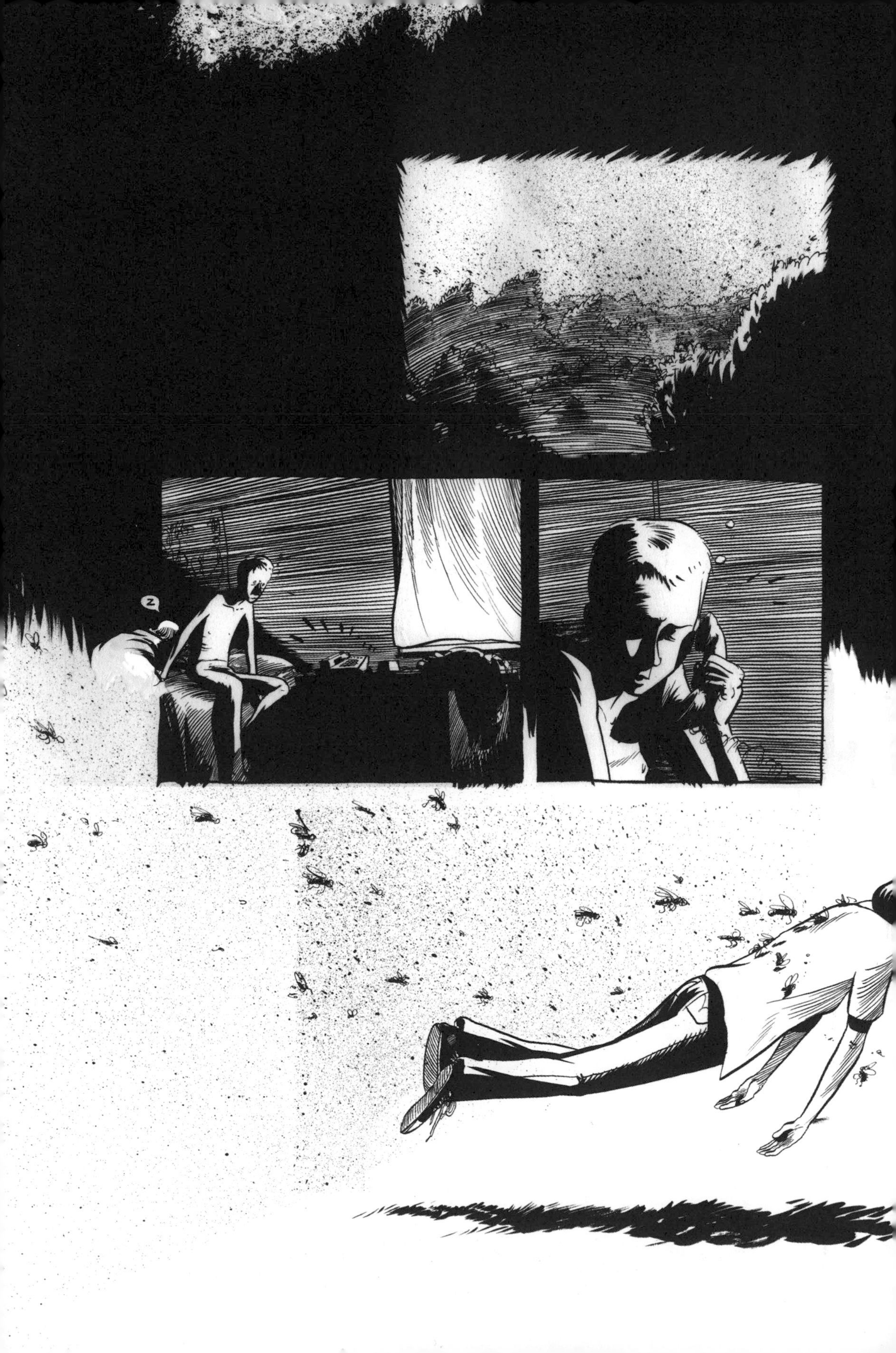
Z

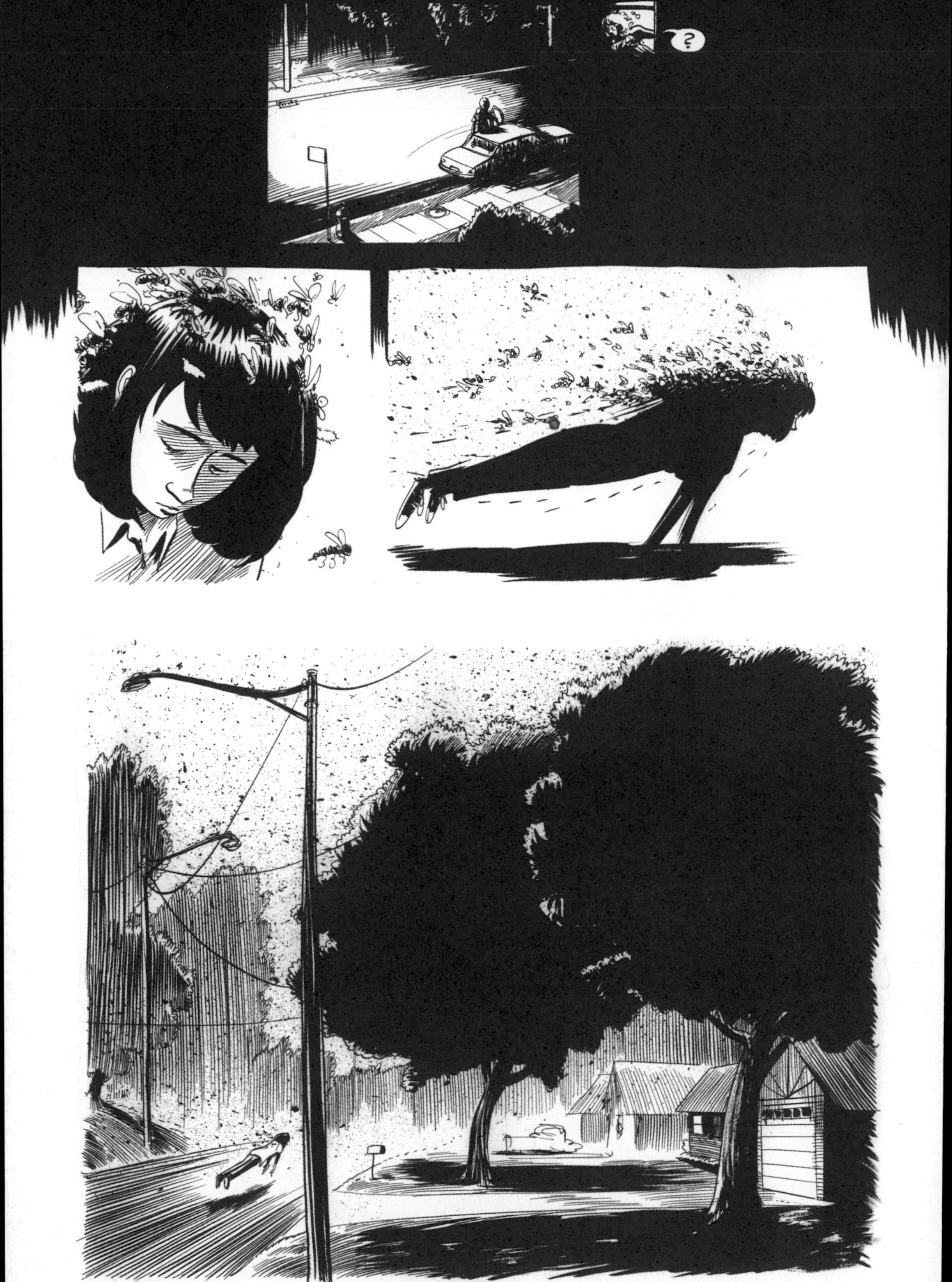
?

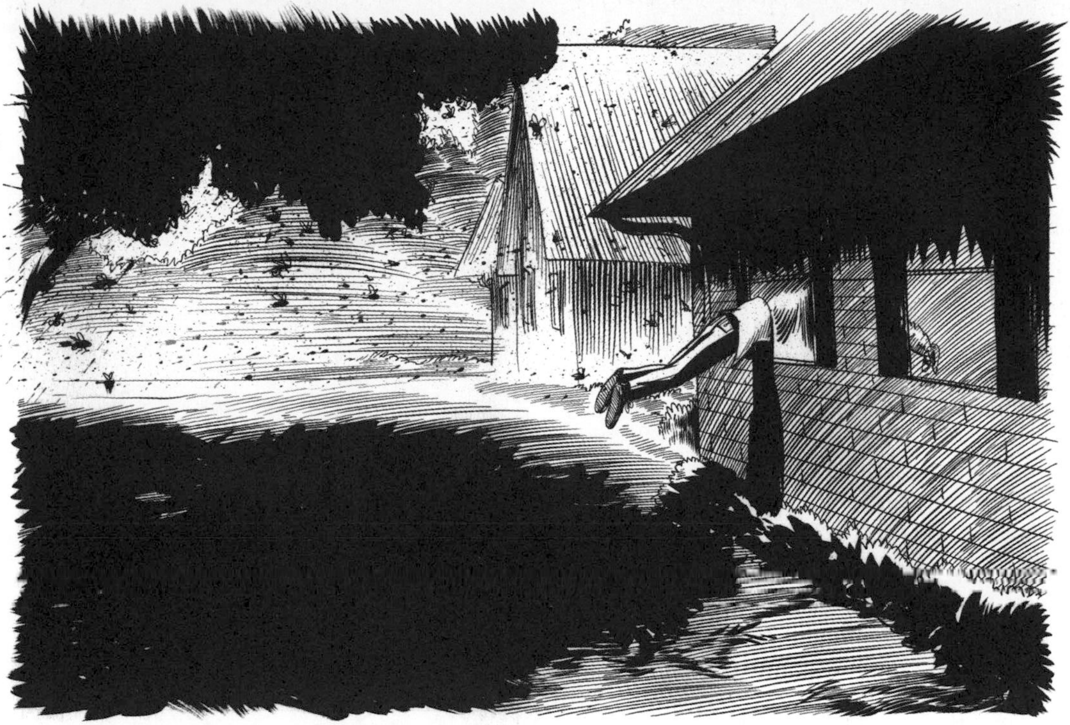

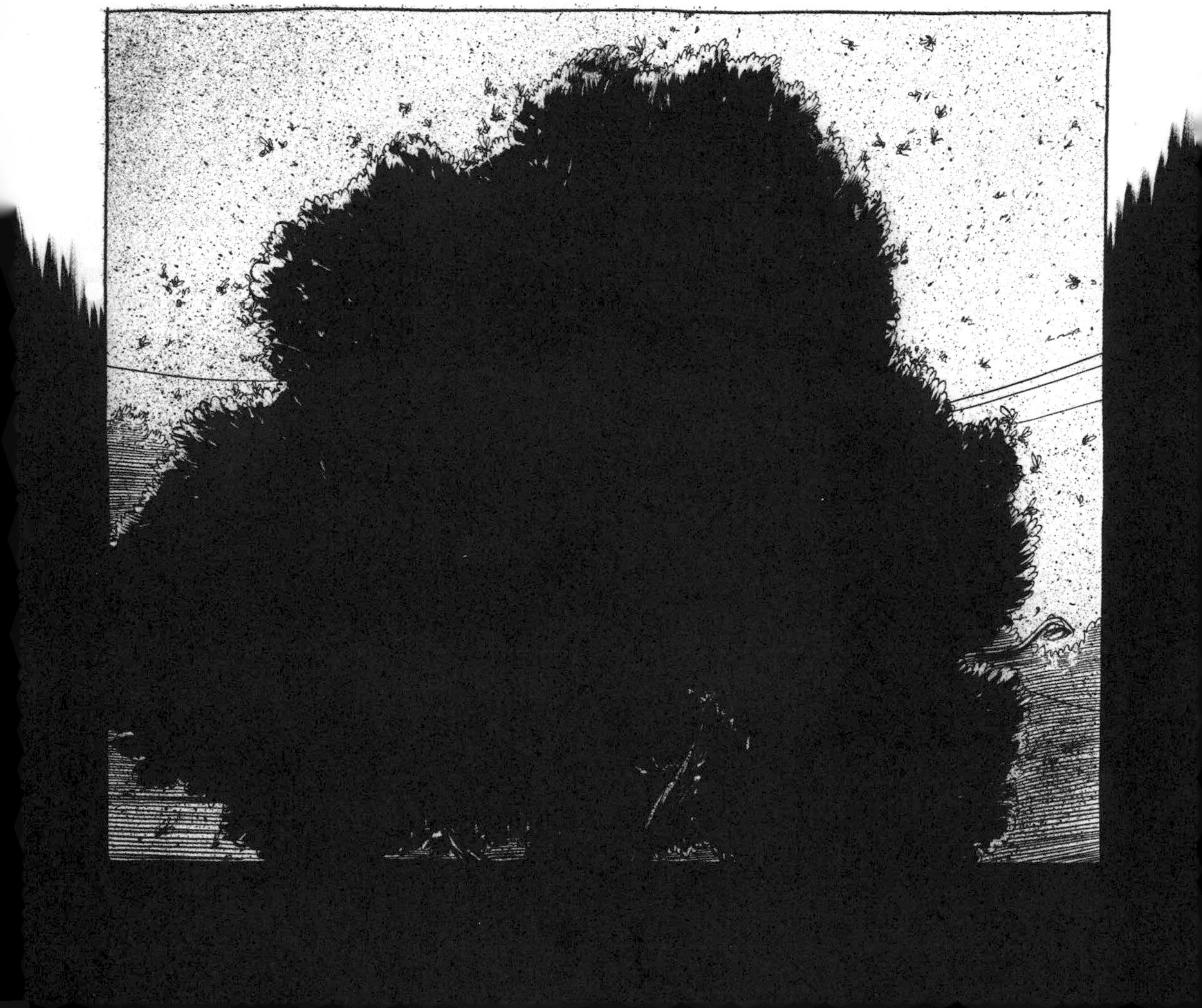

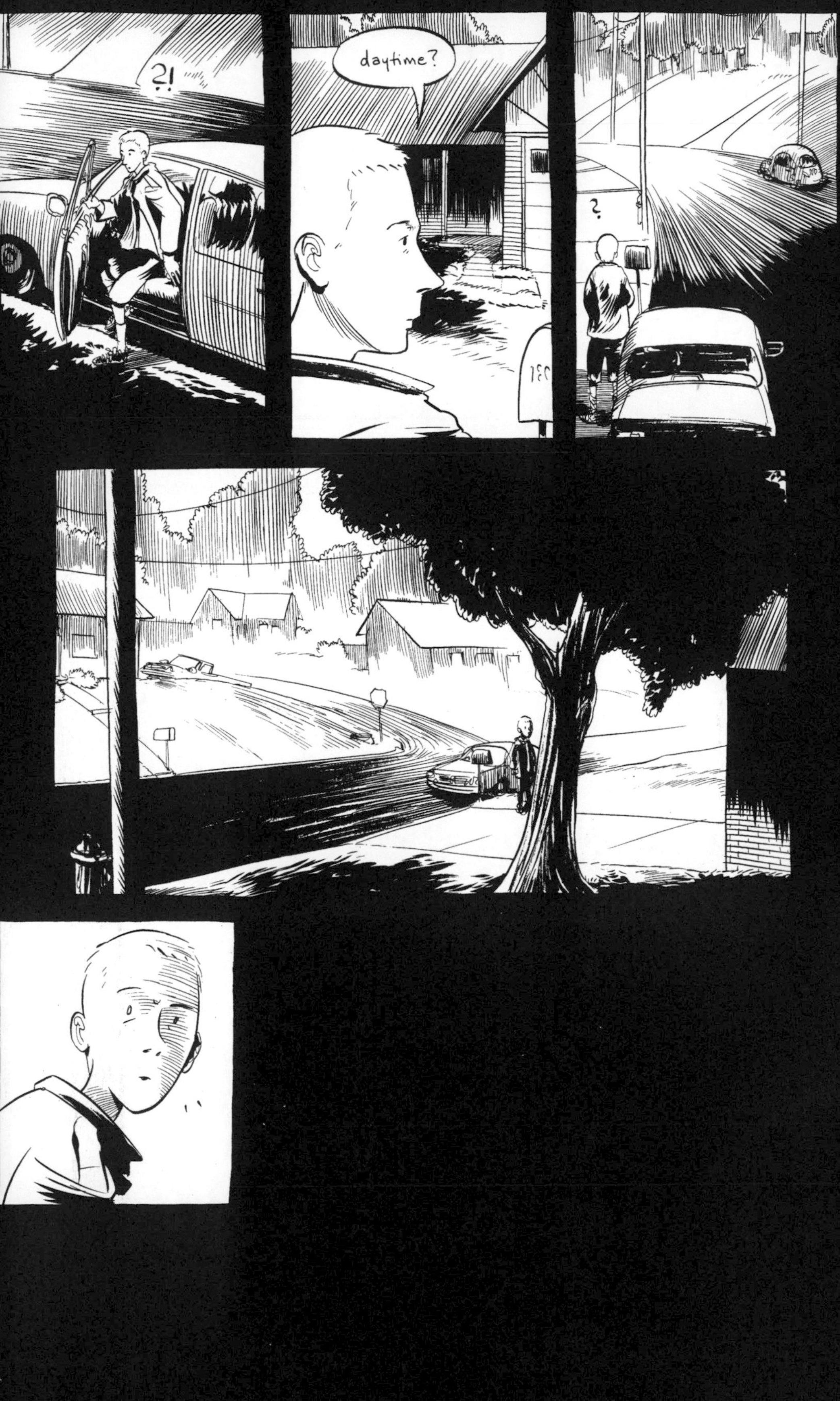

?!
daytime?
?

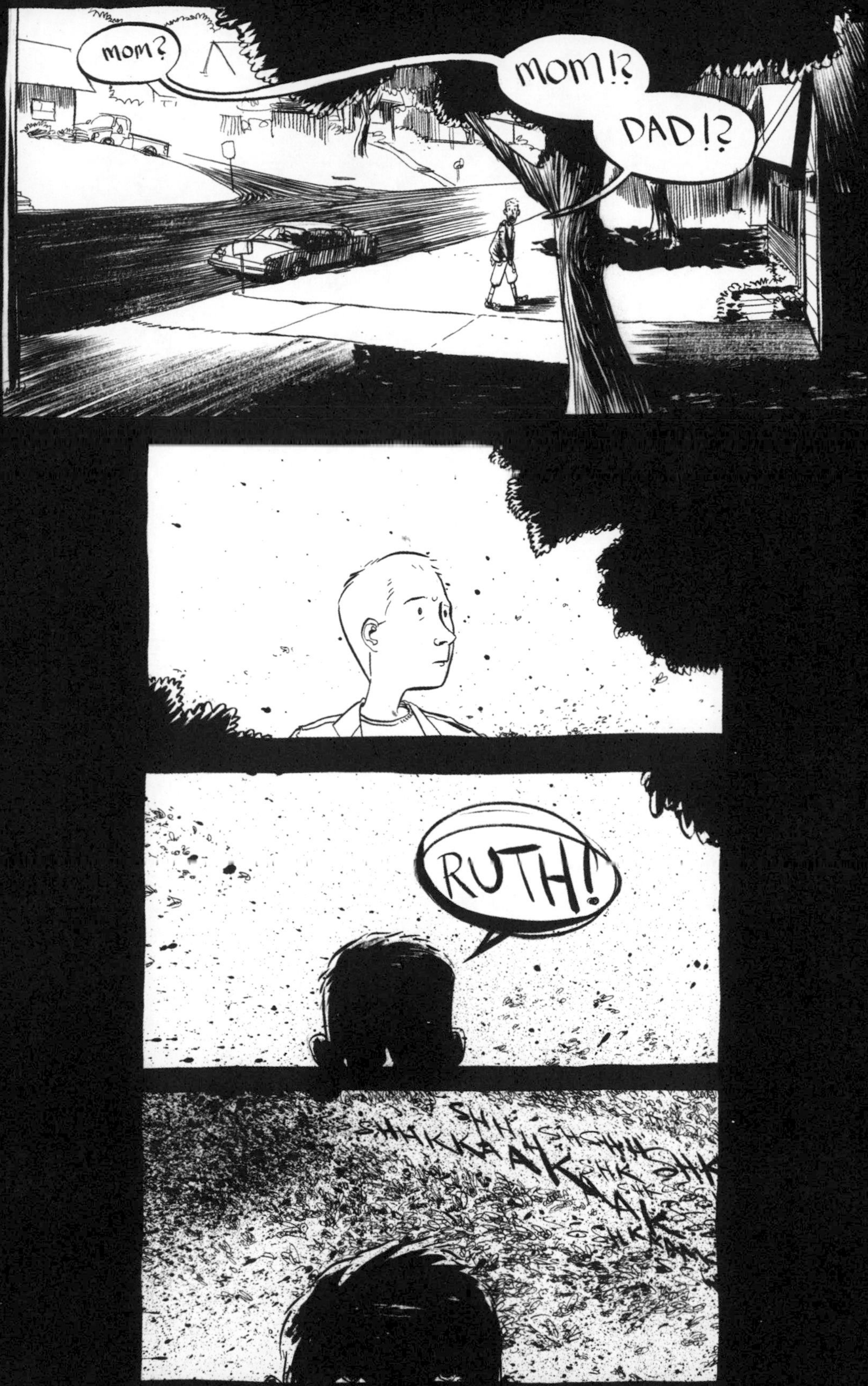
mom?
MOM!?
DAD!?
RUTH!
SHH
SHHKKAAK
SHK

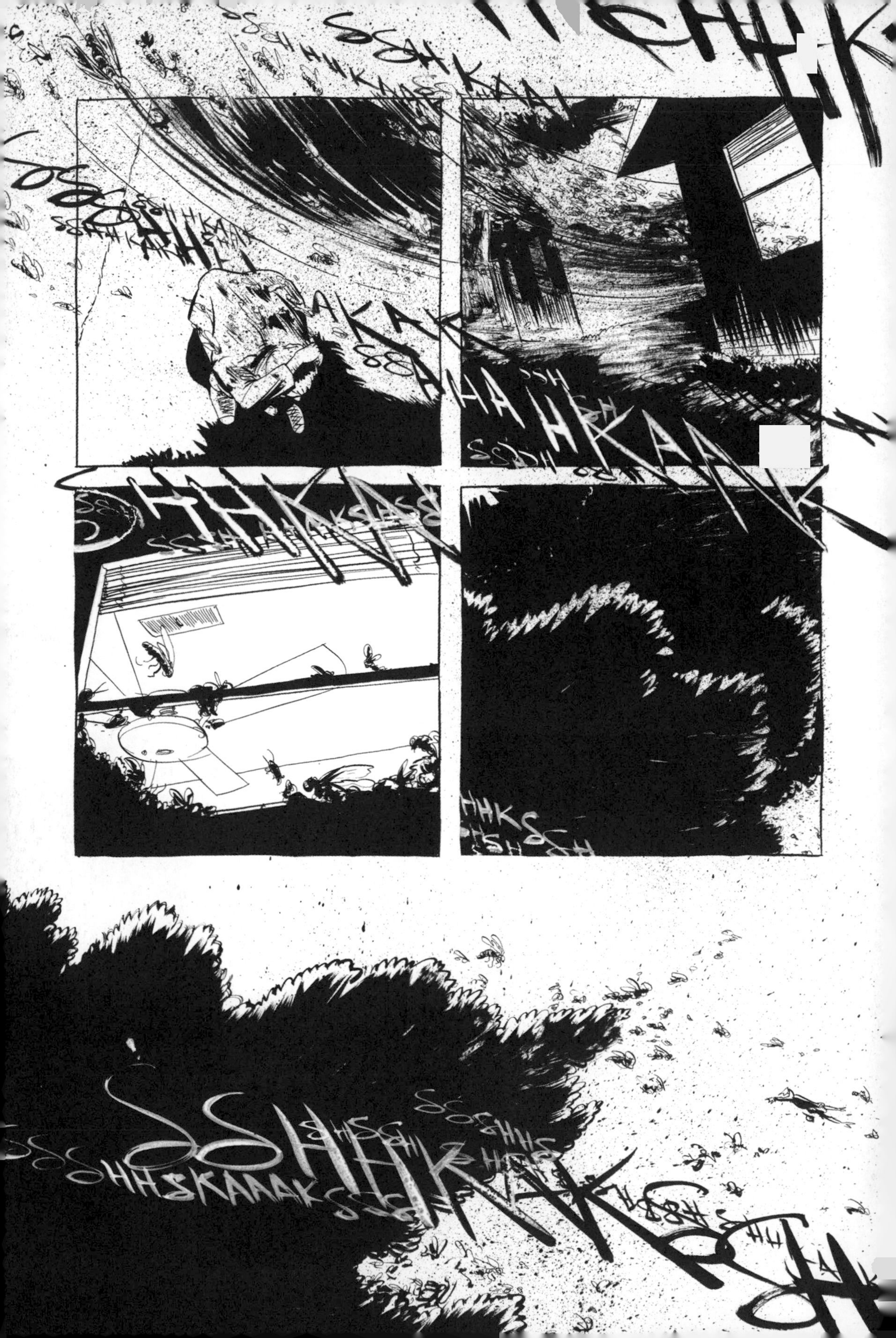
HHSKAAAKS

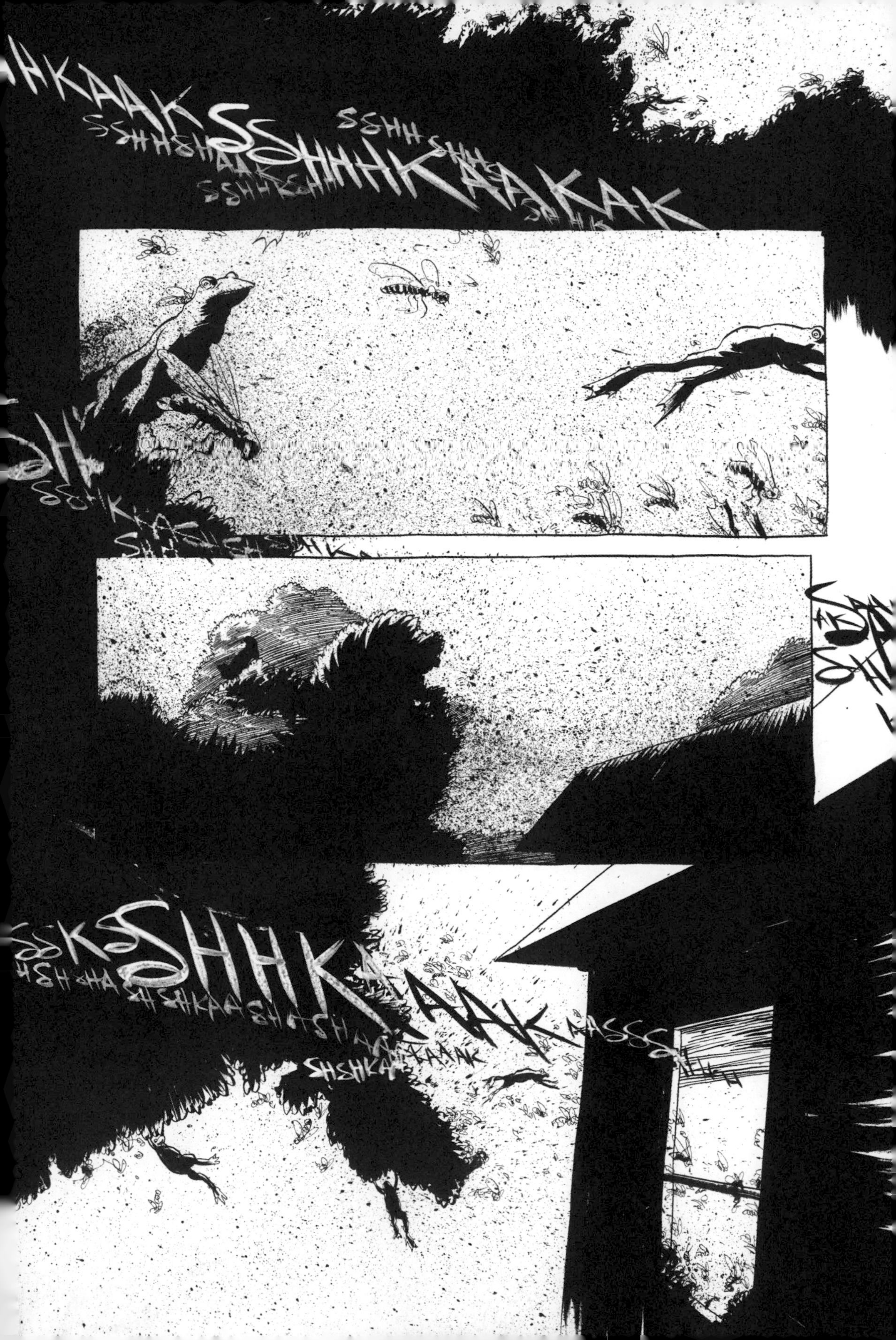
HKAAK
SHHHKAAKAK
SHHKAAAK

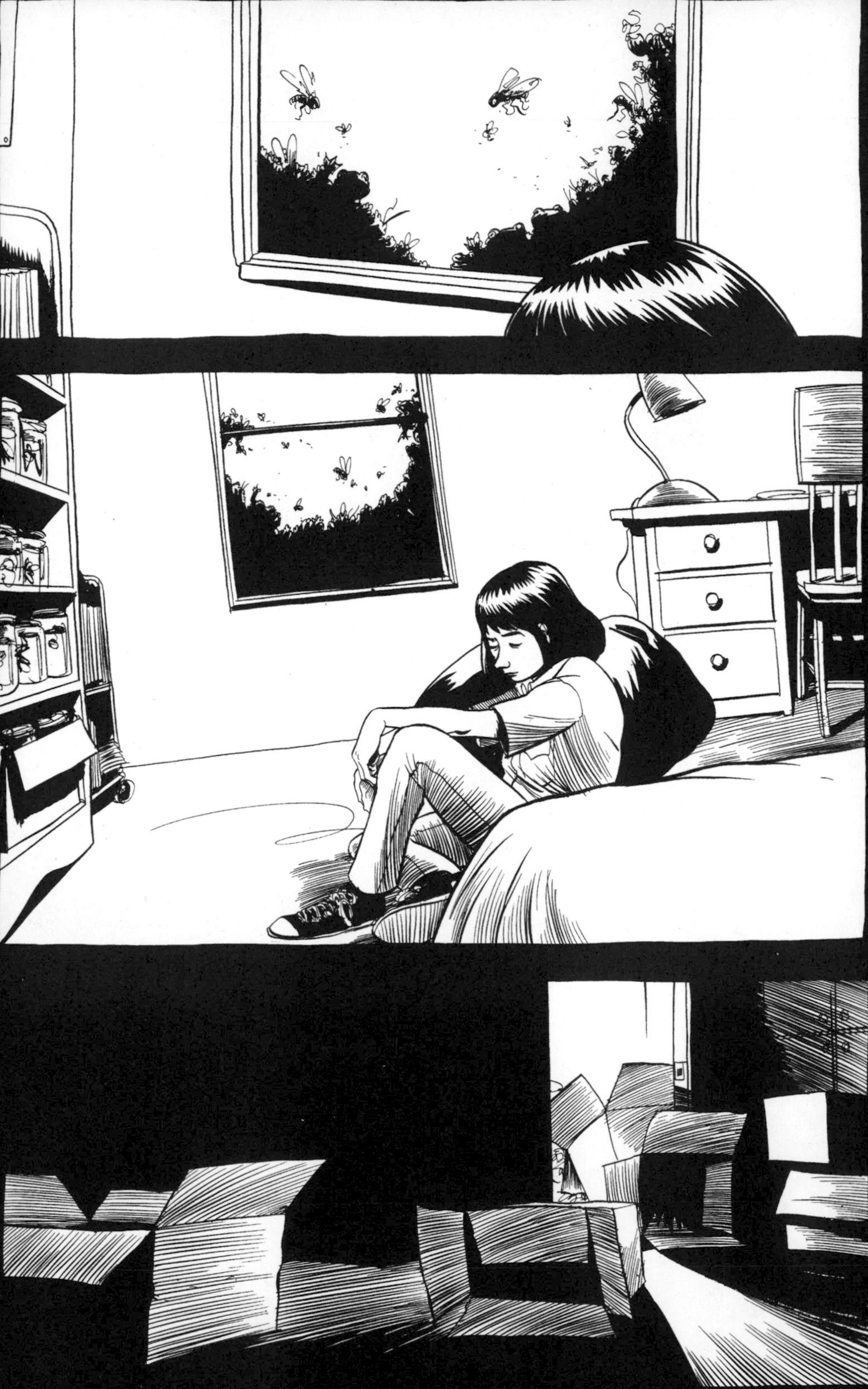

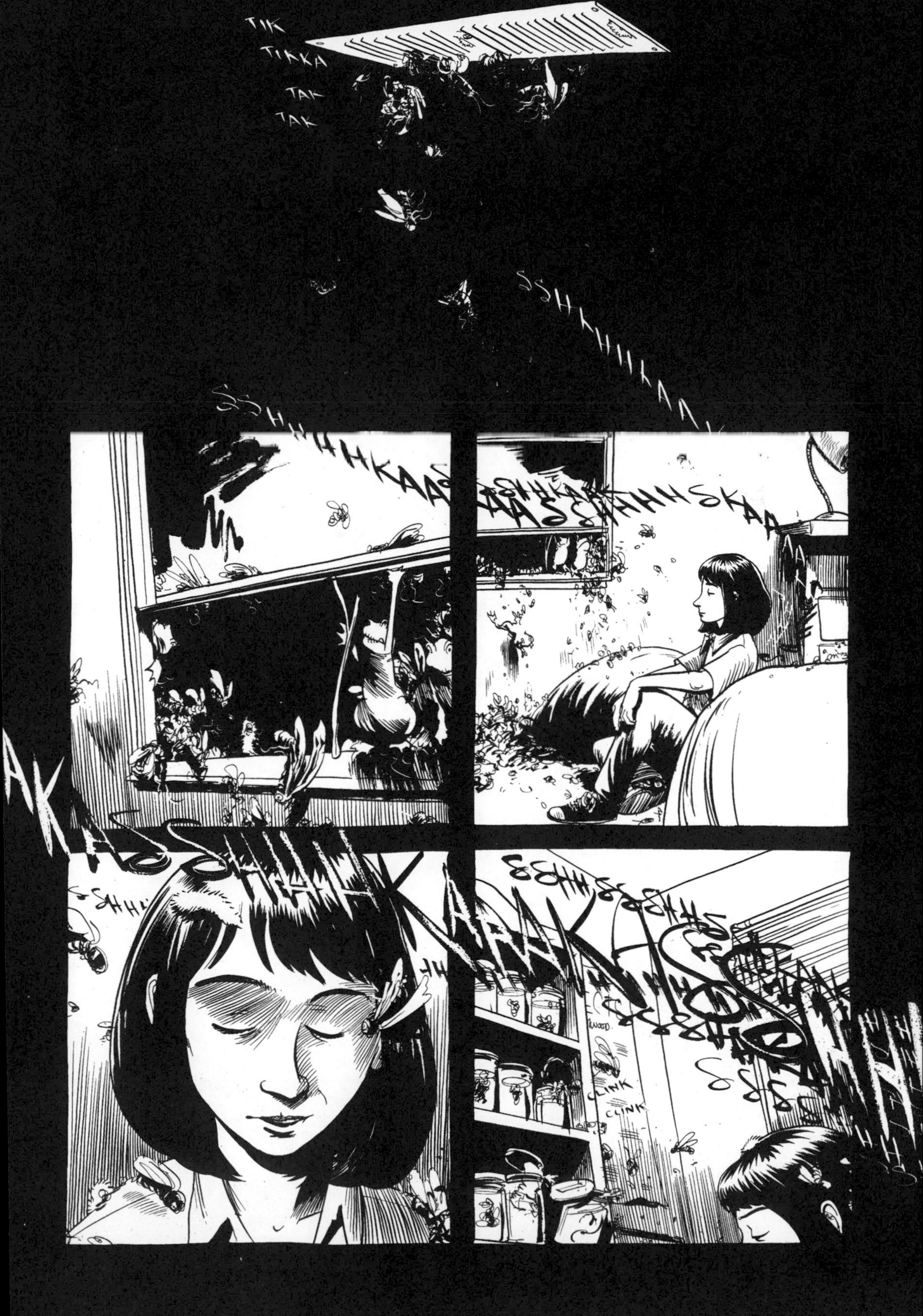
TIK
TIKKA
TAK
TAK
CLINK
CLINK

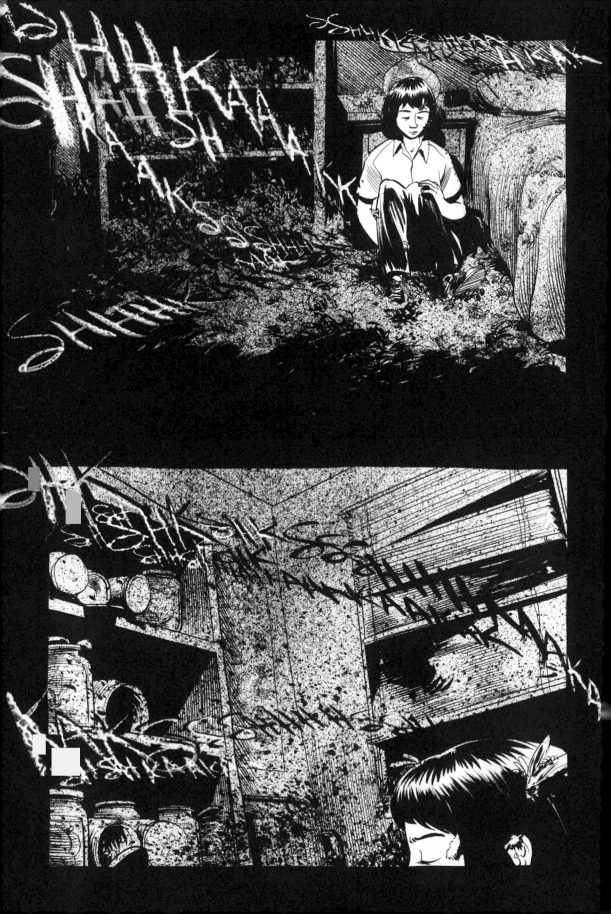

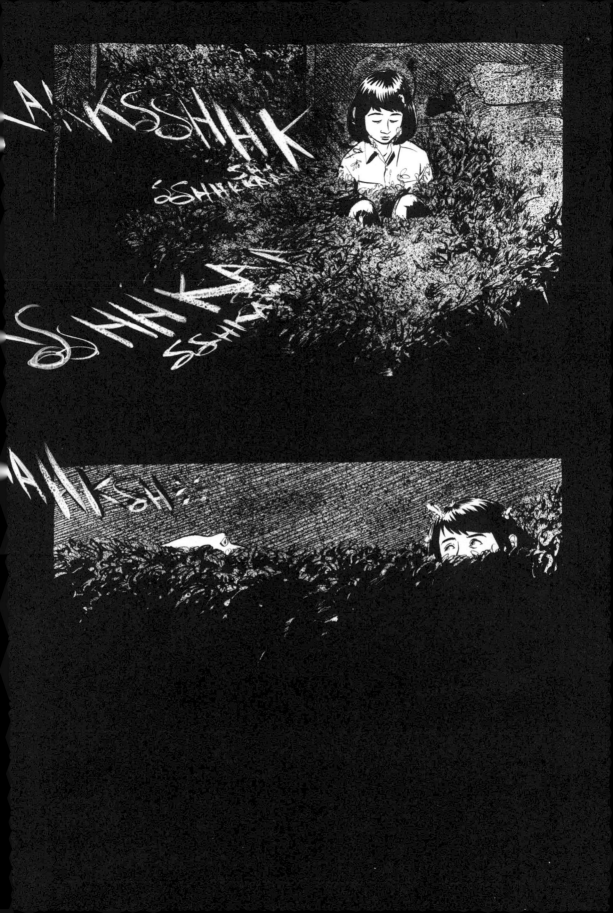

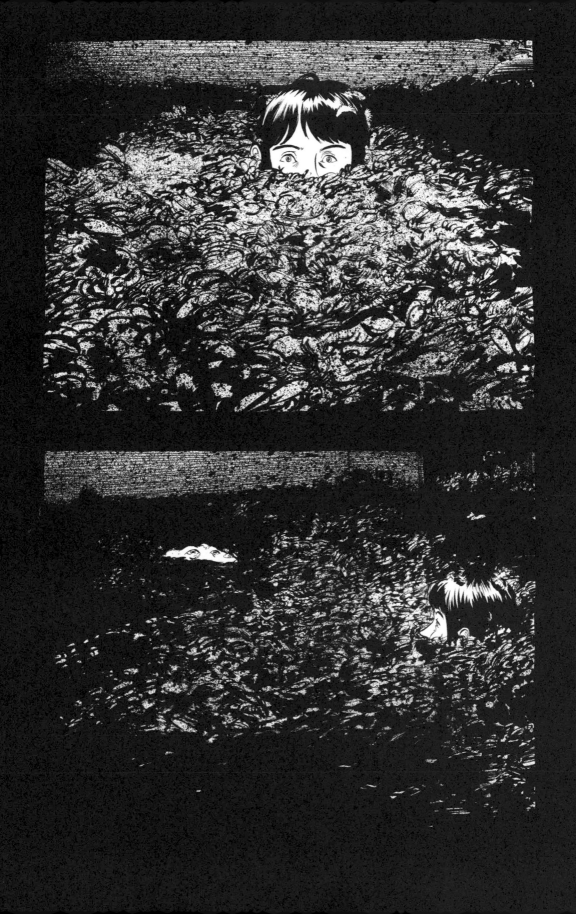

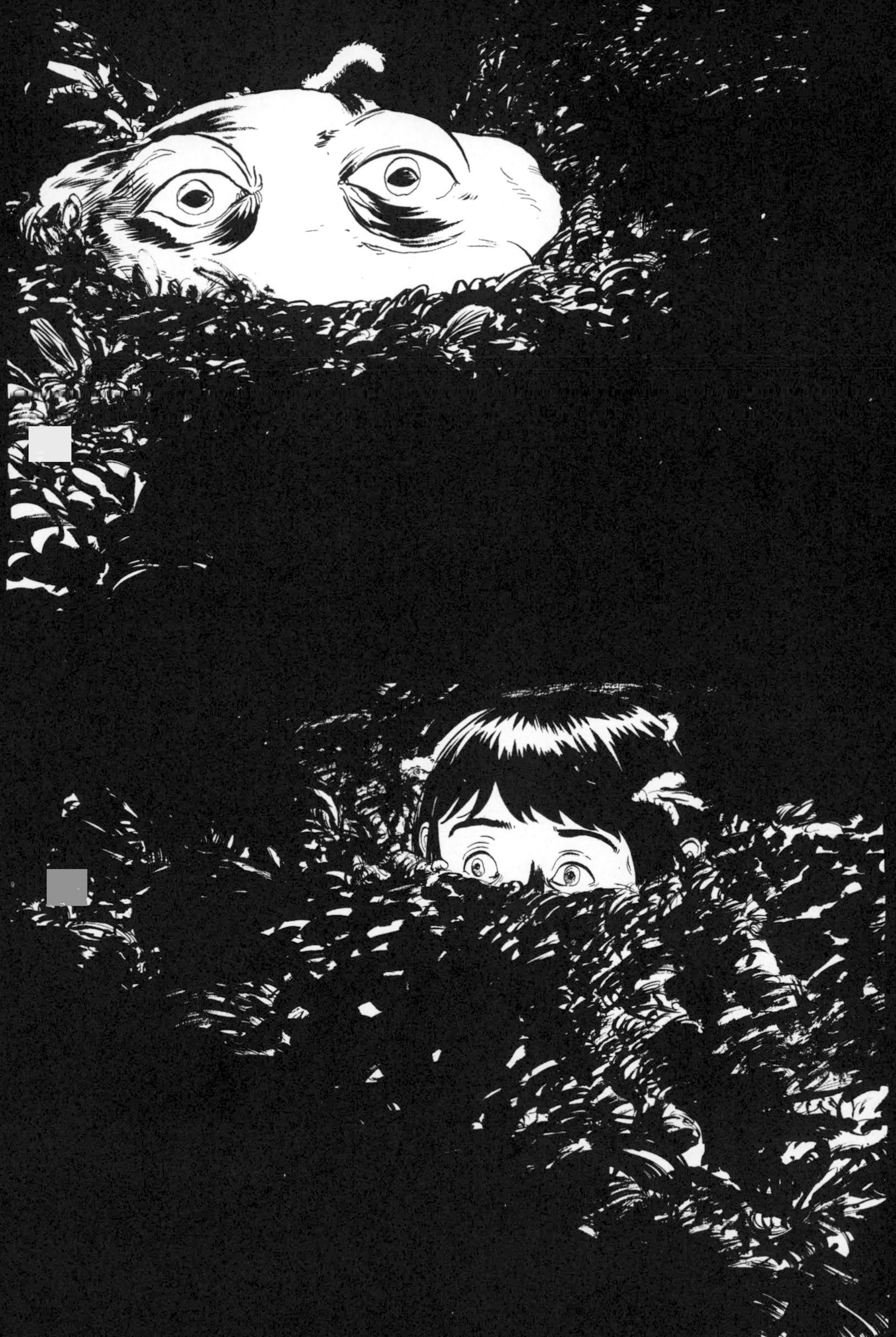

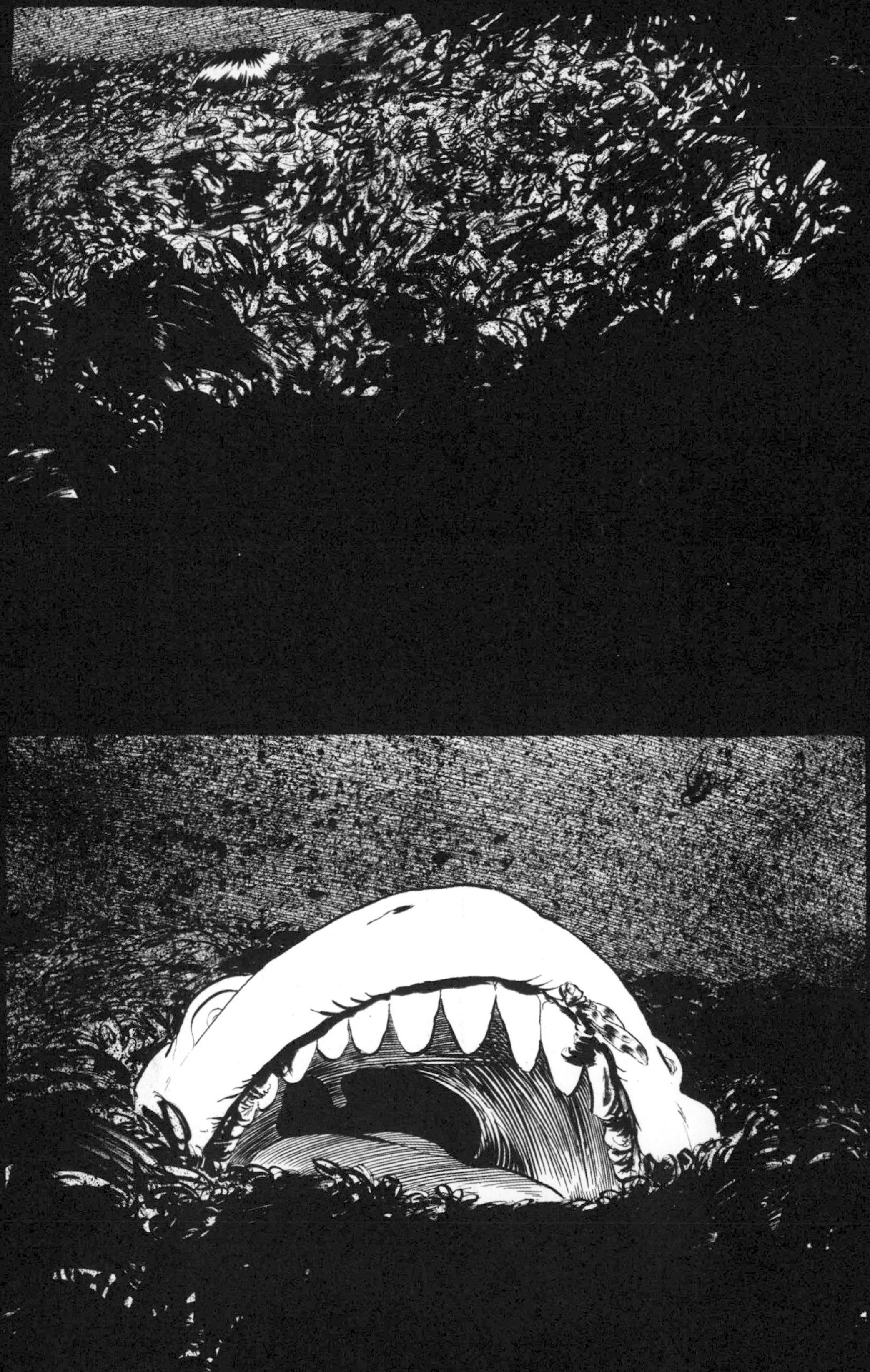

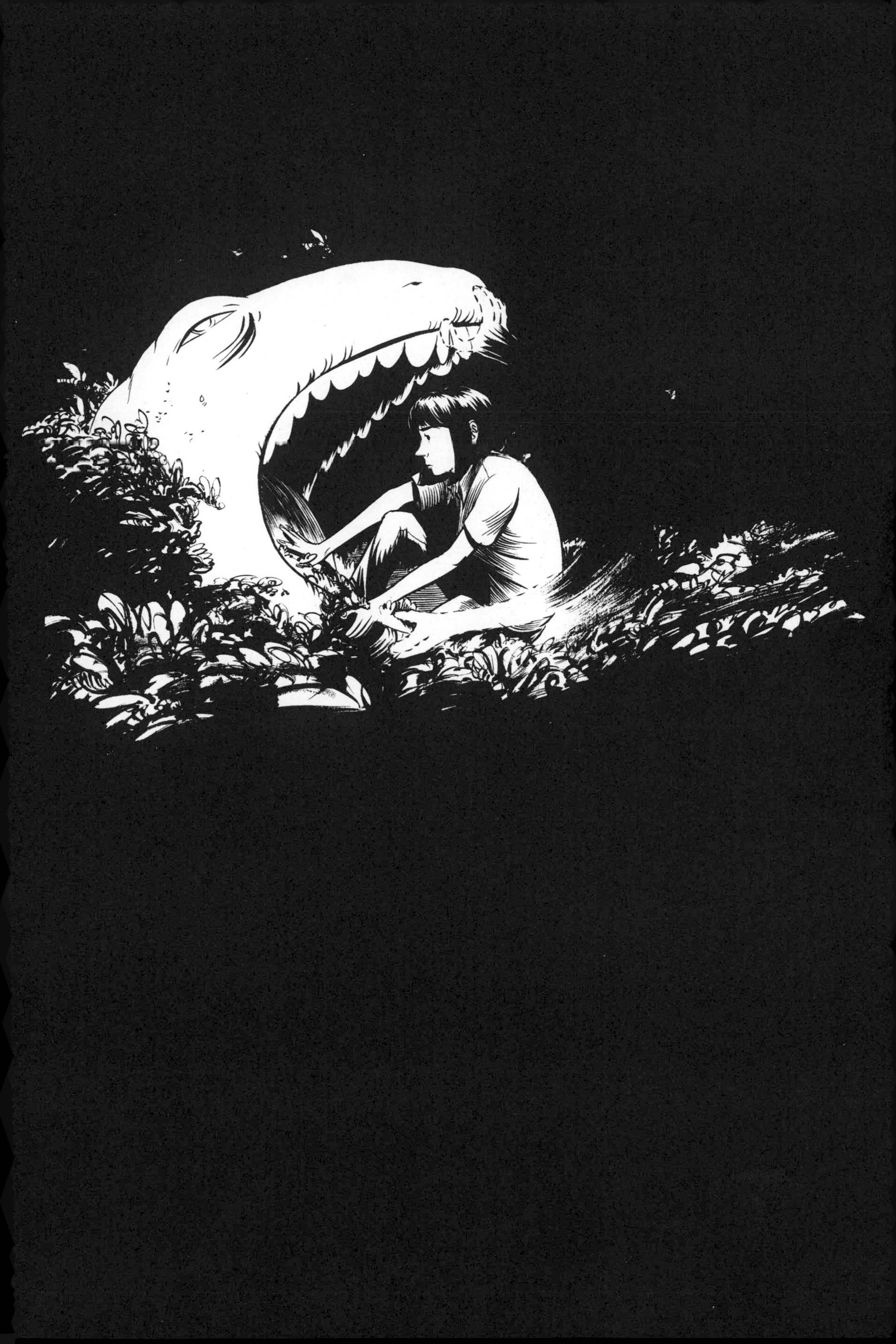

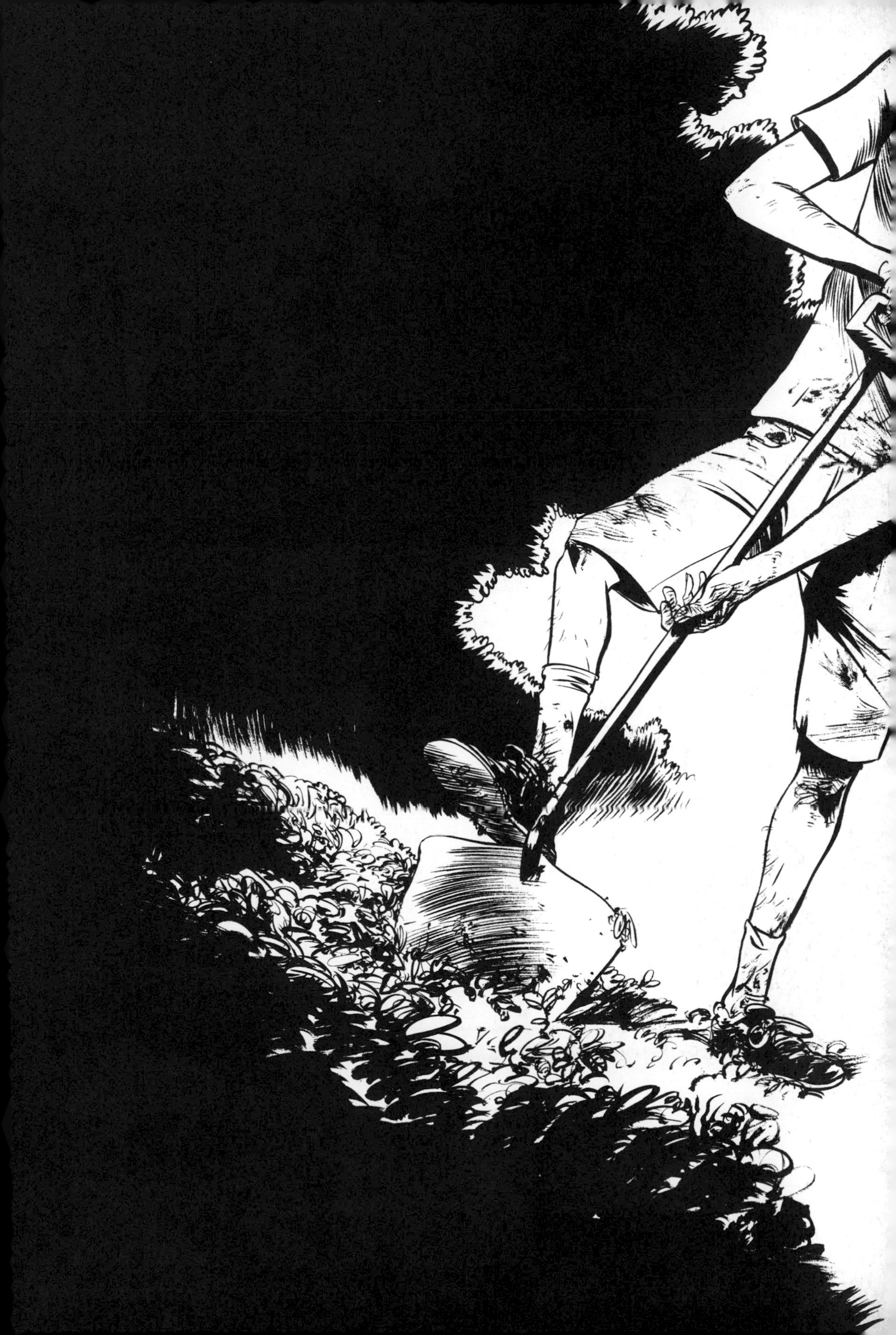

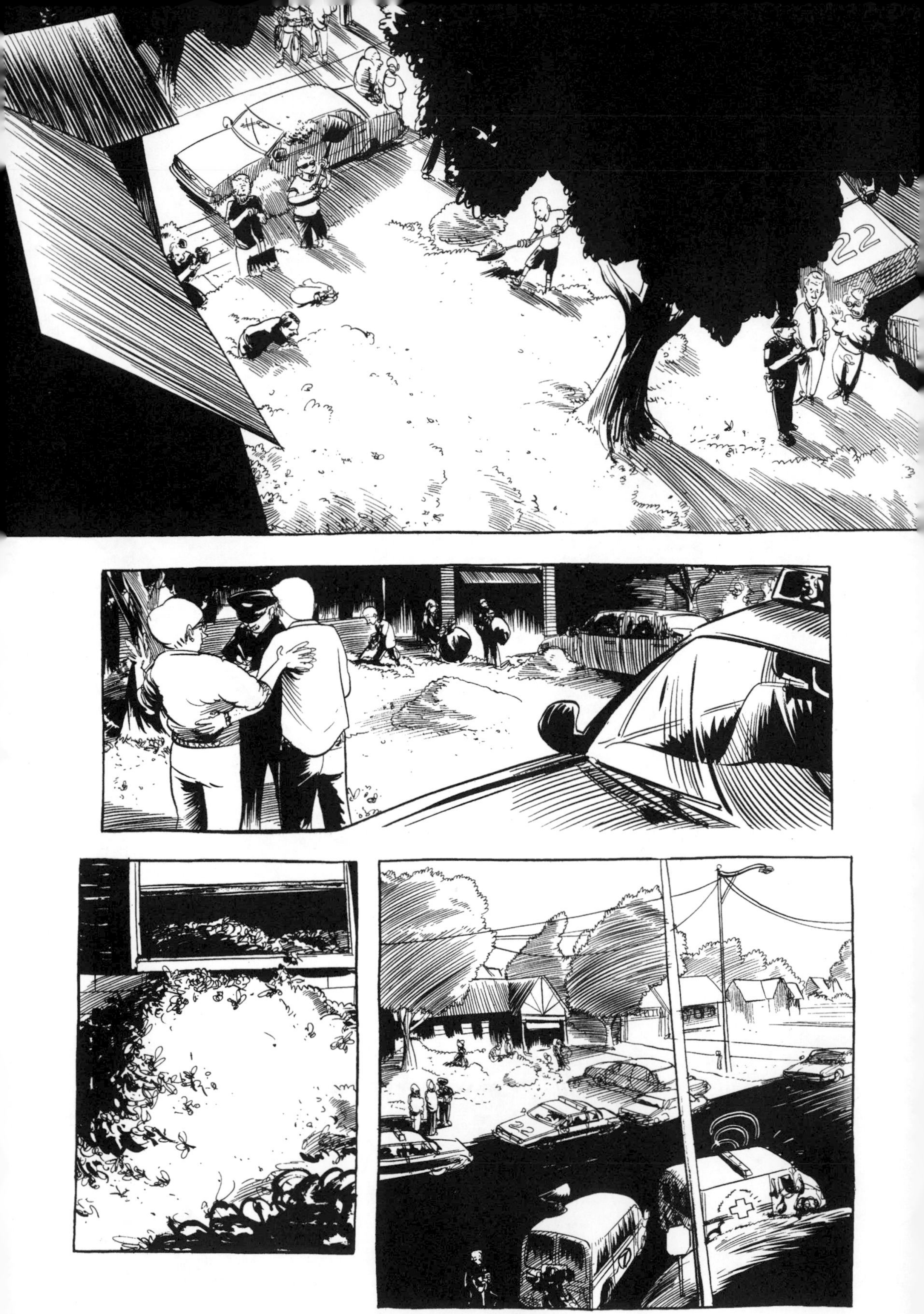
22

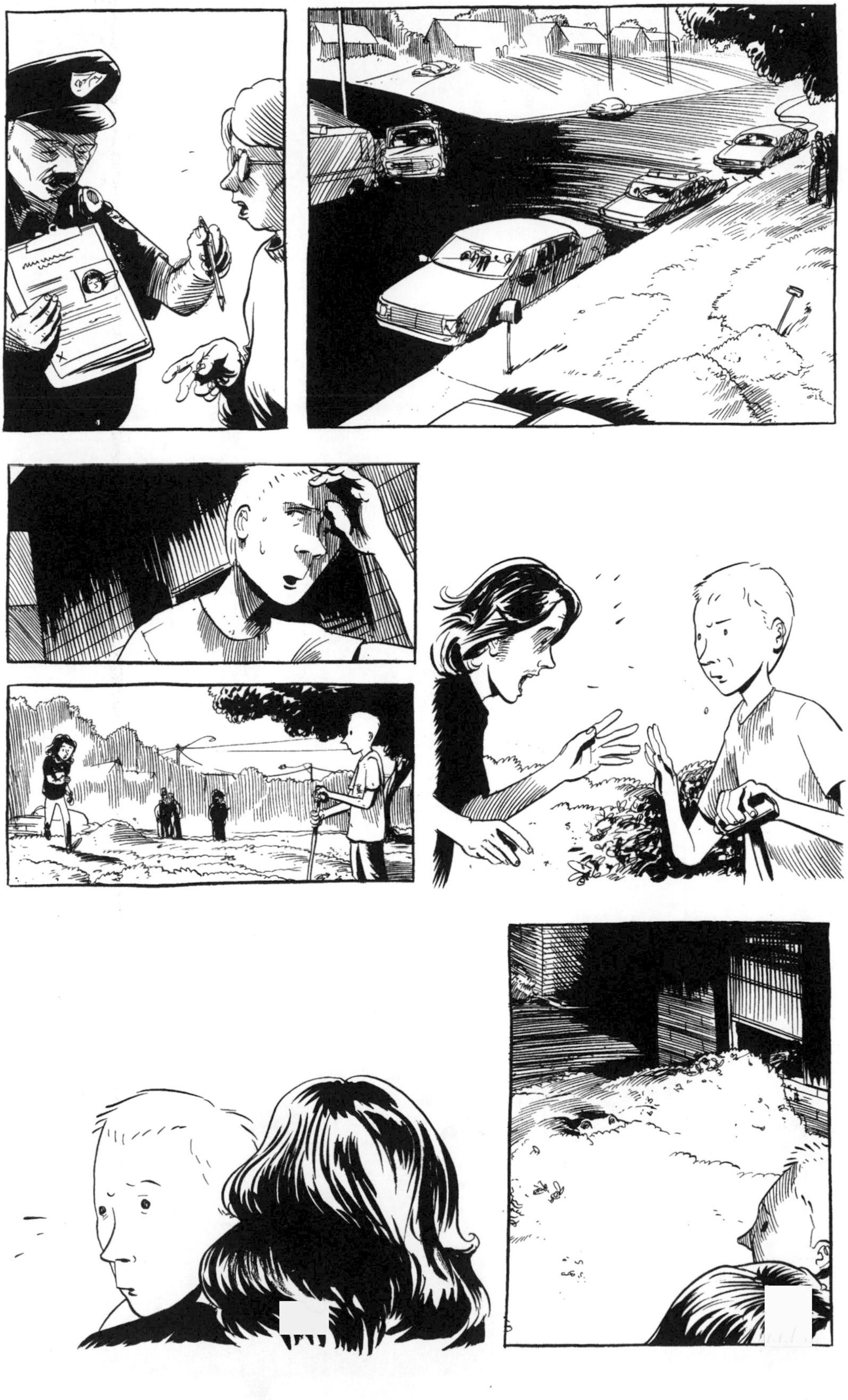

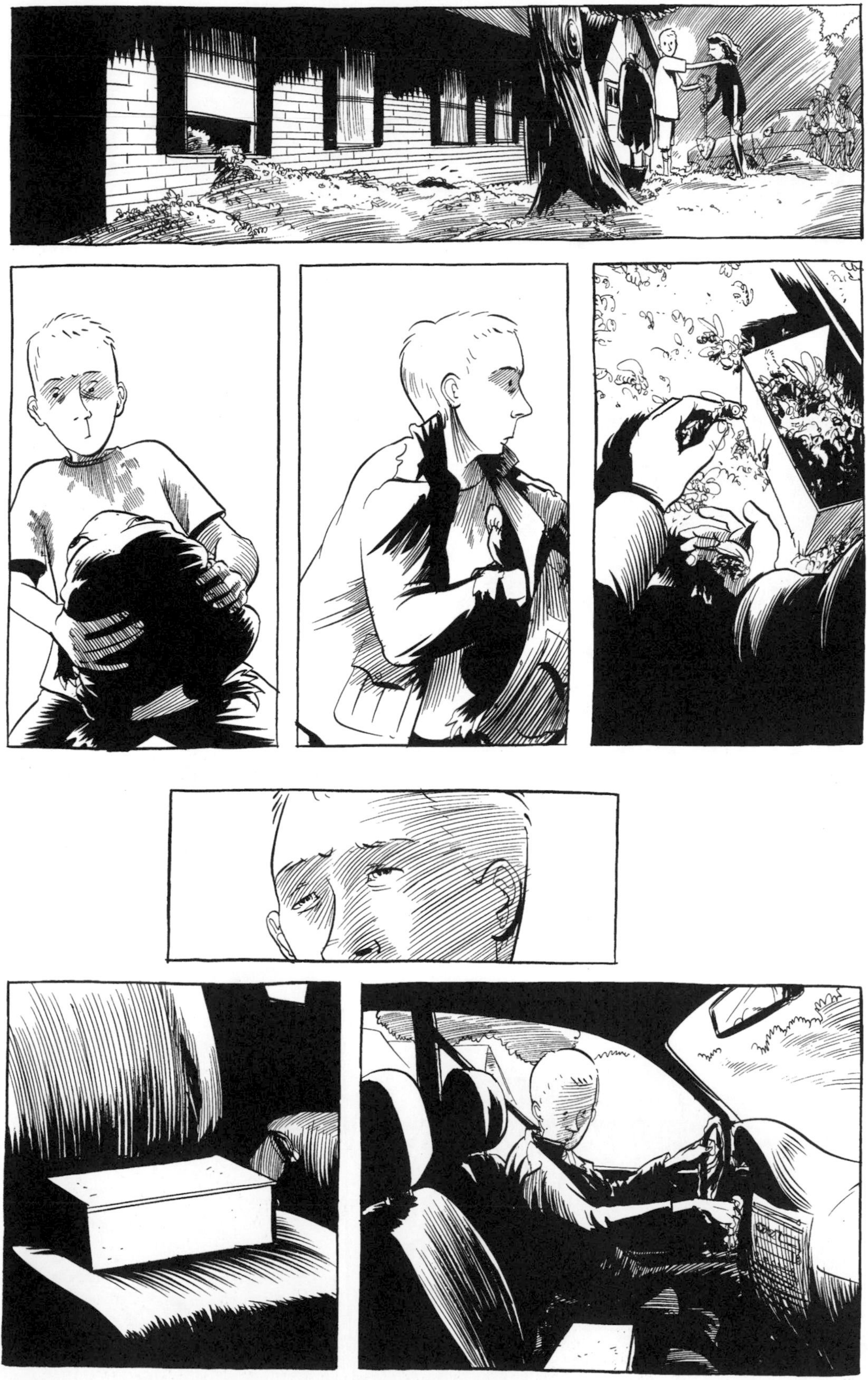

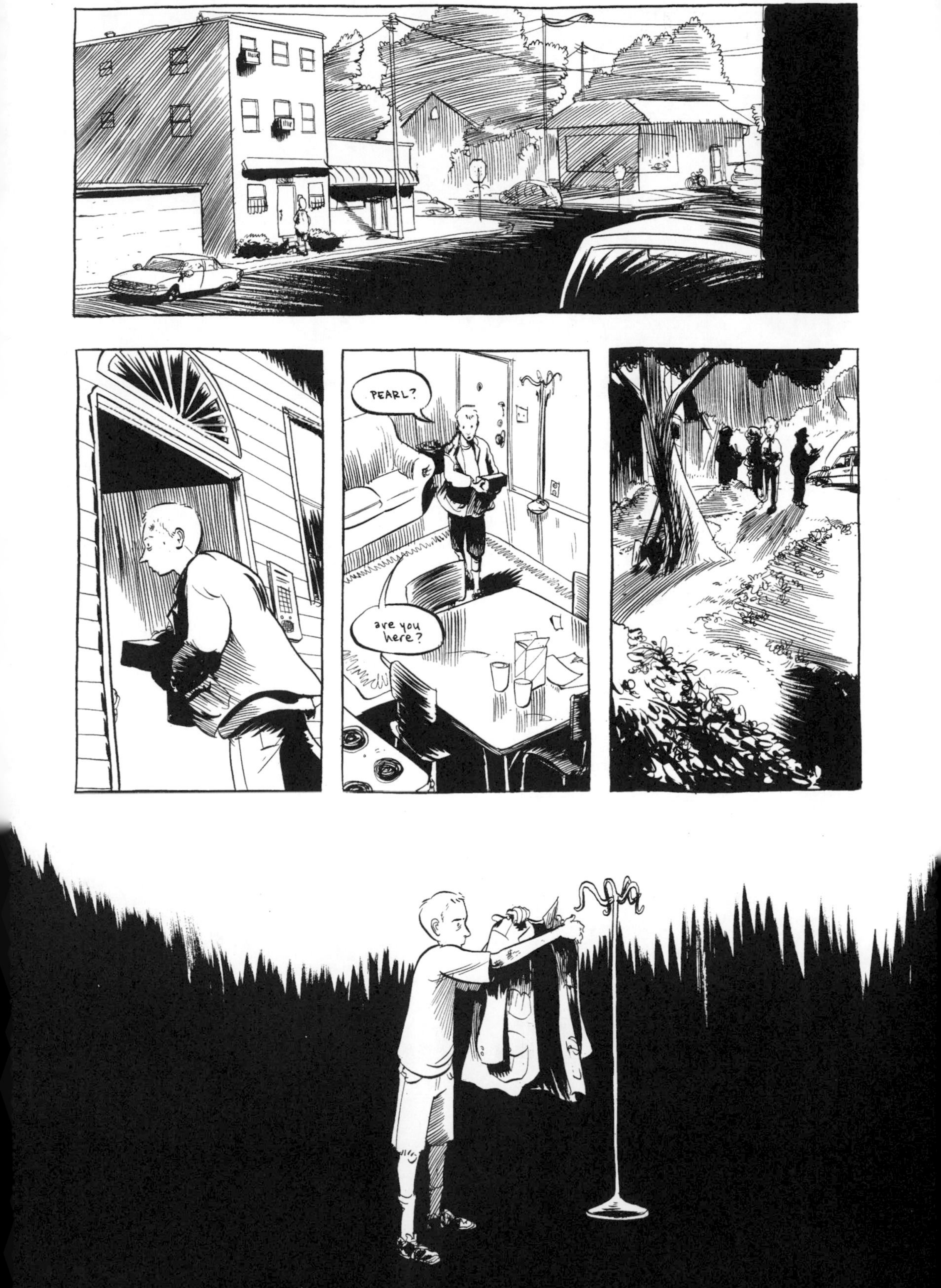
PEARL?
are you here?

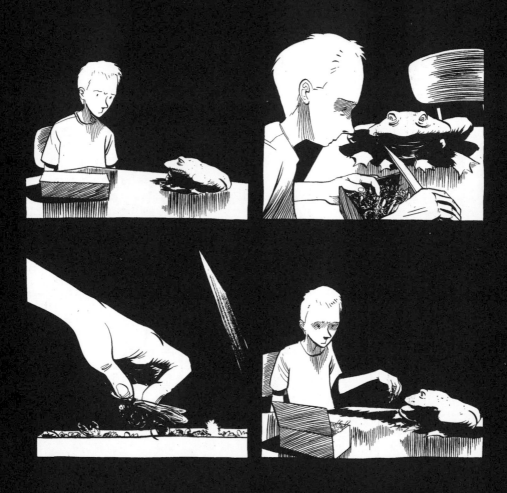

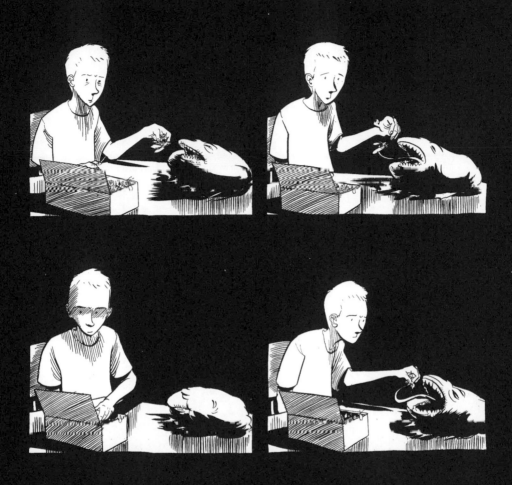

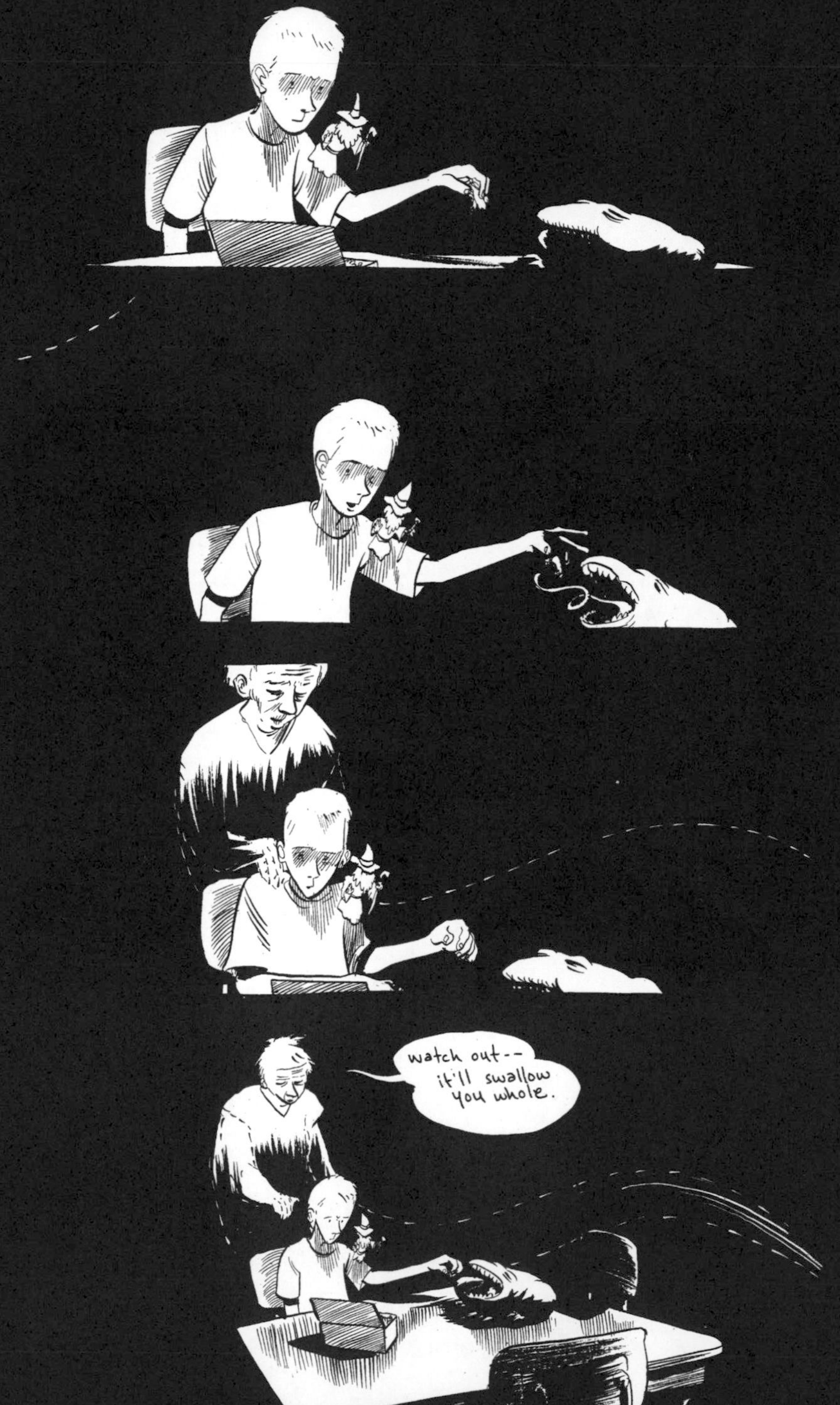
watch out-- it'll swallow you whole.

NATE POWELL was born in 1978 in Little Rock, Arkansas. He began self-publishing comics and zines in 1992 at age 14, and graduated from School of Visual Arts in 2000. His work includes Please Release, Sounds of Your Name, It Disappears, Tiny Giants, the Walkie Talkie series, and contributions to Meathaus, Paper Rodeo, and Eisner-nominated Syncopated anthologies.

Since 1999 Nate has worked full-time for adults with developmental disabilities. He also operates DIY punk record label Harlan Records, and performs in the bands Soophie Nun Squad, Boomfancy, Wait, and Divorce Chord. He does not eat meat, but does drive way too much.

THANKS for all the INSPIRATION,
SUPPORT, and good CONVERSATION:

erin tobey, ryan seaton, rachel bormann,
michael hoerger, nathan wilson, tim scott, mike lierly,
maralie a.-milholland, eli monster, mike taylor,
travis fristoe, aaron cometbus, kristine barrett,
matt tobey, marea noël, lisa merva, amy karr,
natalja kent, mara bethel, andrea zollo, mike kirsch,
farel dalrymple, alec longstreth, al burian,
samantha jones, melissa number one, patrice poor,
joe biel, sparky taylor, kerri snead, brood X cicadae
of 2004, the poltergeist in my massachusetts house,
chris staros, brett warnock, and all at top shelf,
and my family.

WRITE ME! → PO Box 3382
Bloomington IN
47402 USA
seemybrotherdance@yahoo.com
www.harlanrecords.org

this is for E.T.

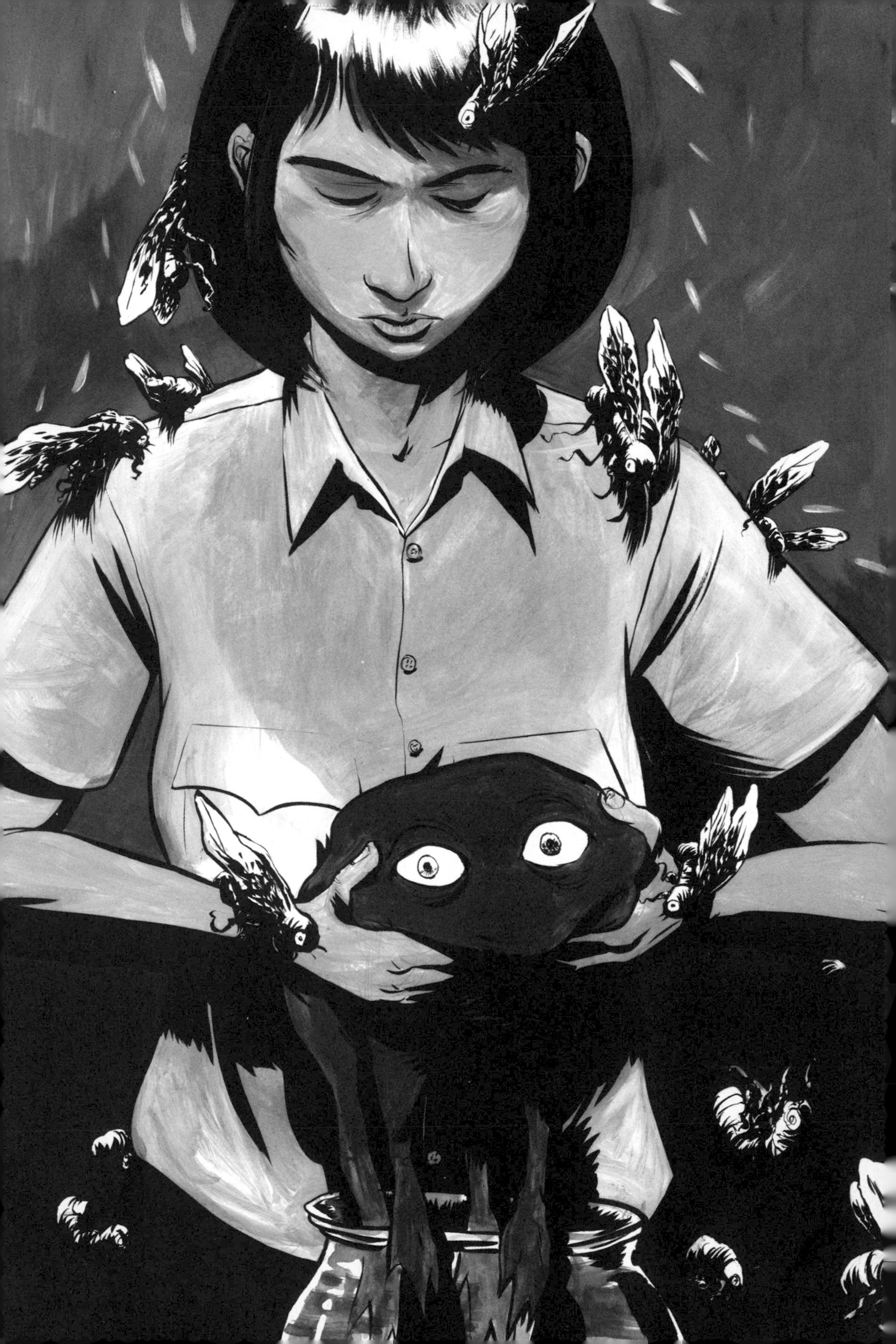